J.P. Rodgers was born in Co. Galway. He left school at fifteen and at age sixteen had the first of his many letters read on Ireland's popular Radio Éireann programme 'Dear Sir or Madam'. In 1963 he joined the mass exodus of Irish people who went to England in search of employment. He worked there as a bus conductor before emigrating to Australia in 1970.

In 1978 he moved back to his childhood home near Williamstown, Co. Galway, where he still lives with his wife.

'A heartrending story'   *Irish Mail on Sunday*

'Moving and ultimately uplifting'   *Irish World*

'A testament to the power of love'
Nottingham Evening Post

'Few stories are as tragic, yet inspirational, as this one'
Western Daily Press

'We urge readers to take a look at this story of the triumph of love over adversity. And we challenge you not to have a tear in your eye by the final chapter'
Northampton Chronicle & Echo

For the Love of My Mother

JOHN RODGERS

headline
review

First published in Ireland in 2005 by MacRuairi Art
First published in the UK in 2006
by HEADLINE PUBLISHING GROUP

First published in paperback in 2007
by HEADLINE REVIEW
An imprint of HEADLINE PUBLISHING GROUP

1

Cataloguing in Publication Data is available from the British Library

(ISBN) 978 0 7553 1593 2

Typeset in Bembo by Palimpsest Book Production Limited,
Grangemouth, Stirlingshire

Printed and bound in Great Britain by
Clays Ltd, St Ives plc

Headline's policy is to use papers that are natural, renewable and
recyclable products and made from wood grown in sustainable forests.
The logging and manufacturing processes are expected to conform to the
environmental regulations of the country of origin.

HEADLINE PUBLISHING GROUP
A division of Hachette Livre UK Ltd
338 Euston Road
London NW1 3BH

www.headline.co.uk
www.hodderheadline.com

ACKNOWLEDGEMENTS

Writing my first book was never going to be easy. Getting it published was even harder. I would like to say a special thank you to Diane Banks my literary agent who gave me a new lease of life. To my editor Jo Roberts-Miller at Headline Publishing Group, a special thank you - you were a joy to work with; to Helena Towers, Bernard Dive and all the staff at Headline, thank you. To my good friend Chris Keane who read the first three chapters and said those magical words, 'John, I think your ship has come in', and to Maureen Keane, who always gave me her wholehearted support – this book is for both of you. Claudia Jennings, who typed up the early drafts for me, you were great to work with. To my son, Óisin, who rescued all of my material when my computer crashed on Christmas Day, well done, you'll go a long way. To my daughters Róisin and Síle, thanks for all your help correcting when it was so badly needed. A special word of appreciation to my wife Julie, I'm glad I married you. My good friend and photographer Steve Lilley, who kept the electronic wires burning, many thanks. And to the Irish World newspaper, many thanks, it was a joy to write for you.

INTRODUCTION

M Y LIFE COULD best be described as a total disaster. Whichever way you look at it. I've wanted to do so many things, tried so many projects – some good, some bad – that either petered out or were left unfinished. In essence what I'm trying to say is, I was probably the most successful failure ever to come out of Ireland. All my life I've wanted to write a good book. And although I've the makings of a book gathering dust somewhere in the house, it is not of the most pressing subject. True, there are plays, poems, short stories – bits, I might add – but all without direction. But now, as I approach the autumn of my life, I am going to make one gigantic effort to write a good book and lay the ghost of my past, which hangs over my life. But where do I begin? Do I start with an account of a solitary day in my youth, or with the story of my mother, whose life, interwoven with mine, is what really haunts me? Until I tell her story, all other attempts at writing, I feel, are meaningless.

5 a.m.
27 April 1997
J. P. Rodgers

CHAPTER ONE

I T WAS FRIDAY morning, the seventh day of March 1930, that the whole rotten episode began. It was the kind of morning when you wished you'd stayed in bed instead of having to face into the biting cold wind that swept down the littered streets of old Dublin towards the Metropolitan Courthouse, situated in the north of the city.

But despite the severity of the wind and cold, several snotty-nosed little chisellers hung around the old Smithfield Market, next to the courthouse, ready to steal what they could to stem the growing tide of starvation. And for every fleet-footed and successful little chiseller roaming the streets, there were at least half a dozen more tiny infants huddled in the litter-strewn doorways, crying pitifully and begging for alms.

Every now and again the weakest little chiseller of them all was asked to pay the heavy price of appearing before the Court of Justice in the nearby Metropolitan Courthouse. And it so happened that morning that in his private chambers inside the grim-looking Victorian building, the chief justice of the court, Mr Justice Cussens, who was extremely grateful for the indoor warmth, prepared to put on his wig and gown before presiding over the day's sitting.

The minute he opened the door to enter the courtroom, the court clerk gave the order to the assembled crowd, 'Will the Court please rise.' The packed courtroom, made up of solicitors, Garda Síochána and those awaiting trial immediately stood to attention as the judge made a dignified entrance, stepping up to his bench, where he gave the nod to commence proceedings. When the clerk was satisfied that Mr Justice Cussens was ready, he gave the order to the assembled crowd to be seated and called for the first case to be heard.

'Your Honour, the Court calls on Rose Clancy, complainant versus Bridgit Norah Rodgers, defendant.'

A hush descended on the assembled crowd, while discreet nods and whispers passed between Rose Clancy and Garda Michael Corcoran, a young officer who was summonsing on Rose Clancy's behalf. Garda Corcoran then made his way hesitantly to the witness stand, where he took hold of the small black Bible and swore to tell truth, the whole truth and nothing but.

Accepting the judge's offer to be seated, the young officer glanced nervously at his notes before reading out the charge.

'Your Honour, as a result of a complaint received from Rose Clancy, on the twenty-first of February 1930 at approximately two thirty p.m., I proceeded to the market end of Chancery Street, in the said district of Dublin, where I observed a small female child in a very distressed and dishevelled state. She was crying pitifully while begging for alms by holding up an empty vessel and pleading to those who passed by. On further investigation, I ascertained that the child was a Catholic, having been christened Bridgit Norah Rodgers, and whose date of birth was given as the thirteenth day of September 1927 and her address as number 44 North Great Clarence Street, in the said district of Dublin, but who lately appears to reside at Bluebell, Inchicore, in the County of Dublin. Further to my inquiries, I found that number 44 North Great Clarence Street no longer exists, having recently become a derelict site. At present the defendant, Bridgit Norah Rodgers, appears to be in grave moral danger, being without any family support, and her legal guardians are at this time unknown. That, Your Honour, is a truthful account and concludes my statement.'

Chief Justice Cussens cleared his throat before remarking, 'What a state of affairs – when people feel free to discard their offspring like unwanted litter on to the streets of Dublin.'

Turning to Garda Corcoran he added, 'Thank you, Officer, you may step down.'

Garda Michael Corcoran rose to his feet and breathed a sigh of relief, tugged at the lapels of his neat uniform, and returned briskly to take up his position at the rear of the courtroom as the complainant, Rose Clancy was called to the stand.

Dressed in a three-quarter-length navy overcoat, with a matching broad-brimmed hat, Rose Clancy was a spinster, aged about forty-five, with a desire to rid the street where she lived of its unwanted homeless children. She had something of a haughty appearance about her: a sort of cock-of-the-walk look and a thin mouth that seldom smiled. She also had an unflattering gait that made people smile to themselves as they observed her taking the witness stand.

Once the preliminary proceedings were out of the way, Rose Clancy spoke of her discovery of the child and of her desire to rid Smithfield Market once and for all of its street children.

Judge Cussens removed his reading glasses and cast a cold eye over the complainant before enquiring, 'Miss Clancy – if I may call you that? – you're not married, I take it?'

'No, Your Honour, I'm not.'

'Refresh my memory, if you would. I think . . . we've met before?'

'Yes, Your Honour, as a member of the RSPCC I made a previous request to the Court to have a child committed to care. He was a ten-year-old boy who stole two freshly baked soda cakes from my—'

'Oh, yes, yes! How could I forget?' interrupted the judge as an aside, before asking, 'What can you tell me about Bridgit Norah Rodgers?'

'Your Honour, Bridgit Norah Rodgers, I've learned, is an

illegitimate child. No one seems to know who her real parents are, and the register shows her birth mother as a Colleen Rodgers whose cousin Mary Harte of Bluebell, Inchicore, is supposed to be looking after her—'

'Sorry to interrupt, but you say, "No one seems to know who her real parents are", then go on to tell me her birth mother is Colleen Rodgers. There's a contradiction there, surely?'

'Yes, Your Honour. Colleen Rodgers is the mother but I—'

'And where is the mother?'

'She is supposed to be living in London. I believe she ran away.'

'And what about this cousin? Why can't she take care of the child and not have her traipsing the streets like something out of . . . out of a Dickensian novel?'

'Your Honour, Mary Harte has six children of her own. She works as a fruit seller in Smithfield Market because her husband is laid up with tuberculosis.'

'Thank heavens *she* didn't go to London as well or else we'd be overrun with abandoned infants. What state of health is this child in at present? Does anybody know if she's been seen by a doctor?'

'Your Honour, the child has been examined by my own doctor and is in good health, although she is somewhat undernourished,' Miss Clancy replied.

'How old is this child and where is she now?'

'She is two and a half years of age and, if it pleases Your Honour, the child is here in the courtroom,' said Miss Clancy, turning to point to where a small frail-looking girl was playfully trying to kick a ball at the feet of Garda Corcoran, who was keeping an eye on her. 'At present she is under the temporary care of the Children's Hospital in Harcourt Street, but as they are unable to accept responsibility for her further welfare, a suitable place will have to be found for her elsewhere.'

Once again, the judge removed his horn-rimmed glasses and

peered down into the body of the courtroom where he observed Bridgit Norah Rodgers pick up a small red ball and dance around with glee.

'Ahem! An elfin child, if ever I saw one,' he remarked to no one in particular, before turning his attention to the complainant seated in the witness box. 'Miss Clancy do you wish to say anything further?'

'Your Honour, if it pleases the Court, I request that an order be made to have all of the street children in my area sent to state institutions where I have no doubt they will receive due care and attention, as well as some sort of religious and educational training.'

Judge Cussen's plump jovial features assumed a grimace as he remarked, 'I don't know if it necessarily pleases this Court, but it is quite clear that an order of some description will have to be made in relation to this child. But before you step down, Miss Clancy, may I also add that however well-meaning your intentions were, I would ask that you yourself give serious consideration to establishing some sort of a local refuge where these "street children", as you call them, can be taken care of, instead of having them continuously brought before this Court. That will be all, Miss Clancy,' he added, pushing the file relating to the matter to one side before entering into a whispered conversation with the clerk of the court.

Miss Clancy, meanwhile, cocked her nose in the air as she plodded down from the rostrum, before making her ungainly way to the back of the courtroom where she stood awaiting the verdict. Holding her head high, she smiled drily, as the chief justice picked up his gavel before bringing the weight of it down three times on the bench.

'I shall reserve judgment in the case of Rose Clancy versus Bridgit Rodgers until three o'clock this afternoon.'

On hearing this, Rose Clancy again had a private word with Garda Michael Corcoran before disappearing out the door of the courtroom, leaving the child in the police officer's care. The garda was only too happy to take the child's pleading hand and escort her down a side street to a café where they both had tea and biscuits.

At precisely three o'clock, a mere handful of people sat lounging around the courtroom as the judge returned to give his verdict.

'In the case of Miss Rose Clancy, complainant, versus Bridgit Norah Rodgers, defendant, the Court finds that Bridgit Rodgers, a child under the age of fourteen years, having been born – as far as can be ascertained – on the thirteenth day of September 1927, and who lately resided at Bluebell, Inchicore, in the County of Dublin, and who on the twenty-first day of February 1930 was found at Chancery Street in the said district, *begging for alms*; and whereas the council of the said county has been given an opportunity of being heard; and whereas this Court is satisfied that it is expedient to deal with the said child by sending said child to a certified industrial school; and whereas the religious persuasion of the said child appears to be Roman Catholic, it is hereby ordered that the said child shall this day be sent to St Joseph's Industrial School at Clifden, County Galway, it being a school conducted in accordance with the doctrines of the Roman Catholic Church. The managers this day state that they are willing to receive the said child, there to be detained from and after this day, the seventh of March 1930, until, but not including the thirteenth day of September 1943. And it is further ordered—'

'Ah Jezzus, Your Honour! Are your bleedin' mad or wha' . . . ?' interrupted a loud voice from the body of the court as Mary Harte, a heavy-set middle-aged woman, suddenly ran forward from where she had been loitering in the doorway and tried to rescue the child standing next to Garda Corcoran. 'Her mother will go bananas if she finds out her little chiseller—'

'Order! Order!' came a loud reprimand from the bench as

Justice Cussens began to beat the desk with his gavel. 'I will not allow this disturbance in my court!' he added, as a mêlée broke out when the gardaí tried to stop Mary Harte from gaining access to the child, who was now crying pitifully and clinging to Garda Corcoran.

'Ah, order, me bleedin' arse! What do yous lot know about childer? Yous never even saw a bleedin' fanny in your life—'

'Order! Order! Remove the assailant from this courtroom immediately . . .'

By now, two or three hefty gardaí were carrying a screaming Mary Harte out through the door and, for a second, a strange silence engulfed the courthouse, before a loud pitiful cry could be heard coming from Bridgit Norah Rodgers, as she clung to the trouser leg of Garda Michael Corcoran, while the flustered judge raised his gavel before bringing it down heavily to re-affirm, 'Judgment as stated, for the defendant.'

The die was cast.

CHAPTER TWO

For some time the young street urchin struggled to come to terms with her new surroundings at St Joseph's Industrial School. The school was a fortress-like institution, perched on top of a small hill overlooking the picturesque town of Clifden, on Ireland's westernmost seaboard, and looking out on to the broad Atlantic Ocean.

Occasionally, on warm summer Sundays, Bridgit Norah Rodgers – now affectionately referred to as 'Bridie Rodgers' by the nuns – and a group of her friends were escorted for short walks out along the famous Sky Road in Clifden. These rare outings were to become a feature of her summer days in St Joseph's, where the broad expanse of sea and sky seemed to stretch for miles and miles.

But her life was anything but rosy. No sooner had Bridie made new friends at St Joseph's than they suddenly left, having been fostered out to new homes. Boys were soon whisked away to help out on family farms, while the girls were often fostered out to ageing couples to fill the gap left after their own families had migrated to England or America. When Bridie's friends disappeared she would sit pining for hours and hours until the Reverend Mother tried convincing her yet again that all was not lost.

'But, Bridie, some day you too will have a new mammy and daddy.'

'And will I have brothers and sisters?'

'Perhaps. You might even have lots of brothers and sisters,' replied the Reverend Mother, Sister Concepta, knowing full well that Bridie could never leave St Joseph's because of the court order; and wondering what kind of family Bridie had that could leave such a gorgeous-looking child, with her mop of jet-black hair, begging for alms on the streets of Dublin.

Months later Bridie would again ask the Reverend Mother, 'But why can't I have a mammy and daddy now? What are we waiting for?'

'Bridie, dear, you have got to be patient and wait for the right mammy and daddy to come along, and besides, amn't I your mammy here? What's going to happen when you go and I'm left all on my own and I'll have no one to sit on my lap and sing "Away in a Manger"? Will you sing it again?'

Bridie shook her head shyly.

'Ah, go on, please!'

'If I sing and play the mouth organ, will you get me a new mammy and daddy?'

'I promise I'll do my very best.'

'And you'll get me brothers and sisters, and cousins and aunties, and everything?'

'It will be awfully hard, but I'll try.'

So Bridie sang the sweet, children's carol.

This bargaining chip was something Bridie Rodgers used often during her long stay in St Joseph's. And although there were many rows between herself and the sisters as she grew older and bolder, her time at the school was reasonably contented until one day she was unexpectedly called into the new Mother Superior's office.

She wondered what she'd done wrong now and whether or not she was going to be punished yet again for some minor indiscretion, like burning the bread or putting too much salt in the butter.

Instead she was relieved and mildly surprised when the

Reverend Mother said, 'Bridie, I'm sure you'll be pleased to learn that for your sixteenth birthday I've found you a job as housekeeper for a wonderful farming family who live in a big mansion known as Conly House. It's situated in the village of Cill Conly, about halfway between Tuam and Galway.'

For weeks some of the nuns had being dropping hints to Bridie about her being free to leave the industrial school on her sixteenth birthday. She'd been so amazed at first that she had not believed them, and yet, when she had asked them straight out if she'd be free on her birthday to leave St Joseph's for ever, they had all pleaded ignorance.

Bridie was amazed when the Reverend Mother added, 'You'll be working for a very wealthy family, the O'Malleys; Gerald and Beatrice. They're a middle-aged couple, with two boys, aged eight and ten, and a girl of twelve. Your job will be to take care of the children, to cook, wash and sew for them. You may, of course, be asked to do a little house cleaning for them from time to time. In return, you'll receive free accommodation, clothing and footwear, and have every Sunday off. They are very nice people and I have no doubt you'll be treated as one of their own. You're leaving tomorrow morning, at ten o'clock, if that's all right with you?'

'What's common-dation?' asked Bridie, looking pleased.

'The word is "accommodation", child – as in to accommodate someone, to give them a free bed. I thought that by now you'd have learned that much at least. It means you get free meals and a bedroom to yourself in return for the work that you do.'

'And do I get paid as well?' asked Bridie, delighted by the sound of the plan. She recalled clearly the nuns teaching that few things in this world are as powerful as money. People could buy goods at will, and the freedom to do this arose from the money in your pocket, which you earned by the sweat of your brow, whether as a kitchen maid, a farm labourer, a village shopkeeper or a city bank manager.

'Bridie, the first thing you've got to learn is that a girl such as you, with no professional training or decent family background, is in no position to expect anything other than free accommodation. You may be entitled to a small wage at some future date, but not just yet. Your present qualifications are limited to a little basic cooking and general housekeeping duties such as washing and ironing. You're probably more suited as a priest's housekeeper but this is all we can offer you now. So if you'd care to go gather up your personal belongings and stack them on your bed, I'll see if I can get you a nice suitcase, and then I'll check that you've got everything you need. I will, of course, be keeping an eye on your progress and I shall be available should you need to write to me for help or advice,' said the Reverend Mother, rising from her chair and escorting Bridie down the corridor.

'You're to address your new employers as "Mr" and "Mrs" and say, "Thank you, sir", or "Thank you, mam",' the Reverend Mother continued. 'You only ever speak when spoken to, and always ask for something by saying "please" or "may I". You've been through all this in school already and now it's time to put your good learning into practice. And I wish you the best of luck, Bridie,' she added as she turned right at the end of the corridor that led directly to the convent situated opposite the school's tall entrance gates.

For a long time Bridie sat in her room in shock and disbelief. 'Imagine, I'm leaving St Joseph's,' she said aloud to herself, before running excitedly across the school grounds to the bakery, where she knew her friend Alice was cleaning the ovens.

'I'm leaving! I'm leaving!' she beamed, jumping up and down; but when she saw Alice's reaction she wished the girl were old enough to join her. Alice still had another year to go to her sixteenth birthday, unless some rural family badly in need of domestic help came to her rescue.

After imparting her news to her friend, Bridie went straight back to her dormitory and began to pack up her bits and pieces. I can't wait to tell the rest of my friends, she thought, as she sat down again. This was the greatest thing ever to happen to her. Her new life was merely a few hours away. She would be free to go for long walks on her own. Free to eat at a nice big table with a family, instead of nibbling whenever she could while trying to mind a large group of young children.

She'd live in a big fancy mansion and have her own bedroom. Not only that, but she'd have a real mother and father, she figured – well, almost. But most important, she'd be able to have a boyfriend. The subject of boyfriends was totally frowned on at St Joseph's, but Bridie had picked up a lot of useful information from some of the unruly young girls who were brought in from Galway city where every girl, it seemed, had at least one boyfriend. She didn't care if he were a farmer's son, a shoemaker, a tinker or a thatcher, so long as she had some nice boy as a friend. Perhaps she might even find a husband and then have lots and lots of children. She danced on the bed again and sang, 'I'm free! I'm free!' as she bounced up and down.

Sister Rita appeared at the door. 'Why are you jumping on the bed like that with your dirty boots? Bridie, your behaviour is ghastly! You're acting like a tramp and an idiot. Now pull yourself together.'

'Sorry, Sister, it's just . . . that I'm so happy. Thank you and the Reverend Mother so much for finding me a job. I promise I'll do everything you and Sister Bernadine told me.'

'Yes, yes. Well, you'd better start as you mean to go on,' said Sister, sternly. 'Oh, and I almost forgot, one last thing,' she added in a barely audible whisper. 'You're to take good care of your chastity. We can't have you coming back in here again just because you've been stupid or careless. You must not, under any circumstances, harbour any impure thoughts or desires because unfortunately the world is full of evil men whose only interest is to possess your body for their own wanton pleasure and destruction. You must never allow yourself to be alone with any man, be it in a house, a field or a country lane. Should you ever find yourself in that position, you must pray for God's guidance and seek help by going to the nearest house. Purity of body is God's greatest gift to you so guard it as if your very life depended on it. Now, where are your clean petticoats and I'll help you to pack?'

'I've it all done,' said Bridie, cheerfully.

And what in God's name does she mean, 'a house, a field or country lane'? Jesus, that one's daft. Won't I be working in a house, and what would I be doing in a country lane? thought Bridie, as she watched Sister Rita make her way down the corridor. She herself went to see some of the other girls, who were working in the kitchen preparing tea for the little ones.

She made up her mind there and then she'd spend the rest of the evening discussing this latest problem with Alice when she finished work. Surely she'd be able to throw some light on this 'wanton pleasure and destruction' business.

At ten thirty the next morning, Bridie, seated on the back seat of a Ford motor car, waved goodbye to all her friends and the staff, who were standing on the gravelled entrance to St Joseph's, waving her their goodbyes. She had witnessed this scene so many times down through the years from the sanctuary of her bedroom window that she had almost given up all hope that she too would one day be driven like a lady to a new place in the country. A tiny tear betrayed her emotions as she looked round and waved one last time to Alice, who stood waving a white handkerchief. Bridie recalled for a moment their days of daisy chains in the big field and a famous lost coin. Oh yes, and the burned cakes, and Sister Bernadine constantly lecturing her, the oul' bitch.

Perhaps she meant well, thought Bridie. Pity it isn't the old

Mother Superior, Sister Concepta, who's standing there, though. I would just love to have hugged her. She understood me better. But what matters now, I've a brand-new home to go to. I'll be living in Conly House.

CHAPTER THREE

THE SCORCHING LATE summer sun shone brightly and a cool breeze swept soothingly through Bridie's hair as the gleaming motor car wound its way through the Connemara mountains, sleek as the birds of prey that were soaring and gliding high above the picturesque valleys.

The driver said they'd stop in Galway, have a nice cup of tea near the beach and be at their destination in three hours.

Bridie wondered what was in the letter that she had been given to pass on to the O'Malleys. Perhaps it was a reference. They'd probably need a reference on her ability to cook. Oh my God, she thought, more burned cakes and soggy soda bread and botched needlework. No, don't be silly, rich people won't need any socks darned, she told herself. Besides, I'll have Sundays to recover and perhaps I can go to the beach – wouldn't that be wonderful? Then I could learn how to swim.

It was almost one thirty. Bridie's stomach did a roll as the car suddenly turned left and wound its way up a long gravelled drive to a big white house surrounded by beautiful trees, flowers and shrubs. On either side of the driveway were immaculate lawns, with bronze statues and a fountain. And beyond were acres and acres of green pasture.

Bridie stepped down from the car as the driver took her small brown suitcase and then escorted her towards the door. Mr and Mrs O'Malley appeared with outstretched arms.

'You're very welcome, Bridie. I'm Gerald, and this is my

wife, Beatrice, and, of course, you've already met Tom, our chauffeur. How are you?' asked Mr O'Malley.

'I'm fine,' said Bridie, as she unwittingly did a little curtsy and shook hands first with Gerald and then with Beatrice, who cast a critical eye over her – or was she imagining it?

Mrs O'Malley thought her new housekeeper was too frail and thin looking for such a demanding job, though she was a very attractive girl with waves of black curly hair. In a way she felt disappointed. She had expected her new housekeeper to appear more mature for her age, and be dowdier-looking.

'I won't be needing you till seven this evening, thanks,' said Mrs O'Malley, turning to address Tom.

'Let me help with your luggage,' said Gerald, taking the suitcase from Bridie as she was about to pick it up, and they all traipsed into the house.

'Bridie, Gerald will take care of your luggage. Just let me show you downstairs and then I'll take you through the rest of the house. You won't be starting work until tomorrow morning. I'm sure you must be exhausted after that long journey and those horrible winding roads,' said Beatrice.

'No, I'm fine,' smiled Bridie. 'The scenery was magnificent, and Tom showed me the Lazy Wall in Salthill. It was unbelievable, watching all those people lying there, sunning themselves. He said that's why it was called the Lazy Wall.'

'Did he now! Hmm, that's our Tom.'

Bridie was amazed at the size of the house for just five people. There was a conservatory, a reading room, a sitting room, a dining room, a kitchen, a scullery and a games room; as well as a laundry and two lavatories. Upstairs was the master bedroom, the children's bedrooms – Sinead, being the eldest, had her own room – the maid's room, where Bridie would sleep, four other rooms and a bathroom and lavatory besides.

Soon the children came in from the fields where they were riding ponies and arranging jumps. They were introduced to their new housekeeper. Bridie was immediately struck by the likeness of the daughter, Sinead, to her mother. She thought it was like looking at Beatrice when she was twelve years old. She had bright blue twinkling eyes, and light-coloured wispy hair so fine you'd almost need X-ray eyes to see the few strands hanging over her face. The boys, Daniel and Darragh, she couldn't figure out because of their mischievous grins.

After tea and sandwiches Bridie was invited to dine with the family for the evening meal before being handed a work schedule for the rest of the week.

Tomorrow, Tuesday, she'd be expected to be up at seven o'clock in the morning to light the fire in the drawing room – because Gerald liked to read for an hour while enjoying a cup of tea. She'd have to cook breakfast for the farm workers and, when they had finished, she'd cook breakfast for the whole family before washing up and preparing her own meal. Then it was time to sort Monday's wash and put the dry clothes into the various wardrobes. She'd have to change and dress all the beds, sweep and dust the rooms before preparing dinner for whoever was in the house.

Afternoons were to be taken up with more cleaning and polishing, before getting the dinner ready for the children on their return from school. Then they did their homework before Bridie accompanied them for fun and games. Wednesday and Thursday were more of the same with a little baking and sewing. Friday was fish day all round, with no meat of any description, something Bridie was well used to. The O'Malleys had fish of a Friday, in one form or another, for breakfast, dinner and tea. To Bridie, Saturday sounded the worst day of the week. Stairs, landings and corridors had to be cleaned and polished in preparation for Sunday's expected visitors. Mrs O'Malley gave Bridie strict instructions to consume her own meals in her own time in the kitchen.

She was surprised and a bit disappointed to receive this cold order, and recalled a little yarn the Reverend Mother had once told her. Her next-door neighbour, she said, had a loyal servant, who, on being invited only to the afters of her master's wedding, bravely replied, 'A bone-picker or plate-licker I'll never be to those who think they are better than me.' Bridie wished that at that moment she could have come up with some similar quick-witted reply for Mrs O'Malley, but she couldn't.

That evening Bridie dined in splendid and sumptuous surroundings, as the dining room was brightly lit and the oval mahogany table laid out in the famous blue of Mason's ironstone china and King's cutlery, which Bridie recognised.

Candles and bottles of red wine adorned the settings as Mrs O'Malley served up prawn cocktail followed by roast beef and sherry trifle. During the meal Beatrice and Gerald questioned Bridie extensively about life in St Joseph's. Bridie had nothing but the highest of praise for her former custodians, as she felt that the O'Malleys were merely digging for malicious gossip that might well find its way back to Sister Bernadine. And while they divulged very little of themselves, it became clear that Gerald was indeed a gentleman farmer with a penchant for rearing horses.

Bridie couldn't wait to snuggle down in her own bedroom, with its new feather bed and hand-embroidered quilt. But when she did and the lights were out, she found she couldn't get to sleep. The day's events kept going through her mind, and then suddenly she was gripped by an awful fear. First, there was the strange silence and stillness that was so different from night at St Joseph's. There was never any noise at the school, but this new-found silence was terrifying, and it was made much worse by minute creaking noises that made her want to sit up and scream. She couldn't make up her mind if it was her room door being slowly opened or someone tiptoeing on the floorboards at the foot of her bed. Several times she held her breath; she was afraid even to breathe because she couldn't see anything.

Yet on and on it went: the awful silence for long periods, followed by faint creaking noises. What if someone was trying to kill her or attack her in bed, she thought. Were the O'Malley children spying on her? Worse still, had Mr O'Malley sneaked into her bedroom? Bridie remembered Sister Rita warning her that, 'the world is full of evil men whose only interest is to possess your body for their own wanton pleasure and destruction.' But what pleasure would they get out of killing her and taking her body? What, she wondered, if Mr O'Malley had come sneaking into the room to take her body away? What would he do with it?

At that moment she heard the creaking noise again and sat bolt upright in the bed, screaming. 'Who's there?'

But nobody answered as she peered into the darkness, expecting to feel hands clutching at her body. She thought the room was starting to spin as she tried to figure out where things were. Where was the door, the dressing table, or the washstand? She closed her eyes and lay back in bed, covering her head with the blankets. She was practically gasping for breath. She thought, that's it, the house is haunted. She had heard so many ghost stories in St Joseph's, and she was now convinced this must be one of those haunted houses. If she ever again saw daylight she'd run away, back to St Joseph's. She could hear footsteps approaching her room now and she started shaking violently. She threw down the blankets from over her head and was about to scream to high heaven when the bedroom door opened and Mr O'Malley appeared, dressed in his night attire and holding aloft a lantern in his hand.

'Bridie, are you all right? I thought I heard someone calling.'

She was so relieved to see Mr O'Malley standing there with the night-light that she was completely lost for words. When she did not reply, he again asked, 'Are you all right, dear?'

'Yes, yes, I think I must have been dreaming,' croaked Bridie.

'Oh. You're all right then. We're just down the hall, if you

21

need anything,' he reminded her, quietly closing the door behind him, and Bridie heard his footsteps retreat down the corridor. Slowly she submerged her tortured body beneath the blankets, closed her eyes and started to say her night prayers once more.

Bridie felt as if she had just nodded off to sleep when Mrs O'Malley shook her in the bed and said, 'Bridie, what's the meaning of this? It's nearly eight o'clock, and the workmen are below in the kitchen waiting for their breakfast. If this is an example of your behaviour after the way you were treated last night then I wouldn't give much for your chances of staying on here.'

'I'm sorry, Mrs O'Malley, I'm sorry. I must have overslept,' said Bridie as she sprang from the bed and proceeded to dress quickly, as Mrs O'Malley left the room, slamming the door behind her.

Bridie was in the kitchen preparing the late morning breakfast, as the three workmen sat around the large kitchen table, well aware of Bridie's slip-up. They were having great fun amongst themselves.

The young, slightly balding farm hand was saying '. . . and did you ever notice when there's work to be done you could stay in bed all day; but when it's your day off, you're up at cockcrow because you can't sleep?'

'I don't know about you,' replied his dark-haired co-worker, 'but if I had a good-looking girl beside me in the bed of a morning, the devil-a-up I'd ask to get.'

'If you had a good-looking girl in the bed and you didn't rise every morning, it wouldn't be long until she'd come running to me, because I'd be up! And up! And up!' replied Baldy, obscenely, as Bridie began to drop the hard-boiled eggs into their egg cups.

'Ah, you dirty bugger. Shut up. That's all you ever think of, sex, sex, sex! I think there's a bit of the farm animal about you.'

'Take no notice of him, girl, 'tisn't a brain he has in his head, it's a cesspit,' said Darkie, winking and smiling at Bridie as she cut some more bread.

Bridie said nothing in response to their coaxing, as she had other things on her mind and was well aware that Mrs O'Malley was hovering around somewhere nearby.

A few hours later she was beginning to feel the pressure of the number of jobs she had to do, which wasn't at all helped by her having continuously to ask Mrs O'Malley where this was or where that was, because she didn't know the place of anything or the household ritual. Much earlier she had decided to do without her breakfast, but she was still struggling to cope after dinner, when she knew she should now be on schedule with her chores. She decided to skip some of her duties and to concentrate on the more pressing ones, like getting ready for the children's return from school. She gave them their tea and helped them with their study before they showed her round the farm. The children were nice and courteous to her, showing her all the horses, sheep and cattle, and telling her that Dad liked reading the *Racing Chronicle*, because sometimes his name would appear along with those of his prize horses.

On Bridie's return, Mr O'Malley asked her how her day had been.

'Fine, thank you.'

'Sorry about this morning. Herself thinks it's a crime to sleep in of a morning, but sure, we all make mistakes some time or other. So don't take any notice of her, Bridie; her bark's worse than her bite.'

As if waiting for an opportunity to intervene, Mrs O'Malley suddenly appeared and said to her husband, 'Oh, there you are!' Then, folding her arms across her chest, she added, 'I hope, Gerald, you had a word with Bridie about this morning. You know, Bridie, sleeping in is not acceptable.'

'Yes, yes, we've just been through that, and Bridie has apologised,' said Gerald, as he abruptly turned to go out the door now that his wife had come in. She, in turn, followed him out and Bridie carried on with her tasks.

Bridie thought she'd love to stick a pin in Mrs O'Malley just to shut her up. After all, what was I supposed to do? she sighed to herself as she finished the last of the day's chores. I feel wrecked after all that and I not getting a wink of sleep for hours last night. And what am I to do tonight if it's the same thing? I just dread the thought of that room. I'll be out of a job tomorrow if I sleep in again. That reminds me, I must check the rota and see what I'm cooking for the workmen and the children. At least the workmen were nice and polite. What were their names again? I like the nice one that winked at me while I poured the tea. He wasn't too bad-looking. I wonder how old he is? Twenty? Twenty-two? Yeah. That would be a good age. But how would I know what was the right age for a fellow or a girl to be together?

Bridie's thoughts were blown to smithereens by the explosive charges in the grandfather clock that stood in the hallway. She decided she'd done enough for one day. She had deliberately stayed hanging about in the kitchen, leaving just enough to do should Mrs O'Malley appear again. Now she'd rinse out a few dishcloths, spread the tea towels to dry and go to bed. She hoped tonight she'd get some sleep and dream about Blackie, the nice workman – that's what she'd call him until she found out his real name. What way did he say it? 'If I'd a good-lookin' girl beside me in the bed of a morning, the devil-a-up I'd ask to get.' Umm. I wonder what that would be like. It would be lovely and cosy and safe, like when I jumped into Alice's bed that night during the thunder and lightning. And next day I had to listen to a lecture from Sister Bernadine: 'Bridie, what you did at your age was very wrong. It's a bad habit to get into, as it can only lead to sin.'

Neither Alice nor I could ever figure out what she meant. Anyway, she can't stop me now. Imagine, I can do what I want, go where I want. Perhaps I'll go somewhere on Sunday. I could visit Tuam or Galway, I suppose. I'd love to go to Tuam. But how will I get there? What if I can't ever leave here and there's nobody to bring me anywhere? Surely they wouldn't leave me here all day on my own, would they?

It was getting late, but the O'Malleys hadn't gone to bed yet; Bridie could hear the steady drone of their voices downstairs. She lay in bed, reliving the horrors of the night before, expecting them to return at any minute. She tried to think about Blackie, but it was the presence of Mrs O'Malley standing over her bed that morning that kept intervening. She couldn't concentrate on anything else. She found herself listening in the dark for the creaking noises she'd heard before. All was quiet. In fact it was much too quiet, apart from the occasional voice coming from downstairs. And when she thought about the stillness of the night, the feeling of terror that had haunted her the night before started to creep back again. She had survived it, she told herself, only because she wasn't tired; whereas now she was exhausted after the day's exertions.

What, she wondered, was she going to do to get some sleep? She could get up, go downstairs now and tell them about the noise. Then she heard the chairs downstairs being moved about and people were saying, 'Good night, see you tomorrow.' They must have had visitors. The O'Malleys were coming upstairs. It was too late to say anything now. Besides, Mrs O'Malley might get angry with her and send her back to St Joseph's. Would she go back to Clifden or should she run away to Galway or maybe Dublin? It was hard to know what to do. If she went back to St Joseph's, she might be kept there for ever, or made to join the nuns and sent to some convent where she would have to look after children for the rest of her life.

Oh my God, there's that queer noise back again, and the

faint night-light that was under the door has gone out. God, it's so creepy in this house, she sighed.

She hugged her shoulders and pulled the blankets up around her neck for added security and protection because she could still feel the goose pimples on her arms and shoulders. She turned over and tried to get comfortable.

Maybe I suffer from a fear of strange houses, she thought. That's silly. If only there was some light I could get comfortable and go to sleep. Could that creaking noise be a mouse or, worse, a rat?

Her body gave an uncontrollably nervous twitch at the thought of seeing a rat emerging from a hole in the floorboards, like she'd once seen at St Joseph's. As bad as that experience had been, she'd still settle for the peace and tranquillity of St Joseph's right now, with her friends sleeping all around her.

Here, in this big house, she was all alone in the middle of nowhere. She forced herself to try to face reality. The O'Malleys lived here, so it must be all right.

God, maybe that's it, she thought. How could this place, this house, even this room, be like St Joseph's? Here I have my own room, my own bed, while in St Joseph's there was always a beautiful comforting sort of noise I never realised existed. Someone was always coughing, snoring, or talking in their sleep. Someone might scream aloud because she was having an awful nightmare of being beaten by her drunken father, but always you could hear the soothing voice of the night nurse as she said, 'It's all right, pet, it's only a dream,' as she tucked the child in again. 'Go back to sleep now.' And if the screaming woke me I'd lift my head to see who it was, then I'd turn over and go back to sleep and I wouldn't be a bit afraid. Besides, several night-lights hung on the dormitory walls. Here there are no lights and no friends, and it's such a small room compared to the one in St Joseph's. Listen, there's nothing; not a sound, except when the creaking starts. Maybe it's from the floorboards in the next room. That's silly, there's no one sleeping in the next room.

Whatever it was, she wasn't hearing it now, and the thought that she was beginning to deal with her fears gave her confidence. She realised for the first time that this was how it would always be; she'd have to get used to it. And, with these comforting thoughts, she turned over and whispered, 'Dear God, thank you for coming to my rescue,' as sleep carried her away on a tidal wave of happiness.

It was Sunday. The O'Malleys were preparing for Mass and had arranged to give Bridie a lift to church. She sat waiting in the living room. On her return she would be treated to dinner with the family. Mr O'Malley had already told her there were some nice sights, if she wanted to get out and about for a walk. The children would show her around. But deep down she was expecting something more on her day off. She thought how nice it would be to get away from the house. She'd been here only six days she told herself; nevertheless she would almost certainly be here for another six days before she could go anywhere again. She was supposed to be free, yet she had nowhere to go. She thought how lovely it would be to go to the cinema. She had seen two films while in Clifden and would love to see another one. But how would she go? Maybe there are no films in Tuam. And if she did go to the cinema, whom could she go with? She didn't have any friends here to go anywhere. Then she remembered the workmen saying something about a dance tonight at the cross.

God, if only I could think who it was that said it, Bridie thought. Oh, yes, 'twas Peter. What did he say? 'They're organising a bit of a ceilí at the cross.' What cross? And who's 'they'? Oh, what did I do with the five shillings the Reverend Mother gave me? I'll run upstairs and bring it with me to Mass, just in case we go somewhere.

They went to ten o'clock Mass in the small village church in Cill Conly. The children wanted to go to the cathedral in Tuam, but Gerald said no. Bridie was disappointed because the children had led her to believe that going to Mass in the cathedral was a regular event. Instead she had to smile and pretend to be happy when introduced to the various aunts and uncles of the O'Malley clan, while everyone appeared to stop and gawk and whisper as she moved around the circle.

'A fine slip of a girl,' the men said.

'Ahem. But does she know how to boil an egg?' asked Auntie Biddy, cocking her snoot in the air.

After Sunday dinner, the children showed Bridie the ancient castle in the grounds of an enclosed orchard where other children came in autumn to plunder the apples. The O'Malley children were strictly forbidden to enter the orchard because some of the high-broached walls of the castle hung precariously, and were a danger.

'. . . Anyway, the apples aren't nice. They're huge green things only good for tarts, not like the beautiful ones we have in Granny's garden. Bridie, do you have apple trees in your garden?' asked Sinead, as they stood looking over a low stone wall at the ruins of the castle.

'Yes, of course, lots.'

'And are there castles near your house?' asked Daniel.

'Not as near as yours, but quite near.'

'Can we go there someday?' asked Daniel, his eyes dancing as the three of them now surrounded Bridie.

'But . . . but . . . where do you live?' asked Darragh, coming closer.

'Oh, it's a long, long way from here,' said Bridie. 'Clifden. Have you ever heard of Clifden? It's in Connemara.'

'Is that in Dublin?' asked Darragh, hopefully.

'You shut your gob. I was talking to her first,' Daniel sneered at his brother angrily.

'No. It's on the coast. It's a beautiful seaside town,' said Bridie quickly, hoping they'd realise that not everyone gets to live near the sea.

'Ah, no. You mean you live by the sea?' said Sinead, excitedly.

'Yes,' answered Bridie, triumphantly, just when she was beginning to think she wouldn't have anything good to say about herself.

'Oh, I want to go there. I've only ever been to Salthill. Can we go and stay in your house?' asked Sinead.

'Well . . . I don't think that's possible,' said Bridie, after an agonising delay.

'But why?' asked Darragh. 'Do your mother and father not like us?'

'Shut your streece. Her mother and father have never even seen us,' interrupted Daniel as he playfully pushed his younger brother out of the way.

'I won't. I won't,' shouted the little fellow defiantly as his older brother laughed and the two of them started to wrestle on the ground, before running across the field.

Sinead was delighted. She now had Bridie all to herself. She prayed the boys would carry on playing on their own, because she liked the new housekeeper, who was so much younger and slimmer than the last one. Sinead was shocked when she realised she herself was only four years younger than Bridie. Out here in the country she thought Bridie was lovely, while at home she seemed awfully quiet.

'Do you have many brothers and sisters?' asked Sinead, as they walked towards the river that divided the farm.

Bridie, caught unexpectedly, didn't have time to think and answered rather hastily, 'No, I have no brothers or sisters.'

'Uck! I'd hate that! You mean you never had a brother or a sister? Who minded you then? Whom did you play with?'

Bridie now felt she had made a fool of herself by telling the truth. Worse still, she felt a strange kind of anguish on hearing Sinead say 'Uck!' just because she was on her own. Perhaps she should have lied. But what, Bridie wondered, would Sinead say if she knew she had no mother or father either? She would have to invent something quick or Sinead might grow to dislike her and no longer be her friend.

'I had a younger brother once, but he died when he was three,' said Bridie.

'Died? What happened to him?'

'I don't know. He just died . . . I think it was the measles or something. Is that the river?' said Bridie, changing tack and realising that she was entering dangerous territory, telling lies.

'Oh, how awful. Darragh and Daniel,' shouted Sinead, as the two boys came into view over the rise, pretending to be galloping horses. 'Bridie had a brother that died of measles, and you've not had measles or mumps yet.'

In an instant the galloping horses came to an abrupt halt, and reverted to curious boys again.

'What's measles?' asked Darragh.

'What's mumps?' asked his brother.

'Measles. You're covered in spots, your eyes, your ears, your nose, your mouth, your chin, right down to you know what. Besides, Mum has already told you,' laughed Sinead. 'And anybody who even touches you or goes anywhere near you gets it straight away. And mumps . . . are great big lumps that cover your face,' she added triumphantly.

'Why do only boys die?' asked Darragh, worried.

'Not many boys die,' intervened Bridie quickly, lest she be accused of frightening the children. 'Only someone who is very ill, too weak, or not able to take their medicine,' she added.

'Gosh. I don't think I've had measles or mumps yet,' said Sinead, thinking that she herself might still be at risk, and that if one of them got it then the whole family would be wiped out. But it hadn't killed Bridie, so it might not kill her if the boys got it.

'But why didn't your mother and father get another boy when your little brother died?' queried Sinead.

'I don't know,' answered Bridie. 'Maybe they were afraid he would die too.'

'Oh, that would be awful. Anyway, I'd rather have a sister. Sisters are more fun,' said Sinead, suddenly grabbing Bridie by the hand, because she knew it would annoy her brothers, who hated girls.

'And I'd rather have a brother. Heh!' snorted Daniel, sneering right into his sister's face. 'Because girls are sissies and crybabies.'

'Come on, I'll race you to the river; then we'll see who's a crybaby,' said Sinead, knowing full well that she could outsprint Daniel any time.

Later, when they all returned home, Bridie decided it might be a good time to write to Alice and Sister Bernadine at St Joseph's, and she went quietly up to her room.

Meanwhile the children, on being asked how they had enjoyed their afternoon, told their mother how Bridie lived in a house by the sea, and how she had invited them there next summer. That they too had loads of apple trees and lived near a castle, and that Bridie had a brother who got the measles and died; and that her father and mother had decided not to get any more boys in case they died too.

'Mammy, does that mean we'll die if we get the mumps or measles?'

'Of course not, dear, don't be silly,' said Mrs O'Malley. 'Did Bridie say anything else?'

'She wanted to know about the dance at the cross, and if you and Daddy ever went, and how old Thomas and Peter are, and where they live and if they have girlfriends. She said she'd love to go to the pictures; that she used to go in Clifden,' said Sinead.

'She said the pictures were like big photographs that moved on a white wall, and that it was real scary at first. But they're not real, but can be very funny or sad, added Daniel excitedly. 'Mammy, can we go to the pictures?'

'I don't know. We'll have to ask your father, and we all know he only likes going to the horse shows. Now, don't you think it's time you got ready for bed? You've school in the morning,' she said, as Gerald came in and proceeded to put his shotgun away in a secure cabinet after an enjoyable day shooting with his friends.

'Oh, there you are. I need to have a word with you about something important later.'

Her words were almost drowned out by the excitement of the children relaying the day's events. An hour or so later, when all was quiet in the house, Beatrice turned to Gerald as he sat reading the newspaper, and remarked, 'I don't think Bridie is the type of person I'd want as company for our children.'

Gerald, somewhat startled, put down the *Racing Chronicle* and looked over the rim of his gilt-framed glasses at his wife.

'Whatever makes you say that?'

'Surely you were startled at the lies she told our children this afternoon. "A big house", my foot! And inviting them there next summer! Surely you don't think that's acceptable behaviour?'

'Perhaps she was only trying to be friendly. After all, she's only sixteen.'

'Upon my word, and a dangerous sixteen at that. Did the children tell you she was asking about the workmen – what they did on their days off and when was the next dance at the cross? Besides, she's not very good at housekeeping. She doesn't know how to bake properly, and I have to constantly remind her to clean up after herself whenever she does the cooking, and you know how tiresome that can be, just keeping an eye on her.'

Gerald picked up the newspaper and started to read to show his distaste at his wife's pettiness.

'You're not listening. You never do. I knew I should have gone to St Joseph's myself and vetted the girls personally, instead of letting them send out a half-trained girl without an ounce of parentage.'

This line was enough to rile Gerald. Knowing he'd get no peace, he flung down the paper and removed his glasses.

'I thought we'd both agreed, we'd consider giving a job to a nice homeless girl after we'd read about their plight in the newspaper. Did we or did we not agree to that?'

'Of course. But she's totally unacceptable. You saw how she behaved that first morning – I almost had to cancel my appointment with the tea ladies – and now these lies. It's not acceptable, Gerald. I will not have my children's prospects tainted by someone whose only ability is to fill them with false hopes and lies; not to mention the fear of death from some hideous disease or other. I think we should both accept it's been a horrible mistake and go for a more mature lady in her early thirties.'

'I don't accept any such thing,' said Gerald in exasperation. 'We've had three different housekeepers in the last five years. They could cook, sew and were very good with the children. But they all left, didn't they? At least Bridie's young. She could become part of the family; she seems eager enough to me, and besides, the children like her, especially Sinead.'

'That is precisely my point, Gerald. She would be a bad influence. This talk of dancing and pictures and farm boys is not good listening for any daughter of mine. What we need is a nice sophisticated girl, a trained nanny, somebody with a proper pedigree. You've said it yourself: you'll not buy a mare unless it's a thoroughbred.'

'Ah, Beatrice, don't talk rubbish. We're talking about people here, and as far as I'm concerned, Bridie's a nice girl. She's attractive, pleasant and the children like her. As far as I'm concerned there's nothing wrong with Bridie that a little chat wouldn't put right. Have a word, if you must. But for God's sake, leave it at that.'

Next morning, when the children were gone to school and the workers had vacated the kitchen, Mrs O'Malley sat Bridie down at the kitchen table.

'Bridie, dear, I feel obliged to inform you that Gerald and I have been rather taken aback by your comments to our children yesterday. Have you anything to say?'

Bridie was dumbstruck. She didn't know what Mrs O'Malley was talking about, but her mind raced to the bridge, the castle, the orchard, the measles . . . surely it wasn't the dreaded talk about the mumps and the measles? She decided quickly it was best to plead total ignorance.

'What do you mean?' she said.

'You, Miss Bridie Rodgers, led my children to believe you were a person of distinguished background, whose parents owned property on the seafront. You claimed you had a younger brother who died tragically as a result of contracting measles, when we all know you were a homeless child sent down from Dublin. You also intimated to Sinead – who, God knows, is an impressionable young child – that you fancied one of the farm hands. That, Miss Bridie Rodgers, Gerald and I find most reprehensible.'

'Excuse me,' said Bridie, her eyes ablaze, 'I said no such thing. I'm only here a week and I don't know anyone. I've slaved every single day and all I did was have a friendly conversation with the children. I asked Sinead about the other workers and what they did in their spare time. That's hardly claiming to fancy somebody.'

'What about the lies?' retorted Mrs O'Malley. 'The so-called parents of yours that don't even exist; brothers that don't exist, and a big house by the sea: that's obviously a figment of your imagination, and you not even owning the rags on your back.'

Bridie could not believe she had been so stupid with the children, but the way Mrs O'Malley portrayed her personal background was like thrusting a knife into her heart, she felt so hurt.

She rose from the table shouting, 'Yes. The very rags you gave me. I'm going to tell Sister Bernadine the sort of person you are.' And with that she ran crying from the kitchen and upstairs to her room.

Mrs O'Malley could barely conceal her anger that such a brazen hussy could treat her like that. She meant to give Bridie a good lecture, but somehow Bridie, who hadn't said a word all week, managed to make her feel small by running away from her. Nobody, but nobody, does that to me, intoned Mrs O'Malley to herself. If that lady thinks she can ignore me after I, out of the goodness of my heart, gave her a bed to lie on and a station to be proud of, then she has another think coming.

Bridie sat on her bed and cried. What's wrong with me? I'm always in trouble, she wept. I can't do anything right. If it's not the baking, it's the cleaning-up after myself. If it's not what I do, it's what I say. Why can't she accept I've done nothing wrong? Surely it's not a sin to pretend I have a mother and father, or a brother who died, she sobbed. Besides, I do have a home if I want, you oul' hag. I'm sure Gerald never said those things. He always seems so nice to me, when she's not there. But he leaves the room the minute she comes in. Sure, he hates the sight of her. I'll write and tell Mother Superior . . . But I already wrote praising the O'Malleys. How can I write again and say I don't like them?

What will I do now? she wondered as she tried to pull herself together and to reason the whole thing out. I'm not going downstairs again. But then maybe she'll throw me out and then I'll have nowhere to go. I've no food; no money except the five shillings. Maybe I should leave now and go into Tuam where there's a convent, and I could work for wages. I suppose

I was wrong to tell the children I had a brother, but I didn't mean it. I never said I fancied any of the farm lads. Saying Blackie was nice — does that mean I like him?

Deep down Bridie knew that it did. But then she liked Gerald and the children, and Alice. Language and words and suggestions are stupid, she thought. Pure stupid. Everything I say or do is twisted. Even Sister Bernadine didn't believe me when I found the two shillings in the nuns' field, and she tried to say I stole it. Now that hag Mrs O'Malley is trying to say I led her children to believe I was a person of distinguished background.

But I *am* a person of distinguished background. I've been taught by the nuns; in a proper school. I made my First Communion. I learned to cook, sew and play the mouth organ, so I'll not let anyone belittle me like that, thought Bridie. I'll stay right here till that bitch says she's sorry.

Meanwhile Mrs O'Malley, with her arms folded, stood looking thoughtfully out of the rear kitchen window. She could see the workmen in the distant fields ploughing-in stubble with Gerald's best horses at the helm. But horses were the last things on Mrs O'Malley's mind. Bridie — what was she going to do with her now? If the workmen weren't to be deprived of dinner, then somebody would have to prepare it, and quick. She, as head of the household, was not going to do it while *that one* was upstairs. But how would she get her down without losing face? The way she saw it, she had two choices: dismiss Bridie instantly and do the cooking herself, which was her preferred option; or apologise straight away and get Bridie down quickly to do the cooking. She considered the latter a horrendous idea. It meant she would have to grovel in order to get Bridie back to work. She turned on her heel and decided she'd do the cooking. She had a bucket of washed potatoes on the table, ready to peel, when the thought suddenly struck her that she would have to do them again tomorrow if Bridie were dismissed. Worse still, she would have to wash and peel, scrub and sew, and bake for the entire week. And if her friends and neighbours ever found out that her home had been reduced to self-catering simply because her new housemaid was here only a week and gone, what would they think? She frowned as she washed her soiled hands. Gerald, of course, would get very cross if he found she'd dismissed *that lady* without his agreement, and after what happened with the last maid that would be unthinkable.

I know, thought Mrs O'Malley, I'll pretend it was all my fault and get it over with for now. Then when I'm good and ready, and when *that one* least expects it, I'll get my revenge.

She went upstairs and knocked on Bridie's door. 'May I come in, please?'

Bridie opened the bedroom door and stood looking at Mrs O'Malley.

'Bridie, I've been thinking. Perhaps I'm not very good at expressing myself. But what I really want to say is . . . I've been a bit hasty. You're only here a week and you've been very good and everything, and we're all very fond of you. So let's just forget everything I've said, and go back downstairs.'

Bridie did not answer. She stood looking at Mrs O'Malley in disbelief. There must be a reason for this sudden change of heart, she was thinking, as her eyes took in Mrs O'Malley's gem-encrusted brooch, fancy earrings, and multiple wedding and sovereign rings.

The hag, thought Bridie, all that's missing is the bag. You're far too grand, missus, to be washing potatoes, cutting cabbage or scrubbing kitchen floors. But do I have a choice? No. But true as God is my judge, Mrs O'Malley, I'll bide my time, wait my chance, and then I'm off.

She silently side-stepped Mrs O'Malley and ran down the stairs.

Bridie soon realised that labouring under Mrs O'Malley was one major ordeal she had not bargained for. She decided, however, not to respond to her continual goading. After much thought she came to the conclusion that she didn't have any choice but to keep her head down and say nothing for the time being. This restriction on herself was most painful in the company of the children, especially Sinead, whom she loved to talk with. Bridie felt she could no longer wear her heart on her sleeve because there was no knowing how her words might be construed by Mrs O'Malley, should the children ever engage in a harmless bout of tittle-tattle.

Instead, Bridie turned her thoughts to the workmen, Peter, Thomas and Seamus. Of the three, Seamus was now her favourite. Although the oldest by far, he had a certain charm that made her enjoy being in his company. Seamus and Peter usually regaled Bridie over breakfast with lurid tales of the local community, where, according to Seamus, the village was rife with snobbery and where the working class begrudged you the steam of their piss. She just loved the facial expressions and witty remarks that went with their recounting of a tale.

Her favourite memory was of Seamus's belief: 'Nothing good ever came out of Cill Conly, because it's the sort of place where if the neighbours have anything at all against you, they'll bide their time, and then give you the full contents of their steaming piss-pots in the face of a morning when you least expect it. And if you're lucky they might even rush out and plead it was a pure accident, while deep within their hearts they're just delirious with pleasure at having scored a direct hit. For days and days their household will simply revel in the sordidness of it all. So don't say, girl, you haven't been warned. Don't say.'

She was warned too by Mr O'Malley that the local village was not the place to be seen at a Sunday crossroads dance. There everyone would know she was a stranger. And it was only fair she should know the place was full of lecherous-looking men well past their prime, so that if she were ever to consider going to a dance, then the place to go was Cross or Toureen across the border in County Mayo.

But Bridie never got to go anywhere except when the children were taken to the cathedral in Tuam, which was very rare. Her only social contact was preparing tea for the weekly visitors and listening to the daily episodes of the farm workers, as they pulled up noisy chairs to attack breakfast each morning.

It was Thursday and Bridie was on her knees, cleaning the stairs and dreaming of a possible romantic interlude with Seamus, who had said he was going to the dance at Cross on Sunday night. It was only four miles away. Perhaps she should consider walking there herself. It's high time I got to see a bit of the world, she thought. Sure, I think I'll go on my own, one way or another.

Suddenly, she was aware of a disturbance behind her, but she was too late to avoid the handle of the brush as Mrs O'Malley laid it across her back.

'What's the meaning of this?' (wallop!) she began. 'You've ruined my best blouse with your blasted iron.' (Wallop). 'Don't you know you can't iron a silk blouse if the iron's too hot?' she shouted.

Bridie ran for protection to the top of the stairs.

'I didn't know! Mrs O'Malley, I didn't know!' she pleaded, retreating hurriedly, but Mrs O'Malley continued to lash out.

'You're nothing but a wastrel; thrown out of the industrial school by a shower of nuns. I should have known better than to hire the likes of you.'

Bridie turned, her eyes ablaze. Pointing a finger at Mrs O'Malley, she said, 'If you hit me once more—'

Wallop! 'How dare you point a finger at me?' hissed Mrs O'Malley, as she hit Bridie a short sharp crack across the hand. 'Go to your room at once,' she ordered as she closed in on her.

Bridie saw this as a very dangerous move, and knew she might get a severe beating in the confines of her room. So, acting purely on instinct, she shot forward and bolted past Mrs O'Malley, almost knocking her back down the stairs.

Bridie stood for a fleeting moment in the relative safety of the hall, looked up and shouted, 'I won't. I won't. You can get some other body to do your dirty work.'

Mrs O'Malley, recovering her balance, started to come quickly down the stairs as she screamed at Bridie, 'Come back here at once! Come back here, now!'

But Bridie had shot out the rear door and was running for dear life down the long gravelled drive. She kept running until she was out of sight of the house and then she climbed over a wall and into a field in case anybody saw her. Struggling to get her breath, she sat down on a rock and started to sob. This in turn led to a fear that her hand might be broken, for it was now slightly swollen. Besides, her back ached and stung whenever she moved.

She stayed there, sitting on the huge boulder for a long time, till a cold chill took hold of her and she knew she'd have to seek shelter. Lightly dressed, she soon realised she had no clothes, no food and no money. She made up her mind she was not going back to that house again. But somehow she had to get her clothes and money. She had nothing else to wear and was powerless without them. A light rain was starting to fall. She knew she'd have to do something quickly. Using her vague knowledge of the area, from the walks with the children, she decided to go by a circuitous route back to the farmyard, where she'd hide and shelter until she could go into the house and get her belongings.

Better still, she might ask Peter or Seamus to get them for her. Otherwise she would have to stay hiding until tomorrow morning because the children would be around in the evening, and Mrs O'Malley was not due to go visiting anywhere until tomorrow.

Terrified of the animals in the field, she scurried along by the ditch, climbed over a barbed-wire fence, crossed a little stream and was now only one field away from the hay barn, where she planned to hide for the time being. Inching her way slowly along by the nearest fence, she made a short run across the farmyard and into the barn.

She was now more frightened than ever, being so close to the house and possibly to being discovered by the O'Malleys. If that happened she knew her chances of freedom were slim. They were, in a way, responsible for her care and they might not let her go.

For what seemed like a long time, Bridie stood hiding behind the half-open door, peeping across the yard in case anyone came out of the house. After a time she thought she heard someone coming, and tiptoed upstairs and hid in the rear of the building. She'd gone into its furthest corner when she heard one of the workers whistling his way casually into the barn. If she tiptoed out to the top of the stairs and peered down she might see what was happening below. But from the whistling she thought it was Peter and not Seamus, whom she'd prefer to see. After a while the whistling stopped and she thought whoever it was had gone out of the building. She was thinking of venturing out when suddenly an uncontrollable urge to sneeze came over her. She put up her hands quickly to smother it but only succeeded in muffling the sound. This was followed immediately by another and another. Then she knew someone had heard her and was coming to investigate because she could hear him tiptoeing up the stairs.

'Who's there?' said a voice, which Bridie recognised instantly as Peter's, and gave a sigh of relief because she felt sure he would not betray her to the O'Malleys. 'Who's there? Is somebody there?' the voice asked as it moved tentatively closer to where she hid.

Bridie thought she'd better answer, lest somebody else hear him talking. She whispered loudly, 'It's me! Bridie!'

Peter came within feet of her before he saw her form in the hay. He turned and stood sideways so that he might better see who it was.

'Bridie!' he exclaimed loudly. 'What are you doing here?'

Bridie could not answer. The words just lodged in her throat. She wanted to burst into tears, to tell someone how Mrs O'Malley had beaten her like a dog, and that she had a pain in her heart far worse than anything she'd ever known.

'Are you all right?' Peter asked as he moved closer. 'Did Mrs O'Malley say something to you?'

Bridie nodded and started to cry, as Peter stood beside her. He could see she was very distressed and placed an arm around her shoulders to reassure her. For a few minutes she sobbed uncontrollably, burying her head in his chest as she babbled on, telling him what had happened. After some time she recovered her composure and Peter forced himself to remove his arm and stand aside, because he could not trust the wayward feeling creeping into his body. But when he looked at her dishevelled face, her pleading eyes and tender red lips, he was overcome with an insatiable desire to seize her face between his hands and kiss her passionately.

Bridie too had felt a strange sort of comfort while she rested her head against his chest. She had distinctly heard the heavy boom of his heartbeat and felt the strength of his comforting arm around her shoulder. She straightened herself up to brush the hay from her hair and petticoat and, as she did so, Peter saw the shapely outline of her body. It was too much; he could not control himself any longer. He suddenly seized her pale cheeks and turned her face up to the light to admire her porcelain beauty for a lingering moment, before planting his coarse stubbled chin on her face and kissing her moist red lips.

For a split second Bridie was in a daze and did not know

what was happening. Then a surge of excitement swept through her body as she realised she was being kissed for the very first time and it was everything the Galway city girls at St Joseph's told her it would be. Peter's strong arms were wrapping themselves about her shoulders as his eager lips sent shockwaves through her system. Without realising it, she placed her hands on his shoulders to tell him to stop, but instantly conflicting signals emerged to tell her to wait a second, followed immediately by an urgent message.

Stop! Stop! But she couldn't, because Peter was now nuzzling her neck, nibbling her ear, while all the time pressing her closely to his firm body. She felt a warm shiver of excitement that sent flesh-quakes down her spine.

'Stop, please!' she whispered nervously. 'Stop it, Peter, please!' she cried, as she tried half-heartedly to push him away.

Peter hesitated for a second but when he began to kiss her again, and his strong arms again moved to explore her body, she lost control. She could feel the strong muscles of his thighs and body as he squashed her ever closer to him. His hands were everywhere, as a strange tingling sensation took control of her, and she savoured his hungry searching lips once more. His body reeked of a strange odour that wafted into her nostrils and put her head spinning. Then a gust of shame swept over her, because he was now exploring the naked flesh of her body as she begged him to stop.

'Peter! Peter!' she pleaded. And when she realised his strong hands were tearing at the flimsy material of her undergarments, she again cried aloud, 'Stop! Stop!'

But it was useless because in an instant his powerful arms had raised her clean off the ground, and as he again kissed her passionately on the lips, she was forced to cling desperately on to his shoulders as he forcibly spread her legs and wrapped them around his waist.

This single act was like nothing she had ever imagined. It

sent a bolt of excitement through her entire body, and an urgent request to her brain. What was he doing? Was he trying to smother her to death? Why was he now panting and breathing so hard? His legs and lower body were trembling uncontrollably.

She was about to force her mouth away somehow and scream, 'Stop it, Peter! Stop it!' Instead it was a scream of mercy she unleashed followed by a faint cry, when the hot pole of his excitement plunged straight into her lower body, and she cried out, 'Ah! Aaah! Peter! Peter! Stop!' She felt at that moment as if some sort of mortal wound had been inflicted; like a knife thrust deep into her flesh that sent hot waves all over her being. Suddenly she was gripped by the most awful fear that the man she knew and trusted *was* now going to kill her. She too was gasping for air because her whole body felt as if it had been set on fire, and when a faint voice called out, 'Peter! Is that you?' she thought she'd surely die. For a moment, she felt his taut body turn to stone before he let her aching limbs slowly dissolve away from his grasp.

Again, the voice asked, 'Peter! Is that you?' Sinead came inquisitively into view. And Peter turned his back quickly to hide his shame. And a cold sweat suddenly enveloped his body as, he barked urgently, 'Stay! Stay! Stay where you are, Sinead. I'll be out in a second.'

'Is that you, Bridie?' asked Sinead, tentatively after a pause, feeling that her friend Bridie was in some sort of a dilemma, so she stood her ground at the top of the stairs, peering into the darkness.

'For Christ's sake, go down, Sinead. I'll be out in a second,' roared Peter.

Sinead turned and ran downstairs and into the house as Bridie tried rearranging her clothes as best she could, and Peter turned abruptly and disappeared almost as unexpectedly as he had appeared.

What was she going to do now that Sinead had seen her there in the hay, Bridie wondered. She felt physically sick at the thought that she had been discovered with Peter. Bad enough that Mrs O'Malley would soon know, but she felt positively guilt-ridden and dirty after what had happened. She was terrified even to move, and when she did, she thought she felt something oozing down the inside of her leg. She plucked up the courage to step into the light and examine herself. She was shocked to discover she was bleeding. She almost fainted at the thought that she was on again after only two weeks, when it was only meant to happen to her every four weeks.

Menstruation from what the nuns had told her, was part of being grown up. They had explained that her body would undergo major changes: from that of a young girl into that of a mature woman. But why was it happening to her again so soon? She felt weak and dizzy, and rested her body against the giant stack of hay.

Her head was now spinning and she could not think clearly. She told herself she must have committed some awful sin by allowing a man to kiss her like that. But surely it was all Peter's fault. But why had she allowed him to do it? He must have cast a spell over her body. Sister Rita had said, 'The world is full of evil men whose only interest is to possess your body for their own wanton pleasure and destruction.' Did that mean her body was possessed by some evil spirit? It must be, Bridie thought, because she felt torn apart, battered, bruised and broken. She hated the O'Malleys, she hated the children, she hated Peter, but most of all she hated herself because she was a coward who let other people abuse her, mentally and physically. She just wanted to lie down and die, and never wake up again. Oh God, maybe, just maybe, it was all a bad dream and this day never happened.

But when Mr O'Malley suddenly appeared at the top of the

stairs and made his way over to her she thought she'd surely die of shame and embarrassment, because she knew it was only the beginning.

Later, as she lay half asleep in bed, and was still struggling to erase the day's horrible events from her head, she heard a lot of shouting and noise downstairs. Then a gentle knock came at her door.

It was Mr O'Malley. He came in, stood beside her bed and asked, 'Are you feeling any better?'

Bridie nodded. She was. In fact she felt much better since she'd had a hot bath and a change of clothes. She just wanted to rest now and get her thoughts together, and see where she was going to go from here. Mr O'Malley had brought her into the house, where Mrs O'Malley had suddenly become very concerned for her welfare. She insisted she rest herself for the remainder of the evening, and told her she could have tomorrow off. Tomorrow off? That was a major treat to look forward to. She made up her mind then that she was going to walk into Tuam and decide her future.

'Do you mind if we talk?' asked Mr O'Malley, a worried frown on his face.

Bridie shook her head.

'Would you like to tell me what happened? And start from the beginning,' he urged after a momentary pause.

Bridie didn't feel much like talking, but she wondered if Mr O'Malley knew what Mrs O'Malley had done. She thought it best to say nothing at all. But then the prospect of being able to put the record straight and tell him about his awful wife was too good to ignore.

She lay, looking out blankly at Mr O'Malley, as he spoke.

'I understand that, maybe, it's not easy and that perhaps you'd like to talk to someone else. Would you like me to get a doctor?'

But Bridie did not feel bad enough to need a doctor; although her back and arm were still sore – not to mention the rest of her body. She pulled the bedclothes about her shoulders and lay staring up at Mr O'Malley for a few moments. She didn't know for sure if he was a nice man, or just Mrs O'Malley's husband pretending to be nice. What if she told him everything and he didn't believe her? Then there would be two people who hated her. It didn't matter whether she stayed or not, she still wanted people to like her. Surely that was not too much to expect. Nevertheless, there was that niggling fear that everything was going against her. The nuns, Mrs O'Malley, Peter, and now Mr O'Malley; he might be no better, she thought. Even the children, particularly Sinead – they would now hate her. How could she ever again meet her face to face without recalling how Sinead had caught her in that distressed state in the hay barn?

Mr O'Malley was studying her. He said softly, 'You've a lot on your mind. Sometimes it's good to talk. It soothes the spirit, calms the fears.' After a long pause he continued, 'You got up today and made the breakfasts and the children went to school and I went to Spring Field. What happened then? Where did it go wrong?' he urged.

'It's your wife, Mr O'Malley. She's horrible and I don't like saying it,' cried Bridie as her eyes welled up and she started to sob. 'She's the cruellest person I ever met, who treats me like a beggar. I wouldn't do to an animal what she's done to me.' She sobbed uncontrollably, letting her tears flow. 'She treats me as if I'm a piece of dirt in off the street. She calls me names and today she beat me with the brush. I had to run away because I knew I'd stick a knife in her if she didn't stop. I don't want to hurt anyone, but she's always at me. Look what she did to my arm.' Bridie pulled up her sleeve and showed him the red swollen welt. 'And she hit me across the back . . . just because I made a mess of a blouse I'd never ironed before,' she sniffed, as she dried her eyes with the sleeve of her pyjamas.

A shocked and distressed Mr O'Malley looked at her flushed expression and was himself struggling to control his own emotions. He knew this girl was telling the truth; that, if nothing else, Bridie was a person of substance. He rose from the chair and turned to face the bedroom window so that she could not see his tortured face. He had to accept that his wife was now pushing things close to the edge, that perhaps it was time to face reality. She had already been the cause of several staff members leaving Conly House, and now she was resorting to violence; the latest bout having led to an assault by one of the farm hands.

He turned round and leaned against the wall to face Bridie again. Then he asked her, 'What happened then? After you ran away?'

Bridie told him how she ran down the road to get away from the house, but then decided to return for her belongings and to hide in the hay barn until she could get her clothes. Bridie turned her face away from his prying eyes as he waited for her to finish.

'Then what happened?' he asked, a resigned look spread across his already pained expression.

But Bridie could not tell anyone how she had shamed herself before the world by being caught red-handed in the most vile unladylike position by Sinead, his own flesh and blood: a child that she herself was meant to be minding. She closed her eyes because it was all so revolting. Mr O'Malley came and sat on the edge of the bed and placed his hand gently on her tiny closed fists, but Bridie pulled her hand away quickly and said, 'Please don't.'

It was as if his hand had stung her. She didn't ever want to feel a man close to her again. A chill went down her spine at the thought of what had already happened when she thought she could trust someone.

Mr O'Malley rose from the bed. 'I'm sorry, Bridie, I know it must be very difficult for you to even discuss it,' he whispered.

'You don't have to tell me everything, and I'd appreciate it if you called me Gerald. It's just that I need to know where I stand. I have to look after the staff and make sure everyone is treated equally and with respect. At the same time I need to know if someone is stepping out of line.'

After a pause, he asked the question that really galled him, because Sinead had said: 'Dad . . . I caught Peter and Bridie kissing in the hay.'

'Did Peter take advantage of you today or is something going on between you?'

Bridie did not answer but slowly gathered the blankets about her before turning over to look away. Gerald saw it was time to go. As he quietly left the room, he already knew the answer, but he had other things on his mind.

He walked wearily down the stairs and went into the reading room. He would have to think. If Bridie had been assaulted – and he felt sure that she had – then what? He decided very quickly that Peter was guilty of assault, Beatrice was guilty of wounding and he himself was guilty of neglect and of allowing his house to become a place of ill-repute where a hired staff member had to run away, only to return and be sexually assaulted by another member of the household. Gerald buried his head in his hands. He was ruined, destroyed, or as close to it as made no matter, he told himself. If this got out, if word spread, then he was finished entirely because no self-respecting man or woman would ever want to work here again. He would be shunned in the local community.

For a long time he paced up and down the room, trying to decide what to do. His only hope of salvation was to be strong and resolute, to do the right thing. The time for reflection had long since passed. If he didn't act now, there was no knowing what might happen next. And by doing something positive now, at least whatever was relayed in village gossip, it could be always said that he did what he could.

Bridie was sent immediately, on the pretext of a holiday for a few days, to stay with Gerald's sister in Tuam, while he arranged a new working schedule for Conly House. But not before he had a long and heated discussion with Peter, who denied any improper behaviour towards Bridie. He described what transpired in the hay barn as mere horseplay. But Gerald was adamant. Peter would have to go, and go he did, to be replaced by a young chap from a neighbouring village. And gone were the hearty breakfasts before commencing work in the morning. Gone were the days of boiled bacon and cabbage and, worst of all, gone was the freedom ever to set foot in the house again, or to mix with any of the household staff. Instead the farm hands sat on milking stools in the stables, come hail, rain or shine, with their sandwiches and bottles of cold tea. And it was widely rumoured that Mrs O'Malley was gone to America for an extended holiday.

Bridie was persuaded to return after a few days when Tom collected her and she was asked by Gerald to put forward her ideas for the reorganised running of the house.

'Bridie, as you can see, the situation is anything but ideal at present, but I appreciate you returning after what has happened. However, we must all do what we can, especially for the children. I would like you to continue working as normal. My sister, Mary, will be only too glad to come over and relieve you on your days off. And besides, the children will be delighted to see a little more of their auntie. So I hope we'll all get back to normal as soon as possible. I cannot, however, guarantee that you will be able to remain with us. I can't say for definite how long my wife will be away. But in order to give you a start in life and in readiness for any plans you might like to make, I am putting you on an income of two and sixpence a week plus your keep. How does that sound to you?'

'Fine,' said Bridie, and a warm glow of satisfaction spread across her pale face at the prospect of earning her first pay.

Bridie now had more time to herself, and felt she might be able to enjoy a little bit of freedom about the house; to go places, to make new friends; to go to Tuam or Galway, or even Dublin. The nuns had told her in school that she was from Dublin. Perhaps she should go there and see for herself.

Who knows, I might even find my mother and father? Not that they'll be much good to me now, she thought, But still, 'twould be nice to know where I come from. If I started to save a few shillings I could soon get the train. But first I want to be able to buy my own clothes and get my hair done.

Her plans were working out well. She had no more workmen to feed and the children were at school most of the day. So, every room in the house was now spotlessly clean and a smell of beeswax wafted from the antique furniture after she did her rounds each morning.

One day, Bridie heard a heavy knock at the front door. Gerald was away at Ballinasloe horse fair, and she wasn't expecting anyone. She opened the door, and there stood Peter, half smiling.

'Oh, how are ya? I just thought I'd come to see how ya are . . .'

'I'm fine,' said Bridie, surprised to see him and wondering what he wanted, because he wasn't supposed ever to set foot inside the door again.

She stood looking at him for a moment, then he asked, 'Can I come in?'

'Gerald is not here. Do you want to see him?'

'No, no,' Peter answered quickly. 'Someone told me he was gone to the fair and I thought I'd stop by to see how you were, you know,' thinking to himself maybe he could renew the friendship; that's if she hadn't taken things too badly last time.

Bridie was very aware of his body language and half closed the door lest he should try to barge his way in. She suddenly had a fear of the man, as all the memories came flooding back:

the arm around her shoulders, the sudden kiss, the excitement in his body and the way his hands wandered all over her.

Without realising it she had almost trapped herself between the door and the jamb in an effort to keep him out.

'No, no. I never want to see that man again,' Peter elaborated. 'This was something between you and me. He should never have interfered. I like you, and I want to be friends. We were always friends, weren't we?' he said, hoping she'd open the door and let him in before anyone saw him.

If she was in the house on her own, he might just be able to get at her again, and now that he saw her in the flesh, he knew that he had been right all along: she was indeed a beauty, and he would give anything to get her in that position again. He might never ever get another chance, as Mrs O'Malley would surely get rid of her the minute she came home, and God knows where Bridie would end up. He thought she might be a bit cross with him because he knew he'd been a bit hasty the last time, but then again she had seemed to enjoy the experience.

Bridie was looking at his shifting restless eyes and sensed that he was capable of doing the same thing to her all over again. She was now positively petrified. She had trusted him before and thought he'd be sympathetic to her problem. But when she thought of the way he had treated her and spread her legs, she felt herself getting weak at the knees. It was frightening the way he seemed to have some sort of strange effect on her. Now she thought of Gerald. He had warned her that nobody was to be let into the house in his absence – only the children, and Auntie Mary, who was not due till this evening. Gerald was a kind and decent man, she thought: she would do what she was told, and he had said nobody, but nobody, must ever be allowed in while she was on her own, especially any of the workmen.

She summoned up the courage to say, 'I must go now. The

children will be coming home from school and I must get their dinner,' surprising herself at how quickly she came up with an excuse.

'Arrah, they're not due home for ages yet,' he laughed, trying to seem relaxed and cheerful.

The idea was to get inside the door. He'd ask for a drink of water. That should do the trick. Then he could walk in ever so casually, talking by the way, and then . . .

'Oh, they're getting off early, and Auntie Mary's coming over and stopping for a few days to help clean the house,' lied Bridie, beginning to feel her confidence coming back.

'Home early?' said Peter, alarmed that his plans might be about to fail. 'Why would they come home early?'

'I don't know,' answered Bridie, thinking she had put her foot in it. 'Oh, the teachers sent word yesterday to say they'd be letting them out early. I must go now, or Gerald will be cross with me if the jobs are not done. I'll tell him you called.'

'Oh, no! Jesus, no! Don't say I was here,' said Peter, alarmed at the thought that she could be so stupid. 'I only came to see how you were. I thought we'd have a little chat.'

He was disappointed that his timing had been so bad and that there was the ever-present danger that he might be caught in the act again by one of the children. He had only just managed to convince Gerald the last time that nothing unseemly had happened between himself and Bridie; that he had merely had his arm about her, reassuring her after her beating at the hands of Mrs O'Malley; convincing himself in the process that the reason for his dismissal was because he dared to side with Bridie.

At that moment the rumbling of a horse cart on the gravelled drive could be heard as one of the workmen turned in the gateway from the main road on his way back from town. Peter turned to look and a sense of urgency crept into his voice as he ran to grab his bicycle which was leaning against the wall.

'Don't tell anyone I was here. I'll see you again, Bridie. Good luck,' he said, as he jumped on his bike and disappeared down the bridle path that ran from the back of the house.

'Oh, thank God for that,' sighed Bridie as she returned to the kitchen. If he comes round again, what am I going to do? I'll have to tell Gerald he called and that I wouldn't let him in; he'll be pleased about that.

But Gerald was not at all pleased to hear that Peter had the gumption to call around in his absence, proving he was right to dismiss him and even more correct in his beliefs that he should warn Bridie never to let anyone into the house.

Bridie continued to live in fear that Peter would return, by fair means or foul, and when Mrs O'Malley returned home unexpectedly, she felt as if one evil person was being replaced by another.

But Mrs O'Malley was now a much-changed person. She appeared more at ease with herself and those around her. Nevertheless, she spent days and days in her room, and Gerald instructed Bridie to carry on as normal. Beatrice was on medication and he himself would take care of her.

By degrees, and after a few months, the lady of the house returned to something like her old self. Then one day she approached Bridie with a rather strange request.

'Bridie, we're going into Tuam tomorrow. Gerald and I think you too should come along for the drive. We're going to the doctor's. You haven't had a check-up since you've been here, have you?'

Bridie, somewhat surprised, replied. 'All right.'

'It was Gerald's idea. He thinks we should all have regular check-ups as TB is now so rampant in the country.'

Bridie decided that if it kept her ladyship quiet, then she was only too happy to go along. Besides, it would be a rare treat to be going somewhere after all the months of monotonous housework. The only place she had been since she came to work in Conly House was to a showjumping event in Athenry with Gerald and the children. Apart from that she went to Mass every Sunday and wrote to the Reverend Mother when she came home.

When they arrived in Bishop Street, Gerald, Beatrice and Bridie all traipsed into the waiting room and, after a lengthy wait, Bridie was called in to the surgery and given a thorough examination. Bridie didn't particularly like having doctors examine her as she felt it was all such an invasion of her privacy, particularly as she wasn't ill or anything. She couldn't understand why it was always men who had to examine girls, but then maybe there were no lady doctors. Sometimes she thought they could be off-handish enough, especially that time when the nuns thought she might have had appendicitis. But thankfully this doctor was much nicer and though he didn't say an awful lot, she didn't feel too bad about it when it was all over.

Afterwards, Gerald insisted on taking them to a nearby hotel where he treated them to tea and some lovely sponge cake. Then, after a quick shopping spree, they all returned home. Bridie thought the news concerning Mrs O'Malley might not be good, as both she and Gerald were extremely quiet on the way home, but nothing was said. But she herself was in good health, and that was all that mattered.

That evening Gerald asked Bridie to make a pot of tea and to join him in the reading room. When she had done this and sat down to face him, she got the distinct feeling that something awful was about to unfold. There was something about the way Gerald watched her pour out the tea that convinced her she was being sent back to St Joseph's. He had told her before, he could not guarantee that she would be able to remain with them, so it looked as if, once again, Mrs O'Malley was calling the shots; even though she no longer interfered with Bridie, except to call for her medication.

'Bridie, I'm afraid I have some disturbing news,' Gerald said, sitting down, elbows resting on his knees, and rubbing his hands together as if trying to soothe away some pain or other.

Bridie thought: this is it. I knew I was right, but little does he know, I'm not going back to St Joseph's – no, never. I'll say nothing, just go along with whatever he suggests. I have some clothes and money, and can run away for the first time in my life.

'I think I know what it is,' said Bridie, a resigned look on her face that caught Gerald by surprise.

'You know?' he queried, with a raised brow as a wave of relief swept over him and transformed the corners of his mouth into the faint outline of a smile.

'Yes,' she added confidently. 'I have to leave. You're sending me back to St Joseph's. You said before, I might not be able to stay, remember?'

Gerald's features collapsed into a heavy scowl and his heart gave a painful lurch that he'd been so taken in by Bridie's innocence; that he was, after all, going to be the conveyer of bad news. Get it over with quickly, he told himself, and stop beating about the bush.

'Bridie, you're pregnant. You're expecting a baby. The doctor says you're seven months gone; which means you're due in eight weeks.'

Pregnant? Pregnant? But how could . . . ? The words sent a shiver down her spine. Seven months! Eight weeks! She felt faint. The doctor . . . ? So that's why he quizzed her as he placed his hands gently on her abdomen. But how could I be . . . ?

Gerald was saying something but she didn't hear because it was all coming back. She was still cleaning the stairs; Mrs O'Malley, was shouting and hitting her, and she was running down the drive, climbing stone walls, and then making a disastrous decision that would lead her to the hay barn. She could clearly hear and see it – her garments being torn and then Peter lifting her like a rag doll and her cry for help. *Stop it, Peter. Stop.*

She could still feel the pain, and now the shame. She closed her eyes for a split second to shut out the world, because she didn't want to recall that day again. Yet here it was now being thrust at her, forcing her to accept what had taken place, whether she liked it or not, because she was pregnant. Pregnant, she thought. Only mothers get pregnant; how could she be pregnant? She wasn't married. She had never been to a dance in her life, not even a house dance. A baby . . . ? She stared at Gerald.

He was looking back at her and saying, 'I'm so sorry it turned out like this.'

But she wasn't listening, only studying his lips as he spoke. She had allowed a man to kiss her, and now she was pregnant. It was Peter's. She was going to have his baby.

She was still in shock and bewilderment when a smiling Mrs O'Malley came in and said, 'Congratulations, Bridie. I understand you're going to be a mother.'

Gerald sprang to his feet. 'Beatrice! Come. Bridie needs time to herself. We'll go into the other room,' helping to escort his wife out.

After a few minutes Gerald put his head around the door and said, 'I'll just leave you for a moment. I'll be in again to talk it over so try and relax.'

Bridie nodded agreement.

The more she thought about it, the worse it got. How could she have a baby, in a house with the likes of Mrs O'Malley sneaking about in her slippers? She might harm the child. She couldn't very well run away now, because she'd only be settled somewhere and then the baby would be born, and nobody, not even a priest, would want a housekeeper if she had a child. It looked as if she'd have to stay with the O'Malleys for the rest of her life. The mere thought of it was enough to make her sick. Unless, of course . . . she got married, but she didn't have a boyfriend. Unless Peter . . . ? Did he have a girl? Nobody had told tell her anything when she'd made discreet enquiries, although there was a suggestion that he was married. But Bridie didn't believe it. He didn't behave like a married man the way Gerald did. And if he wasn't then he might marry her, she thought. But suppose he was cruel to her and beat her like some of the fathers whose children had to be put into St Joseph's? She would not under any circumstances marry someone who'd do that to her.

While working in Conly House, Peter had seemed so nice, always ready to make her laugh, but then in the hay barn he had changed. One second he had his arm soothingly around her shoulder, the next he was forcing his lips on hers. She closed her eyes again to squeeze out the memory.

She heard a gentle rap on the door. It was Gerald coming back into the room with two glasses on a tray.

He gave one to Bridie, saying, 'I don't approve of young ladies drinking, but under the circumstances a little sherry will help you get over the shock. In fact it will help you relax while I outline a few things to you.'

'I don't think I should,' said Bridie. 'I don't drink.'

'Nonsense,' interjected Gerald. 'It's just for medicinal purposes, and we all need help at a time like this.'

Bridie pretended to be shocked at the taste of the sherry, but she had sneaked a little sip of it once before when she was on her own in the house and had already made up her mind that she didn't like it. But she'd better drink it now whether she liked it or not, she thought, as Gerald eased himself into a chair the other side of the coffee table.

'You were very close to the truth, Bridie, when you said you'd be leaving,' he began. 'I have to be straight with you and tell you that you can't stay on here indefinitely, because of the children. It would be unthinkable for you to have your baby here, and even if I allowed it, I don't think Mrs O'Malley would.'

Bridie coughed and nearly spewed her drink when she heard

she was expected to leave at a time like this. So she'd be going back to St Joseph's after all.

'Are you all right?' asked Gerald, as she continued to cough and splutter.

'Yes, I'm fine,' she answered hoarsely as she accepted his handkerchief.

'Of course we'll make proper arrangements for you to go somewhere safe, where you can have your baby in comfort; where you won't have to worry about anything. You'll be well looked after, I promise you that.'

'Am I going back to St Joseph's?'

'Only if you want to. I'll arrange for our local parish priest to call around to discuss a few things with you.'

'The priest?' said Bridie in surprise.

'Yes. I think he's in a better position than I am to advise you on your best options. I know he's helped one or two others in similar situations. Of course you don't have to go yet, not for a couple of weeks, anyway,' said Gerald, trying to reassure her.

'But he'll send me to St Joseph's, and I don't want to go back there again,' said Bridie, a look of distress spreading across her pale complexion at the thought of living among the nuns again, and looking after screaming, pitiful-looking children.

And now that she was old enough she would probably have to help feed and care for every single one in the school. The thought of having to cook for scores of children and wash, dress and feed them − not to mention caring for her own − where she'd never have a minute's peace or privacy, was too frightening. And with no freedom or prospect of ever meeting anyone to marry or having a family of her own.

These thoughts were reverberating round her head as Gerald said, 'There are several places around the country where they give care and assistance to unmarried mothers. As far as I know, you should be free to choose. As a matter of fact, there's a place right here in Tuam, but I don't want to cut across anything the priest might advise. So why don't we leave it and see what he says? In the meantime, I best go back to work; you can stay on here and rest a while.'

'Yes,' said Bridie, 'I'll be out in a minute,' starting to feel buoyed by the drop of sherry; happy that she could now think for a moment in private.

The phrase 'a family of my own' seemed to be taking root in her thoughts. Suddenly she realised the words had a meaning beyond her wildest dreams. She almost jumped out of her chair with joy.

'I'll have a family of my very own,' she whispered. 'I've never had a family and now I'm going to have one. I've never had a father, a mother, a brother, a sister, a niece or an uncle. I've not even had a first cousin, a second cousin, and not even a thirty-second cousin; but now I'm about to have a son or daughter.' She raised her eyes to heaven and whispered, 'Thank you, God, for sending me someone. I'll have my very own family; I don't care whether it's a boy or girl. I'm going to be a mother. Imagine. I'm going to be a mother.' She smiled to herself as she stood up to go back out to the kitchen.

'This way, Father,' said Gerald, as he showed the priest into the reading room. 'She'll be with you in a moment.'

His Reverence could hardly wait to see the new housekeeper. He wasn't sure if he had met her or not. No doubt, he surmised, she's another one of them ready to lie by the ditch with every other—'

'This is Father Michael, our parish priest,' said Gerald, escorting Bridie into the room. 'Bridie Rodgers, our housekeeper,' he said, introducing her to the priest. 'I'll leave you two to have a chat. Beatrice will join us later and we'll have a cup of tea.'

'That would be lovely,' Father Michael answered, sitting down.

Gerald left the room, closing the door behind him.

Although she was extremely pale, Father Michael thought Bridie had some noble qualities about her. Her raven-black hair greatly enhanced her wide eyes and high cheekbones, which gave the impression that she might be of Spanish origin.

'And how are you, Bridie? I think I've seen you in church,' said Father Michael, as Bridie sat down opposite him.

'Fine,' said Bridie, her mind made up that she'd listen carefully but say as little as possible because she didn't really trust priests. She'd seen so many of them visiting St Joseph's Industrial School and they were always planning to put someone in or take someone out.

'So, Gerald's been telling me what a wonderful job you do here; that you're able to cook and look after the children.'

Bridie smiled shyly, waiting for his pastoral advice. She thought he looked much older than he appeared in church on Sundays, where he ranted on, occasionally thumping the pulpit with his clenched fist to hammer home the point. 'Drink is the work of Satan himself, his very own brew, drawn from the tainted waters of the River Liffey.' His words made history in the parish where people loved to spread the Gospel and took the priest's words literally, particularly if they were of a controversial nature.

'How long have you been here now?' he asked her.

'I'm . . . I'm here eight months, Father.'

'And before that you were in St Joseph's?' said His Reverence, thinking: it won't be too long till you're back there again.

'Yes.'

'Would you like to go back?' asked Father Michael, with a smile.

'No, Father, I don't ever want to go back there.'

A little touch of arrogance, thought the priest, but he said nothing for a moment as he sat looking at her as if in deep thought. Then he said, 'Of course, a girl in your predicament has precious few options. You do realise that, don't you?' He lowered his head, glaring across at Bridie, as if to emphasise the point.

Bridie said nothing, but continued to stare back, eyeball to eyeball. Finally he gave way and said, 'Would you care to tell me how you got into trouble in the first place, Bridie?' And he sat back, stretching his long legs across the floor, waiting for the story to unfold.

Bridie looked at him and wondered how much he already knew. Gerald must have told him something about it, and she certainly did not feel like telling such a sordid story to a complete stranger, so she made up her mind to be curt in her reply.

'Got into what trouble?' she asked, pretending to be surprised.

Dumb as well as stupid, were the first thoughts to enter the priest's head as he gave her a look that said, don't mess with me, lady, for I have the power to make life most uncomfortable for you.

'Pregnant? How did you come to be pregnant, child?' he growled.

Bridie could tell from the look he gave her that he was not at all impressed, and she started to revel in his discomfort. After all, it was really none of his business, so she decided to make life a little more difficult for him and await his reaction.

'Do you want the full story or part of it?' she asked brazenly.

'Why, the full story, of course,' he replied, as he drew in his spider's legs and sat up with interest, so he might better absorb the gory details.

But Bridie knew she had pushed out the boat too far and that she could get into very deep water indeed if she told the whole story. She had no desire to tell him anything. And if she did, it would be about the way she was treated by Mrs O'Malley. But she also knew she could never betray Gerald by telling the priest about his awful wife. Gerald was too good to Bridie and she would not like to bring pain and suffering on his family. Besides, how was she supposed to tell him about Peter? No way was she going to tell him anything about that.

'There isn't that much to tell,' she said, and watched Father Michael's eyes roll back in his head. 'I was caught off guard by one of the workmen,' she added quickly.

His Reverence waited for her to continue and when it wasn't forthcoming, he asked, 'Which of them?' in an exasperated tone, showing his distaste at her shillyshallying.

'Peter. Peter Murtagh,' she replied with glee, knowing full well that Gerald would probably have told him this already.

'Peter Murtagh?' he repeated. 'I don't know any Peter . . . except . . . Where is he from?'

'I don't know. He used to work for Gerald. Gerald dismissed him,' said Bridie, surprised that he didn't already know that. She thought priests knew everything, and everyone's business, especially within the parish.

'Is it the Peter Murtagh that worked here for Gerald?' he asked.

'Yes.'

Father Michael sat bolt upright, a look of horror on his face, his piercing blue eyes casting a look of disbelief at Gerald's housekeeper.

'Bridie! How you could say such a thing? I'm absolutely appalled that you should tarnish the good name of one of my parishioners.'

Bridie, completely taken by surprise, sat in momentary shock. Then her blood started to rise.

Father Michael went on, 'I know Peter Murtagh. He happens to be a very respectable man: a married man, as a matter of fact, who takes great care to provide for his family . . .'

'Well, he can take great care of mine so,' said Bridie sarcastically.

'I will not listen to lies from a servant girl like you,' replied the Reverend Father, thumping the arm of the chair. 'It's a damn lie, and you know it. The truth of the matter is, Bridie, you do not know who's the father. But you choose the most convenient candidate, which in this case happens to be Peter Murtagh . . .'

Bridie, devastated by the attack, jumped to her feet and shouted, 'It's not a lie! It's not a lie! Ask Gerald; he'll soon tell you,' and she ran for the door.

But His Reverence, belying his age, sprang like a panther to try cutting her off at the door, pleading, 'Bridie, please! Leave Gerald out of it. This is strictly between the two of us. I'm here to advise you. Besides, you don't even realise what you're saying,' he added, holding her firmly by the arm.

Bridie, suddenly terrified of the man and the way he tried to control her, managed to get the door slightly ajar and screamed, 'Geraaallddd!'

Gerald, on hearing the commotion, came running down from the top of the stairs.

Bridie, her head sticking out of the room, was about to shout, 'He's calling me a liar,' but the words lodged in her craw when the children and Mrs O'Malley came running out of the kitchen, before standing abruptly to gawk at her.

Gerald, seeing something serious was amiss, ordered his family back into the kitchen before returning quickly to enquire what was the matter.

Father Michael, who was beginning to perspire under an uncomfortably tight collar, turned as red as an overripe strawberry as he tried to explain himself.

'I'm sorry about this Gerald, it's—'

'He called me a liar. He doesn't believe—' intervened Bridie.

'Wait. Wait,' said Gerald authoritatively, showing the palms of his hands in mock surrender. 'Let's discuss this in a reasonable manner. I hate to see people squaring up to each other in a pugnacious fashion.' Having closed the door behind him, hands on hips, he asked, 'What's the problem?'

His Reverence spoke up quickly. 'Bridie here seems to be making some sort of an outlandish claim that one of my most respected parishioners is the father of her child.'

'Is she now?' asked Gerald, in obvious annoyance. 'And who might that be?'

'Tell him what you're after saying,' said Father Michael, indicating to Bridie with a nod of his head.

'I told him it was Peter Murtagh; and you know it as well. But he doesn't believe me. He thinks I'm not capable of telling the truth,' added Bridie.

'Shush, shush. Let's not have a slanging match here. As far as I'm concerned, what's done is done. We're here to plan a way out of a very unfortunate situation, not to decide who is right or wrong,' said Gerald with a great deal of self-control.

'Gerald, I couldn't agree more, which is why we can't have a decent man's name dragged through the mire. Peter's an honourable man – even you know that,' said the priest, looking directly at Gerald.

'I knows a lot of things; too much for my own bloody good, if you'll pardon the expression, Father,' responded Gerald, peeved that what was meant to be a charitable call was instead turning into an act of recrimination. If there was one thing he detested it was politicians or the clergy refusing to face facts or to administer fair play. 'Now let's get one or two things straight. I asked you here, Father, to help arrange suitable accommodation for this young lady, so that she might have her child in comfort—'

'Certainly, certainly. I'll be only too glad,' interrupted His Reverence.

'One moment, I'm not finished, Father, and when I am,

you'll have your say,' said a visibly shaken Gerald, with a raised palm and a furrowed brow. 'When I asked you here, Father, I confided only that a young lady was in trouble. I did not mention who the child's father was, other than to say that I suspected it might be one of my men. I had no desire to bandy anybody's name about. And while we're on the subject, Father, there are many things in life that we just have to accept as fact whether we like them or not. And as you correctly pointed out, Peter Murtagh is a very popular man, a regular churchgoer and everything. But he's the father of Bridie's expected child. Not only that, but he's also reputed to be the father of two other children in the parish. Surely, you're aware of that, or have you chosen to turn a deaf ear?'

When Bridie heard Gerald speaking in such forthright terms, she could hardly conceal her glee, but managed to stand quietly in the centre of the room, though her hands fidgeted with the pleats in her skirt. And when she heard, Gerald say 'two other children', she could not resist taking a sideways glance at His Reverence. He stood solemnly, his head held high in an air of defiance as she watched him take out his handkerchief and mop his brow before contesting Gerald's words.

Father Michael thought he had known the O'Malley family well, but was never really privy to their thinking and was shocked that they too should suspect Peter Murtagh of such a distasteful act, and Peter's wife already expecting their fifth child.

'Bridie, there must be some mistake, some misunderstanding,' the priest began. 'After all, when a girl is young and free, it's only natural that she develops a keen interest in the opposite sex, be it out walking, visiting or at a dance. And where large numbers of people congregate like that at a crossroads dance, who's to say for certain who is the father of an expected child? Gerald, you're well aware of the number of times I've preached about having to break up young couples that I found in compromising positions by the side of the road.'

At this point, His Reverence paused for a deep breath. He'd been caught so unawares he didn't really know what he was supposed to say. He was more used to people latching on to his every word and looking up to him with the greatest of respect. After all, he thought, I'm supposed to be in charge of the parish; I'm the one who decides who's right and who's wrong. So it looks like once again I'll have to emphasise the seriousness of the situation.

'Like I've said, I've had to wallop them home from the side of the road with the crook of my blackthorn stick, and I got very little thanks for it.'

Gerald had heard enough. He was sick of listening to this rabble-rousing approach to a subject that required a degree of compassion. He intervened sharply, 'Listen, Father, I'm sorry I brought you here. I think it's better for you to go home because there's nothing more to be said. Thanks for calling. Oh, and in relation to Bridie, we'll make our own arrangements,' he added, turning to open the door and show Father Michael out.

'But it's no problem! No problem! I can arrange whatever you want! I'd be only too glad to help . . .' replied Father Michael, coming forward reluctantly.

'Thanks,' said Gerald.

'Thanks,' added Bridie, unable to resist a parting word and giving Father a wan smile at the door.

'But . . . but why wasn't it reported to the guards?' he asked, trying to claw back lost ground. 'It's such a heinous crime.'

'It was reported directly to me. And we have witnesses,' replied Gerald, with obvious satisfaction as he stood at the door and politely waved Father Michael out.

Two weeks after the priest's failed mission to assist Bridie, Gerald arranged for her to be taken into the care of St Mary's

Home for Unmarried Mothers in Tuam; run by the Bon Secour order of nuns.

Bridie, however, did not like the idea of once again being under the supervision of a group of nuns and this bad feeling was fuelled in no small way by the fact that she now felt aggrieved at having to leave Conly House under such a dark cloud. Ever since that memorable walk through the farm on her arrival, things had never been the same. When Mrs O'Malley accused her of telling lies to the children, Bridie immediately felt at odds with everyone except Gerald. Now it was even more painful trying to avoid eye contact with Sinead, and to hide the growing bulk of her pregnancy, which she had vaguely thought might be the result of her efforts to put on more weight because everybody thought she was too thin.

So it was with a sense of relief that she woke on her last morning in the big house. It had been agreed that she should leave quietly while the children were still in school; and on their return, they would be informed that Bridie had to go to Dublin to look after an elderly relative. When Gerald entered the sitting room to check on Bridie's readiness, he was touched to find her kneeling on a rug, ticking off a number of horses on the racing page.

'Bridie,' he said, 'I want you to know you've been a great help to us here. Personally, I was very happy with your work; but regrettably, fate – call it what you like – wasn't very kind to you. Who knows? Maybe it's for the best,' he said smiling lamely, as he took out his wallet.

Bridie felt embarrassed to be caught idling on her last morning and stood up quickly to respond. 'Thanks. I enjoyed working here too,' she lied. She didn't know what else to say.

Then Gerald, going forward, took Bridie by the hand and said something very strange. 'Here's a little something for yourself, for a rainy day,' shoving a crisp one-pound note into her hand. 'Now I want you to remember this, Bridie: always take a little gamble in life . . .' He had her tiny hand clasped in his as he looked into her eyes. 'I can tell you now that you'll never be rich; but then again, you'll never ever be poor, because someday, perhaps years from now, when you least expect it and need it most, you are going to win.'

Then, looking up at the clock, he said, 'Now, have you got your things? I think it's time to go.'

'Thank you,' said Bridie, as they both made their way out of the room.

Getting into the car beside Tom, she turned round and waved to Mr and Mrs O'Malley, as the car slowly pulled away down the long gravelled drive.

CHAPTER FOUR

A STRANGE EERIE feeling seemed to transcend the decaying walls as Bridie waited patiently to meet the new matron of St Mary's, Sister Hortense. What it was about the place that gave her such a feeling she did not know; and the appearance of bowed elderly nuns carrying dilapidated old iron bed-ends and sunken horse-hair Victorian couches along its musty-looking corridors did nothing to allay her fears. On the one hand, it was as if the Church was now going to dictate the shape and pattern of her life to come, just when she thought she had left it all behind in St Joseph's; and on the other, it was as if she could feel the presence of a thousand ancient ghosts roaming about the place. Bridie shivered nervously and tried to drive the demon thoughts from her head, but they would not go. Suddenly she looked around in terror as she distinctly felt something touch the back of her long black hair.

'Jesus!' she cried aloud, as she jumped up and looked about the wide hall leading to a long narrow corridor. 'What's wrong with me? Am I going insane?'

There was no one there. She sat down and placed her hands about her shoulders for support. She now felt something was happening to her and she prayed that the matron would come quickly. Instead, she felt a strange power enter her body through the soles of her feet, like a warm tidal wave that did not stop until it had moved up her entire body, as if she had slowly submerged herself in a steaming hot bath.

She was now positively petrified and stood up to flee from the building, but before she could make up her mind which way to run, a miraculous sound cast a hypnotic hold over her, the most tranquil sound she'd ever heard. It was a beautiful church choir, and came from somewhere within the building. So sweet and melodious was its rendition that Bridie raised her eyes to heaven to thank God, and luxuriate in this spiritual healing. By the time the hymn was finished she felt a small miracle had taken place because she was no longer afraid. It was her favourite hymn, and it was such a coincidence that it should come to her aid at this time.

> Be not afraid, I go before you always
> Come follow me and I will give you rest.

As Bridie gazed out the window and thought about the words, she heard someone say, 'You must be Bridie.'

She wheeled round and saw a serene smiling sister extend a welcoming hand. 'How are you, dear? Sorry to have kept you waiting. I'm Sister Hortense, your matron.'

'I'm fine,' said Bridie, accepting Sister's welcoming hand.

'Shall we go into my office?'

'I don't mind,' answered a relieved Bridie, as she followed Matron down the long corridor and into a small ill-furnished room, badly in need of repair.

'Here, take a seat,' said Sister Hortense, referring her to a small spoon-backed chair, 'and I'll get you a cup of tea.'

She went to the door and called to a maid going down the corridor, 'Annie, would you ever tell Mary Wade to bring me a fresh pot of tea, please?'

Turning round, she opened a big red book that lay on her desk and ran her forefinger down the middle pages before stopping to digest some relevant details. 'I see you've spent most of your life in St Joseph's.' She raised her eyes to Bridie and asked, 'Was there any particular reason for that?'

'No, I don't think there was.'

'And then you went to work in Conly House,' said Sister, closing the book and pulling up a chair behind her desk to face Bridie. 'Strange that no family ever came to foster you out.'

Bridie, who couldn't think of anything to say, stared back at Sister Hortense. She hoped she wasn't going to hold it against her, just because she wasn't one of the lucky few.

'Perhaps it was your own choice; did you like living in St Joseph's?' asked Sister, thoughtfully.

'No. I would have left . . . but nobody ever seemed to want to take me out,' replied Bridie, feeling sorry for herself, then realising that maybe she was saying the wrong thing; that it sounded awful: 'nobody wanted me'. 'It just never happened,' she added quickly, hoping Sister didn't notice the inference.

'And you get on well with people?'

'Yes, I think I do,' she said, delighted she had an opportunity to redeem herself.

'Oh, you do, you do?' responded the matron, as if quelling any lingering doubts she might have had. 'Mr O'Malley spoke very highly of you; said you were good with the children.'

Bridie permitted herself the bones of a smile at acknowledgement that she was good for something. At least somebody wanted her.

'The poor man, I think his wife has her problems?'

'I think . . . she . . . has,' said Bridie hesitantly.

'Never mind,' said Sister Hortense, reassuringly. 'You'll be fine here with us. Now when is your baby due?'

'I'm not sure. I think it's about five weeks.'

'Wonderful. You'll soon have it all over. Dr Waldron is our resident doctor and he does his rounds every day, just in case anyone has a problem. So you need have no worries about the birth. Now, have you thought of a name?'

'I haven't made up my mind,' said Bridie, surprised at the matron's caring attitude.

'Of course not. There's plenty of time for that yet. Besides, we have a small booklet here with plenty of names to choose from. I'll get one of the girls to give it to you.'

'Thank you,' said Bridie, delighted that there was a human face about the place.

'Tell me, do you have any relatives at all?' An air of deep concern crept into Sister Hortense's voice.

'No,' responded Bridie, somewhat alarmed. 'I may have, but I don't know of any.'

'That's no problem; I just wanted to know if you had a relative who might like to adopt your baby. But then, if you did have relatives, you probably wouldn't have spent all those years in St Joseph's. On the other hand, you might be better off without them, because people don't always get on with each other.'

This sent alarm bells ringing in Bridie's head. Why would a relative adopt her child when she could rear it herself?

Sister Hortense, reading Bridie's mind instantly, tried to put her at ease by saying, 'If you had somebody to care for the child, then you'd stand a far better chance of getting a job, and a far better chance of meeting up with a nice young man. Not many men are willing to take on a mother and child, you know.'

'Can't I keep the child myself? I don't want anybody else to rear it,' said Bridie, a hint of desperation in her voice.

'Of course you can. But first we've got to pray for a safe delivery,' intoned Sister, detecting Bridie's highly strung attitude. 'Time enough to plan for the future when the baby arrives. It's you we must worry about now. I'll arrange for Dr Waldron to see you first thing tomorrow morning. He's very good with expectant mothers, you know, and he'll know almost to the hour when the baby is due.'

She stood up to take the tea from Mary Wade, who hesitated with a tray at the door. 'Thank you, Mary. This is Bridie Rodgers; you'll probably be working together from time to time in the kitchen. When Bridie has finished her tea you might arrange to show her around, please, and I'll get Annie Kelly to give you a hand with the dinners.'

The girls nodded agreement before Mary left the room, and Sister took up the conversation again.

'As you are probably aware from your time in St Joseph's, we have a fairly strict routine here, Bridie. It's designed specifically to be of benefit to the mothers and their children. You're expected to rise at seven a.m., each morning and attend to your own child before going out for an early morning walk around the grounds. You must attend Mass in the chapel each day and then help to feed and bath the children. For the first three months your priorities lie with your own child at all times, though you're expected to leave it in the nursery during the day, only returning to feed it whenever necessary. All other times you're expected to help in the running of the home, in return for free care and attention. How does that sound?'

'Fine. I like working with children, so I'll look forward to it,' said Bridie proudly, delighted to see Sister's warm expression at having someone with experience to help.

'Good. So shall we leave it at that for now?'

'Yes, Sister.'

Sister Hortense told Bridie to wait there for Mary Wade to show her around, while she went scurrying off down the hall.

During the late afternoon, when Bridie started to help out, she felt much more apprehensive, for there was a great deal of lamenting from grieving mothers in the corridors. She watched in horror as two nuns forcefully removed a mother to another section of the building.

Soon it was time for tea, and then they all knelt in the rest room to say the rosary.

A walk in the garden, for those who could, was considered a must before everyone went to bed. Then, Bridie found herself stationed halfway down the dormitory, beside a middle-aged woman with a wild look in her eyes. Bridie wondered if the woman was all right, or if there was something the matter with her. At the same time she could see a group of young girls huddled together in a corner. They appeared to be trying to console a young girl who was crying. The middle-aged woman seemed to be studying Bridie as she undressed. Bridie was mortified that a complete stranger was looking at her and tried to ignore her by facing the wall.

'How yah?'

Bridie half turned to look at her and the woman said, 'Is this your first day?'

'Yes.'

'I'm Margaret, but everyone here calls me Madge. Are you with me, *a grá*?'

'Yes,' said Bridie, somewhat relieved, and getting into a sunken old iron bed that felt as if it might collapse at any moment.

'You'd need to push that bed closer to the wall or it will fall asunder, *a grá*.' And in a flash she was out of her bed and gave Bridie's bed such a drive, Bridie thought the bed would go straight through the wall.

'Them beds have seen more births and deaths than Methuselah. Is that better now?'

'Yes,' said Bridie, wriggling as if to test it.

The woman tumbled into her own bed and addressed everyone in the dormitory in a loud voice. 'Remember now, girls, this is the workhouse. You'll have no airs or graces around here. No amount of grand talk will change that. We are what we are, *a grá*: workhouse women.'

Bridie watched everyone's head in the room turn and give a little smile.

Madge turned to Bridie. 'This is the workhouse, didn't they tell you that when you came in?'

Bridie looked, but said nothing, trying to decide if it was even safe to be in the same dormitory, never mind in the next bed to this woman.

'This is the worst place in Ireland that a woman can be. It's worse than jail. You can be in jail, *a grá*, for stealing a neighbour's hen or a new bicycle, and be out after six months. But here it's for life because we're mentally deranged. The workhouse,' she sighed, looking at Bridie. 'Surely to God you know that?'

But Bridie did not answer. Instead she pretended to be looking round the dormitory.

'Oh, aye, this is as low as you can get. What did you say your name was?'

Bridie looked again at the woman and smiled to herself at the thought that she could hardly go any lower. Her bedsprings were almost touching the floor as she replied, 'Bridie. Bridie Rodgers.'

'You mean Bridgit. Always use your proper name. It's more respectable, *a grá*. Not that you'll be needing it in here because, like I said, we're all mentally deranged. That's why we're here. We're fallen women and fallen women are put away for life.'

This line struck a disturbing chord in Bridie, and she asked hesitantly, 'What's fallen women?'

'Fallen women? What's wrong with you, *a grá*?' asked Madge, as she sat up straight in the bed and looked at Bridie as if talking to an idiot. 'Are you stupid or something?' she said loudly so that anyone who had ears could hear.

The girl across the room from Madge shouted, 'Madge, leave her alone. She's only a young girl; give her a chance,' and turning to Bridie, she added, 'Take no notice of that lady. That's just the old name for this place . . . and don't pay any heed to her,' she added with a wave of her hand.

''Tis the truth,' retorted Madge angrily. 'Honesty is the best policy. I tell no lies.'

But Bridie was beginning to feel she'd heard enough; that there was, undoubtedly, some truth in what Madge was saying: We're all in here *because we're mentally deranged*. Bridie had made up her mind that Madge was disturbed to some degree. But what about herself? Was she mentally deranged too, if she was sent to a place like this? No, she decided. She was here because she was going to have a baby. Peter Murtagh's baby. So that must be what a fallen woman is.

'A woman with a baby,' said Bridie quickly to Madge, lest she catch her embarrassingly with another query.

'That's right, missus. A fallen woman is a person of cheap morals, who lays down her body in any oul' haggard, to be used and abused until she becomes pregnant. Then she's thrown into the workhouse to keep her off the streets for the rest of her life. So there you have it, missus.' Madge heaved her ample bosom beneath the bedclothes and looked up at the cracked, fungus-strewn ceiling. 'We're two of a kind, *a grá*,' she continued, turning her head to Bridie, 'although speaking for myself, mind, I gave me body away with a heart and a half, because me oul' fella wouldn't agree with me seeing poor old John Joe. So I climbs out the winda . . . is it Biddy or Bridie or Bridgit I calls you?'

'Bridie.'

'Begging your pardon, Bridie . . . so I climbs out the winda in the dead-a-night to stay at my true love's. Instead we ended up sleeping rough in the hay, because his mother, God be good to her, had a face like a sow and wouldn't let us get married. In the end poor John Joe went to England, promising me the sun, moon and stars, and I've not seen sight or light of him since, *a grá*. And I'll be whipped entirely if they don't let me outa here soon to see my adopted daughter . . .'

'Is that you, Madge Courtney, spreading them fairy tales again?' intervened Sister Hortense as she came silently down the aisle. 'Girls, what are you doing out of your beds?' she added as she clapped her hands and set about turning down the oil lamps hanging on the walls.

'They're no fairy tales, Sister, and well you know it,' replied Madge as she snuggled down amid a sea of creaking, squeaking bedsprings. 'I know the history of this place since the time 'twas built. Sure, me great-great-grandfather built this poorhouse. A master carpenter he was, as was his father before him, and his father before him, going back, back, back, back . . . right back to St Joseph . . .'

'Madge, that's enough of that now!' snapped a stern-looking Sister Hortense, as she held aloft her oil lamp at the foot of Madge's bed to show her displeasure.

Madge raised her head slightly, showing her two mad eyes over the blanket. 'Beggin' your pardon, Sister, I was just tellin' Bridgit or Bridie here, I don't know where we'd all be if it wasn't for the Sisters of Bon Secour,' turning her head, 'isn't that right, Bridgit?'

'That's enough of your shenanigans. Now go to sleep,' said Sister as she turned briskly to leave the dormitory.

But Bridie had closed her eyes when Sister first came in and was pretending to be fast asleep. Inwardly she was laughing like she'd never laughed before, and was already looking forward to the next day, as the distant sound of Tuam's town hall clock rang out the last hours of her first day.

She'd only been there five weeks and was already filled with dread and apprehension about her future. There were so many thoughts going through her head. Mary Wade was aware of this as they changed and dressed the beds in the dormitory, well away from the tears and heartache that filled the day room on an almost daily basis.

'When's your baby due?' asked Mary, as they both stretched a clean white sheet across a bed and began tucking it in neatly at the corners.

'The doctor says it could be any time now, and I think he's right. I feel as though it's getting very near. But I could be wrong.'

'If the doctor says it's near, then you can be sure he's right. He's spot on every time. What do you think you'll do with it?'

'I don't know. Some of the girls said I should put it up for adoption; others reckon it's better to have them boarded out in the West of Ireland when they're five or six. But to be truthful to you, Mary, and I hope you won't say anything, I don't want to part with my baby at all. I want to keep it myself. I'm so looking forward to having my own child.'

'Well, speaking from experience, I decided to put my Patrick up for adoption so that he'd have a good home, and I wouldn't have to part with him then when I'd become too fond of him. I had me mind made up long before he was born. I could see what it was doing to the mothers here who had to part with them after a year,' said Mary, as they stood facing each other.

'And where is he now?' asked Bridie, thinking this must have happened a long time ago because Mary Wade was getting on in years, by the looks of her.

'He was in Sligo for a while. A lovely middle-aged couple that couldn't have any children came and adopted him. He was three months old at the time. I found it very hard at first, but I'm over it now, thank God, and I've a job here as long as I like. I don't want to leave here because I've nobody belonging to me, and I couldn't face the world on my own. Besides, I like it here.'

This was the exact opposite of what Bridie felt herself. Ever since she'd had that horrid feeling on arrival in St Mary's, she'd been unable to shake off the belief that there was something intrinsically evil about the place that made the hair stand on the back of her head.

Mary, meanwhile, felt as though she was talking to the wall because Bridie wasn't paying the least bit of attention to her.

She had that faraway look in her eyes. It annoyed Mary and she knew she'd enjoy her own company much better if she could get rid of Bridie: ask her to go for a walk or tell her to rest for a while or something.

'Where was I?' asked Bridie, embarrassed to realise she'd lost the run of the conversation.

'We were talking about your baby,' said Mary, annoyed that her own child didn't merit a decent discussion. She bent down quickly in anger to gather up the soiled sheets. 'Why don't you take a little rest now or go out for a breath of fresh air, Bridie, and I'll finish up around here?' she added as she crossed over to the other side of the room.

'Oh, I couldn't do that and leave you on your own . . .'

'No, no, it's all right; sure, we're nearly finished. Off with you, while you have the chance,' said Mary, praying silently that she'd go and leave her in peace.

'Oh, all right, maybe I'll go for a walk. Seems to be nice outside now. But are you sure?'

'I'm sure, I'm sure,' said Mary, hurriedly as she beat a few pillows into shape and then watched Bridie disappear down the long corridor.

Mary sat on the bed nearest the corridor so she could hear anyone coming, and took out the butt of a Woodbine cigarette. She had only two left and was afraid Bridie would have wanted one if she'd stuck around and then she wouldn't have any left for the night.

Bridie went for a short walk by the perimeter wall, and round to where some of the inmates were seated on a low stone wall sunning themselves, amongst them Madge Courtney. At times, Bridie felt that there was a lot more to Madge than met the eye. She had already informed Bridie that her daughter, Sarah, had been adopted a few short months ago, when she was five years old, and Madge believed that she was being reared somewhere in County Galway. But the nuns would not disclose her whereabouts to mad Madge other than to say the child was doing well, because they were legally bound to withhold such vital information.

'How yah? It's a new pair of boots you'll be getting, Bridgit, not a new baby if you don't put an end to the walking,' said Madge, as Bridie drew near them, smiling broadly.

'I wouldn't mind a new pair, but then I like wearing these because they're very comfortable.'

'Push over there, girls, and show a bit of respect for the one that reared ye,' said Madge, as the girls tightened up along the wall, tittering and giggling as one of them was almost pushed off as Bridie sat down at one end. Bridie thought some of the girls looked very young, certainly no more than fourteen or fifteen.

'Doesn't the ivy over there look lovely?' said Bridie, to no one in particular.

'Well, it's said that the ghosts of six Irish soldiers haunt this place, since they were executed by that very wall. You can see where the ivy never grew and never will again. And 'tis well I know it, Bridie, because I have seen their ghosts marching to the sound of beaten drums at daybreak.'

'Ghosts! Ghosts! Will you shut up, Madge? You're always trying to frighten us,' said one of the two young girls, getting up and running inside.

The blood drained from Bridie's cheeks too, and she felt a slight tremor in her body at Madge's words. She didn't want to hear them because deep down she had the feeling they were true.

So she said to Madge, 'Why does everyone seem to talk about ghosts in this place?'

Madge turned quickly and said, 'Because it's the truth, *a grá*. Have I ever told you a lie?'

Bridie looked into her piercing blue eyes but said nothing in case the woman grew violent, because she still couldn't make up her mind whether Madge was the full shilling or not.

'Have I? Have I ever told you a lie?' Madge asked more force-fully.

'No, no, you've never told me a lie,' said Bridie meekly, wishing she would just tone down her monotonous voice, because it was beginning to get on her nerves.

'No, *a grá*, I have not, because we're two of a kind. Fallen women. We're supposed to be mentally deranged. Oh, aye, it's all arranged,' she sighed, 'all arranged to hide the truth. And when I think of all the poor children that must have died here during the famine,' she added, shaking her head and folding her arms across her ample bosom as if going into a trance. 'Imagine being put into the workhouse, the poorhouse, just to die. Oh, they were dark, dark days. Orra-worra-worra-worra, when I think of all the stories me grandfather told me. Died all along the road, so they did, only for the weak to arrive and find this place was a hundred times worse than their own homes. The workhouses were riddled with the cholera and the pox. They couldn't wait to bury the dead, so they couldn't . . .'

Bridie didn't mind listening to Madge when she wasn't so wound up, but now she was beginning to wish Madge would shut up, because she just wasn't in the mood. While she was walking the grounds Bridie thought she was getting cramps, but she wasn't sure. Now she thought they were slowly getting worse, or was she imagining it? But the famine was a subject she was very interested in, having been told about it at St Joseph's, so she sat quietly listening to Madge as she rambled on.

'. . . That evening, as the lad threw the bodies into the coffins, he came to a man who moaned, "Wait! Wait! I'm not dead yet." "You're a damn liar," said the grave-digger. "The doctor knows best." What did he do, *a grá*, only fired the creature into the wooden box, singing: "Rattle his body over the stones, he is a pauper nobody owns!"'

But Bridie was on her feet, a tortured expression on her face as she bent over holding her tummy.

'In the honour of God, Madge. Stop. Stop . . . Oh! The pain! Hold me hand. Quick. Quick. Oh God . . .'

Twelve hours later the nurse delivered a seven-pound baby boy to Bridie, who cried out in agony, and then with joy on being handed the tiny infant.

'Thank you, Sister. I never thought I'd be a mammy. Isn't he lovely?' she whispered, as tears of happiness filled her eyes at the thought that she had produced such a beautiful child after all the distress.

'What are you going to call him?' asked the sister, showing her how to put the child to her breast.

'I think I'll call him Patrick or John. I can't make up my mind, yet.'

'Why not call him John Paschal, after the feast of the Passover? Besides, the name Paschal is French, and as the Bon Secour sisters originated in France, it would be a nice name.'

Bridie took her sound advice and had the baby christened John Paschal, almost two weeks after the birth.

They stayed together for three months in the nursery, where Bridie helped with the feeding and bathing of all the other children.

Just before she was due to be moved into the main building where the older infants and mothers were segregated, Sister Hortense summoned her to the office.

'Bridie, I think it's about time we discussed your baby's future, and of course your own. What are you going to do with the child?'

This was a conversation Bridie dreaded, because she didn't know what was the right thing to do, though she knew that if she gave the baby up for adoption she might never see him again.

'I want to keep the baby myself,' she blurted out.

'Yes. Well, in an ideal world that would be wonderful, but in this situation, it's one that I don't think will work; quite simply because you haven't got a home to go to. Secondly, you have no means of support, and last but much more importantly, you're destroying any chance of future happiness you might have of being free to find a husband and get married. You must have thought of those things,' said Sister Hortense with a very concerned look.

Of course Bridie had thought of those things – indeed, she had thought of lots of things – but she could find no answers. If she kept the baby and could get away from St Mary's, where would she go? How could she find a job and look after the baby? She would be at the mercy of the world, and without friends or protectors. She was thinking of staying in the home for a while and looking after the baby herself, and maybe after a while she could leave to go somewhere else . . .

Sister Hortense was looking at her and asking, 'Well, Bridie, what are you going to do?'

'I'll stay on here working . . . and keep my baby,' answered Bridie hesitantly.

'I know, but that won't work either. There are already one hundred and twenty girls here – thirty-five in the maternity wing alone. We can only keep on four or five full-time staff and they have to be trained. And even if we could keep you on, Bridie, you would not be allowed to keep your child. This is a full-time job – twelve hours a day – and keeping a child as well wouldn't work. Now there are a few people I know who would love to adopt a little boy, and I think you should consider it—'

'I won't give him away,' said Bridie, determination creeping into her voice.

'Fine,' said the Sister, not in the least surprised at her attitude. In a way, she secretly admired mothers like that because she felt it was an indication of superior motherhood. Some mothers would go to any lengths to protect their offspring, and it was the parting of these mothers and their children that caused her most unhappiness. But, what could she do when they didn't have a place to go?

'Your mind's made up then? You're sure about that?'

'I am,' said a relieved Bridie.

When she had gone back down to the nursery, Sister Hortense came up with an idea of her own. Who knew, there was still a chance for the mother, the boy and the adoptive parents, she thought.

A week later, Bridie was summoned to the Matron's office again and was surprised to see Mr O'Malley waiting to greet her. He handed her a big box of chocolates and, kissing her on the cheek, he asked,

'How's the baby?'

Sister Hortense excused herself for a few minutes and left the room.

When the pleasantries were over, Gerald added, 'Bridie, how would you like to come back to work with us again?'

Bridie, taken completely by surprise, just looked at Mr O'Malley, her mouth half open, and replied, 'I . . . I don't know.'

'Well, you're quite welcome. We'd be pleased to have you back. We have an elderly lady who comes and helps every day, but the children miss you a lot and we must find someone who's willing to live in again.'

'But what about the baby? The children might not like me bringing John Paschal home,' said Bridie, thinking that maybe they'd get jealous of him or that Mrs O'Malley might not have much regard for her now, after all that had happened.

Mr O'Malley's gaze fell as he said solemnly, 'Yes, we were hoping you might put the baby up for adoption, as rearing a baby as well would not work . . . as things are at present.'

Bridie wasn't sure what he meant, but she knew by his expression and behaviour that John Paschal would not be welcome at Conly House. And if she couldn't bring the baby then she certainly wouldn't go herself. She was almost ready to cry at the thought that Mr O'Malley could even think such a thing.

'I'm sorry, Mr O'Malley, but I must stay with the baby,' she said, turning quickly on her heel and running out the door just as Sister Hortense was about to come in.

Some uncontrollable instinct made Bridie rush down the corridor to the nursery where John Paschal lay gurgling. Picking him up, she held him firmly to her breast as the tears rolled down her cheeks.

Hugging and nuzzling him, she paced up and down the floor for a long, long time, whispering softly, 'How could anyone ask me to give you up, pet? I'll never ever part with you, son, as long as I live. I'll never ever part with you,' she repeated as she again kissed the top of his frail bumpy head and he began to cry.

The mothers feeding the infants around the nursery turned and looked on as Annie Kelly came over to Bridie and said, 'Are you all right? Is there something wrong?'

Bridie shook her head tearfully.

Then Mary Wade came and, placing a comforting hand on her shoulder, asked, 'Bridie, why are you crying?'

But Bridie could not tell her. She didn't think she could ever tell anyone about the awful pain that was festering in her heart: how she herself never ever knew the love of a mother, and did not have a single moment's recollection of being hugged or kissed by a mother or father, and now that she had someone to love for the first time in her life people were planning to take that joy away.

She turned and sat down to feed the crying infant and gave a huge sigh of relief. She felt she'd come so close to losing her child for ever. Right now she didn't want to talk to anybody. She just wanted to be left alone with her son and to get on with working in the home. But she knew that forces were ranging against her and that sooner or later something bad was bound to happen. She'd had a sense of foreboding ever since she'd first set foot inside the front door. And now she would have to be constantly on her guard.

Chapter Five

I N THE DAYS and weeks leading up to John Paschal's first birthday, Bridie tried to spend more and more time with him. There were constant rows between herself and the nursing sisters in the nursery because she continually overstayed her welcome in the day ward. The regulations stated that infants should only be breast-fed when necessary – at most, three times a day, and only for half an hour each time. But Bridie loved feeding and caring for John Paschal and often stayed longer by pretending to help the overburdened staff so that she could be near him.

During these precious moments she would continuously comb his hair into a fancy quiff, which, she noticed, had a beautiful gold-like streak running through it. On a few occasions she managed to spend most of the day with him, pretending that he wasn't well and that he needed her attention. But the nursing sisters soon grew wise to her motherly ploys and put a stop to them.

The days were now long and sunny, and the birds sang as the St Mary's inmates went to early morning Mass and joined in the singing with the church choir. It was the only time in an otherwise cold, hard existence when both staff and inmates felt truly at peace with each other. Then it was back to dealing with the screaming infants, the scrubbing and the sewing.

Bridie was working in the kitchen, helping Mary Wade, and had decided to ask her a few questions if the opportunity arose.

There was a continuous cycle of expectant mothers coming in and then leaving for God knows where, and rumours were rife. It was widely accepted that children were being sold to wealthy childless couples in Ireland, England and America. It was even said that the mothers were being sent to work in places in Dublin, Cork and Galway, and that some of the mothers were put into mental institutions because they would not accept the loss of their children. Others were said to work in big houses in the country, and children not adopted at birth were put into foster homes between the ages of three and nine years. Their mothers were never again informed of their whereabouts and had no more contact with them.

But amongst the mothers themselves it was felt that fostering out their children was by far the best option – from a mother's point of view. Most of the children appeared to be fostered out in County Galway, they said, so there was always an outside chance – slim though it may be – that you might meet up with your child again.

Trying to extract any worthwhile information from a reliable source was Bridie's greatest problem. Those she felt should know something didn't seem to know anything. And those who might know something were either too afraid to say anything or wouldn't tell out of jealousy, and those who were in a position to tell you everything about how the system worked couldn't be trusted because they were the nuns' pets and were the most reviled people within the home. Every little detail, no matter how insignificant, usually found its way back to the nuns and in particular to the Mother Superior. Bridie knew that Mary Wade was Sister Hortense's pet so she set about fishing for information, as they were both up to their elbows in flour.

'Do you ever hear from Patrick now, or how he is?' asked Bridie, innocently.

Mary was somewhat surprised and looked sternly at Bridie, who kept her eyes firmly fixed on the mixing bowl. Mary did not like to be reminded of her son; especially by someone whom she knew would be gone out of the home in a matter of weeks, and who really didn't care about how her son was.

'No. Why do you ask?' said Mary, curtly.

'Oh, I was just wondering,' replied Bridie. 'Were you ever told by his foster parents how he was getting on or anything? It might help me make up my mind about my own son,' she said as she raised her eyes and looked pleadingly at Mary.

This line cut no ice with Mary. 'You'll have to do what we all had to do, and that is give up your baby, and pay for your sins.'

This reply shocked Bridie so much that she was on the verge of picking up the mixing bowl and hurling it to the floor, but suddenly she thought better of it and said, 'Well, excuse me, but I refuse to pay for a sin I did not commit. I'm here because of what someone did to *me*. Why does everyone here just accept that you can't keep your own child? It's my baby and I'm the one who should decide its future . . .'

'There's no need to lose the run of yourself,' said Mary. 'Remember you're no better or worse than any of the other girls in here. We're all a bit unfortunate in some way, otherwise we wouldn't be here, would we?'

Bridie instantly realised she'd lost her whole plan of action and that she had made a complete mess of things. Getting on the wrong side of Mary Wade was akin to committing suicide, so she replied, wearily, 'Yes, you're right.'

Then Bridie decided to play her trump card by saying, 'You know, I really admire yourself and Sister Hortense. You're so good to all the mothers. I'm sure if you both had your way, you'd change the rules. I thought you'd be the ideal person to give me advice because, to be truthful, I don't know what's going on here. But I do know that handing over a child is a big decision and I know that by now you must have a good idea of what's right and wrong.'

Mary was scraping away the heavy dough from between her fingers with the blunt knife, as she looked across at Bridie. She thought, Bridie, you're smarter than I imagined. Anyone that'd seen you hanging around with mad Madge would take you to be a real *amadán*.

'Would you like a cup of tea?' she suddenly whispered as she glanced at the other girls working in the huge kitchen.

'Oh, I'd love one,' answered Bridie, who felt that she had scored a direct hit. She now knew that Mary was going to say something, but Mary continued working in a businesslike fashion.

'Girls,' she said, turning round, 'you can stick these in the oven now.'

She then beckoned Bridie into an alcove where they usually weighed the flour and oaten meal, and where no one could really see what was going on.

As Mary Wade pushed a cup of lukewarm tea towards Bridie, she said, 'You're right, it's probably the biggest decision you'll make in your life, and I envy you this minute.' Bridie said nothing as she looked at Mary, who repeated, 'I really do envy you this minute.'

'Why?' asked Bridie

'Because of your courage. If only I'd thought like that years ago, maybe I'd still have my son. At least I'd know where he was. But no, I was such a fool. I did what the sisters told me to do but now it's too late to do anything else,' she sighed.

Bridie immediately felt guilty for reminding Mary of her past and distressing her, so she added quickly, 'No. You mustn't start to think like that. You did the best you could at the time. Could Sister Hortense not help you?' she asked, realising she was asking this question for her own benefit.

'No. Unfortunately she was away on retreat when I gave up the baby and it didn't bother me too much that time. But ever since it has haunted me: how I gave up my beautiful little boy without a fight. Sister Hortense was very good to me and tried again – only last year – to trace the couple. They're in America somewhere, but no one knows where they are. So I'm warning you, Bridie, don't give up your baby for adoption or you'll never ever see him again. I don't know how the adoption system works because I've never been outside these four walls except once, but some of the older mothers, who've been in here once or twice, said they knew lots of children in Tuam who were reared here in St Mary's and then fostered out to complete strangers. Some children are sent over to England and America just to get them out of the way, because their father's name – usually some big shot – would be destroyed if anyone ever found out. So they pay a lot of money to the nuns to keep the whole thing quiet.'

'I heard that,' said a relieved Bridie, knowing how close she could have come to giving up John Paschal so she could go and work for the O'Malleys again. 'Could Sister Hortense do anything to help me, do you think?' she asked, half afraid she might overstep the mark by querying Mary's personal relationship with the nuns.

'I can't say,' Mary replied, as she turned round to rest herself against the small table and fold her arms across her white calico apron. 'I know she's the only one who gets anything done around here. When she first came here from Glenamaddy, you know, this place was a tip and she has transformed it as best she could. But some of the other sisters! They'd near cut you with a knife, they get such perverse pleasure from watching the mothers suffer.'

'How do you mean?' asked Bridie in surprise.

'Do I have to spell it out for you?' Mary whispered. 'If Sister Imelda or any of the other sisters don't like you, they make you hand over the child yourself for adoption and then watch you go demented.'

'Oh, but that's horrible,' said Bridie fearfully.

'I know, but we live in a horrible place. Oh! Where'd you get that?' she said in delight, as Bridie offered her the butt of a Woodbine cigarette, half afraid she'd refuse it after she herself specially cadged it off one of the mothers for this very purpose.

Mary Wade seized the fag, lit it and dispelled a blast of smoke towards the rotting fungus-stained ceiling, before adding, 'By making the mother do that, they will always be able to say, "Well, you handed over the baby yourself for adoption so don't blame us if you're suddenly feeling sorry for yourself." And, of course, they're right, you did hand him over.'

'And what happens to the mother? What do you think they'll do with me?' asked a worried Bridie.

'Oh, you're for the madhouse; you're for the asylum,' said Mary, relishing an opportunity to take a rise out of Bridie. 'But make sure to bring a length of rope, so you can hang yourself,' she added gleefully, much to Bridie's consternation.

'Mary! What are you doing there? Have you not finished the bread yet?' asked Sister Imelda, as she came silently into the kitchen and almost caught them unawares.

Mary dropped the fag instantly and ground it into the floor before nudging it under the table 'We're just finished,' she and Bridie replied in unison. 'We're just tidying up now,' added Mary, lest she be seen to be lacking in her responsibilities.

With that, Sister Imelda went towards the other girls preparing meals on the long tables, and checked the bread in the ovens.

Just as the sister was coming through the door, after Mary had said, 'You're for the madhouse,' Bridie felt dizzy. Immediately Sister Imelda had departed she took a few faltering steps out towards the lavatory in the corridor.

She thought she'd never get there. For though she knew Mary's words were spoken in jest, Bridie believed that in certain instances, mocking was catching and a curse was now trying to take control of her. She locked herself in the lavatory and sat down as she broke out in a cold sweat. It happened so suddenly it terrified her. It was as if she were in some telepathic mode and knew that John Paschal would be removed at any moment. She felt that if she did not do something, she would suffer at the hands of some unseen power that would sweep part or all of her along its evil path for ever.

I must be possessed by some evil spirit, she thought as she tried to get her breath and struggled to swallow her spittle. At that precise moment she made up her mind that though she and John Paschal might be parted in body, they would never be parted in spirit. And to ensure that, she knew she would have to be on her guard twenty-four hours a day for the remainder of her stay.

For the next week Bridie spent every possible moment she could with John Paschal, because she knew the hour was near. She and John Paschal had now been thirteen months together – mothers and babies were separated at thirteen months.

On Sunday evening Bridie was summoned to Sister Imelda's office. Earlier in the day, Mary had informed Bridie that Sister Hortense was in Dublin for a few days, so Bridie did not like it at all when she had to face Sister Imelda in her office without recourse to the matron.

'Bridie, I have some good news for you,' Sister Imelda began. 'You're going to Galway tomorrow morning: there's a lovely job waiting for you.'

Bridie looked at Sister Imelda for a long time, before she asked, 'Does that mean I'm leaving for good?'

'But, of course. You'll be a free woman. Isn't that what you want?' said Sister, with a sarcastic smile.

'What about John Paschal?' asked Bridie feebly, forcing the words from her drying vocal cords.

'What about John Paschal?' repeated Sister Imelda.

Bridie was fit to jump up and grab Sister Imelda by the hair, but she told herself she must keep absolute control and suffer the pain, and not let Sister Imelda succeed in upsetting her.

'Will he be coming with me?' she asked, knowing full well that he wouldn't.

'Really, Bridie, you can't be that stupid. You know very well that you wouldn't survive out there on your own. You'd be back inside here within a year – with another baby,' she replied in an exasperated tone, before adding firmly, 'No, John Paschal will remain here until he is old enough to be fostered out, or until a suitable home can be found for him. So you need have no worries: he will be well looked after.'

'Oh, thank you, Sister. You know how much he means to me; and I appreciate how much you have done for both of us,' said Bridie, plucking up the courage to ask for the unmentionable. 'Sister, I'd like to ask a special favour – only because I know you'd like to help me,' she lied brazenly as she watched Sister Imelda raise her eyebrows in dismay. 'I'd like you to send me John Paschal's new address wherever he is being sent when the time comes.'

Sister stood up and stared down at Bridie for what seemed an age. She was amazed at her cheek and her seemingly calm acceptance of her sudden departure to Galway. What a welcome change, she thought to herself. But rules were rules, and she had no desire to break them now that Sister Hortense was considering retirement and she herself was next in line for promotion. With regard to this lady, she could never make up her mind whether she liked her or not. She often thought there was something devious about Bridie. And now here she was making demands.

'Bridie, as much as I'd like to help you, you know full well that your request is out of the question. Were I to say yes, then every other mother in Tuam would want the same treatment; so I'm afraid the answer is no. Besides, all contact between mothers and their children is strictly forbidden once fostering or adoption has taken place. Now, if you don't mind, I'd like a little time to read my breviary. I've had a long day in the absence of Sister Hortense.'

Bridie stood up and proceeded to escort Sister out of the office, planning one more desperate plea.

'Sister, can I stay in the nursery for tonight? Please?' she begged.

Sister looked at Bridie as if she were insane. 'Really! You know, Bridie, you're trying God's patience – not to mention mine. Go, child, out of my sight this instance,' waving her away with the back of her hand. 'I don't care where you sleep, it's up to the night sister.'

Bridie flew through the corridors like some demented woman and pleaded with the night sister, who let her take John Paschal into bed with her.

For ages and ages Bridie sat up in bed, cradling John Paschal, hugging and kissing him and trying to control her emotions, knowing that these were going to be their last hours together. She didn't want him to close his clear blue eyes at all, so that she could sit and gaze at him all night long. But eventually he grew tired and cranky, and cried for his feed, which she gave him, and then at last he fell asleep. Bridie combed his quiff of golden hair one last time before gently laying him beside her on the bed as the night sister did the rounds of the nursery with her lamp.

'Time to get some sleep, Bridie,' she whispered. 'Tomorrow's another day, and don't forget your prayers.'

But Bridie could think of only one thing: tomorrow morning, when John Paschal would be gone out of her life for ever. She didn't know if she would ever see him again. The mere thought that she might not caused her more pain that night than she could ever have imagined. She went through his few personal belongings: a little suit, a teddy bear Sister Hortense had given him, and her own hand-knitted Blue Boy. But none of these things seemed appropriate as a keepsake to take with her. In the end, tear-laden eyes overcame her and she fell into a restless sleep.

She woke with a start from a horrible dream, as Sister Anunciata, the ward sister, was removing the child, and telling Bridie it was time to get up to get ready for Galway. For a split second, Bridie was in a state of panic as she made a protective grab for John Paschal. She'd dreamed that she had cut off the child's ear because a spirit had told her that if she did that, then the child would return. Nobody would be able to claim they had fostered out John Paschal, because part of him was missing. If Bridie kept the ear then one day he would return to her and the union would be complete.

Bridie was so relieved to see his ear intact, yet so struck by the message in the dream, that she was utterly convinced it had a valid meaning.

Sister was saying, as she picked up the sleepy infant, 'It's time for you to get dressed. Your car will be leaving shortly and you have to go down for breakfast yet.'

Bridie tried to wrestle the crying child away from the night sister, as she pleaded, 'Please! Please! Give him back to me, just for five minutes.'

Nervous mothers in nightgowns, infants at their breasts, came together and started crying pitifully in the centre of the room, each looking at a premonition of their own sad days to come.

Then a lone voice cried out, 'Ah, Sister!'

This encouraged another mother to add, 'Go on: give her another chance.'

But before any dissent could foment, the night sister had turned on them in an aggressive manner.

'Go back to your beds, the lot of you, and look after your own children; 'twould be more in your line. Bridie Rodgers, you should not have been allowed to sleep here last night. Look at the trouble you're causing now,' she shouted as she tried to back away from the grasping hands of Bridie.

'But there'll be no trouble if I can hold him; just five minutes,' pleaded Bridie desperately, as she started to grapple more forcefully with Sister for possession of the child.

Sister Anunciata managed to turn round and get away from Bridie, the child secure in her arms. She went towards the tiny medicine room situated in the corner of the nursery as the grieving mothers started to close in all around. Bridie spotted a pair of gleaming chrome scissors on the small medicine table. Quick as a flash she slipped the scissors into her dressing gown, as Sister Anunciata turned on the mothers with renewed aggression.

'I said, go back to bed, all of you, this instant, and don't be so nosy! Bridie, will you please go and get dressed and stop making a fool of yourself? If you'll just do that, I might let you hold him for a second.'

Bridie went and started to dress quickly.

Sister Imelda came in and, looking around, said, 'Bridie, are you not ready yet? Your porridge is waiting below.'

Bridie ignored Sister Imelda, while she finished dressing and brushing her hair, all the time thinking frantically about what she was going to do.

When she'd finished dressing she went towards the sisters, who, having finished changing the child, were watching her every move. With outstretched arms, and trembling emotions, Bridie asked, 'Can I hold him now?'

Sister Anunciata looked suspiciously at her, as she herself tried to control the whimpering child in her arms. She answered, 'On condition that you hand him over immediately without creating a scene.'

Bridie nodded in agreement, unable to speak as tears began to well up. Taking a firm hold of her only son one last time, she walked across the room towards the bed, as every mother in the nursery clung desperately to her offspring, helplessly watching Bridie and John Paschal's last goodbye.

Bridie lay the little boy down on the bed as the tears rolled down her cheeks, and reached for the scissors she'd put beneath the pillow. Just as the nursing sisters suspected she might be up to something, she took the scissors and cut off the quiff of the child's hair, which she had so lovingly trained for months. Kissing him quickly on the cheek and forehead, she sobbed hastily, 'Goodbye, John Paschal, goodbye. Some day, please God, we'll meet again.'

Sisters Imelda and Anunciata, on seeing the glint of the scissors, came running frantically to grab Bridie, who struggled free and ran down the corridor.

The young mothers, deprived of a last farewell, cried out, 'We'll mind him for you, Bridie. We'll take good care of him.'

They immediately went as one to honour their commitment, while Bridie, unable to look back, disappeared at the end of the corridor, forced to part now, and perhaps for ever, with the only true love she had ever known.

CHAPTER SIX

T HE EARLY MORNING sun rose majestically into a deep blue
sky, slowly peeling away the early morning dew that hung
over the tribal city. And as the last residue of dawn faded, it
revealed a bright sparkling city awaiting the arrival of yet more
visitors to its scenic shore as a black 1937 Austin motor car
came into view.

This was Galway, where city transport buses vied with each
other for the right to carry day-trippers to its famed Salthill
Strand. The black car, however, was not holiday-bound, and
came to an abrupt halt at the city end of College Road, where
it parked alongside a high stone wall. The three occupants on
the back seat looked questioningly at each other but said
nothing. They didn't know where they were, and they didn't
dare ask.

This must be it, thought Bridie as the two nuns in the front
of the car got out, and opened the rear doors to escort the
three girls to their new place of work.

'*There's a lovely job waiting for you,*' was the one thing that had
stayed in each of their heads since they'd left Tuam, almost an
hour earlier.

And here they were, standing at the bottom end of a steep
hill, with a neat row of red-brick houses directly facing them.
Bridie noted the green and white metal nameplate attached to
the end house that said 'Mary Magdalene Terrace'.

The girls looked anxiously around at the high imposing wall.

They shivered nervously despite the warm summer sun as each waited patiently to be handed her small brown suitcase.

The 'job', thought Bridie, must be in one of those houses, because there are no shops, no hotels and no hospitals here. Nothing.

Then a sudden notion struck her that she should run away while she still had the chance. Why should she go working for the nuns? Couldn't she find her own job somewhere in Tuam, and be near John Paschal? But then again, she might not get a job in Tuam or Galway, and she'd have to sleep out, because she had nowhere else to go. Besides, she didn't think she had the energy to run away after such a restless night and the struggle she'd had this morning just to say goodbye to her son. And as she looked sideways at the other two girls accompanying her, she thought, if the new job is good enough for them, then it's probably good enough for me.

She followed the two nuns as they walked ten short paces before unlocking a small entrance set in a massive oak door. Once inside, the girls looked in awe at the picturesque grounds before them. A huge, impressive, two-storey, stone building stood thirty yards away and to its right was a winding path leading via stone steps to a beautiful grotto dedicated to the Blessed Virgin. And further to its right again was a small enclosed graveyard, housing numerous black-painted iron crosses.

A graveyard! What in the name of God was a graveyard doing here? This place must be some kind of a church, the girls thought.

But the Magdalene Home Laundry in Galway city was a bit like St Joseph's Industrial School, Clifden: a place steeped in religion. Rare religious artefacts adorned every single room, and religious garments from the four corners of the province were sent here to be cared for, as well as dirty laundry from the region's tourist resorts, hotels and guesthouses.

Once inside the main building the girls were ushered into a small office and told to wait.

Almost immediately a stout nun with a rugged complexion came into the room and said, 'Good morning, girls.'

'Good morning,' replied the girls sheepishly.

'All the way from Tuam. Did you have a nice trip?' she asked, as she sized them up and began rubbing the backs of her large blue hands as if trying to inject some life-blood into them.

'Yes, Sister,' they answered with no great enthusiasm.

'Now, I'd like to get your details, if I may. I'm Sister Antonia, the Mother Superior. Any problems you may have, you come straight to me,' she said sternly, before going behind her desk and opening a great ledger, which stood out amid a mountain of receipt books.

Then looking straight at Bridie, she pulled up what looked like a heavy throne to support her ample posterior, and said, 'Now, young lady, what is your name?'

'Bridie Rodgers.'

'Bridie Rodgers,' she repeated, entering her name in the great book. 'How old are you, Bridie?'

'Seventeen.'

'Seventeen. And your address?'

Bridie looked nervously at the Mother Superior, but said nothing. She didn't know what to say.

'Your address, dear? We'd like to know your address and next of kin, who you are and where you came from, just in case someone comes to take you out; although I doubt very much if anyone cares.'

'Dublin,' replied Bridie doubtfully. The problem was she didn't know what she was supposed to say. She didn't know if she had an address any longer. She didn't want to say St Joseph's, she didn't want to mention the O'Malleys, and she didn't know whether she should say Tuam because it seemed she was no longer living there.

'Dublin,' repeated the red-faced sister. 'Is that it? No house, street or suburb?'

'No, Reverend Mother,' replied Bridie.

'You were born somewhere in the slums, I expect. Do you have children?' she asked.

'I have a one-year-old boy: John Paschal.'

'And I take it he is still in Tuam?'

'Yes, Reverend Mother. Will I be able to go and visit him?' asked Bridie, without giving the idea any great thought.

The Mother Superior put the gold embossed fountain pen back in its holder, as her already ripe complexion visibly flushed in anger at Bridie's outrageous suggestion. Then joining her hands as if about to pray she leaned back in her monumental chair and said, 'My dear! Let me explain one thing in the clearest possible language. You are now resident in the Magdalene Home Laundry: an asylum if you like; a place of refuge for the unloved, unmarried and unidentified. It is not a three-star hotel where guests can come and go as they please. You are here because nobody wants you, or because of your past sins. Here, we help you to atone for the sins of your past life or else you face eternal damnation in the eyes of God for ever and ever. Here you have an opportunity to make your peace with God. You are all his servants and from this day on are penitents in the eyes of God and must do his will. Furthermore, you are in the finest place in the whole of Ireland; safe and secure from the evils of the outside world – which by now you all know only too well.'

Then, taking a deep breath, she continued, 'Bridie Rodgers, the task facing you in particular is a daunting one. But my job as a servant of God is to ensure that you learn from your past, and lead a better life. As for any children you may already have, I have no doubt that they will be well looked after. It would serve no useful purpose whatsoever to entertain family visits. On the contrary, such visits would only help to sow the seeds of dissent, doubt and disarray.'

Then more gently she added, 'Now, can we get down to business? Please remember, the sooner you all settle into your new posts, the easier it will be for everyone.'

Looking directly at the girl next to Bridie, she asked, 'And what is your name?'

'Noreen Donnellan.'

'Address?'

'Kilbeg, Winnamstown.'

'Where is that?' asked Mother Superior with a furrowed brow.

'County Galway . . . it's near Castlerea.'

'You mean, Williamstown?'

'Yes,' answered Noreen, growing uneasy.

'Yes, what?' growled the Mother Superior.

'Yes, it's Winnamstown.'

'It's "Yes, Reverend Mother" to you! You are to address me at all times as "Reverend Mother"! Do you understand that?' barked the Mother Superior.

'Yes, Reverend Mother,' replied Noreen nervously.

'And it's pronounced "Will-yams-town". As far as I know there's no such place as "Winn-ams-town". So get that into your thick skull now!' Then, turning to the book again, she said, 'And how old are you — all the way from Will-yams-town?'

'I'm fourteen.'

'Fourteen, Reverend Mother!' roared the good Mother. 'We'll stay here all day if we have to; so get it right. Have I made myself clear?'

'Yes, Reverend Mother,' said Miss Donnellan as she shifted uncomfortably from one foot to the other.

'And what, may I ask, brought *you* to Tuam?'

'The parish . . . priest put me in . . . Reverend Mother.'

'Why did he put you in?'

'I don't know . . . Reverend Mother, yet.'

'Were you beaten by your parents in Williamstown?'

'A biteen, yet. I mean yes.'

'A biteen,' repeated Mother Superior. 'Perhaps you didn't get half enough. Maybe that was the problem. If you addressed your mother and father the way you addressed me, then I think I'd be giving you more than a biteen.'

Then turning to the third girl the Mother Superior asked, 'And what is your name please?'

'Josephine Finn, Reverend Mother.'

'Age?'

'Twenty-one, Reverend Mother.'

'And your address?'

'Lurgan, Dunmore.'

'Lur-gan,' she replied, writing it in the big book. '*An bhfuil Gaeilge agat?*'

'*Níl.* I can speak a little Irish, Reverend Mother.'

'But you have a baby?' said Sister Antonia, an air of sarcasm in her voice.

'No, I haven't, Reverend Mother,' said Josephine, emphasising the word 'no'.

'And why were you in Tuam then?'

'I was told it was only for a while – that I'd be given a decent job somewhere.'

'But why were you sent to Tuam in the first place? It's a home for expectant mothers – or were you ill-treated too?' queried the sister, detecting a rebellious tone in Josephine that made her blood pressure rise.

'No, Reverend Mother,' replied Miss Finn, who was beginning to dislike the Mother Superior more and more.

Josephine hated all nuns and priests because they seemed to lead such perfect lives. Any lingering hopes Josephine thought she had of ever becoming a saint in civilian life were dashed the day she met Cathal Swanick. Her whole world was turned upside down when she refused to stop seeing him – just because he was a Protestant. And the more her parents demanded she give him up, the more determined she became in her belief that she would not. So they enlisted the help of the parish priest, who promptly had her forcibly removed from her home and sent to Tuam. She was determined not to divulge any of this to Sister Antonia, who was now looking at her and awaiting an explanation.

When nothing further was forthcoming, Sister said, 'Am I to take it that you were removed from your home because you were something of a rebel? A nuisance perhaps or company keeping?'

'No, I wasn't,' replied Josephine in a manner that reflected her wounded pride. She wasn't going to tell anyone anything; it was no one's business but her own. She didn't want the nuns or any of the other girls to know what went on in her past life because pretty soon herself and Cathal would run away to England and get married. Cathal would surely come to her aid, she thought, although he had not shown up when her parents kept her at home after they forbade her ever to see him again. But this was different. He would surely come to her rescue now that the whole parish would know that she had been forcibly removed from her home and put away by the priest. Perhaps she would write to him now that she was in Galway, and see what happened. But then Cathal's father might see the letter and urge him to have nothing at all to do with her. No, no, Cathal wouldn't let her down. Sooner or later he would show up and whisk her off to England, so no one in the parish would ever know where she was and she could live happily ever after.

'Disobedience,' sighed the flushed Mother Superior, as she leaned back in her great oak throne and studied the three girls standing before her. 'Let me remind you girls, the world is full of disobedience coming in that door; but I can assure you it abounds with meekness before it goes back out again.' Then coming out from behind her desk, she scowled at them as she summoned in a loud voice from her office door, 'Sister Philomena.'

Sister Philomena appeared as if by magic and the Mother Superior said, 'Will you please arrange to have these girls assigned as quickly as possible? Perhaps you can find work for them in the kitchen and let Lilly MacAlastair and Peggy Neary go back on calender duty.'

The word 'calender' rang an immediate bell with Bridie. She knew the machine was for smoothing out sheets and blankets in a laundry. So this place must be like St Joseph's and St Mary's. But the Mother Superior said this was an asylum, a place of refuge for the unmarried, unloved and unidentified.

I'd better stop thinking and say nothing and see what happens, thought Bridie, as the three of them followed Sister Philomena down the corridor towards the rear of the building and into another room.

Handing each of them a white uniform and cap, a small towel, a bar of carbolic soap and two pieces of linen cloth, Sister Philomena whispered softly, 'They're for your monthlies. Take great care of them as they are only given out once a year. They will not be replaced should you lose them. And make sure to keep all of your personal possessions in your bedside locker at all times. Also, I must warn you that smoking is strictly forbidden. Please remove your clothes now and put on your uniforms. You don't have to remove everything, just your outer garments. You can change the rest later this evening after you've had a hot bath.'

Then all of their good clothes and personal items were put into their small brown suitcases and taken away. But Bridie did not part with her son's lock of hair. She now had it wrapped in a piece of paper and safely tucked into the cup of her bra until she found a more suitable place for it.

Down in the kitchen the inmates were busy scrubbing pots and peeling potatoes.

Sister Philomena called to two of them, 'Lilly! Peggy! Will you please go back to the laundry and help sort out the Tuam and Ballinasloe baskets? These new girls will take over here.'

Then turning to Bridie she said, 'What's your name?'

'Bridie.'

'Bridie! Will you come with me, please, and I'll show you what to do? Girls, I'll be back in a moment.'

Sister Philomena led Bridie down to the steam room where she was shown what clothes to iron. Half an hour later the three new inmates were shown where they'd be sleeping, by Sister Stanislaus, the ward sister.

There were three large dormitories upstairs: St Teresa's, Our Lady's and the Sacred Heart. Bridie and Josephine were going to sleep in Our Lady's, while Noreen Donnellan was going to be sleeping across the corridor in the Sacred Heart.

On their return they were given tea and bread in the kitchen and taken on a guided tour of the laundry by Sister Philomena. They were shown the large industrial calendars, the rows of galvanised wall sinks for hand-washing, as well as the steam room, the ironing room, the recreation hall upstairs, the church tucked away neatly at the back of the main building and the convent.

During their dinner break, all the girls in the laundry went outside to absorb the fresh air and sunshine. Bridie was amazed at the crowd of people huddled together, nattering in little groups, all of them clad in long white calico gowns and silly-looking white caps. Apparently these were new uniforms, or so the girls told Bridie. Some girls were walking around by the perimeter wall, linking each other in twos and threes, while some of the nuns walked around behind them with their rosary beads in hand, or knelt at Our Lady's Grotto in prayer. Two or three elderly penitents were tending the nuns' graves, and looking after the flowers in and around the walkways. But Bridie had eyes only for her comrades. She wanted desperately to compare notes, but above all to make friends with the two new girls.

Josephine Finn waved wildly when she spotted Bridie and rushed to join her, dragging Noreen Donnellan with her.

'Oh God, what do you think, Bridie? The kitchen's horrible; I'm not staying here. What are you doing?' asked Josephine with urgency.

'I'm in the ironing room, ironing shirts. I don't mind ironing, but the girl I work with has been here ten years and was never out once, not even for a day, and she said some of the girls were here an awful lot longer,' answered Bridie with even more urgency, as Noreen stood listening and looking all around her.

'We work with two oul' ones. They hardly spoke to us, did they, Noreen?' asked Josephine, turning to her young friend.

'No. They seem to creep or shuffle about the place. I was afraid to ask how long they'd been here. They looked like zombies to me. To tell you the truth, I think they're a bit gone in the head.'

'And one keeps forgetting where she leaves things,' added Josephine.

'Why don't you ask if you can come over to the ironing room with me?' suggested Bridie.

'Do you think it would work? They'd never let the two of us out of the kitchen,' said Josephine doubtfully.

'Well, you could try,' suggested Bridie. 'Tell them you worked with me in Tuam.'

'But I didn't, and I'd be no good ironing.'

Then Bridie spotted her workmate and called out, 'Julie, these are my friends that I was telling you about: Josephine and Noreen. They came in with me this morning.'

Suddenly another group of girls came rushing to their side, asking excitedly, 'Are ye the new girls?' 'Where are ye from?'

They were wondering if they knew this one or that one, a brother or a sister or a cousin. Did they know the village? How far away from it did they live? But when Bridie inadvertently said she didn't really know anyone or any of the named villages because she'd only been free herself a few short months, they all looked away in silence before hanging their heads. These long-forgotten inmates craved news of the outside world. Did their mothers or fathers really know where they were? Where were the fathers of their children who caused them to be put in there in the first place? Even more important, where were the children, who, like Bridie's, had been forcibly removed from their breasts at dawn and were now living only God knew where? Some of the girls, who were forcibly parted from their brothers or sisters as teenagers, were beside themselves for news of their relatives. Were they married, or living even? Did the new girls know anything at all?

No. Bridie and company knew nothing. Looking at the sea of anguished faces, Bridie felt as if she was betraying each one of them. If only she knew someone in Gort, Mountbellew, Boyle, Strokestown, Belclare – or Tuam, even. But no, she felt utterly useless that, after coming into this strange place from the outside world, she could not answer a simple question.

'Bridie! Do you know my brother, Billy? Billy Reilly, from Tuam? He's real tall, good-looking, with blond hair. Billy Reilly! Everyone knows Billy! He goes to midday Mass in the cathedral every Sunday . . .'

'No. I don't think—'

'But you must. You must know him. Everyone knows Billy!'

'No. I don't. I'm sorry.'

'But I thought you said you came from Tuam?'

'Well, I do . . . I mean . . . I did. But I was only in St Mary's Home for Unmarried Mothers and before that I was in St Joseph's Industrial School in Clifden.'

'Oh! So you're . . . you're . . . one of us!'

Then a small spectacled nun, head down, walked slowly by, clanging a little bronze bell to round up her troops and get them back to work.

Lining up four abreast they filtered through the narrow doorway, each lost in a sea of self-doubt, loathing and pity; before fanning out in the corridor to go and work in the washroom, the steam rooms, the ironing room, the dormitories, dispatch room, the bakery and the kitchen.

For some at least, they were midway through their first full day working in a lovely new job in Galway.

It was almost two weeks later, as she made her way back to Our Lady's dormitory, that Bridie felt the first real pangs of loneliness. After standing behind Sister Stanislaus as she unlocked the dormitory that housed fifty penitent inmates, Bridie slowly made her way to her bed, beside the steel-barred, painted window, and flopped down with sheer exhaustion. She had been on her feet since seven o'clock that morning. It was now half-past nine of a fine July evening, and most of the women were already in bed, Bridie being one of the last. She had ironed scores of shirts, not to mention numerous other bits and pieces. She never wanted to see another shirt as long as she lived. She was even too tired to think at first, and when she did, all she could think was, how was John Paschal? Her son, her own flesh and blood, had been snatched away from her – despite her best efforts. She felt as if someone had severed part of her own body. When she thought of his smiling, cheerful expression and his fancy quiff, which she had so lovingly trained, she reached into her blouse and pulled out a small pouch, which she had stitched on to her Sacred Heart scapular and which held the precious lock of golden hair. She kissed it good night as she did every night.

Soon she heard faint footsteps approaching. It was Josephine Finn, over for a chat. Bridie was too tired to talk, but she didn't like to say anything to Josephine, who was now sitting at the foot of her bed. As she did so, somebody from the other end of the dormitory whistled loudly, but Bridie and Josephine decided to ignore the taunts, as to respond to them would only create mayhem, as they had seen happen during the week.

'How did you get on today?' asked Josephine.

'Oh God, 'twas shocking,' Bridie yawned. 'I was standing there like a statue all this day, ironing, ironing! And now my feet are killing me.'

'But at least you have someone right to talk with. I'll go mad in that kitchen. I will, I swear! Three times I've asked Sister Philomena if I can go and work with you and all she says in her squeaky clean wouldn't-put-a-finger-in-a-fanny voice is, "Patience, dear, patience."'

Bridie, meanwhile, was looking straight at Josephine and thinking how really beautiful she was with her faintly freckled face, crowned with a mass of blonde hair, which now hung in ringlets about her shoulders. She was imagining what she must have looked like as a child, and then she was away on another train of thought herself; playing with John Paschal in the nursery at St Mary's. But when she heard Josephine saying something about being stuck in this place, she sat up in bed because she knew she'd get no peace until they were both exhausted from all the yapping.

Josephine was saying, 'Bridie, you're not listening. What am I going to do? I don't want to be stuck in this place for ever.'

'I don't know,' answered Bridie, but I was just thinking, 'if you started making a mess of things in the kitchen they might think you were no good and move you some other place.'

Josephine's eyes lit up and she exclaimed loudly, 'Yes, yes! That's it! That's it!' And with that she sprang from the bed and proceeded to the centre of the floor where she whirled and twirled like a ballerina, singing. 'Somewhere Over the Rainbow.'

But then an ageing cranky inmate, woken from her slumber, put paid to Josephine's song: 'Would you ever shut up and let a person get some sleep?'

But she in turn was instantly drowned out by a chorus of, 'Ah, Grumpy, leave the girl alone. You're sorer than a boil on a bear's arse. Let the girl sing.'

With that, everyone started to laugh and two or three of the more brazen ones jumped from their beds and began pulling the bedclothes off Grumpy Moran's bed.

'Take no bleedin' notice of that rip,' said Molly from Dublin as she sat crocheting on her bed, 'If you want to sing, love, you sing.'

And for a time it seemed as if pandemonium would reign as everyone started shouting and throwing pillows or pulling at each other's bedclothes.

The appearance of Sister Stanislaus, bursting through the door, vigorously swinging her bell, brought proceedings to a sudden halt.

'Girls!' she exclaimed. 'I'm ashamed of you. You're behaving like a gang of hooligans.'

The silence was deafening until Molly piped up, 'Sister, how do you spell that?'

The dormitory erupted into peals of laughter again, as one or two of the more brazen inmates tried to intimidate Sister Stanislaus; but she was too alert for them and soon locked the dormitory door for the night.

Bridie felt elated that Josephine had such a beautiful voice and, together with the other girls, tried to cajole her to sing again. But she ignored their pleas.

And then the lights went out, leaving the inmates screaming as they grabbed each other and tried to find their beds in the semi-darkness.

Soon everyone was fast asleep except Bridie. She knew she'd had a bad day and, judging by what her workmates were saying, she would have many more. She also knew she couldn't keep going like this with no hope, no plan and no future; with nothing to look forward to. The tales she'd heard of life in the Magdalene Home Laundry were too frightening even to contemplate. She began to twist and turn in her bed in an effort to erase them from her mind, trying instead to devise a master plan. Never mind about anyone else, she would try to look after herself from here on in, she decided.

The small bronze bell made a heavy clanging noise as Sister Stanislaus shook it vigorously.

Jesus! thought Bridie. That bell has the most irritating tone I ever heard. I swear that bitch Stanislaus gets pleasure out of wakening everyone at this hour of a morning.

When Sister Stanislaus had left the room, Bridie turned over and curled up beneath the blankets. She felt so tired and so wrecked that she didn't want ever to get up again. She felt very apprehensive about effecting her plan so quickly, but she decided she'd better get up anyway.

When Josephine Finn came by her bed and asked, 'Are you ready?' Bridie jumped up and grabbed her soap and facecloth from her bedside locker.

As the two of them left the dormitory, they could see other girls in the corridors fighting over towels. This ritual was repeated on an almost daily basis, as the inmates tried to procure fresh towels from wherever they could. Several girls had already been beaten black and blue by the nuns when it was discovered they had helped themselves to a nice range of hand towels sent to the laundry for cleaning, which resulted in everyone being afraid to procure even a small silk handkerchief for her own use.

Down in the washroom, Bridie was once again struck by the appearance of the worn-out elderly penitents as they went about their ablutions in a silent robotic fashion. Their haggard, grey, unsmiling faces were a stark reminder to all that, sooner or later, life in the Magdalene Home Laundry took its toll. For a brief moment Bridie stood in the queue and watched two inmates from Our Lady's dormitory turn in unison from the washbasins and press towels to their thin wan lips, then amble out of the washroom, oblivious to those around them. Bridie wondered if they had ever been kissed; somehow she could not imagine it.

She knew by now that they would shuffle back to their dorm-itory and get dressed slowly, then go to Mass and receive the Blessed Sacrament, have their breakfast and never say a solitary word to anyone. Bridie had found out that these women were only in their forties, and it sometimes frightened her even to look at them, before glancing at her own reflection in the wash-room mirror, as everyone kept commenting on how pale and tired she looked. It was a relief to Bridie to know she had a plan of action in place for her freedom this morning.

When Josephine and Bridie had finished washing they returned to their dormitory and got dressed for work before making their beds.

Then Bridie turned to Josephine and said, 'You go on down-stairs. I'm staying here.'

'Why? Are you sick?' asked a startled-looking Josephine.

'No, no. It's something I have to do. I'll be down later.'

'But Sister Stanislaus will notice, and you might be punished,' said Josephine.

'I don't care,' said Bridie. 'I just want to be left on my own for a while. I'll be down later, I promise. But don't say anything to anyone.'

When Josephine went out and Bridie was left on her own, she looked about the large dormitory and thought it had a surreal atmosphere about it, despite the fact it had a large statue of the Sacred Heart at one end of the room. For a moment she thought it could be classed as a hospital, with its fifty-odd beds, but on closer inspection she thought it looked more like a prison with its heavily barred, painted windows. And when Bridie pictured Sister Stanislaus, with her numerous dangling door keys by her side, locking all the dormitory and interme-diary doors, she suddenly felt frightened. She walked tentatively towards the door in case it should be locked. It wasn't. For what seemed a long time she hung around listening for any approaching sounds, and when she heard the intermediary door in the corridor being unlocked downstairs and the mouse-like movements of the sister's garments, she scurried back to her bed.

Sister Stanislaus came in and said, 'What's this, Bridie? You're late . . . and have not received the Blessed Sacrament this morning. Is something wrong?'

On hearing these placid words Bridie thought perhaps she should abandon her plan. Maybe she was being foolish; that no good would come of it. But then how would she explain her absence? She'd better say something. Now was her chance.

'No, Sister, there's nothing wrong . . . except . . .'

'Except what?' demanded Sister Stanislaus.

'I don't know if I'm ever going to see my baby again.'

'Aw, come, Bridie, don't be silly. That's all in the past now. You'd do well to leave it all behind you. You're starting a new life for yourself here, and you have an awful lot to look forward to. Look at all the wonderful friends you've made. Friends anyone would be proud of. So come on down now and have your breakfast: I won't say a word to anyone.'

But when Bridie heard the words 'don't be silly. That's all in the past now', she felt such heartache that John Paschal's existence didn't merit a care or a thought to anyone but herself that she knew she had to see her plan through. 'I'm sorry, Sister, but I refuse to go to work until I know when I can go and see John Paschal,' she said, looking Sister straight in the eye.

'That's all very fine for you to say, Bridie, but when the Reverend Mother hears about this she will not be very pleased. Do you realise you may be deprived of your privileges? Being allowed to sleep in a dormitory of your choice and not having to scrub linen all day long is a perk I'd be very slow to lose,' said Sister authoritatively, pushing her pale white hands into the deep folds of her long black sleeves.

Bridie stared at the floor for a long time before meeting Sister Stanislaus's eyes again, but said nothing.

'Well, are you coming down with me or not?'

'No, Sister,' replied Bridie, realising she had now embarked on her plan and would have to see it through.

'Fine. In that case you give me no choice but to report your disobedience to Mother Superior,' said Sister Stanislaus, turning on her heel and hurrying out the door.

But she very soon returned to inform Bridie that the Reverend Mother wanted to see her in the office right away. Bridie followed Sister Stanislaus down the long corridor, feeling somewhat elated that she was at last making a stand for herself.

When she went into the Reverend Mother's office, the hard-faced Mother Superior looked at Bridie with disdain, as Sister Stanislaus remained standing next to Bridie, like some prison guard.

When the Mother Superior spoke, it was with a gruff voice. 'I understand you have a problem, Miss Rodgers.'

'I . . . I don't really have a problem.'

'Well then, what are you doing here?' she growled. Then, looking directly at Sister Stanislaus, 'I thought you said she refused to go to work?'

Bridie spoke up promptly when she realised she was losing ground and was being pitted against Sister Stanislaus.

'I refuse to go to work, Reverend Mother, until I know when I can see my son, John Paschal, or if I'll ever be allowed out of here.'

'I see,' said the good Mother, starting to tidy up her office desk as if Bridie were merely a distraction. 'So we have not one, but two requests from you, Bridie Rodgers. Is that correct?'

'I want to know how my son is,' said Bridie, changing the emphasis slightly.

The Reverend Mother stopped work instantly and looked at Bridie. She knew she was dealing with a novice, so she availed herself of the perfect opportunity to get her full contingent back to work.

'But why didn't you just come out and say that? I could have told you: your son is fine. I was speaking only yesterday to Sister Hortense,' she lied, 'and she informed me that your son is thriving. He's just fine. You have absolutely nothing to fear. Now, can you be a good girl and get to work, please, because I'm afraid we're very short-staffed this morning on account of the nuns' retreat.'

Bridie knew that she had said the wrong thing. She couldn't very well make a demand now, after what Mother Superior had said. Her son was fine and that was all that mattered.

'Thank you,' she said rather tamely as she stood up and was escorted all the way down the corridor to work by Sister Stanislaus, who uttered not one word.

Down in the ironing room there was an air of excitement, with everyone wanting to know where Bridie was or what had happened to her.

When she returned and told them what she'd done, Julie Murray said, 'You were silly to bother your head, *a grá*. Sure, that one wouldn't take a blind bit a notice of an'thin' anyone said. Sure, she's only an oul' cod,' she added as she began carefully folding up another ironed shirt. 'You should have told us *f*what you were plannin'; and we'd have told you *f*what to do.'

'But what else could I do?' asked Bridie, somewhat perplexed.

'Sure, if we'd known, we could have gone and supported you and . . . and . . .'

'That's right,' chipped in Lilly MacAlastair. 'You were lucky the Superior Ass didn't put you on a starvation diet. At least if we were with you they couldn't starve us all because then there'd be no work done. Mr Hehir, the van driver, he said, the one thing the nuns hated was the prospect of a strike; that they have to have the clergy's laundry done, no matter what . . .'

'And besides, they'd have no money for the bishop,' added Julie.

'Money? For what bishop?' asked Bridie, feeling really annoyed that she knew nothing, and that no one had bothered to inform her.

'The money they charge the hotels in Ennis, Gort, Kilrush an' ever'*f*where,' said Julie. 'Sure, they make a fortune,' she continued, 'and give it all to Bishop Frown. He comes here then at Christmas and we all have to kneel down and kiss his oul' ring . . . an' the devil . . . stuck-a-thin-him.'

'Yes,' agreed Lilly, 'and we like a right shower-a-eejits polishing his size-ten shoes and washing his smelly oul' underwear all year.'

'Sure, glory be to God Almighty, Bridie, where's the sense in that? 'Tis him should get down on his two bended knees and kiss our feet,' continued Julie good-humouredly.

'Our arses, more like,' corrected Lilly.

'Oh my God, will ye stop it!' cried a disgruntled Peggy Neary, as she began pounding down the heavy steam iron, trying to press her own religious views on all and sundry. 'Ye know well it's all for the good of the Catholic Church. That some day, please God, we'll all get our reward in heaven.'

'Reward, how are you?' echoed Julie. 'If you ask me, we're livin' in hell already 'cause none of us can get out.'

'May God forgive you, Julie,' snapped Peggy Neary.

'You'd want to watch who you're talking to, Bridie, around here, 'cause the place is full of spies,' said Lilly MacAlastair, tipping a wink at Bridie.

'And what's that supposed to mean?' bellowed Peggy, wheeling round.

'Oh, Peggy, we don't doubt you for one minute, but it's strange how the last time we planned to go on strike, the nuns knew more about it than we did,' said Lilly, matter-of-factly.

'But that had nothing to do with me, Lilly, I swear to God, cross me heart and hope to die,' said Peggy, making a fleeting gesture of a cross on her chest.

'But *f*why do the nuns always give you nice clothes an'

ever'thin', an' we're left wearin' nothin' but oul' rags?' added Julie mischievously

'It was a bloody parcel! From home! I already told you . . .' screamed Peggy defiantly, as the sound of the dinner-hour bell reverberated through the laundry. 'If I told you once, I told you a thousand times, 'twas a parcel!' she reiterated as her laughing colleagues were already scrambling out the door.

'Bastards!' swore Peggy, as she finished folding and putting away another freshly ironed shirt. 'Just ye wait till I tell Mother Superior, just ye wait,' she mumbled.

Bridie was feeling somewhat down after another long day at work, and wanted desperately to be alone with her thoughts. After carefully considering the chapel as a quiet place of refuge, she decided instead she'd hide behind Our Lady's Grotto out in the laundry grounds. Surely there wouldn't be anyone there at this hour of an evening. All she wanted was a quiet moment to get away from everyone and have a fag in comfort.

She began by walking casually around by the perimeter wall of the enclosed grounds and peered through the heavy iron and barbed-wire gate leading to the nunnery field where two of the young penitents and a nun were turning out the cattle after they had been milked. She then stole up by the back of the grotto and stood leaning against the stone wall, well away from the prying eyes of the nuns in the convent, and took out the butt of a Woodbine cigarette she'd found in the pocket of a shirt. After a few wholesome drags she was surprised by the unexpected appearance of Julie Murray.

'Oh! There you are! An' I searchin' all over for you. Sure, I was wonderin' fwhere you'd gone,' said Julie. 'Fwhat are you doin' here? Fwhere'd you get the fag?'

'Oh, I found it somewhere,' said Bridie, annoyed at being discovered.

'Come on and we'll walk around to the front of the grotto,

'cause the nuns can see ever'thin' outa them windas, and if they see us hidin' behind Our Lady, they'll think we're up to some-thin'. The best place to talk is the nuns' graveyard. Sure, they think we're prayin' for them then, the oul' eejits,' she tittered, as they started out.

Bridie had earlier in the day witnessed a relay of penitent women, under the directorship of the Mother Superior, pluck the neat pastures of grass that grew between the rows of head-stones. So there was nothing else for them to do now but pretend to pray. Bridie and Julie both stood facing one of the graves, so that anyone looking out of the convent windows would think they were a pair of religious zealots. Bridie admired Julie's cuteness and regretted not having thought of the idea herself.

'Bridie, I'll never stick it here. Kneel down there now,' she ordered, 'until you hear my confessions.'

'Well, you've stuck it ten years,' said Bridie, kneeling down and joining her hands as if in fervent prayer. 'Look at me. I'm only here a few weeks. Do you think we could ever run away or climb over the wall?'

'I don't know! Sure, you'd want to be mad in the head to stay here, *a grá*. And madder again, I'm thinkin', to get away. Only one young one managed to get clean away. And one died in a laundry basket. Sure, scores-a-girls tried, but them oul' raps-a-nuns cut off their hair and left them black and blue. God forgive me, Bridie, but I hope them oul' nuns rot in hell. Oooh! And to think some-a-them girls had such beautiful features,' she lamented. Then turning to look at Bridie she continued, 'Do you know what it is, Bridie? I think I must be goin' mad. I really think I am.'

Bridie was so taken aback she could say nothing. She didn't want to dwell on such horrible thoughts.

'Ten years! Sure that's enough to drive anyone mad,' added Julie, as if to reinforce her argument.

'But you're not. You're not,' said Bridie, trying to reassure her. 'You're just upset, that's all, and you have every right to be. You're here a long time. But why are you in here anyway? You never told me and I didn't like to ask,' she added hesitantly, feeling that she could converse more openly with Julie now that they were friends.

'We'd better keep walkin' 'cause them nuns hate to see two friends together,' said Julie.

When they were out of the graveyard and walking silently by the perimeter wall, Julie stopped abruptly, glanced around and whispered, 'Bridie, I have to tell you something awful. Promise me you'll never ever tell a sinner, because if the nuns knew about it, I'd never ever be let outa here.'

Bridie felt privileged at the thought that she was now going to be entrusted with some terrible secret. 'Julie, you can trust me. I promise,' she said with all sincerity.

'Oh, I was a silly girl! A silly, silly girl!' lamented Julie. 'Sure, I had no sense!' she began to whisper emotionally, as they both started to walk, slow unified steps, their arms neatly folded, their heads bowed in contemplation, along the winding circular path that zigzagged its way around the scenic grounds. 'There was twelve of us in my family, an' then Daddy died. I was very young then; around thirteen or fourteen, an' I hadn't a coat or a gansey to put on me back.'

As she spoke, she pulled out of her sleeve a lovely silk handkerchief, which was trimmed in red lace and that had the letter J boldly embroidered in one corner, her very own creation, and began dabbing her eyes with it.

'An' then I saw a beautiful red coat hangin' in a shop winda, an,' you know, Bridie, I dreamed-a-that coat, night, noon an' morn.' Suddenly she stopped and turned to Bridie, sobbing pitifully. 'I ran into the shop an' stole the coat. I'm a thief, Bridie! I'm a thief! I'll never get out of here now. Oh, what am I going to do?' she cried, as Bridie looked around embarrassed in case anyone saw them. But the only ones there were two nuns reading from a prayer book the other side of the grounds.

Bridie, surprised by this admission of guilt, linked her friend by the arm and said, 'It's all right! It's all right! No one knows and besides, you're not a thief. You only took that coat because you were poor. I'd have done the same myself, I swear. And anyway, it was a long time ago. So how did you come to be here?'

Julie, drying her tears, mumbled, 'The guards were called and said I'd have to go to jail. But the priest stopped them. He said I was too young an' told my mother she'd be better off without me: that he knew a place in Galway that'd soon smarten me up. So he put me in here. For four years, he said, an' I'm here since. Sure, they must plan to leave me here for ever. I'll never get out now. Never, ever.' She started to cry again.

For the very first time, Bridie saw the enormity of her own predicament within the confines of the Magdalene Home Laundry, and was stunned into prolonged silence.

Julie, meanwhile, began to wish she hadn't told Bridie anything as it seemed she was now ignoring her, not having said another word.

When finally they returned to the dormitory and were locked up for the night, Bridie lay awake for hours and hours. She couldn't sleep because the whole spectre of her life began to unfold like some long-forgotten horror story. The memory of her childhood in Connemara, the beatings at the hands of Mrs O'Malley in Conly House, her forcible separation from John Paschal, and her removal to this house of refuge from which no one could escape.

She was terrified the way her future seemed to be shaping up. As things stood, she surmised she didn't have a future. But the most horrible thought of all then entered her head: the sayings of Madge Courtney, or 'mad Madge', as they liked to call her in Tuam. A fearful chill crawled up Bridie's spine at the thought that Madge's words were a prophecy. 'We're fallen women,' she had said, 'and fallen women are put away for life . . . This is the worst place in Ireland that a woman can be. You can be in jail, *a grá*, for stealing a neighbour's hen or new bicycle and be out after six months.'

If the guards had put Julie Murray in to jail that time, she'd be out by now, thought Bridie. But here it's for life because we're all mentally deranged. Oh God, that must be what's wrong with Julie! Didn't she say that very thing this evening: 'I think I must be goin' mad'! Maybe she didn't steal a coat at all. Maybe she imagined it.

Bridie's already tired and worn-out body developed a cold sweat as the words 'We're all mentally deranged' echoed over and over in her head.

Jesus, we must all be mad, she thought. That's why they lock the doors and put bars on the windows, and paint them: so we can't see out and no one can see in. If I got sick now, would they let me out? I think I'm going to die this minute, I really do. I must have a fever. Why am I now so hot? And if this place went on fire, we'd all burn alive cause no one can get out. Julie? She's here ten years. Ten years! Oh God, what am I going to do? What hope have I? And the old women, they're here all their lives. They don't even send them home when they die. They bury them here. That must mean I'm going to die here in the Magdalene. Oh God! Oh Jesus, Mary and Holy St Joseph, please come to my aid this night, she cried softly, as she crept out of bed and made her way down the dorm-itory amid the sleeping, snoring heads to seek solace and comfort with Julie.

But when she reached Julie's bedside she was shocked to discover somebody else was sleeping with Julie, and a strange sickly feeling came over her; yet somehow she managed to prevent her jelly-like legs from folding beneath her. She didn't want to talk to Josephine Finn, who was nearby and who was asleep anyway, because she didn't think she'd be able to understand.

Bridie made her way slowly back to her own bed and lay down once more. She asked herself if this whole thing was a nightmare. She had thought things were bad in St Joseph's when she had no mother or father, or brother or sister. She thought things were bad at the O'Malleys, when she felt the weight of the broom across her back; and she'd never ever forget the pain in her heart the day her son was taken from her. But this: 'the worst place in Ireland that a woman can be' . . .

In desperation, she clutched her rosary beads and tried to pray, but however hard she tried, her mind could not get away from those haunting words: 'The worst place in Ireland that a woman can be'. So she made a pact with God that she'd say one 'Our Father', one 'Hail Mary' and one 'Glory Be to the Father' if tomorrow would bring her a better day, and with that plea ringing in her head, she fell into a deep, deep sleep.

Sister Philomena came in hurriedly through the swing doors of the ironing room and requested Julie and Bridie to go with her to the storeroom.

'The new girls must have got them mixed up somehow, because several items of precious altar cloths from the bishop's residence have gone missing, as well as some of the sheets from Ennis,' she explained, as she stood among the stacks of linen cloth. 'I want you to check all the codes and see if you can locate them. Then put them into a basket and take them over to dispatch.'

'Yes, Sister,' replied Julie and Bridie, delighted to be away from everyone, a welcome break from their everyday routine.

It's the perfect time, thought Bridie, to find out who's sleeping with Julie. All morning the thought that Julie had another close friend had been distressing Bridie.

'You know, Julie, I couldn't sleep a wink last night,' she said as they both started checking the mountains of folded altar cloths and clean white sheets, which had codes and initials neatly hand-sewn into a corner of every item.

'Thanks–bit–o–God, I slept like a log.'

'So I went down to you late last night to have a chat, but there was somebody else with you,' said Bridie.

'What do you mean, someone with me?' replied Julie, going through the layered folds of material to find the initials, then stopping to look quizzically at Bridie.

Bridie knew by Julie's face that she was as puzzled as herself, and began to think that perhaps she was imagining it all.

'I went down to have a talk with you because I was having the most awful nightmare about this place . . . but when I got to your bed . . .' hesitated Bridie.

'*F*what are you on about?' said Julie, pulling out one of the missing cloths with a vengeance.

'There was someone sleeping in your bed, so I didn't say anything,' said Bridie, delighted that she had had the courage to confront Julie.

'Arrah, you must be ravin'!' said Julie, continuing to stack one neat pile of linen on top of another.

'I'm not raving! Far from it!' answered Bridie, emphatically. 'I couldn't see who it was in the dark, but there were definitely two people in your bed.'

'Sure, there was no one in bed with me. An' anyway, isn't it me own business who I sleep with?' she frowned. After a momentary silent recollection, she rejoiced, 'Arrah, it must be Harry! I brought Harry back last night,' she laughed. ''Twas Harry you saw.'

'Harry? Harry who?' asked Bridie, horrified that Julie might have sneaked in one of the delivery drivers, although she couldn't see how that was possible because you couldn't even smuggle a packet of cigarettes into the laundry without the nuns knowing about it.

'Harry! Me teddy bear! Sure, he's as big as mesel'. I call him Harry after a fella I knew. Some of the girls asked me weeks ago, could they borrow him for the night, and he's been doin' the rounds ever since. I had to bring him back from St Teresa's dormitory because Margaret Sherry was trying to keep him. Sure, the poor devil's worn out, but I have him back now and I'm keepin' 'im,' she tittered.

'God, that's a good one!' laughed Bridie with relief. 'I thought it might be Noreen Donnellan or Josephine Finn. I was killed wondering.

'No, *a stóre*, 'twas only Harry. Lord, if he was real, wouldn't it be wonderful?' She paused dreamily. 'I'd tie him to me bed and keep 'im for ever. But sure, *ƒ*where's the use in talkin'? I'll soon be eleven years here now, and no one cares!' she sighed. 'No one cares!'

Bridie watched Julie shuffle over to the storeroom door where she listened attentively for a moment before returning to the centre of the room.

'If I tell you a secret, will you promise to keep your mouth shut?' she whispered.

'Of course I will! Why wouldn't I?' Though Bridie wondered what else Julie had done and if she herself would be able to cope with all the secrets.

'I'm goin' to try and get out of here because I don't think I can stick it another minute.'

'Get out!' exclaimed Bridie in amazement.

'Yes. I'm goin' to run away. Climb over the wall or somethin'. An'thin' to get away from here.'

A surge of excitement that something was about to happen, and that she herself might be part of the plan, brought a sudden flush to Bridie's cheeks.

'When are you going?' she asked, holding a set of priest's vestments in her hand in case Sister came in and caught them talking.

'Sure, I haven't the foggiest, but I remember once, 'twas months and months ago, I was walkin' down the corridor and I happened to look down the nuns' corridor and didn't I see the big door at the front of the grounds wide open. You could see straight out on the road. Sure, I should have run, I suppose, and got away because I'd be afraid to try and climb over the wall. It's awful high the other side and I might get kilt.'

'Oh I know,' said Bridie, recalling how frightened she was at the forbidding wall the very day she first came to the Magdalene. 'Would it not be easier to escape across the nuns' field at the back? Maybe we could then catch a train or something.'

'Sure, the only time we're out there, the nuns walk beside us while we're on retreat, sayin' the rosary an ever'thin' and if we as much as whisper a word, them trumps'll give one a skelp across the back-a-the head that'd knock you kickin'. Sure, they nearly kilt me once, because I started titterin' an' ever'thin'. Some ould eejit was standin' on the railway embankment shoutin' over at us. "Ah, Jaysus, will you look at the seagulls, and the oul' penguins. Look at the penguins," he was sayin'. Sure, we were all in stitches and the next thing I got such a clatter across . . . the—'

The sound of sandalled feet across the floor alerted the girls.

Sister Stanislaus came in, cheerfully exclaiming, 'Bridie, a letter for you,' handing her a small white envelope. 'Put it away now and don't open it until you've finished your work,' she added.

'Oh, thank you, Sister. What a lovely surprise,' said Bridie, studying the envelope for a split second before slipping it into her pocket and wondering who could possibly have sent her a letter.

When Julie saw Bridie getting a letter and she there only a few weeks, she was full of despair. No one ever wrote to her except her own sister, Kay, otherwise known as Sister Rosario, who was a nun in America and who only ever wrote at Christmas.

'Sister Stanislaus! Are you sure there's no letters for me? I never seem to get an'thin' from an'one.'

'Julie, dear, you know there are never any letters for you. So why do you keep asking? If there's any letter you shall be the first to know,' said Sister, gliding out the door, rosary beads clinking at her side, a small handful of letters held tightly to her breast.

Julie turned to Bridie after a momentary pause, and whispered, 'Aren't you going to open it?'

'Do you think I should?'

'Sure, it's your letter, Bridie. They can't take it off you.'

Bridie took out the letter and quickly tore it open as Julie stood guard at the storeroom door. She pulled out a small square photograph of a child sitting on the grass. Bridie immediately kissed the image of her son.

'Oh, Julie! My prayers have been answered,' she sighed, as she held the photograph for a moment to her bosom, while raising her eyes to heaven in appreciation of the power and glory of the Almighty.

She checked the envelope again for some form of correspondence but there was none. Not a word. Then she turned over the photograph and read aloud, '"To Bridie, best wishes from all in St Mary's xxx."'

She could barely conceal her glee at having got a picture of John Paschal, yet was mystified at the lack of any letter, and when she turned to Julie to show her the photograph she saw she had her back turned and was making believe she was busy folding clothes. Bridie knew it was not the time to share her photograph as she could sense Julie was being torn apart at not having received any letter.

After a while Bridie said, 'Why don't you come for a walk this evening, and we'll talk about your plans?'

Julie turned round and, placing an armful of clean fresh linen along with what Bridie had already sorted, mumbled, 'Plans, me arse! Sure, I'm sick of plans. They never work,' before going over to the door once more to peep out.

When she came back she said, 'If you're ever caught by the guards they leave you black and blue, and then the nuns give you the works ƒwhen you're brought in. They cut off all your hair and ever'thin'. Sure I'd look like a convent, an' ever'one laughin' at me.'

Bridie herself smiled at the word 'convent', knowing Julie was trying to say 'convict', and the idea of seeing Julie, hair cut to the scut, with a ball and chain around her ankle, appealed to her own sense of humour.

'Sure, besides, ƒwhere can I go? Me mother mustn't want me. If I wrote once, I wrote a score-a-times, and as for the rest-a-the family . . .' she sighed, 'only God knows ƒwhere they are now. So there's no use in plannin', *a grá*. 'Cause we've all supped with the devil.'

A few days later, as Julie was sent from the steam room to help out in the kitchen, she chanced to look down the short corridor leading from the main hall and noticed to her amazement that the huge laundry van was just pulling out on to College Road, and that the big oak door was wide open. For a split second her heart pounded in her chest at the prospect that escape was so tantalisingly close. She stopped in her tracks and looked furtively around to see if anyone was watching. The coast was clear. She ran like an alley cat up the short corridor leading to the Mother Superior's office, crouched down beneath the glass-panelled door and scurried out into the yard. She ran across the front grounds leading to the main exit and in an instant found herself out on College Road, where she momentarily froze, before deciding to turn right and go straight into the city. Running as fast as she could, she thought she'd surely choke, gasping for breath. On and on she ran and into the fair green in Eyre Square. She glanced quickly round, but no one was following her. She stopped in disbelief at what she had just done.

'I'm free! I'm free! Free at last,' she gasped as she turned again to face into the city after spending nearly eleven years as a penitent in the Magdalene Home Laundry.

CHAPTER SEVEN

THE REVEREND MOTHER was busy in her office making phone calls and writing letters when she happened to raise her head to seal an envelope and thought she saw what looked like a blip of white flee past the bottom of the window in her office door. Moving quickly, she went to the door in the hope of apprehending one of the nuns listening or spying on her. But when she opened the door there was no one there. Then she thought she caught a brief glimpse of a white calico gown disappearing to her left out on College Road. She didn't know who it was, but the speed at which the thing moved told her it must be one of the girls in the laundry – escaping. She rushed out and was halfway across the grounds when the driver suddenly appeared, ready to slide the heavy oak door back into position, but not before he was grilled and reprimanded by the Mother Superior.

'But I was in the front of the van, checking the delivery dockets. I didn't see anyone,' he said.

'Seamus, if I find out one of my girls has gone missing, then your career as a van driver will be in the lap of the gods. You're to report to my office on your immediate return. Have I made myself clear?'

'Yes, Reverend Mother,' answered a puzzled-looking Seamus.

Sister Antonia could scarcely believe that one of her inmates would run out the gate. They didn't have the brains, the guts or the courage, she thought, not after the way I dealt with them last time. That must be, what, a year ago or more, but now someone had undoubtedly escaped, perhaps two or three. My God, what would the bishop say if he heard about this? She moved quickly and went back into the laundry where she ordered an immediate head count, and after a considerable delay it was ascertained that Julie Murray was missing.

Sister Antonia phoned Eglington Street Garda Station.

'May I speak with Sergeant Ruane, please? It's very urgent.'

The duty officer collared Sergeant Ruane as he was about to go out the door. '. . . She says it's very urgent, Sergeant.'

'Women!' he grumbled as he grabbed the phone. 'Sergeant Ruane speaking.'

'Good morning, Sergeant. I'm so glad to have got hold of you. I hope I'm not inconveniencing you in any way. But unfortunately one of my girls has gone missing. I think she's gone straight into town.'

'Sister Antonia! What a surprise. I haven't seen or heard from you in ages . . . It sure has. It sure has . . . Now what's this about one of your girls? . . . What? . . . Missing? Are you sure?'

'Yes, I'm sure, Sergeant, and she's no pushover; she's a bit of a wild one. Her name's Julie Murray. She's from Kilmaine, and will probably try to go home . . . About twenty-five, I'd say, of stocky build, with shoulder-length fair hair, but she may still have it pinned up beneath her cap.'

'Leave it with us, Sister Antonia, we'll see to it. She won't go far.'

'Sergeant, you're an angel. I'll ring you later to see how you're progressing.'

When Bridie heard that one of the inmates was missing she could not in her wildest imagination have visualised it to be Julie Murray, despite the fact that they had discussed that very subject only days earlier. But after it was indeed confirmed that Julie was missing, Bridie became very despondent that her friend could do such a thing without giving Bridie the opportunity to escape with her. She didn't know whether she was happy or sad that Julie had managed to escape, but she felt that Julie had cheated her in some way. That she had all along concocted some well-laid plan to go it alone or with the able assistance of someone on the outside. But who would help her?

Julie Murray wandered back out on to Shop Street for the umpteenth time. She didn't really know where she was, but thought that the buildings looked vaguely familiar. First she thought Moon's shop was on the right-hand side of the street and now it seemed on the left, and there was Lydon's lovely restaurant again. There must be more than one of them, she thought. And the smell of their freshly baked scones and the sight of their strawberry tarts in the window made her ravenous with hunger.

She moved on down the street, but kept looking over her shoulder. She had to dodge into shop doorways continuously as she saw several nuns from her own Sisters of Mercy order making street collections. Her greatest fear was that she'd be spotted by one of them, so she decided to take to the side streets again. She kept asking herself where she'd go, because she couldn't stay in the city. Someone was sure to see her. If only she could get away. She didn't have any money except a half-crown, but that was hidden in her dormitory locker and of no use to her now. Worse still, she had no food and no clothes. If only she could change out of her white gown she might not be recognised. She took off her cap and, after careful consideration, decided she'd catch the bus to Kilmaine. But every bus she saw appeared to be packed with tourists bound for either Salthill or Mervue. If she found the right bus she'd tell the driver she'd lost her purse or, better still, say her mother was meeting her at the bus stop, then when she got near home she'd jump off and hide. It was her only hope. She could not go down to the bus station as it was too close to the Magdalene, and wild horses would not drag her in that direction. She'd keep walking and walking until she found the right bus.

Sergeant Ruane made up his mind once and for all that he was going for a bite to eat. Since coming on duty it had been one hurried cup of tea after another. In the meantime he'd added another name to the city's growing list of missing persons. He had already issued the description of Julie Murray to his men on the beat. Strange, he thought, that she hadn't yet been sighted in or around the bus or rail terminals. It was four hours since she'd been reported missing. But he was going for a feed now, no matter what.

He was making his way towards the outer door when the phones started hopping again. God, he muttered as he fled the station, crime! It gets worse everyday.

He was about to cross the road on his way to his favourite eatery when something interesting caught his eye. It looked like a young nurse had walked right by Garda headquarters. He stopped in the middle of his stride to ogle her as she made her way through the throng. A sturdy piece, he thought by all accounts. But not at all like the starched uniform of the 'come-to-bed' nurses he knew so well from the regional hospital. She wasn't a nurse, so she must be a chemist, or a bakery assistant. No. He wasn't convinced. Yet, she had such a shapely rear, he wished he could have caught a better glimpse of her to see if he fancied her.

Watching her progressing down the street he thought she didn't seem to be going anywhere in particular, just ambling about. Perhaps she's on her lunch break. But the way she was looking up at the buildings, it was as if she was never in town before. He was in two minds whether to pursue her or not, in the hope that, if she proved any way attractive, he might be able to set up a date. But the sudden ear-splitting sound of a brazen cyclist's bell made him jump out of the way and jolted his wayward mind into a broad sense of reality. Would the girl ever be the one from the Magdalene, the missing 'Mag'? He immediately set off at a fast pace down the street, then slowed as he neared her.

Now, he ambled along behind her, the frayed hem of her long white gown and her shoulder-length fair hair as good as confirmed his suspicion. His heart skipped a beat at the prospect that he himself might be the very one to apprehend her. If he managed to do so, it would be a considerable feather in his cap. He decided he'd use the same ploy he always used when chatting up women. The sight of the Garda uniform worked every time as far as females were concerned.

'Excuse me, madam. Excuse me,' he called out.

Julie Murray wheeled round when she heard the male voice directly behind her. She stared transfixed. A guard! A bloody guard! she thought. She was about to plead, 'I didn't do anythin', I didn't do anythin',' when the officer said, 'Haven't I seen you somewhere before? You wouldn't be Julie Murray from Kilmaine, by any chance?'

When Julie saw the smirk on his face and heard him mention Kilmaine, the awful nightmare of that fateful day when she stole the coat came back to her in a flash. He would arrest her now and throw her into jail. The thought of that made her turn and run for dear life.

For a moment Sergeant Ruane stared in awe, then his brain slipped into top gear, and he pursued her down the street at an almighty rate. 'Christ, it's her! It's her! It's the missing bloody Mag,' he mumbled excitedly.

As he caught up with her he reached out, grabbed her by the sleeve and said, 'Not so fast, Maggie! Not so fast!'

Julie Murray, terrified of being put into jail, reacted instinctively by sinking her teeth into the officer's long bony fingers.

'Bitch! You poxy bitch!' barked Ruane, giving her the full force of his good hand into the side of the jaw. 'If that's how you want to play it, Maggie, then I'll give you plenty of it,' he shouted, grabbing her forcefully by the collar, as she was about to stumble to the ground.

In an instant he had her arm twisted up behind her back, and gave her a good kick in the arse as she screamed in agony. He then began to lead her back to the station. Julie, unable to plead for mercy, just screamed with the severity of the pain as several onlookers stood watching in bewilderment at the city's enforcement officer successfully apprehending his prey.

When Julie realised she was now inside a Garda station, she did everything in her power to escape. The thought that she was going to be sent to prison as a thief was too much for her. Several times she sought to break free and each time she was met with a blow of a heavy truncheon.

When Sergeant Ruane felt that she had calmed down sufficiently, he relaxed his grip on her, only to find she again tried to break free, but she was subdued by a few more blows to the side of her body. Soon a small number of newly recruited officers had gathered round to look at her, as their leader boastfully outlined his recipe for success.

'As you can see, this is a perfect example of how we should all go about our duty as members of this force. Keep your eyes open! Keep your wits about you! And I can guarantee, you'll keep one step ahead of crime!'

When the Reverend Mother received a phone call from Sergeant Ruane, informing her that he had apprehended Julie Murray, she was overcome with joy. She would not now have to inform the bishop that one of her charges was missing. But she felt somewhat disappointed when the sergeant informed her that as he himself was very busy right now 'his officers' would be returning Julie Murray to the Magdalene Home Laundry in a Black Maria. She recalled instead his last visit to her office when she had distinctly felt the flush of excitement on seeing his handsome features. She wished for nothing more than to see his rugged face again, as she leaned back momentarily in her comfortable oak throne. It was, what, six months ago? She remembered vividly him standing right beside her, in his impeccable uniform with its gleaming silver-crested buttons. The mere closeness of him gave her a thrill beyond her wildest imagination, and when he gently placed his peaked cap with its sparkling Garda Síochána emblem on her desk and accepted her offer of a nice cup of tea, she felt as if they were sharing in some strange symbol of power. It must be something to do with the coming together of Church and State, she thought: the combination of their uniforms; an officer and a nun. We were so close to each other, she sighed. They say opposites attract: male and female; one soft and pliable, the other big and strong . . . hard as—

The phone rang interrupting her dream. She let it ring for a moment, praying it would stop, but its incessant clamour had killed her passion instantly. She grabbed the offending object with distaste.

'Mother Superior.'

'The delivery driver has gone without the Ennis shirts, what will I do?' a voice asked.

She paused. 'One minute, I'll be down right away. Drivers,' she sighed. 'Stupid, bloody drivers.'

When Julie was led in handcuffs out of the Garda van and not into jail but into the care of the Magdalene Home Laundry she could not believe her luck. She went meekly down the long corridor, escorted by the Mother Superior, Sister Stanislaus and Sister Philomena. She was brought into a small room, occasionally used as a storeroom and told to sit on a chair. She already knew the awful punishment that awaited her, so she made up her mind that she would take her beating like a man, no matter how painful, rather than give satisfaction to the Mother Superior, who was instructing Sister Stanislaus to cut off Julie's hair.

If there was one thing the Mother Superior relished it was

the power she had over her entire flock. She had learned a long time ago that supremacy was the only rule to guarantee an orderly house, and was proud to have inherited this attitude from her father, who had ruled their home with an iron fist. Many a time she had witnessed her mother go down on bended knees and beg for mercy when his favourite shirt wasn't ironed or his dinner wasn't on the table when he came home from a cattle fair after a few well-earned pints. When he threatened to break loose, she herself would hide in the broom press beneath the stairs, and watch as her father removed his broad trouser belt and beat her mother. In no time at all everyone would be running hither and thither at his beck and call. And later, when she'd emerge mouselike from her hiding place, her father would ruffle her fair hair and give her a few sweets from his coat pocket as an acknowledgement of her having supported him.

Now she had succeeded in turning the Magdalene Home into a virtual fortress by following her father's regime, and it was her intention to keep it that way.

When at last Julie emerged from the torture chamber, it wasn't the fact that she'd been beaten within an inch of her life — despite the pleas of Sister Philomena — that pained her most, it was the sheer humiliation of having had her hair cropped. As if that wasn't bad enough, she then had to get down on her bended knees and join the nuns in prayer by offering up five decades of the rosary for her own intentions, so that God might grant her the wisdom to see the errors of her ways.

It was late that balmy August evening when Bridie, Josephine and the rest of the gang returned to their dormitories to find Julie Murray, the supposed escapee, sitting crying on her bed.

'Julie! We thought you had escaped,' they cried.

But Julie could not speak. She didn't know if she could ever face them again, because she knew she had let them all down by upsetting the cosy little arrangement they had of living and working together. Worse still, she felt like some hideous monster when the girls all gathered around her, some of them tittering at her grotesque appearance. She knew she looked awful as she had stolen a glance at her savaged features in the mirror. She had a badly swollen jaw, a black eye, and a naked skull, not to mention a multitude of other marks on her body that no one would ever see. She felt as if part of her inner being, her self-respect, had been torn away. Worst of all, she could not restrain her hands as they continually explored the flat contours of her bony scalp while her lower lip quivered uncontrollably.

For a long time, Bridie and Josephine sat beside Julie, trying to ward off her many inquisitors, and when at last dusk fell and all but a few of the inmates had gone to their beds, Bridie held Julie's hand.

'Remember, Julie, we're your friends! We'll always be here. It doesn't matter what the guards or the nuns do to you, they can never take your friends away from you.'

'*F*why is it . . . I have such misfortune?' she babbled. '*F*why is it?'

'Shush, pet,' said Bridie, as she gave Julie's hand a gentle squeeze. 'Some day, please God, we'll all be free: don't ever forget that. I met a man who told me that in the end I'd win, and that I'd be very lucky. And do you know what, Julie?'

'*F*what?'

'I believe him because he was the nicest person I ever met. His name was Gerald. I'll never forget him and I know that some day his words will come true.'

While all of this was going on, Josephine was sitting listening and thinking to herself, there's something about Bridie Rodgers. What it is I don't know. And when Julie suddenly seized the back of Bridie's hand and kissed it, Josephine was filled with a powerful emotion that somehow galvanised her own flagging spirits. If ever she was going to test her own mettle it was now, she told herself, while, at the same time, feeling so useless at being unable to offer any consolation to Julie the way that Bridie had. After what she had just witnessed, she felt she herself needed consoling too. These inmates all needed each other's support and friendship.

'Listen,' she said, standing up to face the few friends who had not yet retired to bed, 'there's too much gloom around here. Feck the nuns and feck the laundry! We should all stick together, and not let the nuns get the better of us. What we need is to keep the faith. Smile! Smile! as Judy Garland would have sung . . .'

'Oh, Josephine! Please! A song,' intoned Bridie.

'Oh, please, please! "Somewhere Over the Rainbow",' begged Lilly MacAlastair, and others joined in the pleas to hear Josephine sing.

But Josephine could not look her friends in the eye: to do so would be to drown in their sadness. Instead she turned and began to walk slowly away as the quivering, faltering tones of her favourite song rent the air . . .

Hours later, Josephine still lay awake in her cosy bed, happy in the knowledge that she had enthralled her audience. It was the first time, she thought, that she'd been truly happy since she'd been put into the Magdalene Home Laundry. She was beginning to despair of ever getting out to nurture her dream of becoming a great singer. But now she could begin to believe in the lines of her own lay. Some day, somewhere, I'll be back with you, Cathal, my one and only love, she thought.

CHAPTER EIGHT

I T WAS ALMOST ten o'clock in the morning, and Sister Stanislaus was on her way to supervise the cleaning of the Sacred Heart dormitory when she thought she heard the swish of clothing and sandalled feet behind her. On looking round she was met by a breathless Mother Superior.

'Sister, I'm so glad I caught up with you. I need to speak with you urgently. Could you please come to my office in ten minutes?'

'As you wish, Reverend Mother. I'll show the girls what to do, then I'll be down straight away.'

'Thank you, Sister,' said the Mother Superior as she hurried back down the corridor.

Trouble, thought Sister Stanislaus. I smell trouble; either she's in trouble or I'm in trouble.

When they pulled up their chairs to face each other in the office, the Mother Superior said, 'Sister, I may need to call on your support tomorrow. That Murray One, the escapee, did you know she has a sister who's a nun in California? Well, seemingly she's home on holiday. What harm, but she phoned me late last night to say she's coming in to see Julie tomorrow.'

'A sister? A nun?' feigned Sister Stanislaus in reply.

Sister Stanislaus knew that Julie Murray had a sister called Kay, who was a nun known as Sister Rosario. Julie was forever giving out about her; how Kay would never write to her, except maybe at Christmas. Sister Stanislaus got a great thrill out of this, believing she had far superior knowledge of the penitents in general than the Reverend Mother ever possessed.

'Coming to see her! Tomorrow!' she exclaimed. 'But what are you going to do?'

'What are we going to do?' echoed the Mother Superior, emphasising the word 'we'. 'I've spent the whole morning praying for guidance. I thought perhaps you might be able to come up with some idea to stall that lady.'

'You'll have to say she had some kind of an accident – working in the laundry,' suggested Sister Stanislaus, relishing the prospect that the Mother Superior might have landed herself in hot water.

'Are you suggesting we break the eighth commandment?' she smiled vaguely as her chubby fingers danced on the desk. 'Remember, "*Thou shall not bear false witness against thy neighbour*". Bearing that in mind, whatever excuse I come up with must stand on its own merits in the eyes of God and man.'

'Yes,' bowed Sister Stanislaus, struggling to acknowledge her Superior's undoubted wisdom. 'But what are we going to do? We could postpone the visit.'

After taking the idea on board for a few seconds the Mother Superior said, 'No! That would be to postpone the inevitable. In any case, I gather Sister Rosario hasn't got the time, and I haven't got the patience. I think I'll have to leave it,' she added, and stood up promptly, which signalled that the meeting was over. 'I'll probably think of something. But I need to know, Sister, that I can count on your support tomorrow, whatever I decide to do. You do realise that under no circumstances must Sister Rosario be allowed to see Julie in her present condition?'

'I understand,' replied Sister Stanislaus meekly, because she knew that to disagree with anything the Mother Superior said could lead to her being transferred to some enclosed order, where prayer commenced at four a.m. and where promotional prospects were non-existent. At least here in the Magdalene Home she was a ward sister, looking after the welfare of one hundred and fifty penitent women. As well as that, she could read her breviary every night while quietly pacing the corridors, and still be privy to the goings-on in the women's dormitories. Many were the snippets of information she gleaned, which helped prevent the penitents going on strike and led directly to a strengthening of security within the Magdalene Home Laundry. So all in all, she thought, it was always best to agree with the boss, even though she didn't always approve of some of the ill treatment meted out to the workers.

Because of Julie's physical condition, Bridie knew she would not be escorting her friend on their late evening walk of the enclosed grounds, so she decided instead to slip away quietly into the chapel where she could have a quiet think by herself. As usual, three or four nuns from the convent knelt close to the altar in silent prayer. As Bridie tiptoed into the second last pew, they all got up to leave, their heads still bowed reverently as they passed by. Bridie wondered how on earth they could devote their entire lives to constant prayer with nothing to look forward to: no husbands, no children, no freedom. On the other hand, she thought, the chapel was such a peaceful place of worship it must surely be good for the soul, which was the reason she was here herself. But as she studied the beautiful glow of the red sanctuary lamp she realised prayer wasn't the real reason she came.

The photograph of John Paschal, she thought. Who could possibly have sent that? Sister Hortense? Mad Madge, or the other girls? I must write and thank them. But whom do I thank? If I write to Madge or one of the other girls, I could be getting her into trouble – unless it was Sister Hortense herself who sent it. And according to the girls here, no parcel or letter ever goes in or out of this place without the nuns knowing exactly what's in it. And if they don't like it, it gets the bin. Funny, I thought it strange how there was no letter or anything with that photograph, even a few lines. Lilly said that's probably why it was signed 'Best wishes from all in St Mary's' – so that the Mother Superior wouldn't actually know who sent it. I'll bet anything it was Sister Hortense, thought Bridie. Didn't the Mother Superior – or Super Ass herself, as they call her – say to me, 'Your son is doing fine'? What did she say again? 'I was speaking only yesterday to Sister Hortense and she informed me your son is thriving.'

Strange too how Sister Hortense was talking about me and John Paschal on the phone, if one could believe that rap. God, I must write now and thank her for sending the photograph. That's what I'll do. I'll write and thank Sister Hortense and I'll sign it, 'From all the . . .' no, I'll sign it, 'Best wishes . . .' no, No . . . I'll say, 'all the staff . . .' No, no, no. Why am I making such a mess of it? Just say, 'Many thanks for the beautiful photograph of the baby.' That way no one will ever know who sent it except Sister Hortense. I'll also say, 'Please write soon again, with best wishes from all in the Magdalene.' There, that's it. That way, if it *was* Sister Hortense, only she will know and write back again.

And how about writing to Gerald in Conly House, while I'm at it? I can't very well write to 'Mr and Mrs O'Malley', and besides I wouldn't write to that bitch. God forgive me. But if I write to Gerald and she finds it, then he's in trouble. If the Mother Superior here finds out I'm writing to a man – a married man at that – then I'm really in trouble. Lord God Almighty! Is there no way out?

While she was thinking these thoughts, she almost jumped out of her skin with fright when one of the sisters suddenly appeared and whispered in her ear, 'Sorry, but we must close the chapel now.'

Bridie nodded agreement, and smiled humorously to herself: God I'd better leave quickly, while there's still a way out.

Midday Angelus bells rang out across the cathedral city as Julie Murray's sister, Sister Rosario, arrived at the entrance to the Magdalene Home. A small petite creature, she was swathed from head to toe in white, which enabled her to cope with the searing heat of the scorching Californian sun. She was escorted by one of the sisters into the lavishly furnished parlour to meet the Mother Superior.

Sister Antonia extended a limp fleshy hand, smiled graciously and said, 'Sister Rosario, dear, it's so good to see you. You must be exhausted after all the travelling. Have a seat and I'll get one of the sisters to fetch us a nice cup of tea.'

'Thank you, Reverend Mother,' bowed Sister Rosario.

The Mother Superior then went across the corridor and gave whispered instructions to one of the young novices before returning to join Sister Rosario in the parlour.

'How was your flight? Did you have a nice trip?'

'It was wonderful. I flew into Dublin on Monday, and then I went by bus to Arklow, where I had arranged to meet with an old friend of mine who used to work in the Franciscan Order. We used to have such wonderful times together,' smiled Sister Rosario. 'Then my friend drove me up to Howth where we stayed overnight with some more friends. And this morning I travelled down to Galway.'

'How sweet. Did you come on the train?'

'Yes. I caught the eight thirty from Westland Row Station, and only for some kind gentleman I would have had to stand most of the way down, it was so overcrowded. And, of course, it was late arriving.'

They were settling down nicely, discussing current affairs, when there was a knock at the door.

'Sister! You're a topper,' said the Mother Superior, as

the young novice left the silver tray on the large mahogany table.

As the Reverend Mother began pouring out the tea she asked, 'And what, Sister Rosario, may I ask is the nature of your own particular vocation in California?'

'Our Order, the Sisters of the Most Holy Rosary, takes care of deprived children; particularly those from the ghettos, where, as you probably know, there's a large population of ethnic minorities.'

After listening to Sister Rosario for some time, the Mother Superior pushed her empty cup to one side, awaiting an opportunity to intervene.

'How interesting that we should both lead such similar lives. And, of course, you're correct, it's not an easy task – what with all the responsibility and everything. And believe me, Sister Rosario, some of the adults under my present stewardship can be far more demanding than any group of children. Especially as none of their relatives seems to give a hoot about their welfare; saving yourself and one or two others.'

'Oh, yes! It's so sad, isn't it? And how is my sister Julie getting on? I hope she doesn't cause you any trouble. I'm so looking forward to seeing her after such a long time.'

'Hmm, I'm sure you are and I can well understand. You know, she's been through so much. But Julie is a fighter, and given plenty of time and with God's help, she'll come through,' said the Mother Superior, with a deeply furrowed brow that had Sister Rosario moving uncomfortably in her chair.

'You mean, she's not well?' suggested Sister Rosario, fearing she might have misinterpreted what the Reverend Mother had said.

'Oh. I'm so sorry. Please forgive my ineptness. How could you? How could you have known of her mental illness? Perhaps I should have warned you on the phone. It's just that I'm loath to convey bad news to anyone. I'm afraid your sister Julie has been through a horrid time this past while and is in no condition to see anyone.'

On hearing this, Sister Rosario turned pale, before leaning back in her chair as a bad memory came flooding back to her; how, many years ago, she'd written to the Magdalene Home and enquired about her sister's welfare with a view to having her brought out to join her in South Africa as a lay worker. But according to the Mother Superior, she was then something of a rebel, who required constant care and attention, and which in hindsight probably explained Julie's long rambling letters to her, which never seemed to make any sense. And now it seemed as if nothing had changed, nothing at all.

'But why didn't somebody tell me?' asked Sister Rosario, shocked by the news that her sister was still a problem after all these years.

'Unfortunately you didn't leave any forwarding address, dear. And if I remember correctly, you were working in South Africa at the time,' said the Mother Superior with suppressed glee. You do know she suffers from schizophrenia? Which means she's prone to conflicting ideas and emotions.'

Sister Rosario felt at that moment as if she had been betrayed – betrayed by the Reverend Mother, betrayed by her very own sister, and by the whole world in general.

She reached for the crucifix attached to the long crystal rosary beads that hung round her waist and made the sign of the cross, whispering, 'Lord, protect us from all harm.'

'Amen,' replied the Mother Superior, duplicating Sister Rosario's religious rite.

Recovering her composure, Sister Rosario added, 'I'm sorry, Reverend Mother. How was I to know Julie was causing you so much pain and suffering? Please accept my humblest apologies and convey my deepest gratitude to your Sisters of Mercy order, for their due care and devotion in looking after her. And to think . . . I was contemplating taking her out of here, and bringing her to the States with me. But I figure that's the end of that now. Is there any possibility that I could see her . . . for a few moments?' suggested Sister Rosario, as an afterthought.

The Reverend Mother, who'd thought she was already over the worst, now sensed a direct challenge to her authority. In order not to lose any more ground, she told herself she must remain calm and collected.

'Oh dear. How kind of you to suggest helping her in that way. I'm sure she would have loved the idea of joining you in the States, to start a new life. Regrettably, Sister, she is no longer in a fit state to see anyone. Besides, it would be too upsetting – and, believe me, I know – for a family relative, a loving, caring blood sister such as yourself, to see her now. As you undoubtedly remember, Julie was once as pretty as a flower, and perhaps it is God's wish that you should remember her so. Were I to allow you in to see her now, I know full well that you would go away with a heavy heart and, like I've already told you, I'm loath to convey bad news.'

Then, lowering her voice to a whisper, she continued, 'The doctor suggested she be put into a mental institution for her own good. But after careful consideration I sought instead the advice of an expert counsellor in Dublin, and he informed me that with time and careful medical attention she could make a good and complete recovery; particularly in her own natural surroundings. And were I to let you in to see her now, just think what it might do to her already disturbed mind.'

Julie Murray's sister began to rise ever so slowly from her chair. She had heard enough. Close to tears, she extended her small delicate hand to the Reverend Mother. 'What can I say? Words fail me – except that I'll remember you all in my prayers. I'll write on my immediate return to the States and you can keep me posted on her condition.'

Before leaving the home via the small exit door, Sister Rosario turned to the Mother Superior once more and, taking the Reverend Mother's hand, she inclined her head graciously and said, 'Thank you so much for all you've done, and may God bless you.'

Then she quietly melted into the city, vowing never to return to the home. Her mother, it seemed, had been right all along: Julie had brought nothing but shame on the entire family. Sister Rosario's long-held belief that Julie had been unfairly treated by her mother was now blown to smithereens by this latest revelation. There was nothing she could do for her now but remember her in her prayers. In fact, she thought it only right that she should remember all of the 'Maggies' in her prayers. For it seemed to her they were all in urgent need of divine help.

Chapter Nine

It was Sunday, and there was a distinct air of fulfilment wafting its way through the marbled halls of the Magdalene Home Laundry. Faces seemed brighter as the penitents gathered to converse in huddled groups at the top of the great wooden staircase, or in one of the huge dormitories of Our Lady's, St Teresa's or the Sacred Heart. They reminisced and told jokes and there was the added lilt of laughter.

Julie Murray was happy because she was the proud possessor of a span-new half-crown, given to her during the week by Sister Stanislaus on behalf of the Mother Superior, who let it be known that she was a tremendous worker and deserving of special recognition.

When Julie heard her name being called out in the long corridor she was at once filled with dread that she must have done something wrong. But when Sister Stanislaus gently pressed the large silver coin into her hand and whispered, 'The Reverend Mother would like you to have this; for your hard work and dedication,' she stared at Sister Stanislaus for a moment before blurting out, 'Does . . . ever'one . . . Do we all get one?'

'Shu! Don't be silly. It's for you, dear: you alone, because you deserve it. And remember, you're not to tell anyone. Promise me you won't say a word.'

'I promise.'

But of course Julie told everyone eventually, and soon they all looked at each other as if to say, 'But what about us?'

In spite of this, however, they were all happy because it was widely rumoured that a film was going to be shown at Christmas, which was only just around the corner.

Bridie too was pleased; more so because everyone else seemed happy and, despite one's best efforts at always grumbling, these things have a habit of rubbing off on one another.

Earlier in the evening Bridie had returned from walking a lonely furrow in the picturesque grounds. Of late, she had taken to wandering off on her own more and more in an effort to find peace and solitude. But she was not alone: walking in front of her were other penitents, quickening their step so that they too could retain some semblance of privacy. Likewise, other girls drifted in and out of Bridie's wake, for there was no other way. From morning till night they worked, ate and slept together, seven days a week, three hundred and sixty-five days a year. At night they were caged in congested dormitories, which made them sick of the very sight of each other. If only they could be alone with their thoughts they might see a way out of their terrible dilemma.

Likewise, Bridie was constantly at war with herself for her indecisiveness in confronting the nuns about her son, John Paschal. Several times she had written to Sister Hortense in Tuam to enquire about him, but no response had been forth-coming. She chided herself for going about things the wrong way. Perhaps she hadn't put the right address on her letters, but surely to God they'd get there anyway – that's if the letters ever left the Magdalene in the first place. Who knew? But what she did know was that she was thoroughly fed up with being a nursemaid to Julie, Josephine and a host of other girls. For some strange reason Josephine Finn in particular thought Bridie could wave some magic wand with regard to her and Cathal Swanick. But no, she couldn't. She couldn't cure anyone's ills.

So for that reason alone, and to help retain her own sense of sanity, she made up her mind once and for all that she was going to confront the Mother Superior tomorrow morning and demand her freedom. The least the Reverend Mother could do, she figured, was to allow her out on a short visit to see John Paschal. She had had enough of their authoritarian ways and she was tired of writing to the nuns in St Mary's and getting no reply. It was time she tried some other way – only this time, she decided, she'd be a lot cuter and less formal than the last time. First thing tomorrow morning she'd stay behind in chapel until all the penitents were gone, and then she'd confront the Mother Superior and hopefully shame her in front of the other sisters into letting her out to see John Paschal. Bridie had thought long and hard about telling her close friends but had decided that it was too personal a matter, and that no good could come from enlisting their support.

Now, as a group of her friends sat nattering around her bed in Our Lady's dormitory prior to going to bed, she pushed the thoughts of freedom from her head as one of the girls claimed excitedly that she could hear the faint sound of music. They all fell silent, before rushing headlong towards one of the tall windows. And in a matter of seconds four of them were crammed tightly up on the narrow window-ledge, trying to peer out through the tiny spyholes they had previously scratched on the painted glass of the stoutly barred windows that afforded a panoramic view of the city's rooftops.

They all listened attentively to try to discern the source of the sound. Some were of the opinion that it was just fairground music, provided by Duffy's or Fossett's Circus in Eyre Square. Others were adamant that it came not from the city fairground, but from the Hangar or Seapoint Ballrooms way out in Salthill, because the music was so faint.

'It must be the Hangar Ballroom,' said Josephine Finn, 'because it sounds like a waltz to me. They'd never play that kind of music in a fairground or circus. It would be too slow.'

'I think you're right,' said Bridie, struggling to maintain a toehold on the cramped window-ledge as she clung desperately to Josephine's shoulders in order to catch a glimpse of the twinkling city lights. 'Oh, I know what it is now,' she added excitedly. 'It's "Danny Boy". I used to play it on the mouth organ when I lived out in Clifden.'

'I didn't know you could play,' interrupted Lilly MacAlastair, somewhat delighted. 'Will you play it now? I'll run down and get the mouth organ, and we'll all have a bit of craíc,' she added excitedly as she jumped down from the window-ledge and ran to where she had a mouth organ gathering dust at the back of her bedside locker.

Meanwhile, Josephine Finn disentangled Bridie from around her shoulders and eased herself gently down from the window-ledge because she didn't really want to think of 'Danny Boy'. The very name was enough to remind her of her own Danny Boy, Cathal. She was remembering how, the one night she had been allowed to dance the night away at the village carnival, she had met Cathal Swanick. Yet this harmless act was enough to ignite the rumours that spread like wildfire through the whole parish: how she was doing a line with young Swanick, a direct descendant of the wealthy Protestant landowners who had driven Josephine's ancestors off their land three generations ago for non-payment of rent.

Josephine was not even aware who the good-looking gentleman was when she first laid eyes on him, but had very politely accepted his offer to buy her a mineral after a flurry of dancing. She remembered all too clearly her grandfather's vivid description, when she was growing up, of the painful evictions. But, due to it being such a sore subject – as far as her mother was concerned – it was deemed better to sweep the whole thing under the carpet and let bygones be bygones. Besides, all that was years ago. How was she supposed to know that the gorgeous fella she met at the dance was related to the tyrant landlords? As far as Josephine was concerned, he was a perfect gentleman.

But when she continued to meet Cathal by devious means, her cantankerous father and, in particular, her grandfather threatened to have her sent to Australia, where she would be forced to live with her equally cantankerous aunt.

'Are you mad?' her father bellowed over and over again. 'They took possession of our cattle and land and drove our people to the very edge of extinction; and for all you know Josephine, they are now planning to take possession of you, our only daughter. I swear to God, Josephine, if you as much as look in that man's direction one more time, I'll have you put away for life.'

Josephine kept her promise and for all of four weeks restricted her movements. But when she met the lovely Cathal, purely by accident, while out shopping in Tuam, they were drawn to each other like magnets. They both slipped quietly into an adjoining alley, on the pretext of parking their bikes, and in an intimate hurried conversation they considered how best to overcome their particular dilemma and meet up again. But before they could develop any worthwhile plan they were interrupted by the unexpected appearance of their local village postman, who soon relayed the news to all and sundry that Josephine Finn and Cathal Swanick were still courting. By the time her father got to hear the news, the story had grown out of all proportion and she stood accused of far more than she was ever guilty of. As a result she was immediately seized by her parents, with the blessing and aid of the parish priest, who had her sent to the women's home in Tuam, from where she was quickly transferred to the more secure Magdalene Home Laundry in Galway city.

Now Josephine was beginning to have grave doubts about 'her Cathal'. How was it that he hadn't been to see her or come to her rescue? Or was he too under some sort of family pressure to have nothing to do with a Catholic: any Catholic?

'Josephine, *a grá*, will you sing us a song an' stop your oul' daydreamin' while we're waitin' on Bridie; sure, that one's as slow as Christmas,' said Julie Murray in an effort to get a bit of entertainment going.

Josephine shook her head and smiled drily, saying, 'I'm not in the mood. Some other time.'

Instead she knelt on the floor with the other girls gathered around the bed, as Bridie tried playing the mouth organ. For a long time she struggled for the correct key for 'Danny Boy', but somehow she seemed unable to concentrate, as a strange sensation began to gnaw at her conscience, slowly seeping through her entire body. It had taken hold of her the minute she threw her arms tightly around Josephine's shoulders to peep out of the window. It was an overwhelming desire to relive her worst moment when Peter took advantage of her in the hay. And as her lips slid rhythmically over the metallic instrument, she wished with all her heart that she could instead respond to his hot passionate kisses by pursing her lips along his stubbled jaw. For a mere second she closed her eyes and thought, God, I'd give anything right now to feel that awful hardness in his body again.

'Bridie! Bridie!' interrupted Julie. '*F*what are you at? You're pure useless. Sure, I thought you said you could play that thin'.'

'And I can. I can . . . if only you'd give me time. Arrah, here, play it yourself. I'd rather talk,' replied Bridie angrily, as she threw the mouth organ on the bed.

'Ah, go on, go on. Play it. Play something. It doesn't have to be "Danny Boy",' the girls pleaded.

'No, I won't,' answered Bridie.

For a few moments there was a strained silence. Julie knew she had hurt Bridie's feelings and had put a stop to whatever fun they might have had. So she decided she'd better say something quickly to relieve the tension.

'I wonder *f*what it's like to go dancing in the Hangar Ballroom. Would that be the same as a carnal?'

'You mean a carnival,' corrected Bridie quickly, anxious to show she knew a thing or two and to get in a dig at Julie.

'That's *f*what I said,' cut in Julie.

'No you didn't, you said "carnal". It's not "carnal" it's "car-ni-val".'

'Sure *f*what does it matter? A car-a-nal is a car-a-nal,' replied Julie, blushing and trying desperately to say the correct pronunciation.

'No. No, I don't think it's the same,' said Lilly MacAlastair, intervening to ward off a row amongst her friends because she knew Bridie and Julie were very loyal to each other, and she didn't want to think their friendship could be threatened over a stupid little word that was supposed to mean fun or happiness or something.

'No, I'll tell you,' continued Lilly, 'the Hangar and Seapoint are fierce big dance halls, like, and carnivals or caranals,' she laughed, 'are big tents that are put up out in the country for country people. But I'm not too sure because I was never at a carnival.'

'Well, I was,' said Julie, delighted to inform all and sundry, now that the tension had eased. 'Sure, me older sister used to go ever' year that it came to our village. She used to work in the ladies' cloakroom and she brought me with her once, when I was fourteen. Sure, 'twas fierce excitin' and ever'thin'. Talk about people,' she added dreamily, recalling the glorious atmosphere.

Josephine, meanwhile, was sitting sideways on the floor, her head resting on the backs of her hands the other side of the bed. She was watching Julie's every gesture, and listening to her every word. But when she heard Julie describe the music, the twirling, rhythmic dancers, in her own tin-pot way, and how some of the older girls were bold enough to put their arms lovingly around the men's shoulders during a slow dance, she quietly stood up and went to hide in the lavatory, because each descriptive word of Julie's was like a hammer-blow to her chest, chiselling away at her heart. She didn't want to be reminded. She knew only too well what it was like to have somebody sweep you romantically off your feet as they waltzed you round and round until you were delirious from the thrill of it all.

What, she was wondering – as she made her way down the dormitory, her head hanging in distress and her arms folded tightly across her bosom – what if Cathal Swanick was at home at that very moment, getting ready to go to some dance, and him there standing preening himself in front of some gilt-edged mirror in the Big House? What then? And what if, in her absence, he had arranged to meet some other girl at the dance? What if, at the end of the dance he offered to buy her a drink and then they made their way to a discreet corner to hold hands, while siphoning bottles of Clada orange? What then?

On reaching the seclusion of the lavatory, Josephine rushed into the cubicle and slammed the door shut, threw herself down on the hard wooden seat and buried her head in her hands, crying aloud, 'No! No! No! He wouldn't.'

But despite her best efforts at suppressing her emotions, her ruby-red lips quivered uncontrollably and the overflowing tears rained down her pale cheeks as she begged Cathal to come and take her away: to rescue her from that place of horror, occupied by gangs of lecherous-looking women and dark ghostly creatures of the night, masquerading as the Sisters of Mercy.

Bridie, in an effort to drive the wanton thoughts from her own head, asked Lilly, because she was from the city and was a good bit older than the rest of the girls, what one would have to do or say to meet a nice fella at a dance. But the minute she opened her mouth to ask the question she knew that wasn't what she had meant to say. She'd meant to say something that would get the thoughts of men out of her head once and for all, and in particular the thoughts of Peter. But somehow she couldn't drag herself away from the subject.

Lilly's eyes lit up at the prospect of coaching her friends as they lay all around her, eagerly awaiting her response.

'Well, it all depends, Bridie. Sometimes it's very easy and sometimes it's very hard to meet the right one. Half the time the men are drunk and slobbering all over you. That's the worst time, because they start mauling you just because you refused to dance with them. And the smell-a-drink: sometimes, it'd knock you kicking. But then again you might see a real nice-looking fella, and he'll ask everyone to dance but you – and you after refusing half the country while waiting for him, only to be told by some smart Alec that you'd make a lovely statue if only you'd brought along an oul' rosary.'

Her admirers tittered knowingly, and settled themselves like cats around a warm fire, as she went on.

'No, the best thing, I found, was to stand at the very front of the crowd; that way you can keep an eye on the fellow you're after and he can see you. But whatever you do, don't move out of that position – even if it means crossing your legs – because then he won't know where to find you.'

All of the inmates laughed, as they warmed more to Lilly's favourite subject.

'An' if you did get one,' asked Julie brazenly, 'would you go outside with him the first night, or tell him you'd see him again?'

'Oh, you'd have to go outside the front door at least, because if you didn't then you can be sure some cheap hussy would come along and whip him right from under your nose. The golden rule is that if some poor eejit asks to buy you a mineral, then that means he'd like to take you home – only because he thinks you're a right good thing. But whatever you do, don't let him out of your sight; not even to go to the toilet. If you do, and your fella is left standing around on his own and another girl happens to sidle up to the bar, next thing, your buckeen is weighing her up and she's weighing him up and before you can say "Jack Robinson", the two of them will have slithered down to the other end of the hall and the next bloody thing she's sitting like a peacock on the bar of his bike, the two of them going hell for leather out of town and ready to climb into the nearest hay shed . . .'

Bridie's heartbeat quickened considerably at the thought of climbing into a hay shed and having some fella kiss her passion-ately before nibbling her ear and making her go all wobbly at the knees. She could feel herself blushing now at the mere thought and prayed that the other girls didn't notice her.

Julie too was starting to remember her rare romantic inter-ludes of a Sunday afternoon at the village cross down in Kilmaine, where all the young girls would gather and wait for the lads, who usually came from miles around, tearing down the dusty roads on their bikes at wicked speed; showing off and trying desperately to impress everyone.

'Down fwhere I lived, we used to meet at the bridgeen ever' Sunday,' said Julie.

'That's right,' piped up one of the younger girls. 'We used to do that too, and some of the lads would chase us across the fields . . .'

'Wait a minute, *a grá*, till I tell you me story, about this fella,' continued Julie, keen to reveal the saucy details. 'There was this fella I knew an' he'd give the girls sweets an' ever'thin' if they'd lift up their skirts and let him have a look. He was a biteen wild, like. But sure, all the girls were mad after 'im. God forgive me, but I was always prayin' he'd ask me, like, 'cause he was gorgeous-lookin'. But then one day fwhen he got me on me own, an' the others were messin' over the road, he asked me, like, but fwhen I said no, he said something awful . . .'

'He asked you what?' interrupted Lilly, in an effort to absorb the juiciest details.

'What do you think?' quipped Bridie, laughing at Lilly's concocted innocence. 'To lift up her skirt, of course!'

'Sure! Wasn't it awful,' acknowledged Julie, blushing at the thought that she was now divulging her innermost secrets. But what the hell? she thought as she continued. 'Anyway, fwhen he asked me, I said no, an' do you know fwhat he said? He said he'd pull the knickers off me. Sure, I got afraid an' started to run for dear life – over the road and him after me like a . . . like a . . . a wild jackass. I ran across a big field, an' him still after me. But then I think he must have seen somethin' 'cause all of a sudden he stopped, like. God! If only I'd had the good fortune to fall in the long grass,' she tittered heartily before adding, 'I should have let him catch me, I suppose, 'cause some of the girls reckoned he was a great kisser. Lord, I'd have given an'thin' to see fwhat he was like. An'thin' . . .'

'Troth, he might have given you more than you bargained for. Men! Oh, they're all the same!' laughed Lilly heartily. Then, recovering her composure, she continued, 'But do you know what they say? And I think 'tis true: that the women are worse than the men! I had this friend once, out in the country. She was about eighteen, and she was telling me that her friend Mary was stone mad after this fella who used to go fishing beside this bridgeen every Sunday. Seemingly, all the girls were mad after him, and they used to write dirty messages on bits of cigarette boxes and throw them down at him, hitting him on the head and everything; and do you know, he used to read everyone of them. But he'd never ever ask anyone of them for a date, or arrange to meet them at a dance or anything. Then this girl Mary – well, she hung around one Sunday until everyone else was gone. She was trying desperate to get your man to meet her at the dance. And do you know what he said to her and he looking straight up under her skirt? He said, "I'll meet you at the dance if you take off your knickers and throw them down to me now." And on the virt' of my oath, didn't she up with the skirt and off with the knickers and threw them down to him, and he never again as much as bid her the time of day after that. So now, where would you be going without a bell on your bike?'

'God! I don't believe it. She actually threw down her knickers at some fella?' queried Peggy Neary in disbelief and disgust. 'That lady should be in a mental hospital; she couldn't be right in the head.'

'Arrah, what are you talking about? She's probably sounder in the head than you or me. She's still out there, and we're the ones that are locked up,' replied an angry Lilly.

'I hope they landed on his nose. At least he could use them as a handkerchief,' added Julie mischievously because she knew it would horrify Peggy.

'Oh, Julie, that's disgusting. How could you say such a thing?' cringed Peggy, springing to her feet and blessing herself, before walking away from her foul-mouthed colleagues.

'Are any of ye hungry?' asked Lilly, jumping from the bed and rummaging under it for her slippers.

'You know, I'd love a cut of bread. Do you think it is too late to sneak down now?' asked Bridie, who had no sooner asked than the sound of the bedtime bell came echoing along the corridors.

That meant they had just fifteen minutes to get ready before the lights went out and the dormitory doors were locked for the night. Not enough time for them to sneak down to the kitchen, or across to the rear of the nuns' convent in search of scraps of food.

'Ah, well, we'll have to do without it,' sighed Lilly as she slipped her bare feet into a pair of tatty slippers, and the rest of the gang dispersed to their own sleeping quarters, saying, 'Good night girls.'

'Good night.'

'Oh dear, oh dear,' yawned Lilly. 'I'm as tired as a dog.' Then gathering her bright red cardigan about her to ward off the late night chill, she added, 'The end of another long week. And as usual it's a penny for our thoughts, Bridie, another shilling for the bishop, and a lifetime's penance for our sins.'

Bridie said nothing, because she was remembering how she had a date with destiny in the morning. Hoping desperately to talk her way to freedom. It was all or nothing now, she thought.

She was in the midst of a long queue as the priest gave out the Blessed Sacrament; her head bowed and her hands reverently joined together as if in prayer. But prayer was the last thing on her mind. Bridie, was trying to say the Morning Offering, reverently: 'Oh my God, I offer up to you all my thoughts, words, actions, sufferings of this day for thy greater honour and glory, through Jesus Christ Our Lord, Amen.' Thoughts? Words? Actions? Sufferings? They were nothing but a jumbled-up heap of words, circling around in her head. How can I possibly offer up to you all of my suffering? she thought. I would and gladly, if only I could get out of this place. All my thoughts – how can I control my thoughts? Words – are they the same thing? Dirty words? Impure thoughts? It's the work of the devil himself, egging us to commit sin: at least that's what the priest keeps saying to me in the confessional.

Bridie raised her eyes to scan the length of the queue. Only three more to go before it was her turn to receive Holy Communion, then she'd go back and kneel down and accept the priest's blessing. And then they'd all file past her on their way out, leaving her to succeed or fail in her mission to leave the Magdalene Home Laundry forever.

She looked up and saw the priest looking fervently into her eyes as he held up the Sacred Host, saying piously, '*Corpus Christi*.'

'*Amen*.'

She opened her parched mouth to receive the precious wafer

and tried desperately to swallow the flesh of Our Lord. But it stuck like glue to the roof of her mouth, and no amount of licking, or coaxing could shift it, until it slowly dissolved into a thousand fragments and disappeared down her dry gullet.

The early morning Mass now over, the inmates were filing past, wondering why Bridie Rodgers was showing off; gone all religious like, with her head buried in her hands.

She's not right, *that one*, thought Julie Murray. But I'll soon show her.

She gave Bridie a strong playful puck as she passed by and whispered, 'Get up, out-a-that, you oul' *amadán*, and don't be makin' a show of yoursel'.'

But Bridie remained still, and when she thought the last of the girls had gone out, she turned her head and stole a glance at the chapel door and saw Julie staring back at her.

For what seemed an eternity, the seven nuns prayed on in silence at the front of the altar. Even the priest had come out from the sacristy, having already removed his vestments and extinguished the altar candles. Despite all the waiting, Bridie didn't think she was ready to put her well-thought-out plan into action – even when she saw the nuns rising from their pews before they each went down on their knees and bowed before the glowing tabernacle. Now they were gliding down the centre aisle as if they were mere shadows; and led as always by Sister Philomena, who stopped to enquire if Bridie was all right.

She nodded, she was, and then rose hurriedly to follow the nuns out.

They were moving at such speed down the gravelled path, Bridie almost had to trot after them before calling out, 'Mother Superior . . . I mean, Reverend Mother.'

The fleeing angelic-looking sisters froze in their tracks before craning their veiled heads to look back at Bridie. But before Bridie could make up her mind what to say, the Reverend

Mother signalled with a wave of her hand to the rest of the nuns to go about their business.

Then, turning to look at Bridie, with a sour, tainted expression, she snapped, 'What is it?'

'Please, Reverend Mother, I want to leave the laundry . . . for good. I have to be with my son, John Paschal.'

The Reverend Mother's shoulders trembled slightly as a result of the early morning chill, and she buried her hands deeper into the black folds of her sleeves, before replying, 'Why aren't you down in the laundry? You should be working by now instead of gallivanting around the place. Does Sister Philomena know about this?'

'No, Reverend Mother, I thought—'

'This is neither the time nor the place. Now, please, go back to your work. I'll deal with you later.'

Without any further ado the ageing Mother Superior turned and was gone. For a moment Bridie stood in bewilderment, her anger mounting that she had once again failed in her quest to flee the laundry. Not only that, but she felt so belittled by the Reverend Mother's response: *I'll deal with you later.*

Was that a threat or did she mean she'd discuss the whole subject at a more convenient time? Would that be today or tomorrow? she wondered as she turned and trudged her way back to the laundry to begin another long day. I swear that lady must be in league with the devil; egging her on to torture the living daylights out of me, Bridie sighed as she entered the rear door of the giant washroom, to the heavy sound of washing machines and trundling laundry baskets.

It was noon and Sister Stanislaus informed Bridie Rodgers that the Mother Superior wished to see her immediately. Bridie made her way apprehensively down the long corridor. She knocked tentatively on the glass-panelled door. Mother Superior raised her bushy eyebrows and beckoned from behind her desk for her to come in. Bridie pushed open the newly painted green door and, in response to another gesture, sat down awkwardly, waiting for Sister to finish writing her letters.

The Mother Superior then added her seal of approval to her great work by licking the large envelope with an even larger, grotesque tongue, before stamping it authoritatively with her ample fist.

Turning to Bridie, she said, 'Now, miss, to get back to this morning, what exactly did you hope to achieve by interfering with my devotions to Our Lord?'

After a lengthy, strained silence during which they both sized each other up, Sister repeated, 'What did you hope to achieve?'

'I wanted to ask you if I could leave the laundry,' said Bridie.

The Mother Superior, acting as if she hadn't heard the reply, blasted loudly, 'Don't you ever interfere with my devotions again, be it morning, noon or night. This is a religious—'

'I'm sorry, Reverend Mother,' muttered Bridie, interrupting.

'I haven't finished,' said the Mother Superior with a vicious glare as she sat bolt upright, wringing her large blue hands in an effort to increase the blood circulation. 'My good lady, you only ever speak when spoken to. As I was saying,' she continued after a momentary pause, 'this is a religious institution, where we, the Sisters of Mercy, continuously pray for the sinners of this world. We have here a convent and a chapel, which is supposed to be a place of refuge for girls – such as yourself – who have fallen by the wayside. We cannot pray for God's guidance if we do not abide by the rules of his Church, two of which, incidentally, you broke this morning, thereby committing a mortal sin. You caused me to break my perpetual vow of silence whilst attending chapel. Secondly, you committed a sin of disobedience by being absent without leave from your place of work whilst under the care and supervision of Sister Philomena.' On seeing Bridie's obvious shock and look of bewilderment she asked smugly, 'Shall I go on?'

'No, Reverend Mother,' answered Bridie, embarrassed, while looking deep into the Mother Superior's eyes to try desperately to detect a glimmer of hope, but there was none.

'I'm sorry, Reverend Mother, I didn't realise—' said Bridie, already feeling sorry for apologising because she didn't want to, but somehow the words had just slipped out. If anyone deserved an apology, she thought, it was herself.

'That's part of the problem, Bridie. You young girls never seem to realise anything . . . until it's too late . . . Now what was it you wanted to speak to me about?'

Bridie had been thinking what she'd love to do, if only she had a scissors handy. She'd cut Sister Antonia's snow-white veil and black habit from around her head and upper body and expose her naked breasts, so all the penitents in the laundry could have a good laugh at the Reverend Mother, going around half naked.

But now she was being jolted into a response. She swallowed hard, trying to summon up her courage again.

She said, 'I want to leave the laundry . . . for good so that I can get a job — and look after my son,' she slowly added, thinking the latter would impress the Reverend Mother.

'Oh dear,' the Mother Superior began wearily, as if she'd already heard that request a thousand times. 'You already have a job, one that you can be absolutely proud of. Besides, you know it's both wrong and sinful to desire that which we cannot have. You, of all people, should know that. We reiterate it time and time again in our schools; of which you are supposedly a past pupil. Have we not made it abundantly clear to you time and time again that all contact between mother and child is strictly forbidden once the separation has taken place?'

Bridie, unable to speak, stared open-mouthed at the Mother Superior. She began to realise for the first time that there was no way out.

The Reverend Mother, seeing the look of despondency

written all over Bridie's pale complexion, leaned forward to press home the point once and for all. 'Sooner or later, you, Bridie Rodgers, will have to accept the fact that you will never ever see your son again. It is God's will that he be taken from you and placed in a safe environment. It is also God's will that you spend the rest of your life here in the service of God; for you have the potential to become a consecrated penitent, happy to spend your life helping others, thereby atoning for the terrible sins of your past.'

'. . . *never ever see your son again*' – Bridie thought her heart would surely stop and break in two. The words pierced her body like poisoned arrows. But when the Reverend Mother added '. . . thereby atoning for the terrible sins of your past,' she could take no more. A force more powerful than anything she had experienced since leaving St Mary's was closing in around her chest and squeezing the life-blood from her body.

She sprang from the chair like a demented woman, screaming, 'No! No! No! It's all a pack of lies.' She turned and ran for the door; wrenched it open, before glaring viciously back at the Mother Superior, who was already standing up. 'I'm going to see my son . . . now . . . one way or another and NOBODY will ever stop me.'

Slamming the door behind her, she ran down the corridor, ready to race out into the yard, around to the front of the building and out over the wall. But then she slowed down and thought better of it. It wouldn't do to end up like Julie. She must not give the Mother Superior the pleasure of beating her senseless should she fail to get away, she thought, and as for Sergeant Ruane, there was no way she'd accept the kind of punishment he had meted out to Julie.

Mother Superior's initial reaction on seeing Bridie bolt for the door was one of elation. She thought she had killed stone dead all desire in Bridie to be reunited with her infant. She was extremely proud of her ability to subdue even the most hard-hearted penitent. There was only one way to do it, she thought, and that was the right way; while they were still young and new to the home. But when Bridie turned on her from the relative safety of the doorway and cast that piercing look of hers, she felt a tremor of fear enter her body. Not only that, but she felt as if that look had pierced God's armour, which was her religious habit, her sacred veil; her protection. Her first instinct was to demand that Bridie apologise for her behaviour forthwith, but somehow she lacked the power. Instead she slumped back into her great oak throne, and came to the conclusion that *that Bridie Rodgers one* was an out-and-out brat: a brazen bitch. But she'd get her comeuppance one of these days.

On further reflection, the Reverend Mother was of the opinion that perhaps Bridie was mad. In that case corrective action would have to be taken. I'd better go down to the laundry now and see what's happening, she thought. That lady's dangerous, I know she is.

Bridie, who was unable to face her friends in her present state of mind, headed straight for the lavatory, where she could hide for a few minutes to gather her thoughts. Instead, she found herself burying her head in her hands, trying desperately to expel the veiled image of the Reverend Mother from her head and the terrible words: 'Sooner or later, you, Bridie Rodgers, will have to accept the fact that you will never ever see your son again . . . Sooner or later, you will have to accept . . .' Bridie banged her clenched fists on the cubicle door as she said aloud, 'That woman is pure evil. I swear to you, God, she's pure evil. She's the devil incarnate.'

After a few moments she tried to pull herself together by pleading silently with God: Get me out of here now and I swear I'll never ask another thing. All I'll ever ask in life is to be reunited with my son. He's all I have in this world. Please, please don't take him away from me now, because deep down in my heart of hearts I know I've done no wrong. Answer my prayers, please, and I promise to be a better Christian. I'll do the nine first Fridays. I'll never ever call the nuns names again behind their backs . . .

Bridie's religious pleadings were brought to an abrupt halt by a gentle rap on the lavatory door. She did not answer but stayed quiet as a mouse, thinking it must be Sister Stanislaus, who probably saw her going into the lavatory. Worse still, it might be the Reverend Mother herself. A second knock came, this time more aggressive.

'Is that you, Bridie?'

Bridie stood up. The voice was unmistakable. She was relieved it wasn't Sister Stanislaus demanding to know why she was gallivanting, but at the same time annoyed that Julie and the rest of the gang could never let her have a bit of privacy. There was just no mercy.

She opened the door and made believe she was adjusting her dress as Julie stood there staring at her, her mouth open.

'Are you sick?'

Bridie stepped out past Julie and walked away, mumbling sourly, 'No! I'm not sick, but everybody else is.'

She went straight into the ironing room and sat down on the nearest linen basket, followed by Julie, who stood beside her asking, '*F*what's wrong with you? Did your one give out to you or *f*what?'

'There's nothing wrong with me – now will you shut up and leave me alone and get out of my sight?' said Bridie, raising her voice so that the other girls in the room stopped working to look on inquisitively.

'Don't you tell me to shut up. I know there's somethin' wrong. No need to take it out on me. Sure, I can see there's somethin' wrong because you look like a ghost.'

'Arrah, I'm sick of you telling me how I look,' snapped Bridie. She jumped off the basket and began pacing the floor, her arms folded tightly. 'I'm pale! I'm sick! I'm thin! And now

I'm like a ghost,' she complained, throwing her hands in the air. 'Well, you'd be like a ghost too if her royal highness told you that you could never ever see your son again.'

'Is it the Reverend Mother?' asked Julie, lowering her voice.

Bridie sat down again, trying to control her own thoughts. She just wished that she could run away or hide in some hole in the ground, and not have to be answering so many stupid questions.

'Who else?'

'But, sure, *a grá*, you should have told me *f*what you were plannin' . . .' suggested Julie, feebly, 'and not be keepin' it a secret.'

'Ah, shut up. It wasn't a secret and I wasn't planning anything. You're a nice one to talk. You ran away yourself and didn't tell any of us,' retorted Bridie angrily, as more of her comrades gathered around to hear and see what was happening. They knew it had to be some disturbing news in order to get Bridie so agitated, for she was normally very quiet – much too quiet and civil, they often thought, for her own good.

'What's wrong?' asked Lilly MacAlastair.

'They just told her she'd never ever see her son, John Paschal, again. Sure, them raps don't care,' added Julie, trying to sound sympathetic.

'Wash, wash, wash till our hands drop off – that's all them bitches ever want.'

'And more money for the arse-bishop,' added Josephine, emphasising the word 'arse'.

'I know,' said Lilly thoughtfully, ''tis terrible. They won't let any of us OUT to see our children, or the little ones IN to see their mothers. Ye know, I think I'd rather be in jail, I would, honest to God. I'd much rather be in jail than have to live in this kip for the rest of me life. At least if we were in jail, we'd know how long we were in for.'

The words had no sooner left Lilly's lips than the Mother

Superior and Sister Philomena appeared at the door. The girls turned abruptly and began to fan out, slithering away back to their posts, save Bridie, who remained sitting defiantly on a linen basket.

'Girls! What's the meaning of this! What's going on around here?'

But the girls were already beavering away on their ironing boards.

'Girls!' bellowed the Reverend Mother. 'Come here at once!'

The penitent girls looked from one to the other before collectively deciding it was better to go forward.

'Now, what's the meaning of this? What's so important that it requires all of you to attend a meeting with Bridie Rodgers, who's quite obviously the ringleader of this little charade? What is it?' asked the Reverend Mother, as the penitent women stood before her, their heads hanging in shame, having been caught so unaware. 'Girls! Look at me while I'm speaking to you! And show some respect.'

Slowly they raised their eyes, as one or two of the other inmates peeped in at them from behind a curtain.

'Now which one of you prime lassies said you'd rather be in jail than in this kip?'

The girls were stunned. Even Bridie, who remained tight-lipped, was amazed that the Reverend Mother had picked up on every word of their conversation.

'Girls,' repeated Sister Antonia in a more measured tone, but with a touch of venom in her voice, 'I repeat, which one of you said you'd rather be in jail than live in this kip?'

The penitent women remained silent, afraid to own up. While telling the Reverend Mother who had made the offending remark might earn one a much lighter sentence than the guilty party, it did nothing at all for one's standing in the ranks of the Magdalene women. To split on a friend or colleague was considered the lowest of the low, and usually resulted in that person being shunned – like Peggy Neary, who was loathed by everyone because she was the nuns' pet and told tales.

'So you've all decided to become model citizens by taking a vow of silence. How interesting,' said the Reverend Mother sarcastically. 'So, we shall see how long it will last. Perhaps you'd all like to offer up your continued silence as penance for your sin. All of you from this moment are forbidden to partake of any food or drink. Sister Philomena will take charge of the fast, and when you are ready to talk she will be only too happy to inform me of your repentance.'

On hearing her name being mentioned as the enforcer of this rule, Sister Philomena cringed with embarrassment. She couldn't understand why she was being used in this way. As a novice, she had spent years learning to carry herself in God's own likeness while absorbing the language of respect and common decency, moving about at all times with dignity and decorum, only to end up being sent here to the Magdalene Home to witness the Reverend Mother herself behaving like a bully. She remembered her first day here all too vividly. She'd been appalled at the inhuman way the inmates were treated. They all had that wayward look of despair about them, she thought, and their dormitories stank of stale body odour, perfume and cigarette smoke.

Now she was being asked to be a party to their punishment by her superior. She must not allow herself to be used in this way, she thought. She'd better say something, otherwise the girls would think she was agreeable to the whole thing. She needed time to think but was afraid to contradict the Mother Superior as she had already chastised her earlier for failing to carry out certain instructions to the letter of the law.

'As you wish, Reverend Mother. I will lock them in their dormitories now,' replied Sister Philomena, knowing that by suggesting such a thing she would at least be saving the peni-tents the ordeal of having to work, while at the same time giving herself the opportunity of smuggling some food in to them later.

'On the contrary, Sister Philomena! They shall pay for their disobedience by continuing to work right here in the laundry where I can keep an eye on them,' replied the Mother Superior.

Bridie, on hearing that her friends were going to be punished because they had dared to enquire about her welfare, jumped off the basket and came forward. At that precise moment she didn't care for all the nuns in County Galway, so she brazenly piped up, 'Reverend Mother, I don't think it really matters who said what because I refuse to do any more work until I know when I can see John Paschal.'

The two nuns, who were already making their way out of the room, stopped and turned back to look at her in amazement, while Julie Murray took a few hesitant steps forward and squawked, 'Yes . . . I think she should be allowed to see her son . . . when she wants.'

Then Lilly MacAlastair added fuel to the fire, saying, 'Yeah! She should be allowed to see her son.'

The Reverend Mother's temper rose to boiling point. Moving quickly forward, she slapped Julie Murray hard across the face. 'How dare you interfere with my authority?'

Slap! Slap, she went again, before Josephine Finn, who couldn't believe what she was seeing, rushed forward to support her friend by lashing out at the Reverend Mother, striking her in the face, but succeeding only in knocking her veil sideways as she screamed, 'How dare you hit my friend like that . . . you bitch?' She lashed out again and again with her tiny fists.

'And how dare anybody stop me from seeing my son?' bellowed Bridie, as she came swiftly to Josephine's aid.

The Mother Superior, seeing the fire burning in Bridie's eyes, knew she was in for the kill, as it were. Bridie was far too dangerous, she thought. A troublemaker for sure. She could clearly see Bridie had the ability to lead others, which was the

Reverend Mother's single greatest fear in the running of the laundry. Bridie could start a strike, as others had tried down through the years. Fortunately, Sister Antonia had managed to outwit them on those rare occasions by planting an informer or two in their midst. Now she would have to submit to them for the time being because of their superior numbers, and then resort to her favourite tactic: divide and conquer.

She could see Sister Philomena had remained perfectly still, with her hands tucked into the neat folds of her long sleeves as if nothing had happened. The Reverend Mother thought, how in God's holy name did that child ever come to take her final vows? She's pure useless. But while craving her support, which was not forthcoming, the Reverend Mother managed to recover somewhat before responding to Bridie and the rest of the inmates.

'Very well, if that's how you feel. Sister Philomena and I will let the matter rest for now; but be assured, girls, I will deal with this later. Meanwhile, you can all go back to work.'

Turning quickly, she left the room, followed by Sister Philomena, knowing full well that the inmates had pulled off a major triumph by taking her down a peg, not to mention achieving a physical assault on her person.

But, she thought, they will be made to pay a very heavy price indeed for their arrogance. Particularly that . . . that . . . Rodgers brat.

Sister Philomena, seeing that the penitents had rescued her from having to enforce the Reverend Mother's law, felt a warm glow of satisfaction that justice had been done. But little did she know that her superior had other things in mind when she invited her to have a cup of tea in her office later in the afternoon.

'Thank you for coming along, Sister. Please be seated,' said the Reverend Mother, before proceeding to bless herself and bow her head as they both joined their hands in prayer.

'*In anim an Athair, Agus an Mhic, Agus an Spiroid Naomh. Amen.* Bless us, O Lord, and these thy gifts which we are about to receive through Christ Our Lord. Amen.'

'Amen.'

'Sister, I've just been thinking,' began the Reverend Mother as she poured the tea into her favourite pale, gold-rimmed china cups, 'that you've been here with us for a while now. I know that it's a far cry from what you've been used to – teaching children, I'm sure, is so much easier. But I just wish you'd show a bit more co-operation with these unruly girls; show more interest in their overall welfare.'

'I'm sorry, Reverend Mother, if I failed you in my duty,' said Sister Philomena, resting her hands on her lap and hanging her head slightly while waiting to be invited to partake of her tea.

'Goodness, dear, you haven't failed. Been a bit lax perhaps, but failed? No. Here, have a biscuit,' added the Reverend Mother, pushing the small decorative plate in her direction, as she continued, 'Failure is something we, the Sisters of Mercy, won't tolerate in the Magdalene Home. It is my duty as your superior to teach you right from wrong. Now, tell me, Sister, what do you think of Miss Rodgers?'

Sister Philomena, caught unawares, paused for a brief moment before lowering her head to answer.

'I'm sorry, I don't know her very well,' she said deliberately, in case she'd be accused of being too familiar with the girls.

'Be that as it may, you saw her behaviour today. What did you think of that?'

'I thought perhaps she wasn't well, that she might be suffering from depression,' answered Sister Philomena, knowing this might be what the Reverend Mother would want to hear, which was why she looked her straight in the eye while speaking.

'How very observant of you, Sister. See! You have the potential to be a good analyst and counsellor. Certainly Bridie Rodgers is not well. However, it's not depression she suffers from, but *madness*,' confided the Reverend Mother, as she leaned forward to emphasise the point, 'and *madness* in the confines of a refuge such as ours is highly contagious and must be stamped out immediately. Today was a perfect example of how a group of affected penitents could take over the entire institution – the chapel, the convent, the laundry – and turn the whole place into a lunatic asylum: a laughing stock. Therefore we must be constantly on our guard and watch out for their ulterior motives. It is God's will that penitents such as Bridie Rodgers be sent to a secure psychiatric hospital as well as those of her friends who aid and abet her in her unreasonable demands. So I'd like you to keep a close eye on Bridie Rodgers, and should she persist in her demands to see her son, then I shall have no choice other than to have her committed to Ballinasloe.'

Sister Philomena's eyes widened in dismay, which did not go unnoticed by the Mother Superior, whose sole purpose in outlining this course of action was that Sister Philomena would convey this very real threat to Bridie Rodgers and her friends. That message would surely take the wind out of Miss Rodgers' sails, because she was not stupid; not stupid at all, Sister Antonia thought.

Sister Philomena left the Mother Superior's office, determined to warn Bridie that unless she toned down her demands right away she might never see her son. Bridie, she figured, already knew that once a mother and child were parted, the chances of them ever meeting again were very slim indeed. What Bridie didn't know was that once the mother was committed to a mental institution, then her chances of ever having a reunion were as good as dead.

After the penitents' resounding success in forcing the Reverend Mother to withdraw her threat of fast and abstinence, they were delirious with excitement. So much so that they did very little work, electing instead every few minutes to appoint a new 'lookout' to guard the door so that they could revel in Josephine Finn's singing and dancing, and speak openly about their plans for freedom. At the rate they were going, they figured they'd all be free in no time, because now the nuns were afraid of them. All one hundred and fifty of them would get together and if they weren't granted immediate freedom they would go on strike. But right now they were more interested in Josephine's sense of humour, as she sang while brandishing a pair of long johns.

> I've travelled about a bit in my time,
> And of troubles, I've seen a few.
> But found it better in every clime
> To paddle my own canoe.
> My wants are small I care not at all,
> If my debts are paid when due;
> I drive away strife in the ocean of life,
> While I paddle my own canoe.
>
> Then love you as yourself,
> As the world you go travelling through,
> And never sit down with a tear or a frown,
> But paddle your own canoe.

The girls grabbed each other and twirled around the floor to the tune. Then Josephine jumped up on a linen basket – which threatened to take off across the room of its own accord if she didn't stop her jigging – and began imitating the Reverend Mother.

'I see you've decided to become model citizens by taking a vow of silence. Perhaps you'd like to offer it up as a penance for your sins. Especially you, Bridie Rodgers, full of buttermilk and cream; or you, MacAlastair, for the night you fooled poor Mick. Oh, what a sight when you undid his fly and out jumped his little dick.'

Amid howls of laughter the lookout shouted, 'The sister! Quick!'

'She can go and kiss my arse,' replied Josephine loudly as she joined her hands and bowed her head as if in prayer.

'I think it's the Reverend Mother!' hissed the lookout. And for an instant all hell broke loose as they resumed hard labour. But it was a false alarm, brought about by a nervous lookout, mortified by their antics and afraid that a severe punishment would await them if they were caught again. For not everyone had confidence in the penitents' new-found sense of freedom.

CHAPTER TEN

HAVING GOT OVER the initial shock of being told by the Reverend Mother that she would never ever see her son again, Bridie turned her thoughts to escape. In the ironing room, carefully running the steam iron down the sleeve of a shirt, she thought perhaps she should make a run for it or climb over the wall. The thought both excited and frightened her. Managing to escape was one thing; managing to stay out was another.

Well, suppose I managed to get out tomorrow or even next week, she thought to herself, what then? Where do I go? I have eight pounds altogether, enough to feed and clothe me for a while. But if I go to Dublin or England, which is where everyone seems to want to go, that'll cost me a fortune. And if I go to either place, I'll be too far away from John Paschal.

She started to sort out another pile of priests' vestments. Thinking of John Paschal again, she reached into her blouse to pull out the small goatskin purse, which hung around her neck and which contained the golden lock of hair and the only photograph she had of her son. For a long time she studied his jovial features; his bob of wavy hair, which she now held in her hand. She was astonished that she had a photograph at all, not knowing exactly who sent it.

She resumed her ironing again and was trying desperately to plan her escape bid when Sister Philomena came into the room unexpectedly. She marched straight over to Bridie's table and began to inspect her work.

As she did so she looked furtively around before whispering to Bridie, 'I've come to warn you. You are in very grave danger as a result of what happened yesterday.'

She again glanced round to make sure none of the other workers could overhear her, before adding, 'It's possible you may be taken away from here without warning and sent to a place far worse unless you curtail your demands immediately. Do not under any circumstances ask to see your son again or get involved in organising a strike.'

With those words ringing in Bridie's ears, Sister Philomena disappeared as suddenly as she had appeared.

Before Bridie could even begin to digest what 'a place far worse' meant, the blood had left her cheeks and she thought she would faint.

Struggling to maintain her balance, she went over to her friend across the room and begged, 'In the honour of God, Lilly, have you a fag? I've just had the most frightening news.'

Lilly looked up in surprise. 'What's wrong with you? You're not yourself at all today,' she said, as she rummaged in her pockets for a smoke.

'Oh God, I don't know, I think I'm in trouble. Won't you promise to come straight over to me after work and I'll tell you everything?'

'I will! I will! Don't I always?' replied Lilly, as she handed Bridie the crumpled blackened butt of a Woodbine cigarette. 'Here! And don't smoke it all. That's all I've left,' she added, as Bridie hurried away.

Lilly looked at the clock and thought, what does that lady want a smoke for at this hour of the day? Won't we be finished working in another half an hour?

When she finished work she arrived back in Our Lady's dormitory, and said to Bridie, 'Well, what have ye got to tell me? What's the big secret?' as Bridie and she began removing their white calico gowns.

'The nuns are threatening to have me put away. Sister Philomena warned me this afternoon. She said they might send me to a place far worse than here if I caused any more trouble or asked to see John Paschal.'

'Are ye serious?' said Lilly, looking at Bridie in disbelief.

'As true as God is my judge! That's what she said. And I'm terrified she means it. What will I do if they send me to Ballinasloe?'

'Ballinasloe! Jesus, they wouldn't send you to Ballinasloe, would they?' queried Lilly, after dwelling on the subject for a moment. 'But isn't Sister Philomena one of them? Why would she warn you? Why should she care?'

'Maybe she feels sorry for us. Did you notice she never lifted a finger to help the Reverend Mother yesterday? So she must be on our side. Why else would she warn me?' asked Bridie.

'Oh, Bridie, they wouldn't send you to a place worse than here! They couldn't do that!' Lilly said thoughtfully as she sat down on the edge of Bridie's bed, a tone of despondency creeping into her voice at the very notion that the nuns held such power over them. 'Ballinasloe! You mean they'd send you to the mental, in Ballinasloe?'

'I . . . I . . . I don't know. God, they'd never send me to Ballinasloe, would they?' pleaded Bridie, beginning to feel terrified.

Lilly, seeing Bridie's fear, tried to console her. 'No, no! I don't think they would – not for asking to see yer child, anyway. Everyone knows that place is only for nutcases.'

But the minute Lilly had said it, she realised that the nuns and priests were capable of anything. Didn't they have poor Julie put into the home because she was wild or something; Josephine Finn because she was in love with a Protestant; and herself because she liked eyeing up all the talent? And if priests could put you away like that for nothing, then they could do anything, she thought.

Josephine Finn and Julie Murray returned from work, happy in the knowledge that they had come to the end of another long day. They were no sooner in the door than Bridie and Lilly waylaid them and brought them up to date on the latest development. And when Julie Murray was asked how best to cope with this latest threat she didn't know what to say. She wasn't really in favour of a strike she said, because the nuns might find out she had helped Bridie and then she herself would be put away. She had escaped once and paid a heavy price for it. As well as that, the Reverend Mother now considered her a valued inmate and rewarded her from time to time with the gift of a half-crown.

'Sure, how can we go on strike?' she tittered nervously. 'Sure, *f*what can we do but keep going and pray to the Lord that some oul' eejit'll take us out-a-here.'

'The only way we'll ever leave here is in a bloody box,' said Josephine resignedly.

'God Almighty above,' said Bridie, looking aghast at Josephine. 'That's it! We'll escape by hiding in one of the laundry baskets.'

'Yeah, that's a great idea,' said Josephine. 'We could all go together.'

'Sure, that's been tried before, ye oul' *amadáns*. And an'way, wouldn't we all smother. One young girl died tryin' to get out like that. They threw all the clothes in on top of her. That's why I'd never try to escape like that,' said Julie cautiously. 'An' besides, we'd be too heavy. The lads would notice the minute they tried lifting the baskets. An' the nuns are always watching out an' ever'thin' since one young girl was caught kissing one of the drivers. Sure, they were supposed to have sent her away to Ballinasloe, because she was never seen again. Lord, I wouldn't mind kissing one of the men, if I thought I could get out,' she added thoughtfully. 'It's all right for you, Bridie and Josephine, nobody would notice your scrawny arses lying in a basket, but sure, I'd have no chance. It would take three men to lift me,' said Julie, laughing at the idea of three men coming to her rescue.

'What's happenin'? What's all the excitement?' asked an inquisitive-looking Peggy Neary as she approached them quietly out of the blue.

'Mind your own business! Now buzz off!' snapped Lilly, peeved that Peggy always eavesdropped on their conversations at the most inopportune times.

But when Peggy insisted, by saying, 'Well, don't let me stop ye,' she really raised Lilly's hackles.

'Go on! Off with ye! We don't want ye around here . . .'

'Go on, buzz off!' added Julie, supporting Lilly, whom she knew hated Peggy more than anyone in the world.

'No, I won't! I can go where I like. It's a free country,' said Peggy defiantly as she attempted to sit the other side of Bridie, because she knew Bridie would never interfere.

Suddenly Lilly, who was facing Bridie, grabbed Peggy by the hair and dragged her screaming to the floor, and in an instant they were both kicking and leathering hell out of each other. Amid a chorus of whistles and catcalls, the two protagonists were locked together, each pulling the other's hair and screaming obscenities.

Bridie, Julie and Josephine jumped up to admire Lilly's efforts. The two assailants were still locked in combat and a large crowd of inmates had gathered round when Sister Stanislaus entered Our Lady's dormitory and rang her heavy bronze bell. The ward sister had caught them fighting, red-handed.

Looking solemnly around the large dormitory, Sister Stanislaus appeared distressed as she spoke haltingly.

'Girls, I have a sad announcement . . . to make.' Again she rang the bell to get everybody's attention. Then, looking directly at Peggy and Lilly, she spoke with an air of disappointment. 'Some of you are a disgrace to the good name of the Magdalene Home Laundry. It saddens me to say you're no better than a pack of wild animals.' After a long pause, she looked around the room, now once more in silence, inclined her head ever so slowly, and, placing her left hand across her abdomen, said, 'I want you all to pray this day for the soul of Catherine Kelly, whom God has called to his side. She has just died peacefully in her sleep.'

An audible gasp filled the air as each of the penitents, as if in a chain reaction, hurriedly made the sign of the cross and muttered aloud, 'Lord have mercy,' their every thought and care suddenly vanished into thin air.

Sister Stanislaus, struggling to control her own emotions, continued, 'Catherine Kelly was a loyal and faithful servant to the Sisters of Mercy. The Reverend Mother and I would like you all to join us in a night of prayer for the repose of her soul. May she rest in peace, Amen.'

'Amen.'

Bridie knew Catherine Kelly was an elderly woman who had spent most of her life in the Magdalene Home. For some time she'd been confined to the infirmary ward and her death was not entirely unexpected. Yet the very thought that someone had died in their midst almost took Bridie's breath away, as she tried to listen to what Sister was saying.

'The Reverend Mother and the other sisters will all be there to lead the prayers. We would like all of her friends and colleagues to organise themselves into little groups of ten; each to devote one hour of prayer at her bedside. Her burial will take place the day after tomorrow after twelve o'clock Mass, in the penitents' graveyard. *Deo gratias.*'

Then, as she turned, about to leave the room, Peggy Neary ran up to her and said, 'Sister Stanislaus, I'm so sorry about my behaviour. It was Lilly's fault. She didn't want me to mix with her friends. If there is anything I can do I'd be only too glad to help.'

Sister Stanislaus pursed her lips thoughtfully for a moment, and replied, 'How kind of you, Peggy. Perhaps you'd like to offer up fifteen decades of the rosary for the repose of Catherine's soul.'

Then, seeing Bridie and Josephine standing together by the window, she went to them and politely asked, 'Josephine, would you be so kind as to sing "Soul of my Saviour" at the funeral Mass? And, Bridie, I would like you to join in the choir, for the singing of "Nearer my God to Thee".'

The two girls could hardly believe their luck at being honoured in this way. They both answered in subdued tones, 'We'd be honoured, Sister.'

And as Sister Stanislaus left the room, Bridie and Josephine felt a warm glow of satisfaction that for now at least the focus was on somebody else and not on them.

It was almost a week before Christmas. Bridie and Josephine were on their usual rounds, walking the well-worn path of the Magdalene grounds, discussing life's ups and downs, when Bridie unexpectedly said, 'I've never heard you talk about dreams; do you believe in them?'

'Oh, I do! I do! I have dreams all the time. But they're usually horrible: about rows at home and everything. But worst of all, are the ones I have about Cathal. Imagine, he never even wrote to me; never answered my letters; nor did my parents. Why did you ask?'

'Oh, it's nothing. It's just that I dream a lot too. But there are certain times when I believe in them, and I know that something good or bad is going to happen. You know my birthday is on the thirteenth of September, and I dreamed a few nights ago that I would see my son on the thirteenth. But I don't know what month. I don't know if it's the thirteenth of January or not. It can't be the thirteenth of December because that's gone. So I was thinking maybe I'd see him in January. And you know, that's the second time I've had that dream since I came here. I don't really know what it all means, but I feel as if thirteen is my lucky number. I don't know why I should dream about it but I did,' said Bridie.

'Good for you! I don't seem to have a lucky number,' replied Josephine despondently.

'Oh, don't be silly, everyone has a lucky number,' said Bridie, giving Josephine's arm a reassuring tug, 'but sometimes it's hard to tell. I don't know how to say this, even though it's the reason I mentioned it in the first place, but I had a lovely dream about you last night.'

'About me!'

'Yes, and it was crystal clear, though very strange. You looked so beautiful – like an angel, in fact.'

'Ah, go on, pull the other one!' said Josephine as she gave Bridie a gentle heave on the shoulder, and they started the short circular walk for about the tenth time.

'Honest to God, Josephine! Cross my heart and hope to die! You were in the laundry, singing away. But there didn't seem to be anyone around, and this man appeared and was watching you for a long time. There was like clouds and things – a sort of mist in the background, with loads of nuns or angels praying for you. Anyway, this man, he was very clear to me. He said you had the voice of an angel and that he would take you away and that you'd become famous. Yet there was something peculiar about him. He only wanted you for himself. I was standing there at the side, watching. It was as clear as day. I could even see myself in the dream, looking at the two of you. But the strangest part of it all was that I could also read his mind, and although he was admiring your singing and listening to every note you sang, he was really looking at your body. He was desperate to have you for himself . . .'

'Oh, Bridie, it sounds horrible! Stop it. You're making me nervous,' squirmed Josephine as she began to feel the cold winter chill. 'Why did you have to tell me that? Could you not have told me something nice? Like that it was Cathal Swanick, or something.'

'Ah, no! It wasn't a bad dream or anything like it,' said Bridie sympathetically, as she gave the back of Josephine's hand a gentle pat. 'I'm not very good at describing things. But I know it was like a prediction and I thought I'd tell you for the fun of it.'

'Yeah, fun, me backside,' acknowledged Josephine fearfully, as they both considered going back in to the dormitory where rehearsals were taking place for the staging of the annual Christmas concert.

The religious festivities of Christmas were long since over; during which time the inmates had been shown a film for the very first time. Its historic showing and the penitents' enactment of it amongst themselves afterwards kept them going for weeks. But now it was back to the usual boring routine of cooking, sewing, washing, ironing and scrubbing for hours on end.

Josephine was one of the many inmates scrubbing the filthy shirt collars spread out on their washboards in the deep galvanised sinks that lined one wall of the washroom. She was singing away to herself while entertaining her co-workers, when an inspector from the Department of Health paid a surprise visit to the laundry. He was doing his rounds, escorted by Sister Philomena, when they both looked into the washroom from the safety of the screened doorway. Josephine was oblivious to the rhythmic scrubbing noise of the washboards and the suds that splashed on to the floor, drowning her sore-infested feet. And as she struggled to balance another soggy heap of wet clothes on the trolley, Mr Fincock was immediately struck by her haunting rendition of 'Danny Boy'.

For a moment he stood with Sister Philomena, observing the girls at their stations; they seemed so unaware of the distractions going on all around them. But when Josephine Finn turned towards him to place another heap of wet clothes on the trolley and he saw her face, he gasped, 'My God!' And when Josephine picked up on the second verse he was forced to shake his head and utter, 'What a waste of talent.'

Her beauty and demeanour, he thought, bore all the hallmarks of a beautiful peasant girl, not unlike the portrait of *The Connemara Girl*, by Augustus Burke, which he recalled from the National Gallery.

Turning to Sister Philomena, he said, 'Do you mind if I speak to that girl? Who is she?'

'I'm afraid, sir, we're not allowed to let any of the girls speak to strangers, other than priests or doctors. But since you're here on official business, I'm sure it's all right. Please wait a moment, and I'll bring her over.'

Sister Philomena went and brought Josephine over to meet Mr Fincock. Josephine found it difficult to walk in her bare feet as they were covered in blisters, due to the endless hours spent standing at the washtub where the soapsuds continuously splashed all over the floor. She and many of the girls had long since given up wearing any shoes or socks because the constant wetting made their feet too soft, causing sores and blisters.

'Josephine, this is Mr Fincock. He works with the Department of Health in Dublin. He'd like to have a word with you,' said Sister Philomena, wondering what he could possibly want with a young penitent girl.

'Josephine, may I ask have you ever sung on stage?'

'No, sir.'

'Well, I think you should. You have the potential to be a great singer. A star in the making, I would say. Of course you'd need a little tuition . . . but that shouldn't create any problem.'

Then he extended his hand and added, 'My name is Bruce

Fincock. I'm involved with the theatre in Dublin. So, Josephine, if you ever decide to come to the city, I might be able to get you into theatre or something. Would you like that?'

Josephine looked questioningly at Sister Philomena before answering shyly, 'I don't know . . .'

'You know we have many fine singers here in the Magdalene choir, and Josephine is one of our finest,' said Sister Philomena.

'I'm not at all surprised,' acknowledged Mr Fincock.

Turning to Josephine, he bowed slightly and said, 'Josephine, it was nice meeting you,' as he again extended his hand.

Sister Philomena began to pray that Josephine would not be whipped off to Dublin to start a new career, or she herself would have some explaining to do to the Reverend Mother for allowing them to be introduced in the first place. And now Mr Fincock was quizzing her about Josephine's lack of footwear.

Walking back towards the main office, Mr Fincock remarked, 'For the life of me, I can't understand why a girl with such talent should be working here. I would very much like to bring her to Dublin – if that were possible,' he added, as the two of them stood aside to let a mini-procession of linen baskets and trolleys trundle down the long corridor.

Sister Philomena, who was holding her hands firmly to her abdomen, replied, 'I'm sorry, sir, but it's her family's wish that she remain here. And nobody has the authority to remove her from the Magdalene Home except her next of kin. As for her feet, we are treating them as best we can. She seems, however, to be allergic to all forms of footwear. I will, of course, pass on your concern to the Mother Superior.'

'Yes, I would appreciate that,' replied Mr Fincock as they went to the office to sign the book.

After what she believed was a miraculous encounter, Josephine lived for months in the firm belief that one day Mr Fincock would return to whisk her off to start a new life in Dublin.

So she sang every day in an effort to improve her voice; only to accept eventually that her saviour was never going to come to her rescue. And though she had considered it daft at the time, she accepted that Bridie's prediction had materialised. A man indeed had come, but he was not the right one.

No, the right man for me, thought Josephine, is surely Cathal Swanick. Besides, he's taller and more handsome. Oh God! Dear God! One way or another, I'll have to try and escape from here or I'll go mad.

In an effort to keep her spirits high, she frequently sang her own songs, while perched precariously on a basket, much to the amusement of her friends. Occasionally, the nuns would watch discreetly from behind a curtain and then try to subdue her because she was keeping her friends from their work.

On rare occasions, if the nuns felt that certain penitents were up to scratch, as it were, they'd slip them the odd shilling or two. Later the money would be given discreetly to the delivery drivers to buy cheap perfume, white socks, or cigarettes so that, come Saturday night, the penitents could dress up and make believe they were at a real live dance in some famous ballroom while listening to *Ceilí House* on Radio Éireann.

Bridie hardly ever received any money. Her friends said it was because she was too proud to succumb to the Reverend Mother's petty games. She did, however, receive two shillings on one or two occasions from Sister Philomena as a contribution towards gifts for her son's birthday, and although she never received any more correspondence from Tuam – after the one photograph – she continued to write to Sister Hortense and send little gifts to her son.

Bridie, now entering her tenth year in the Magdalene as a penitent, was beside herself for news of John Paschal. And it came as a major surprise to her when late one afternoon Sister Philomena whispered that she wanted to meet her later in the chapel because she had some good news to convey.

'Bridie,' she began, 'I've been down to St Mary's in Tuam to collect an unmarried mother and I made enquiries on your behalf about John Paschal.'

'Oh, Sister! How is he?' beseeched Bridie, placing a hand on Sister's arm in nervous anticipation as they stood whispering inside the chapel door.

'He's fine! He's fine! I didn't see him. But I have better news. He's been boarded out to a good Catholic family, in a place called Williamstown. I managed to get the name and address. Here it is.' Sister Philomena handed Bridie a small slip of paper.

'Oh, Sister!' exclaimed Bridie gratefully. 'My prayers have been answered. How can I ever thank you?'

'Remember me in your devotions,' whispered Sister Philomena humbly, 'for we are all sinners in the eyes of God. And I am guilty of breaking the commandments by flouting the Church's teaching on child separation. I need your word of honour, Bridie, that you will not divulge a single word of this to anyone; otherwise I could be expelled from the convent. I've had a word with the retired matron of St Mary's, Sister Hortense. She sends you her kind regards. It was she who went into Sister Imelda's office and got the relevant information for me. Now listen carefully,' she continued softly. 'To make things easier for you in the long term and to open up a line of communication, Sister Hortense is going to officially inform you of your son's whereabouts. That at least will give you an opportunity to write to your son's guardians to thank them for looking after him. Who knows, if you're lucky and his guardians are as responsible as I believe them to be, you may even get a reply. But please remember not to put them under any undue pressure. And I wish you the best of luck.'

It was a bright summer's morning almost a year later that a letter finally arrived in response to Bridie's many pleading letters.

Corrolough,
Williamstown,
Co. Galway
10 May 1955

Dear Bridie,

Just a few lines to thank you for the parcel you sent to John. He is getting big now and was mad about the football socks you sent him. I hope you are keeping well as this leaves us all at present, thank God. The weather is broke again and we are busy at the moment with the turf and everything. I have no more news and will finish for now. God bless and write soon again.

Yours faithfully, Mrs O'Brien

Also enclosed was a note from her son.

Dear Bridie,

Thank you very much for the big parcel. It was wonderful. I liked the lucky bags, the socks and hankies and pencils. Goodbye for now, from your son Paschal.
PS. I almost forgot. I would like more lucky bags because our shopkeeper said he was out of luck and that I was lucky that I knew someone that had lots and lots of luck. Bye.

She was twenty-seven years of age, and that letter was the first correspondence Bridie had ever had from a living relative; her very own son. She read the letter over and over so she could absorb the joyous feeling of the last line: 'Goodbye for now, from your son Paschal.'
Wiping away tears of joy, she did the rounds of her friends,

showing them the letter. They were very pleased and that night they had a little treat in her honour, devouring large chunks of currant bread lathered in creamery butter, which they had stolen from the kitchen.

Julie Murray lay moping about on her own in the quiet of Our Lady's dormitory. She was feeling very depressed and was slowly coming to the conclusion that she'd never again see the sun shine on her horizon. It appeared to shine on everyone but herself, she thought; especially Bridie Rodgers, who now had direct contact with her son and was forever writing to him.

Where does that one get all the envelopes and paper? Sure, 'tis a post office we'd need here. And as for that Josephine Finn, sure, she's worshipped like a God just because she can sing a few oul' songs. Even Noreen Donnellan, the oul' scallywag, managed to get workin' over in the nuns' convent, where she'll be smothered with tea and cakes and the devil knows *f*what. Sure, that oul' carry-on would sicken anyone, she sighed wearily.

And it was on one of those balmy summer evenings, a few weeks later, when children could be heard playing on the nearby city streets, that Julie Murray decided to make a desperate dash for freedom. Climbing over the iron gate leading to the nunnery field, she ran helter-skelter along by the boundary wall to the top end of the field. There she climbed over a stone wall and down a steep embankment that led to the Galway-to-Clifden rail line, where she crossed over the tracks and made her way out on to the suburban city streets. She didn't really know where she was, but decided to keep going anyway to get as far away as she could. That was the one thing they were all agreed on in the Magdalene: if you manage to escape, run as far away as possible.

Only when she'd made her way out into the country did the enormity of her rash decision hit her. *F*where was she going to get anything to eat? Worse, *f*where was she going to sleep? It was dusk when she spotted a neat little haggard on the side of the road. And having had some experience of sleeping in the hay as a child, she was happy to spend the night there.

Next morning she discovered an orchard in the adjoining garden and began stuffing herself with apples before wandering miles and miles over fields and laneways in an effort to get home. She was determined not to speak to anyone so that no one could betray her to the guards because she knew they would be scouring the city, looking for her. But the following day a farmer spotted Julie fast asleep in his haggard. Eventually the farmer and his wife managed to coax her into their house. There she was given a hot meal and some fresh clothes to change into. They asked her where she was going. She told them she wanted to go to Kilmaine, but was afraid that she might be sent back to Galway.

As the farmer and his wife were in no position to take her in, they decided it would be best to notify the Magdalene Home. They knew very little about the Magdalene except that it was regarded as some kind of an institution for disaffected women. They were afraid to leave themselves open to a charge of assisting or harbouring an escapee, who was possibly a mental patient. So they sent word via the Post Office to the city. Soon two uniformed members of the Gardaí and a nun from the Magdalene Home came to collect her. But first they had to give an undertaking to the farmer and his wife that Julie would not be ill treated in any way.

Once more, Julie Murray was returned to the Magdalene Home Laundry. She was about to commence her twenty-second year as a penitent in College Road, Galway.

CHAPTER ELEVEN

I T WAS A Saturday morning and a worried frown masked Bridie's pale complexion. As a mother she realised she had responsibilities to her son, so she was trying to figure out her best tactic for buying him gifts for his eleventh birthday. It was already eleven thirty and she hadn't yet had a chance to have a word with Julie Murray to ask her for financial support. They had had little time to converse since Julie's second escape bid. In Julie's absence, her bed in Bridie's dormitory had been given over to a new penitent, and Julie, on her return, was transferred to St Teresa's dormitory. And although Julie was not ill treated in any way on her return she still had her hair cut off as a form of punishment. Which Bridie thought made Julie more cantankerous in dealing with those around her. To Bridie, however, she was as loyal as ever and they continued to meet whenever it was convenient.

As Bridie continued to iron a big heap of shirts, she asked herself what she should do about John Paschal's birthday. I think I'll put sixpence on Mother's Pride in the three thirty race, she mumbled to herself. After all, she thought, hadn't she picked winners before by closing her eyes and sticking a pin in the long list of runners. Mother's Pride somehow sounded like a good bet. She had read about it in last Sunday's newspaper, which had come in with a heap of dirty laundry. And she recalled Gerald O'Malley's parting words to her in Conly House. 'Always take a little gamble in life.'

But what if I lose? My son will have little or nothing for his birthday, she sighed as she folded up another ironed shirt to add to the twenty she had already done. And today was supposed to have been such a quiet day on account of the bishop's visit to the Magdalene tomorrow. Easy, me arse, she thought. It gets bloody harder by the day. If only I had five shillings, I'd buy John Paschal a pair of black patent shoes. No, they would be too dear. Maybe, I'll buy a nice pair of white socks, a shirt and tie, and some sweets instead. Oh, and I mustn't forget the lucky bags. I have the two shillings Sister Philomena gave me, my own sixpence that I found in the lining of that coat and if I can get the two shillings I know Julie has, then I'll have four and sixpence altogether. I hope she comes in soon because today's the only day I can get the van driver to buy the things I want – if I have the money.

Josephine Finn and Margaret Sherry were waist-deep in piles of bed linen from the City's hotels and seaside resorts. They were about to join Bridie across the room for a quick smoke and a chat when the portly figure of Julie Murray appeared at the door, accompanied by the Reverend Mother looking to see if any department was understaffed.

'Girls, how are you getting on?' asked the Reverend Mother in her dictatorial tone of voice. 'Bridie Rodgers! I thought you'd have those Inniscrone shirts finished by now. Tomorrow is the Lord's Day and, as you know, we try if at all possible not to work on the Sabbath. Miss Finn, what are you tittering about? Is it that you haven't enough work to do?' After a momentary silent pause she added, 'I think, Julie, there's not a lot for you to be doing around here. Perhaps Sister Philomena will find you something.'

Bridie, overhearing the remark, knew her opportunity to talk to Julie was lost unless she spoke up.

'Excuse me, Reverend Mother, I wonder could I have some help? I'm not feeling very good this morning,' said Bridie.

'What's wrong with you?'

'I have a bit of a pain in me side.'

'A pain in your side! Are you sure it's not from tittering or laughing?'

'No, Reverend Mother,' said Bridie.

'Perhaps we should all kneel down and say a decade of the rosary for Bridie Rodgers, who has a bit of a pain in her side. Will we do that, Miss Rodgers?'

'No, Reverend Mother, there's no need.'

'There's no need! Well, then, let's be thankful for that. Who would you like to help you iron out your problems?'

'I don't mind, Sister. Julie will be fine, if that's all right with you.'

'Julie Murray? How very strange that she should be standing right next to me. How very convenient that you two always seem to be together no matter where I go. Still, I'm glad that you didn't ask for His Grace the Archbishop, because he can't come in until tomorrow.'

After a slight pause she added, 'Girls, you have until about one o'clock to finish up here. Then it's down on your hands and knees. I want this place shining like a new pin for His Grace's visit in the morning. Go with Bridie Julie, and I'll see you later.'

The very minute the Mother Superior left them all alone, an air of comic relief filled the ironing room as Josephine Finn jumped straight on to a linen basket and began to imitate the Reverend Mother by draping a large white sheet over her head, while holding it firmly beneath her chin as she began, 'Perhaps we should all kneel down and say a decade of the rosary for Bridie Rodgers, who has a pain in her fanny. Will we do that, Bridie? No, Sister, there's no need,' said Josephine adopting the language to her own liking. 'Well, then, who do you suggest might help you sort out the pain? I don't mind, Sister, any oul' hairy Mick or Danny will do, if that's all right with you? How very strange. How convenient that you two always seem to be together no matter where I go. Girls, you have until one o'clock to get shagged. Now let's all kneel down and pray for Bridie Rodgers, who has a pain in her fanny that can only be cured by a lovely boy called Danny.'

Making an obscene gesture, Josephine suddenly broke into a lewd rendition of 'Danny Boy'.

O Danny Boy, the pain, the pain is awful.
From tit to tit, and all the way down.
My knickers are gone and now my flower is waiting,
'Tis you, 'tis you, will come and I will sighhhhhh,
But come you back and shag me once again . . .

Josephine's friends were so shocked at her powerful booming rendition, they ran to haul her off the basket before she got them all into trouble, though they couldn't help laughing. Still, some of them were terrified the Reverend Mother might have heard it and would punish them later for such filthy language. So they all knuckled down to work again in case the Mother Superior paid another surprise visit.

'Oh dear, oh dear! I think that Josephine Finn's for the birds,' said Julie, spreading a shirt on the ironing board. 'Anyway, how are you getting on? Have you much more to do?'

'Fine. I've only about another ten or twelve to do. We'll have them done before dinner, handy enough,' said Bridie, as she mentally prepared herself to ask Julie for the loan of her two shillings. 'You know, Julie, I was praying all morning that I'd see you around as I wanted to ask you a great favour. I hope you don't mind.'

'Not at all,' replied Julie, manoeuvring her ironing board so that they could have a nice chat while working together.

'You know it's John Paschal's birthday soon and I want to buy him a few things. I was wondering if you'd be kind enough to lend me the two shillings you got from the Reverend Mother. The few pounds I had when I came in are gone. What with gifts for Christmas and the odd packet of fags for myself I'm stone-broke. I'll help you with your own work when you're stuck and give you back the money the first chance I get.'

'Sure, I always give you ever'thin', an' then I'm left with nothin'.'

'I know that, dear,' said Bridie 'and I'm very grateful. But what can I do when the nuns never give me any money?'

'Sure, why don't you try and be nice to them, like me? Then they might give you something too.'

'Arrah! Do you hear what's talking? I'm working here like a slave, the same as you. And that's as nice as I ever want to be to them. I got two shillings last Christmas for a whole year's work, and nothing since. You know, Julie, I think it's so unfair the way some people get paid and other people get nothing,' answered Bridie, clamping down the iron vigorously on a white shirt in suspended rage.

'No disrespect to you or anyone else, Bridie, but sure, didn't the Reverend Mother herself say I was doing the work of two people. And that's *f*why I get the odd few bob,' said Julie.

Bridie felt as if Julie was implying something. She stopped ironing for a second and said, 'Julie, I don't doubt for one minute that you're the best worker in the Magdalene, but to be truthful I don't think that's why they give you the money.'

Julie too stopped ironing to look at Bridie in bewilderment. '*F*what do you mean?'

'You know well what I mean. I think it's because they feel guilty about the way they've ill-treated you. If I was you I wouldn't take a red shilling off them.'

'Sure, and you come beggin' me for money. *F*what are you tryin' to say?' asked Julie, getting up on her high horse.

'Ah! For God's sake! Doesn't the whole world know how they treated you after you tried to escape: cut your hair to the bone and belted you around the place! A week later they're giving you money and telling everyone that the sun shines out of your backside. Great worker, how are you! Isn't it the same—'

'Wait a minute,' interrupted Julie, trying to stem the verbal flow, but there was no stopping Bridie now that she had the bit between her teeth. 'No! No! It's the same thing with them other two up in St Teresa's. Only the other day they belted them black and blue for trying to get out. And from what I hear now the same two girls are being humoured with fine pieces of silver.'

Julie, who was listening in embarrassed rage, suddenly turned on Bridie in earnest.

'How dare you talk to me like that? Who do you think you are? Sure, I should never have been in here in the first place, truckin' with the likes of you. At least I've a home and a mother, when you don't even know ƒwhere you came from. You have a child and you're not able to look after it. Sure, only for the nuns you'd . . . you'd die with the hunger. You're like a beggar; you're always cadgin' off someone every minute and hour of the day—'

'Well, maybe I am always cadging,' interjected Bridie, 'but at least I could never be accused of stealing anything.'

'Oh, shut up! Shut up!' roared Julie, picking up a heap of ironed shirts and flinging the lot at Bridie. 'Here! Stuff your ironing; I never ever want to see you again.' She stormed out of the room and the other girls looked on in embarrassment.

They were upset that two of their closest friends should end up squabbling, particularly after Julie had come to Bridie's aid. Josephine made up her mind she'd go over to Bridie to find out what was happening, but first she'd let the dust settle.

Bridie felt at that moment as if she could have cut her tongue, such was her remorse for having said such things to Julie. She turned her back to hide the pain of what she had just done.

She felt so distressed she wanted to smash the iron against the wall; never to see an ironing board again; to be a thousand miles away from the nearest laundry. Instead she stood quietly pleading to herself: oh dear God and his blessed mother, what have I done? What in the name of God came over me? What will John Paschal think of me if he gets nothing for his birthday? How can I ever hope to see him again when I can't even do that much right?

Josephine, aware of Bridie's distress, came across the room and slipped her arm around her, saying, 'Cheer up, Bridie. Don't let it get you down. You'll soon make it up again.'

'Oh, Josephine, I don't think I'll ever be right! Everyone seems to be against me. The nuns if I haven't the shirts ready, and someone always wants the odd fag I sometimes manage to get off the van drivers. Even the Dublin gang blame me if I don't side with them and threaten the nuns.'

'Shee! Calm down, Bridie! Here's a chair. Sit down a minute. As I always say, Bridie, feck the nuns, feck the clothes and feck everyone else,' said Josephine authoritatively, as she placed a chair behind Bridie.

But Bridie refused to sit for fear one of the sisters would catch her.

'What will I do, Josephine? I worry so much about John Paschal. I could lose him, and then I'd have no one.'

'Here! Sit down a minute and be quiet. I've a small bit of a Woodbine. Here! Have a drag; Margaret will watch the door, while I get a light.'

'Margaret,' she called, 'have you a light?'

Quick as a flash, Margaret darted across to them with a small American lighter she'd found in the pocket of a dinner jacket and handed it to Josephine.

Then she ran over to the door to keep an eye, while Josephine said, 'Listen! You'll have to pull yourself together, lass, and not be falling out with your friends. We should all stick together and help each other. Anyway, what were you fighting about?'

'We weren't really fighting. It's just I asked Julie for the money. You know my son's birthday is coming up and I want to get him a few things.'

'Your son will be all right. He's in good hands, and if he's not, then there isn't a single thing you can do about it.'

'Oh, don't say that, Josephine. I'll have to send him something. He's only a child.'

'OK, OK, calm down; we're all friends here, remember! Now listen, Bridie, I've a lovely pair of white ankle socks. They're way too small for me; you can have them if you like. I was going to wear them for the Bishop's visit tomorrow. And anyway, if the truth was known he'd probably rather be looking at me oul' pink knickers than at my white ankle socks anytime.'

'Oh, Josephine, you're terrible! Better not let Peggy Neary hear you,' said Bridie more cheerfully as she began to pull herself together.

'Isn't it the truth? They say some of them fellas can be as randy as hell. Julie Murray reckons with the thick neck on some of them, they're fit to bull cows. Give me that fag till I have a drag before you have it all gone.'

Bridie gave her the fag, from which she inhaled quickly, before stamping it out on the floor and depositing it in a waste bin.

Then Josephine reached into her blouse, took out her Sacred Heart scapular and said, 'Here! You can have this sixpence. You know I don't really trust some of them bitches at my end of the dormitory, so I carry me money – when I have any – in my scapular,' she continued, handing Bridie a shiny new sixpenny piece. 'Buy what you can and I'll help you make up some sort of a parcel for your young fella. We'll get one of the drivers to post it.'

Bridie was so moved by Josephine's gesture she clasped Josephine's hand in hers, saying, 'Thanks, love. Someday, please

God, when we get out of here, I'll make it up to you. And that's a promise.'

'Ah, never mind. Isn't that what friends are for? I know you'd do the same for me.'

'Of course I would, dear, and I will. Listen, you'd better go back to work before the Reverend Mother comes back and catches us talking.'

'Oh, I suppose so.'

Then, turning round, Josephine asked, with a less than hopeful look on her face, 'Do you really believe we'll ever get out of this place?'

Bridie joined her hands and raised her eyes as she emphatically replied, 'Josephine, as sure as God above is my judge, cross my heart and hope to die, I'm getting out of here and I'm bringing two of my best friends with me; that's you and Julie. We may have our troubles, but that won't ever stop me.'

Josephine, smiled half-heartedly and said, 'Lord God, Bridie, if only I had your faith. If only.'

For what seemed like a lifetime, Bridie and Julie managed to avoid each other, their pride too great to acknowledge that their frail hearts were broken.

Bridie recalled almost every night before she went to sleep the memory of that day when Julie broke down while disclosing her terrible secret. She had kept her promise never once disclosing to anyone that Julie was a thief, until she had referred to it in that horrid argument over money. She now wished more than anything to heal the rift but couldn't bear the thought of apologising over something she thought was totally unfair. The fact that she had to beg and scrounge to enable her to send a few things to her son made it all the more painful that Julie, who had no child, received regular gifts of money from the Reverend Mother. It was, Bridie felt, as if the unmarried mothers were being punished for their sins.

Julie Murray too felt that she shouldn't apologise because as far as she was concerned Bridie Rodgers was too cocky and too proud to accept handouts from the nuns. Not only that, but she treated the nuns with contempt, except maybe that Sister Philomena one, whom she went out of her way to make an ass of, by claiming she needed her son's address.

Anyway, I'm fed up, she thought, listening to Bridie going on about her John Paschal. Sure, you'd think no one else in the world had a child but herself. I could have had one mesel' maybe, if only I had let Harry catch up with me that day in the meadow. He would surely have kissed me, and who knows, I might have ended up with twins. Wouldn't that be great? I'd have two and Bridie only the one. But the way she goes on and on about him, and them lucky bags, 'twould make you soft in the head. But sure, where's the use in me talking? I have no child, and amn't I as well to be giving the money to her to buy him somethin' as waste it on fancy lipstick that poor Harry will never see or that oul' rotten perfume that Josephine said would poison a stray dog? But I'll not apologise to Bridie. Never.

It was a week to the day almost when Bridie and Julie met face to face for the first time as they entered the long corridor. They dropped their heads simultaneously to deny the existence of each other as their hearts pounded heavily in their chests. Every move they made all week was in dread of coming face to face with each other, and of how they might react.

But now, as they were about to draw near, the pain and remorse was excruciating. Bridie looked furtively round to see if anyone was following. There was no one. She lifted her eyes just as they were about to pass each other, and to her dismay found Julie doing likewise. For an instant their eyes met and they froze in their strides, and for a split second they stared at each other before collapsing into each other's arms as their proud hearts melted, and they whispered sorry before kissing each other on the cheek.

'Listen, we'll meet after work,' Bridie said excitedly, breathing a deep sigh of relief that their broken hearts were now partially mended.

It was several weeks later, after a particularly violent fracas during which the nuns had to subdue one of the penitents forcibly and have her sent to Ballinasloe Mental Hospital that Julie decided to slip quietly away of an evening to seek refuge in the chapel. She wanted more than anything to sort out things in her head, because she was becoming even more depressed and disillusioned with life in the laundry. She wanted so desperately to be alone with her thoughts, to see if there was any hope at all for the future.

Having entered the chapel, she had to make believe she was saying the rosary because there were two nuns walking up and down the aisle, reading their breviaries. When at last they left her in peace, Julie stood up and began mooching around before stopping to look up critically at the crucifixion.

She sat down in the front seat and gazed up at the figure of Our Lord hanging there lifeless on the huge cross. For a long time she sat struggling to control her thoughts, asking herself why she wanted to come here. Finally, she admitted it was because she wanted to confront Our Lord; to talk to him face to face and ask him, Are you a real God at all? Are you? Sure, sometimes I think you're a fake. If you're real, *a grá*, why go on punishing me? Sure, haven't I suffered enough already? I've been here now for years and years. I'm wore out saying rosaries, and prayers for the dead, and going to Masses an' ever'thin'. *F*what am I doin' it for? For somethin' I did when I was a young one. I'm thirty-five now. I'm almost twenty-three years here; the best years of my life gone forever. Lord, she pleaded silently, looking at the wounded limbs of Our Lord on the cross, is it fair I've never known the love of a man, or will I ever know what it is to have children? There's Bridie – at least she has a son. She'll have someone when she grows old. All I seem to have is pain and sufferin'. Sure the pain of being called a hoor is shockin'. To think them young brats up on the wall call us hoors! Prostitutes! When I've never even had a man's thing in me. Oh, the scourge of them brats, calling us hoors and Maggies. For the life of me I can't understand how Bridie can laugh. She thinks it's funny. Sure, she's not right in the head, that one. 'They're only a shower of trumps,' says I, and do you know what she said then? 'Julie, they remind me of John Paschal.' Imagine! She said that. She said, 'Julie, I'd give anything to see that much of John Paschal. Anything! Just to see the whites of his eyes, even his little hands clutching the top of the wall.' Sure, there must be somethin' wrong with that lady. It's shocking the way some people think. Prostitutes! I wonder are we really prostitutes? Maybe we are: different kind of prostitutes. The girls from Dublin reckon prostitutes sell their bodies for sex because they can get no work or no man. But by selling their bodies, it's a sort of a job, and that way they can have any man they want. I don't think I'd ever sell my body. I'd do it for nothing. Lord, I'd give anything to know what it's like. Just to do it once. Sure, it must be the same as when I do it with me finger, only bigger. Some of the girls said 'twas smaller, but that anythin' was better than trying to do it on your own. Oh God! I'd give anythin' if only I had a man to love. Dublin Mary said half the prostitutes in Dublin ended up in jail, because they were too rough and dirty. Maybe that means I'm a prostitute too. Sure, amn't I locked up for years? God! Is that them trumps I hear at it again?

In the darkening silence of the chapel, Julie could hear the brazen calls of the carefree city youngsters as they lifted each other up on the high walls to shout obscenities into the Magdalene grounds: 'Up the Maggies! Up the Maggies! I'll give you a penny a look, three pence a go. Show us your knickers, Maggie?'

Julie, rising from her pew, shuffled her way to the centre

aisle and threw her hands in the air, shouting aloud in her distressed state. Dear God, do you know ƒwhat it is? I'm sick-a-ever'thin! Sick-a-nuns! Sick-a-priests! Sick-a-this stinking place! Sick-a-pain! Sick-a-sufferin'! Sick-of-being a penitent woman with cramps in me belly! Oh God! Oh God, I'm so sick of it all. And I have such a pain in me side, and me back, and blood leakin' from me fanny. Oh God! Will the curse ever end? She put a hand inside her coarse knickers, beneath her sanitary rag. She could feel the drip. Her curse was in full flow. She took out her hand and smelled the red menstrual blood on her fingers. It smelled as it always did, vile and disgusting: a mixture of blood and urine, and God knew ƒwhat else, she thought. She pulled a clean handkerchief from the sleeve of her cardigan and stuffed it down her knickers, remembering the embarrassment of one menstruation years ago when she got up from the dinner table. Imagine! I left a pool of blood on the seat. Sure, Lord, what could I do? I didn't think it was due for at least another day. I wonder did the other girls or nuns really know 'twas me? Sure, I hadn't time to wear the rags, and that oul' bitch the Reverend Mother lining us all up again' the wall, askin' which of us soiled our pants, leaving the blood on the seat for one of the chaste nuns to sit on; thereby destroying her sacred image. Image, me arse. I could feel my face goin' red because some of the girls were titterin'. I was full sure they were laughin' at me, until Dublin Mary told the Reverend Mother to shut up. She said that we were only human, and that a small drop of blood never kilt anyone. Oh Lord, to see the two of them rearing up. Mary said that if the Reverend Mother didn't shut her gob, she'd put her fingerprints up her fanny and see how she liked it. Sure the Reverend Mother gave her an almighty clatter; said, 'Stop that vile and disgusting language at once, before I report you to the bishop. How dare you use such foul language in God's house? It's just what I'd expect, coming from the likes of you.' And Mary screamed back, 'It may be vile an' disgustin', but 'tis the feckin' truth, you oul' cow.' Well, the Reverend Mother . . . I thought she'd knock her head off. Sure, they near kilt one another. God forgive me, but I enjoyed every minute of it. Especially when Mary lunged at the Reverend Mother. They were like two cats fighting. Sure, 'twas awful. And Mary screaming at us to help her. 'For Jazzus' sake, will yez help me and not be standing there like a bunch of gobshites.'

Oh, the language, sure, 'twas awful. I never heard anything like it. I suppose I should have stood up for Sister Stanislaus and the Reverend Mother, but sure, that crowd would kill one and I'd be worse off then. In a way, only for that Dublin crowd and Connemara Phil, them nuns would walk all over us. Sure, we'd all be murthered entirely. That Mary sure, she must be as hard as nails. Wouldn't give in or nothin'. Then she made up some dirty ditties and went round shoutin' them out in front of the nuns. They had to get shut-a-her in the end, because she got a can a paint out-a-the storeroom and painted one-a-the ditties on the wall. *F*what was it again? Lord, but 'twas great gas.

> There was an oul' nun from Magdalene
> Asked a bishop to have sex in the pavilion
> Said he, with a frown,
> It will cost half a crown,
> For a bishop's prick is one in a million.

Sure, we were laughin' for a week after it. Lord, I wish I could write like that. But sure, I'm good for nothin'. Look at Bridie, writin' ever' day. *F*what am I goin' to do at all? And *f*what am I doin' here *f*when I should be out the country, in a field with some gorgeous fellow kissin' me? And then he'd pull off me knickers and I'd open me legs and he'd roll over on top of me and squeeze me to death.

Sure, it must be pure heaven to be lookin' up at the sky and then to close your eyes and let him do it.

God, *f*what am I doin', sittin' here, thinkin' them horrible things? Amn't I supposed to be prayin' to Our Lord for my freedom? Oh dear God, haven't I asked you a thousand times to let me out-a-here? I'll ask you one more time, as I get down on my bended knees, to let me out-a-here.

Julie kneeled down in the silent, semi-darkness of the chapel, as a wave of depression took hold of her. Lamenting her wasted years and how she had messed up the wonderful opportunities presented to her when she managed to run away – twice – only to be apprehended and brought back because she hadn't kept her wits about her.

Oh God! Dear God, I think I'm finished. Sure there's no hope, no hope now. I must be an awful sinner to deserve this. Daddy! Daddy! Please! I beg of you, if you're in heaven to ask God for my forgiveness. Please ask him for my freedom. I beg of you, Dad! Please, I beg of you! Do it for me, because if you were alive now I know I would not be here. Sure, me mother must hate me. She must hate me rotten, because she never even wrote to me. Imagine. To leave me here, rottin' away. Please! Hear my prayers. Just once! Please! Please!

By now Julie's tortured thoughts caused her to tremble uncontrollably. She manoeuvred her heaving body so she could lie down comfortably on the seat, bury her head in her hands and let the tears flow. Soon she could feel the warm moist droplets stinging her cheeks, and the soiled unkempt strands of her shoulder-length hair clinging to her face. Only the echoing sound of horse-hoofs traversing the ancient city streets of Galway assailed the peaceful sanctuary of the convent chapel. And a little robin appeared, hopping unobtrusively from one seat to the next, as Julie's troubled mind carried her away on a tidal wave of emotion.

★　　★　　★

It was a glorious midsummer's eve in the picturesque village of Kilmaine as strapping farmers' sons pedalled furiously from the four corners of the parish, drawn like magnets to the distant sound of the carnival music that echoed over the warm landscape. Julie Murray stood nervously outside the huge white marquee waiting for her friend Josephine to arrive, but as yet there was no sign. She studied every lamp-lit bicycle pouring into town until her eyes began to sting from the constant glare. Men! Nearly all men, she sighed, as she watched them arrive in twos and threes, throwing their rusty steeds over the nearest wall with gay abandon before rushing headlong into the dance, so as to have the best chance to shift the cream of the crop. She already knew her own prospects were dwindling with each passing song, for the girls would now be standing four deep in their new shifts and silk stockings. She started to say a silent prayer that Josephine would not let her down, or that she herself would not be left to live at home, like an ancient wallflower, for the rest of her life.

Suddenly, as if by magic, Julie found herself being whisked out of the mob by strong hands. It was Harry, whom she worshipped like a God that had come to her rescue. It mattered not one iota where he came from, she told herself; she had him in her grasp now and she meant to hold on to him. Harry's sunburned face shone like a beacon. His strong white teeth seemed to enhance his rugged complexion, giving him the appearance of a Celtic warrior, and when he opened his mouth to speak and call her by her pet name, 'Pickles', she thought she'd pass out, such was her state of happiness.

'Pickles, I've never seen you looking so beautiful. It's great to see you again. Where have you been? I've not seen you in ages,' said Harry as he began to wheel her around the dance floor, which was already treacherous from an overdose of Lux snowflakes.

'I'm in Dublin, staying with my aunt, but I just love to come home for the caranal,' said Julie excitedly.

'I wish I'd seen you earlier, and we could have danced all night,' said Harry with a broad smile that stretched back to his sunburned ears.

The words were almost too much for Julie. In one fell swoop, Harry had managed to pluck her aching heartstrings, and at that precise moment she felt so delirious with pleasure she wanted to throw her head back and burst into song. If only he'd slow down, she thought.

'Harry!' she cried. 'Why are we going so fast?'

But Harry was oblivious as he waltzed her majestically to the strains of Victor Sylvester's famous dance band. Six uniformed musicians in navy pants and red dicky bows were swaying rhythmically as they blew their gleaming saxophones and trombones, blasting the swirling mass of dancers into a state of romantic hysteria. There must be all of seven hundred people here, thought Julie, as Harry and herself, already perspiring heavily, took a rest. She was aware of big shots' daughters wearing expensive dresses that were crucifying their waists, dancing nearby. They wore pleated frills and ball gowns that swished up around their waists as they spun on dainty legs. Their partners proud as peacocks, waltzed them round and round with strong, yet delicate movements, which made each couple look like fine porcelain figurines.

At the same time, gangly youths and ancient relics of bachelorhood stood all along the top end of the marquee, staring spellbound and toothless at the fleeting exposure of suspended stocking tops and naked flesh. Just when they were about to enjoy another show of leg, the band came to an abrupt halt and announced a short interlude.

Julie counted her blessings as she led her prize catch through the excited crowd to the mineral bar, where they siphoned bottles of Clada orange and agreed to leave after one more dance. Back on the dance floor, Julie slid her long slender arms lovingly around Harry's tall frame and rested her head against his chest, as they swayed gently to the music of 'Galway Bay'. For a moment she closed her eyes and began to recall her first meeting with Harry.

They had been childhood sweethearts a long, long time ago, and this now was going to be the happiest night of her life . . . Then Julie thought she heard someone calling her name.

'Julie Murray, Julie Murray.' She glanced over her shoulder and saw a shadow at the door. A man in black wearing a white collar approached her as the crowd parted to either side. A sudden wave of fear engulfed her as she recognised the parish priest, Father Gilhooley. He'd already taken on the appearance of a madman and was foaming profusely at the mouth as he started shouting at her and waving a huge blackthorn stick.

'How dare you, Miss Murray, destroy the good name of my parish and its people? I will not stand idly by and watch you cavorting and fornicating with some of Ireland's most respected citizens, thereby destroying their good name and character.'

Julie turned to Harry for support but, incredibly, he had disappeared and every Christian in the place was now staring at her. Father Gilhooley, with a hideous crown of white hair and black teeth, was closing in on her, brandishing his stick. Julie stood rooted to the ground, unable to move. She let out a blood-curdling scream, but the people around her just laughed as Father Gilhooley grabbed her firmly by the wrist and brought down the weight of the heavy blackthorn across her delicate shoulders. She fought to get out of his grasp, but his hand was like an ever-tightening vice, which made her scream hysterically. Just when she thought her wrist bone would crumble under the pressure and her bulging veins spurt jets of boiling blood, she broke free from his grasp.

For a few brief moments she lay in a warm saturated limbo as she tried to unravel the mystery of it all. Slowly the stark reality appeared before her eyes and what she saw was worse than death itself. For there was no Harry, no dance, no village carnival, but worst of all, there was no freedom. She stared transfixed at the dimly lit altar, where she'd come to pray. A feeling of sheer hopelessness came over her when she realised it had all been an illusion: a vile deception. For there really was no Harry with that loving smile: only the wicked ghost of Father Gilhooley, somewhere in the distant past.

She dragged her heaving body into an upright position on the hard wooden pew of the tiny chapel and saw the spot where she had been sleeping was awash with her tears. She could again feel the teardrops welling up in her eyes but was powerless to control them.

'Oh God,' she sobbed, 'I can't go on; I'll go insane. I'll kill myself.' Raising her head to look at the tabernacle, she whispered, 'God, I swear on my father's life, I'll kill myself if I can't get out of this place.'

Just then she heard the creaking of the heavy oak door. She looked round and saw Noreen Donnellan enter the chapel.

'Julie! Are you all right? We've been looking all over for you.'

But she realised the minute she opened her mouth that Julie was anything but all right. She'd been missing for over two hours. She could see that Julie had been crying over something.

Julie did not answer but stared transfixed as Noreen approached her in the seat.

'Won't you come back with me now and tell me what's bothering you? I promise I won't tell a sinner.'

Julie rose slowly to her feet and clung momentarily to her friend, before they both turned to shuffle awkwardly down the dimly lit aisle.

The friendly robin hopped before them and out the wide door to freedom.

CHAPTER TWELVE

NOREEN DONNELLAN REALLY began her escape bid the day she was transferred from slaving away in the big kitchen of the main laundry to the more peaceful surroundings of the nuns convent discreetly tucked away to the rear of the Magdalene Home.

Over the years, Noreen had listened to her many penitent friends' sad tales of brave escape attempts, and she had come to the conclusion that they had all failed because of poor planning, though she never had the heart to say this openly to them. Instead, she resolved to work extra hard and to align herself with some of the nuns. Furthermore, she let it be known that in time she wished to become a consecrated penitent. Such inmates were often regarded by the nuns as model penitents, who were prepared to give up their lives for the good of their fellow penitents and the Catholic Church. And after eleven years of dedicated service in the laundry, Noreen found herself transferred to the nuns' convent.

From Noreen's point of view the transformation was unreal. Gone were the hard days of continuously washing and peeling spuds for one hundred and fifty inmates, the endless hours of slaving over hot stoves, baking loaves upon loaves of bread.

Here in her new position she only had fifteen resident nuns to look after: a figure that often rose to twenty or more, particularly during the tourist season. But she always had the assistance of the housekeeper and two elderly penitents to help look after the many visiting nuns and priests who came from all over to pay court to the Sisters of Mercy in Galway.

Noreen Donnellan soon realised that she was better dressed and better fed than at any time in her entire life. Furthermore, because of her good work and reliability, she was often on the receiving end of little gifts of money: a shilling here, a sixpence there, with the odd two shillings or half-crown thrown in for good measure.

In her first month alone, she had saved ten shillings and didn't quite know what to do with it. Later still, when she had gathered five pounds, she began to realise that with proper planning and that kind of money she could perhaps buy her way out of the Magdalene.

Soon she became something of a nuns' pet and, being a trusted member of the convent staff, she was on occasion invited to escort one of the nuns to make substantial cash lodgements from the thriving laundry into the bank once or twice a week. On very rare occasions, she was sent urgently to the nearby post office for envelopes and stamps. And it was during one of these hurried trips that she decided to open a Post Office account. Besides, witnessing all those people in the city streets, going around on their bicycles or hopping on buses as if they hadn't a care in the world, made her more determined than ever to work on a master plan. She knew she had to get away. She'd get one chance, she told herself, and she'd better not make a hames of it. So every two or three weeks she continued to make lodgements to her account when she could, while at the same time making discreet enquiries about train and bus services to Dublin, Cork, Limerick and Sligo.

After ten months, when she considered she was ready to flee, she took full possession of her Post Office book so that she could admire her handy work and prepare herself in earnest for whatever lay ahead. She took the precaution of hiding her savings book under her own bedside locker, secure in the knowledge that no one would ever see it. That was until one morning while she was otherwise engaged the Reverend Mother ordered her staff to rearrange the furniture in some of the rooms. She was overseeing this when she spotted Noreen Donnellan's Post Office book on the floor as she moved her bedside locker to one side. Noreen was soon summoned to the superior's office in the main building to explain her actions.

'Miss Donnellan, I have in my possession a very interesting item. Can you confirm whether or not this Post Office book belongs to you?' asked the Reverend Mother, holding up the pale green book, which had Noreen's name clearly legible on the cover.

'Yes, Reverend Mother, it's mine.'

'And would you mind explaining to me how one of our supposedly forgotten, homeless penitents, in the care of the Magdalene Home, came to acquire the princely sum of nineteen pounds, ten shillings and sixpence?'

'I saved it,' replied Noreen nervously, somewhat dismayed at this sudden turn of events.

'Yes, I can see that. But what I want to know is, where did you get it?'

'Visitors, 'twas the visitors . . . mostly,' said Noreen, as she saw the Reverend Mother was studying her reaction like a judge might study a suspected thief.

'What? In ten months?'

'Yes, yes, Reverend Mother.'

'You're telling me you managed to save nineteen pounds, ten shillings and sixpence?'

'Yes, Reverend Mother, I swear by Almighty God, that he may look down on me this minute: yes, in the ten months.'

'And would you mind telling me why you saw fit to keep this a secret by hiding it under your locker?' said Sister Antonia, holding up the book.

'I was afraid it might get lost, yet.'

'Afraid it might get lost?'

'Yes, yes, Reverend Mother.'

The Reverend Mother was watching her young housemaid like a cat might watch a mouse, trying her best to unnerve her. One false move and she was ready to pounce.

'Visitors, mostly,' she repeated sarcastically. 'Looks like I should have been *charging them* for accommodation. Nineteen pounds, ten shillings and sixpence in fact!'

The Reverend Mother didn't for one moment believe Miss Donnellan. Nobody, she figured, could possibly amass so much money in so short a space of time. Then, leaning across the table, she began a line of cross-questioning she knew would make Miss Donnellan feel guilty as far as her secret account was concerned.

'Noreen, is it true that you wish to become a consecrated penitent?'

'Yes, Reverend Mother,' nodded Noreen nervously.

'Prepared to dedicate the rest of your life in the service of God, by looking after the welfare of the poor penitent women here in the Magdalene Home?'

'Yes, Reverend Mother. I've me name down already.'

'Yes, Noreen, I'm well aware of that, which is why I want you to give me one good reason why I should not confiscate this nineteen pounds, ten shillings and sixpence and have it sent immediately to help the poor, starving black babies of South Africa.'

This suggestion really shook Noreen. She had expected to be reprimanded, punished even. But this was the worst ever. After all her scrimping and saving she was about to be put back down where she had been all her life: destitute, both in mind and in spirit.

She kept her composure only because she had warned herself that major problems could arise; that sooner or later something was bound to go wrong, either inside or outside the Magdalene.

It always did. Now she was beginning to see at first-hand what it was really like to try to escape.

But Noreen figured she still had one ace up her sleeve: one desperate throw of the dice. She wanted more than anything else to see the Reverend Mother's reaction when she dropped her bombshell.

'It's . . . it's for me pension. I'm saving for me pension. Yet . . . when I'm old, don't you know.'

'Pension! Pension!' exclaimed the Reverend Mother, her bulging eyes clearly conveying the absurdity of it all. 'What do you know about pensions, Miss Donnellan? You'll be dead and long gone like myself, dear, by the time you'll need a pension. What a preposterous idea!'

For what seemed a long time the two women just sat staring at each other, like two bantam cocks.

'Who or what put that into your head?' asked the Reverend Mother in a subdued tone of voice as she sat back reflectively, in her great oak throne.

''Twas some of the penitents. They were worried, don't you know, that they'd have no money to live on . . . when they're old, yet. They wouldn't be able to work. They said they might be thrown out on the street, yet, don't you know. But I'll have me own money,' answered Noreen confidently, in the firm belief that for once the Reverend Mother had met her match – all the way from Winn-ams-town.

'Upon my word, Miss Donnellan! If I didn't know you better and the fact that you're very highly regarded by the sisters here, I'd say there's more to you than meets the eye. But seeing as God has granted you the wisdom to see the errors of your ways, and that you're about to become a consecrated penitent, willing to devote the rest of your life to those less well off than yourself . . . I'll give you the benefit of the doubt. Nevertheless, I'll take it upon myself to keep this book in my office for safe-keeping. Should you wish to add anything to it, then you must first get my permission. And you are not – I stress the word NOT – to leave the confines of this building unless accompanied at all times by one of the sisters. Is that clear?'

'Yes, Reverend Mother. 'Tis the best idea, yet. I'd be afraid it might get lost or stolen, don't you know.'

It was days before Noreen could make up her mind whether to shelve her plans for the time being or to go ahead. She also had the added embarrassment of having to ask the Reverend Mother for her book every time she decided to put some money into the Post Office. But soon she hit on the idea of opening a second account and leaving the new savings book at the post office. Then when things had settled down again, she'd reconsider her plan.

She had five pounds in her new account when she approached the Mother Superior early one Friday afternoon. She knew the Reverend Mother would be busy in her office finalising the weekly laundry bill.

Sister Antonia, curt and to the point, rummaged in her desk drawer for Noreen's book.

'How much are you putting in?'

'Two pounds, Reverend Mother,' replied Noreen.

'Who's going with you?'

'I don't know, yet. Probably Sister Margaretta.'

'Here, take those with you and ask her to post them for me, and don't forget to bring your book straight back,' said the Mother Superior, handing Noreen some letters, together with the precious Post Office book.

Noreen breathed a deep sigh of relief once she had the book in her hand. She knew, however she'd manage it, she wasn't going to let it out of sight again, at least not until she had her money safely in her hand. She figured the Reverend Mother might change the rules at the very last minute. Noreen knew she was really up against it and she'd have to devise a way of getting all her money out without any of the nuns seeing her.

And because she wasn't planning on having any of the nuns with her when she withdrew her savings, she came up with another bold plan.

'Sister Margaretta, is it all right if I nip out to the shop, yet? I've to get some writing paper for Bridie Rodgers. She wants to write to her son. She asked me yesterday, don't you know, but I forgot.'

'Yes, but try not to be too long.'

Sister Margaretta had no sooner given her permission than she realised what featherheads they both were. Weren't they going to the post office shortly, and couldn't they have done the two jobs at once? She went quickly to the door, but Noreen had vanished.

Noreen slipped out quickly, leaving the front door in the convent slightly ajar so she could slip back in again. Once outside she ran down to the post office, and it seemed to Noreen about an hour before she came out with the grand total of twenty-four pounds, ten shillings and sixpence in her possession. She slipped the notes into the lining of her skirt and ran all the way back to the Magdalene.

'Where have you been, Noreen? What kept you?' asked Sister Margaretta, a concerned look on her face. 'You know you're not supposed to go outside on your own.'

'Sorry, Sister, I forgot. 'Twas Bridie Rodgers kept me talking. She's thinking of becoming a consecrated penitent. She was asking could I go over and have a chat about it.'

'Bridie Rodgers?'

'Yes . . . yes. She thinks she'd like to join.'

'I wouldn't take that lady too seriously, if I were you. Are you ready? Where are the Reverend Mother's letters . . . ?'

Going back into the post office the second time, Noreen stood well back while Sister Margaretta completed her postal business. Then going straight up to the counter, Noreen nervously handed in the book to her old Post Office account, which now contained only half a crown, and lodged her two pounds. She had little choice but to make a lodgement in the presence of her minder, thereby covering her tracks should things go wrong.

On the way back to the convent, Noreen spoke to Sister Margaretta non-stop, as she was terrified Sister would ask to see her savings book, which had become the talk and envy of all the nuns in the convent since it had first been discovered.

With terrific agility Noreen managed to evade the Reverend Mother for the remainder of the evening, before going across the grounds to see her friend Bridie Rodgers. She had some startling news to tell her.

CHAPTER THIRTEEN

FOR ONCE, SOME of the inmates, the unmarried mothers, the wayward lassies and the destitute, were having a wonderful time. They were sitting in a large circle on the highly polished floor of the Sacred Heart dormitory, recalling their happiest childhood memories and their worst moments.

Out in the corridors, Noreen Donnellan was checking the dormitories, trying to locate Bridie, when she came upon the little gathering unexpectedly. They too were delighted to see Noreen and invited her to sit down and join them. As she did so she listened with interest to Bridie, who was in the middle of her spiel.

'. . . And I remember sitting on Sister Concepta's knee – she was the Reverend Mother out in Clifden – and she had the most beautiful voice I ever heard and was always playing the piano. One evening she sang a lovely song. 'Twas called "Where the Flowers Sweetly Grow", and do you know, for the life of me I can't think of a single word. But I'll never forget Sister Concepta, she was so kind to me.'

There was a brief lull, a silent pause from her audience as they tried to absorb the fact that there could be such a person in the whole wide world as a decent nun.

But before anyone could cast doubt on her judgement, Bridie continued, 'And I know the worst memory of all was the day they took my son away from me. I'll never forget that pain as long as I live, and if I ever get away from here, the first thing

I want to do is to be reunited with my son. Then I'd like nothing more than to meet a nice man and get married, and maybe some day, please God, I might meet my real mother and father.'

'Sure, don't we all. An' maybe if he has a biteen-a-money an' all, 'twon't go astray,' replied Julie Murray, good-humouredly after a strained silence.

Again they all laughed.

'Fair play to you, Murray, ye know how to look for a bargain down in Kilmaine,' said one of the girls, whilst another intervened to ask Bridie if that was the day she cut off her child's hair.

'Yes,' responded Bridie proudly. 'I still have it here.' She reached into her blouse to extract the precious item attached to her Sacred Heart scapular, which she had now guarded for twelve years.

'What are you going to do with it?' asked one of the girls, examining the lock of hair; trying to imagine that it once belonged to another human being living somewhere out there in the big wide world.

'Nothing. I just want to keep it in memory of our time together. You know it would have to be something very special, something extraordinary, for me to ever part with it. But I know a day will come when I'll give it away with a heart and a half, because then I'll have my precious son back.'

'Anyone else?' asked Julie, looking eagerly around to see if anyone else wanted to join in the conversation.

'Noreen, what about you? You haven't said anything,' urged Bridie.

Noreen only had one memory from her childhood, one that seemed to stretch over many years. She didn't really know if it qualified but was eager nevertheless to tell it, because her recollection would carry greater significance for Bridie as her son was now being reared in Williamstown where she herself was brought up.

So, turning to Bridie, she began hesitantly, 'Well, when I was down in Winn-ams-town – that's where I was before I came here – there was this man. Tom Tully was his name, and he used to come to our house to help out with the ploughing and the harvest, don't you know, yet. And the people I lived with were very mean. They'd leather the hell out-a-me if I took as much as a graineen-a-sugar or a thing. I was always starvin' and I'd be wake with the hunger, yet, don't you know. And when Tom and the workmen would come in from the fields for the dinner, I'd be sent out to the street to hold the horses by the head, in the freezing cold. I hadn't a shoe to me name, yet. And Tom would say, "Bring in that child there out-a-the-cold. The poor girleen'll be famished. That's no place for her in her bare feeteen, yet." And when I'd come in, me mother and father – I mean the people that reared me – would be fierce jealous, yet, because Tom would stick a fork into a thick piece-a-bacon, cut it up and say, "Here, take this, *a-gráeen*, and warm yourself up, yet. Then he'd make me sup a big mug-a-hot tay with loads and loads-a-sugar. He'd give me the whole dinner, so he would, yet. He had no children of his own, see. And he'd call me his little pet, yet. If I ever go back to Winn-ams-town, I'm going to see Tom Tully, so I am. Now that's all I have to say, yet.'

'He really sounds like a lovely man. I'd love to meet him,' said Bridie, 'and I'd tell him you were asking for him.'

'You can, yet.'

'I'm afraid I don't have very many happy memories,' said Lilly MacAlastair. 'But I remember one nasty shopkeeper who was rotten to me mother, God rest her soul. Do ye want to hear it?'

'Go on! go on!' urged Noreen.

'Of course we want to hear it,' answered Bridie, as Lilly hesitated because it brought back such an awful memory.

'Sure, haven't we till eight o'clock in the morning,' suggested Julie cheerfully.

'Anyway, there was this nasty shopkeeper,' began Lilly. 'I was only about ten or twelve at the time. Of course we hadn't two pennies to rub together, and you know at that time 'twas a great treat to get a couple of herrings of a Friday. If you could get two or three lovely fresh herrings, you were the bee's knees. Usually me mother would send me to the shop. But this evening we were both walking back from my aunt's house, as me father, God rest his soul, was only after being buried.'

Some of Lilly's friends on hearing this let out an audible sigh, and they hurriedly made the sign of the cross.

'Amen,' nodded Lilly. 'Well, we stopped when we saw this big box of herrings outside the shop window. And me mother pulled out an old newspaper she always had in her bag and picked out a decent lump of fish. And because that time they were all the same price – big or small – she started rummaging through the box for another good one. But I could see the shopkeeper looking out at us with a sour puss on him. So the next thing he comes out and says to me mother, "Listen, mam, 'tisn't your husband's cock you have in your hand now. No matter how much you play with them, they're not going to get any bigger. So just take as many as you want and go."'

'Aw, what a thing to say,' said Bridie, trying desperately to sound sympathetic but not fully understanding what it meant, as the rest of the gang began to gasp and titter and snigger before finally they all broke into peals of laughter. Even Bridie had to succumb to a fit of the shakes before normality was restored and Lilly could finish her story.

'Let her finish. And what did your poor mother say?' asked Bridie, looking around at the smirking faces, while still trying to control her own mirth.

'Ah, me poor mother was mortified, and could you blame her? Well, she threw the herring back in the box and said,

"Here, you can stick this one up your arse, and maybe in God it will choke you."'

At this point the girls lost all control of their senses. They laughed like they hadn't laughed in years. Even Lilly herself had great difficulty trying to convey the point she was making about her offended mother, coming home from the funeral.

'Ah, no, 'twas an awful thing to say, and as young as I was I knew he had upset my mother something awful, because my mother cried all the way home. Anyway, he's dead now, the lousy bastard: I hope he died choking.'

Noreen Donnellan thought the girls would never stop talking and laughing. She was anxious to get Bridie on her own, but she didn't want to make it obvious to the rest of the inmates that she had something to say to Bridie.

Bridie thought it strange how Noreen had just come along and joined in the fun. She had a feeling that maybe she wanted to talk to someone, so she kept a close eye on Noreen and, as if reading each other's minds, they both signalled with a flick of their eyes to move out.

Noreen Donnellan excused herself while Bridie offered to walk her to the end of the corridor. They started walking slowly, linking arms with each other like sisters.

Then, when Noreen thought it was safe she turned to Bridie and whispered, 'I've something important to tell you. Promise you won't say a word, yet.'

'I promise,' said Bridie, wondering what was so urgent and why Noreen had to always say that silly word 'yet'.

'I'm leaving in the morning, with God's help. I've been planning it for over a year.'

'Over a year!' said Bridie in dismay.

'Yes. I've saved more than twenty-four pounds and I'm going, yet.'

'Twenty-four pounds!' exclaimed Bridie in astonishment. 'But how?'

'Shush' urged Noreen, putting her finger to her lips, as her small, childlike frame seemed to be dwarfed by Bridie, who was only about five foot five. 'They'll hear us, yet.'

'But how . . . ?'

'Listen, I haven't time. I told Sister Margaretta I was calling over to visit some friends, yet. They'll be expecting me back any minute. I'll tell you again. If I manage to get away, I'm going down to Dublin, or England, yet. I'll write a letter to you and post it to Mr Hehir, the van driver. He lives across the road in Mary Magdalene Terrace, number fifteen. He'll pass the letter on. He doesn't know yet because I haven't told him. Say nothing to him for three weeks. If there's no letter, don't you know, you'll have to ask 'im.'

'But how are you going to get out?' asked Bridie wondering if all this talk might be in Noreen's head.

'I don't know yet,' answered Noreen shrewdly, not wanting to give her game plan away – even to a friend. 'Won't you say a prayer for me, yet?'

'Of course I will,' answered Bridie. 'I'll pray that everything will be all right,' smiling to herself at the thought that Noreen was about to become a Houdini by vanishing into thin air.

God, she must be a biteen gone in the head, she thought. That lady would never manage to get out on her own. Their whispered conversation was curtailed at that point by the sound of the clanging brass bell as Sister Stanislaus entered the corridor and the penitents began fleeing in all directions back to their sleeping quarters. When Sister Stanislaus's back was turned, Bridie and Noreen hurriedly kissed and bid each other farewell.

'And don't forget to write, because I want to join you,' was Bridie's parting whisper.

Noreen had made up her mind several weeks ago that, if everything went according to plan, when the time came for her to leave the Magdalene she'd tell only one person: Bridie.

She wouldn't tell any of the other girls in the convent because, like herself, they were desperate to court favouritism and, although she wouldn't like to hear anything bad said about her work colleagues, she didn't really trust any of them. She knew that each had her own favourite sister, and if she told one of them she might just tell the nuns out of pure spite. Bridie was different; she was outside that circle. And although Noreen knew one or two of the nuns didn't like Bridie, she was very popular with the penitents. But still, Noreen decided she'd not tell Bridie more than she needed to know. While at the same time she felt they had a certain understanding on account of having come into the laundry on the same day. And now that Bridie's son was being reared in Williamstown, they had even more reason to trust each other.

Noreen Donnellan rose at the crack of dawn, much earlier than usual as she hadn't slept a wink all night. She was full of apprehension and riddled with guilt that she was about to commit a major crime. In a few hours, if she managed to get away, she'd be a wanted criminal, sought by Sergeant Ruane here, there and everywhere.

She tried hard to reason with herself that she was entitled to her freedom, and at twenty-seven years of age still had a chance to start a new life.

But her mind kept wandering back to the fact that she had told so many lies, making fools of the nuns by asking them to consider her to become a consecrated penitent, prepared to dedicate her life to the service of God and to looking after those around her.

After twisting and turning all night, she managed to convince herself that she was doing the right thing. If she didn't see it through now, she might regret it for the rest of her life. She knew failure carried a very high price. If she were apprehended, she'd probably be forever carrying out menial jobs like scrubbing floors all day, or washing up in the kitchen. She'd have her mouse-like hair shaved off and be whipped within an inch of her life by the Reverend Mother, whom she had fooled up to the whites of her eyes.

When she got up, she made a big pot of stir-about, put on the fires, set the tables and did all the usual things before going to Mass, only this time she ate a big feed of porridge in preparation for the long journey ahead.

At early morning Mass she could hardly wait to carry out her last task, one for which she received special dispensation from the priest and nuns: to leave Mass directly after Holy Communion and return quickly to the convent to make the tea. Seven small pots of tea she had to brew, regular as clock-work every morning, so that when the Sisters returned from Mass, the tea was already on the table.

Rushing back from Mass, Noreen attempted to make the tea but was so nervous she failed to complete her task, fearing she would be too late for the train. Instead of finishing the tea, she went straight into the Reverend Mother's private room and removed the spare front door key, which she had previously identified. Grabbing her own coat, she left all her personal belongings behind in her room, together with a hastily written note on her bedside locker: 'Gone to Winnamstown for the day. See you this evening.'

Making her way hurriedly to the reception desk at the front end of the laundry, where the public left their washing, Noreen managed with great difficulty to open the heavy oak door out on to the street and lock it behind her. She scurried like a rat across the road and into the station, where she knew, if the convent clock was right, the Dublin train would be leaving any minute: that's if it hadn't already left. The thought was unbearable.

Fortunately the train was still there. She had about five minutes to spare, she told herself as she queued for her ticket. Miraculously the queue disappeared as people fled with their luggage, and in no time she was doing likewise.

And as the Dublin train pulled out of Ceannt Station, she was filled with such elation on the one hand, and fear of being apprehended on the other, she spewed her guts up before she even reached Athenry.

After what seemed like an eternity to Noreen, the train finally arrived in Dublin's Westland Row Station and from there she made her way via taxi to an address in Phibsboro she remembered from her youth. The woman of the house in Phibsboro was a distant relative of her foster parents in Williamstown, whom Noreen suspected regarded her favourably.

Noreen was going straight in the gate when she met the lady of the house coming out. After a lengthy explanation the woman turned round, put the key back in the door and invited Noreen into her home – where Noreen quickly removed her grey coat and gave a deep sigh of relief that after twelve years' service with the Sisters of Mercy in Galway, she was a free woman. At last!

CHAPTER FOURTEEN

B RIDIE READ THE letter and disposed of it immediately for
fear anyone else might see it, particularly the nuns. As Noreen
didn't leave a forwarding address, there was no reason to keep it.
Noreen said she would write to Bridie again when the dust had
settled, and tell her everything. Noreen was in Dublin but, by
the sound of things, she might be going to England.

I just pray to the Lord that she keeps in touch, thought
Bridie, because I need somewhere to go if I ever manage to
get away from here.

Letters were something Bridie treasured above all. She wrote
every single week to John Paschal and his guardians, Mr and
Mrs O'Brien, pestering them to bring him in to see her. All
of these letters had to go through the Reverend Mother's office
unsealed, so that they could be censored before being posted.
Bridie was forever praising the nuns and saying how much she
liked the place, knowing the nuns would be reading that.

When the letters eventually arrived, the O'Briens were
convinced that Bridie Rodgers was a bit touched in the head,
because so much of her correspondence was unreadable or had
words blacked out. To Mr and Mrs O'Brien, many of the letters
made no sense at all. Likewise, their replies going into the
Magdalene Home to Bridie were steamed open and similar
action was taken. Occasionally some of these letters were considered inappropriate and disposed of immediately.

For years Bridie had been hankering for a visit from her

son, but to no avail. Despite this, she continued to write letter after letter, begging for a visit from her son until one summer's evening her pleas got a rare mention in the O'Brien household.

The O'Briens were seated either side of the cosy turf fire, both lost in worlds of their own. Edward was sitting quietly, smoking his crooked stemmed pipe while reading *Treasure Island*, courtesy of John Paschal's school library. His wife, Catherine, or 'Kate' as she liked to be called, was equally quiet, her knitting needles clicking rhythmically away while she plotted her move.

'You know, I was thinking maybe we should hire a hackney car and bring that fella up to see Bridie, his mother. After all, it's the least we can do.'

But Edward was a million miles away, and his only response was to grunt, for he hated to be disturbed while reading.

'. . . God knows, 'twould be an act of charity to get her off our backs. I'm not able to be writing any more, and besides, I'm sick answering her letters and making excuses.'

'Hmm.'

''Tis all right for you and your "Hmm". You never write anyway, not while you have muggins here to do everything for you . . .'

'Hmm,' sighed Ned, peeved that even in his own house he could never get a minute's peace without herself continuously bedraggling him about something or other.

'You know he's thirteen now. Another couple of years and he'll be gone from us altogether.'

But still Edward's only response was to raise the tempo of his reading to denote his heartfelt annoyance at her interference. His reading became an audible whisper in an effort to silence his wife's endless tongue, which at times he secretly thought was the length of the street.

To Catherine, this was a clear signal that she was winning

her argument and that anything she suggested was more or less sanctioned by him. So she continued to gnaw at his subconscious in an effort to bring him to heel.

'. . . Of course we'll have to buy him a new suit. We can't have him going in there to that place looking like a tramp; what with his mother and the nuns looking at him and everything, he'll have to look his best.'

Edward moved uneasily in his chair. His reading came to an abrupt halt. He removed his spittle-stained pipe and spat into the fire, saying angrily, 'I don't know in the light of Jesus how that tongue of yours can stick it!'

Catherine's knitting needles, which were going at a nice steady pace creating the sleeve of an Aran sweater, suddenly moved into overdrive, as she replied angrily, 'Arrah, God blast it! If one was waiting for the likes of you to do anything, one would be waiting a long, long time.'

Edward, peeved at her accusation, stood up before turning his back to absorb a little comfort from the dying embers of the fire.

'And what's wrong with the suiteen he has?' he asked her.

Kate stopped knitting and looked at him in sheer exasperation.

'Well, look, you're the damnedest man I ever met! Can you not see that jacket of his is too small? Isn't it like a little waistcoat on him, or don't you realise that he's a growing lad? And what's more, if we don't bring him in to see her soon, his shoes will be too small for him and it's a brand new pair he'll need, on top of everything else.'

'Well,' replied Ned, with a resigned look, as he turned and spat into the fire again, 'I don't care what you do; it's up to yourself,' before deciding to put on his jacket and go out into the night.

Within days Mrs O'Brien gave instructions to John Paschal – who usually spent his evenings playing football or gallivanting, as she liked to call it – to write and tell his mother Bridie that he was coming in to see her. Soon.

For years John Paschal had lived in a confused state of mind in relation to his mother in Galway. He couldn't understand why he had to go on writing to her if she was his mother. Why couldn't he go and live with her? As far as he was concerned the whole thing was silly. Wasn't he already living with his mother, so how could he have another? Though there was a time when he thought he could vaguely remember running around with other children with one or two or three women looking after him. But then he thought that was probably another school. He wasn't sure of anything. And when he asked Mrs O'Brien why he had two mothers when everyone else in the world had only one, she told him he was too young yet. That he wouldn't understand. 'Maybe when you're sixteen, you'll understand better.'

Sixteen! But I'll be an old man, he thought. I'll be living in Dublin or England or maybe America. Because I'm definitely not staying on the land, even though my father would like me to. I'll go somewhere where I can see the pictures every Sunday night, and maybe if I'm lucky, get a job. I'll play for Galway. There is nothing else in this world I want more than to play football for Galway.

But now he had more exciting things to think about. He was going to Galway to see Bridie for the first time. He had to write and tell her now or Mammy would have his guts for garters.

Dear Bridie,
    Thank you very much for the lovely letter you sent me. I hope you are in good health as this leaves us all at present, thank God.
    The weather is good. We have the hay saved and some of the turf footed.

Now close your eyes for a second, as I have some good news for you. Mammy said to tell you we are going to Galway to see you on Saturday the 13th.

That is all the news I have for now. Goodbye and God Bless, and write soon.

From your son Paschal

He was in bed trying not to think about his visit to Galway. He wanted instead to finish reading *The Adventures of Huckleberry Finn*. But it was no use, no adventure, no matter how good, could be as exciting as travelling by car to Galway city for the very first time. He had never been in a bus, train or car in his entire life. So he decided instead to curl up beneath the blankets and visualise Kirrane's gleaming black hackney car pulling into the street. Its hidden powerful engine purring away beneath the bonnet as a spasmodic stream of white smoke trailed from its chrome exhaust while it waited especially to transport him all the way to Galway.

When at last the day came, he found to his great joy that he was really on a holiday. He didn't have to do any of the usual farmhouse chores. No milking the cows, feeding of the pigs, or bringing in the turf. Nothing.

'Eat up your breakfast now like a good lad and be ready to go when the hackney comes. We can't have you smelling like an oul' piss pot, and I after scrubbing the lard out of you,' said his mother.

Just when he thought he was fully kitted out in his brand-new suit, Mammy collared him and put a good lather of Brylcreem on his head to try to keep his hair in place and not have it falling into his eyes. And to crown it all, as it were, she placed a triangular-shaped white handkerchief in the top pocket of his suit. When he looked at himself in the mirror he saw that this major white symbol transformed him from a well-dressed country gossoon into a real townie and he felt awfully proud. All he could do now was sit by the window and wait.

The sun shone its brightest as the car sped up hill and down dale. John Paschal sat in the back seat with his mother. He absorbed the fragrant smell of the highly polished upholstery, and he craned his neck to study the chromium-plated circular dials of the dashboard. They were doing fifty miles an hour, but not for long.

Halfway past Tuam they met several herds of cattle, motor lorries and the longest nomadic convoy of gaily painted, horse-drawn tinkers' caravans he had ever seen. This was indeed a breath-taking sight. There were hundreds of piebald horses, donkeys, goats and ponies travelling along the road. And bringing up the rear was a mini-parade of shawl-clad women and what looked like their chimney-swept husbands in corduroy garb. They were seated in the midst of their horse-drawn carts surrounded by leg-bound hens, ducks, and geese as the horses went clippedy-clop, clippedy-clop along the road at a steady pace. Occasionally the chickens would flap their wings in a vain attempt to get away from the deafening sounds of whinnying horses, frisky, braying donkeys and wild-eyed, bleating goats. Then as Paschal knelt on the back seat of the car, looking back at the minuscule, fading spectacle, he was surprised to hear the driver say they were almost in Galway.

Meanwhile, Bridie fretted more and more each hour about her son's imminent arrival. Ever since she'd received John Paschal's letter and had its contents confirmed by the Reverend Mother, she worried about how he would react to her after all these years. Would she recognise him? Would he accept her as his real mother? What if he wasn't nice to her, and wouldn't give her a hug? The whole thing might be too much for him, she thought. He might even get frightened and turn away. Besides, Julie Murray,

Josephine Finn, Lilly MacAlastair, Margaret Sherry as well as Sister Philomena and the rest of the nuns, everyone wanted to meet John Paschal. The way things were going, she thought, she wouldn't get a look in at all herself. She had planned to give him something special. So when Sister Philomena gave her the gift of a few shillings to mark the special occasion, she was very happy indeed.

Suddenly all of Bridie's friends wanted to give him little gifts of their own to mark the occasion too. But Bridie was also worried about her hair, her clothes and her looks, until Sister Philomena surprised her by bringing her into her office for a clothes fitting. Soon everything was arranged.

Bridie could not believe that a bright new day was about to dawn. She was almost too afraid to think about it in case something happened to spoil her happiness – that she'd get sick or that John Paschal would get sick, or, worse still, get killed on the road before she could lay her eyes on him again.

Nervously she paced up and down the Magdalene grounds with her close friends. She had asked the nuns if they could take time off to be with her and to see John Paschal. It didn't matter anyway because all of the penitents were now on their lunch break, running around the place like excited school kids, though most of them were oblivious to Bridie's impending reunion with her son. Bridie prayed that the bell would soon go so that they couldn't all gawk when Mrs O'Brien introduced John Paschal to her. She wanted only her friends to be with her when the moment came. She was shaking like a leaf and asked Julie Murray for the second time if she had any more fags.

'For God's sake, will you slow down? Sure, you must be eatin' them,' said Julie as they paced up and down by the rear door of the laundry like a group of sentries.

But despite Julie's outward show of good humour, she was struggling to come to terms with the fact that Bridie Rodgers was lording it over them all. She was thinking: that one gets her own way no matter ƒwhat. She can write letters galore to her son and no one will say a word to her. How she managed to swindle John Paschal's address out of the nuns I'll never know. An' now they're letting him in to see her, if you don't mind. Sure, that one must be coddin' us all. There has to be some trickery involved. An' if I as much as try to run out the door or try to run away I'm near kilt: murthered so I am. The people around here – especially them nuns – they're gone soft in the head. They seem to think the sun shines out of that one's arse. 'Tis not fair, so it isn't.

'God Almighty, will he ever come?' asked Bridie, as she linked arms with her friend Julie and they continued to walk behind Lilly MacAlastair and Josephine Finn.

Suddenly, they were stopped in their tracks by the appearance of Sister Philomena, calling aloud from the rear door of the laundry, 'Where's Bridie Rodgers? Bridie Rodgers!'

Conflicting emotions surged through Julie's heart at the prospect of her friend's crowning glory. Look at her now, she thought, trottin' off after the nuns' every beck and call: off to meet her John Paschal. And all I'm left with is the devil; and all because no one cares. Sure, there's no justice at all in this wide world.

The nuns were trying to coach Bridie on how to behave, but she wasn't listening, merely bowing her head at everything they said. She too was in a world of her own. She thought of all the days and weeks and months and years when she had prayed for this moment. She remembered vividly how she had dreamed on countless occasions of seeing her son, on the thirteenth. Now it was about to become a reality. She knew it was the most significant number in her whole life. She was born on the thirteenth. Her son, John Paschal, was removed from her after the thirteenth month and now she was seeing him on the thirteenth day of July. Thirteen was her lucky number and always would be.

After a lengthy introduction with the various religious figures, John Paschal began to observe his impressive surroundings. The parlour where his mother and a group of nuns stood huddled together in whispered conversation was adorned with a beautiful array of antique furniture. Mini statues of St Joseph, black St Martin, and St Anthony adorned the massive Connemara marble fireplace, while huge religious pictures hung on the walls, amongst them a large blood-stained crucifix of Our Lord.

It was quite obvious to John Paschal that not only would one not be able to say a swear word to oneself while living here, one would not even think such a thing. These nuns were the holiest human beings he had ever seen. Their soft gentle voices proved their delicate minds could not withstand a minor swear word, let alone a real whopper, like he knew he was capable of delivering. He also knew from what his teachers had told him that priests and bishops, no matter how bad their behaviour in this life, were sure of a place in Heaven. So naturally one only had to take a look at these nuns to know that they too would all march straight into the kingdom of Heaven, while mere mortals like Mammy had to work hard night and day to redeem their souls.

John Paschal was, at that particular time, considering joining the priesthood for that reason alone. But somehow the idea never took root in his head; no matter how many times he told himself he'd like to help the black babies of South Africa, where it seemed you could buy a dozen oranges for a penny. A Jesuit priest visiting his school had divulged this extraordinary secret. He begged the boys not to tell anyone or the whole country would be rearing to join up, to become priests, so they could all go on the foreign missions. John Paschal recalled how he almost signed up there and then when the priest started describing the great problems they had with the vast quantities of grapes and bananas continuously falling from the tall trees, almost killing the natives. It seemed to John Paschal at that time as if everyone else, and especially the priests, had all the luck. And there they were now, before his very eyes, a bountiful bowl of ruby-red apples and mouth-a-peeling Transvaal oranges sitting majestically on the large mahogany table in the centre of the room, waiting to be devoured.

But his pangs of hunger were soon banished by a commotion at the door when a dark-haired woman, surrounded by a cloister of nuns, approached him with outstretched arms, pleading, 'Paschal! Paschal, dear, how are you?' Bridie threw her arms around him and held him for a moment in a vice-like grip.

John Paschal froze. He was unable to speak, even though his mother had instructed him to be on his best behaviour, to say 'yes, ma'am', and 'no, ma' am'. But how could he possibly do that now when a woman he'd never seen before was attempting to squeeze the life out of him, while a gang of dumbstruck nuns – as well as his mother – were watching him like hawks.

'Paschal! You look wonderful! You're so big! And you look so smart in your new suit and everything. Aren't you going to say anything?' said Bridie, holding him at arm's length.

Slowly, Paschal shook his head. No.

'Aren't you going to say "Hello" to your own mother? Paschal! Paschal! I'm your mother,' teased Bridie again.

But John Paschal said nothing. Instead he dropped his head in shame and mumbled to himself, 'No.' All he wanted to do was run away. Because all eyes were still on him, as if he were guilty of some major crime.

'Won't you say "Hello" to Bridie?' urged Mammy, annoyed that John Paschal wouldn't even open his gob; while at home, he'd talk the hind legs off an ass.

'Hello,' said John Paschal, because he knew he'd get the back of Mammy's hand and a right tongue-lashing when he got home if he didn't.

Aw!' exclaimed the nuns. 'Now, can't he talk. Perhaps some day he'll be a priest.'

'Lord, wouldn't that be wonderful?' added Kate O'Brien proudly. 'We'd all be blessed entirely,' while at the same time she was wondering if this whole thing was such a good idea after all.

Inwardly she'd recoiled in horror when she heard Bridie say, 'Paschal! Paschal! I'm your mother!' thinking to herself: you weren't much of a mother to him the day I rescued him from the home in Tuam, and you, miss, not having a penny to your name, a bit to put in your mouth nor a pot to piss in. As far as I'm concerned, he'll only ever have one mother and that's the one that reared him.

After some time his new mother took him on a tour of the picturesque grounds, with their colourful array of shrubs and flower-strewn pathways leading to Our Lady's Grotto.

It was only then that he really observed his new mother for the first time. She was tall and thin – thin as a wisp – with the most gorgeous head of black curly hair that was as sleek and shiny as a raven's wing. And when she spoke it was with a soft soothing voice that made him want to listen to her all day. She had beautiful big eyes with extraordinarily high cheekbones that gave her a Spanish look, he thought. And yet her face was as pale and white as the driven snow. This frightened him because he had never seen anyone so pale, except once when he went to a funeral with Mammy and he had to stand beside the coffin, pretending to pray, but had looked instead at the hideous ghostly appearance of the body. In a way, he thought, Bridie looked like that. She wore a long-sleeved silk blouse and a three-quarter-length navy pleated skirt. She was so thin and frail-looking he thought that she must be very ill, and that the place was some kind of a hospital. The word 'sanatorium' sprang to mind, but he didn't know what it meant. He had heard it used in whispered conversations at home, and was now of the opinion that this was such a place. But when his new mother put her arm about his shoulder and gave him a gentle hug as they walked around, he felt less afraid of her and her condition. But he still couldn't grasp what it was all about. It seemed as though he really had two mothers, the same as some of his school friends had two uncles and three aunts. He knew he had no aunts or uncles, but with this new addition to his family he couldn't wait to tell all his friends about it.

Bridie was at that moment endorsing his belief when she presented him with a small leather purse containing a brand-new pound note. He never had so much money before, and knew instantly that this was the same person who made all his birthdays come true at Christmas and Easter and every other day with her surprise parcels.

She was introducing him to all her friends, as they stood gawking in their long, white calico gowns and white hats, each of them giving him packets of sweets and bars of chocolate. And when Julie told Bridie he was the spitting image of her, her face lit up with a beaming smile. Then, as Bridie made him wave goodbye to all her friends, she led him back into the parlour once again.

'Paschal, dear, I want you to know I'll be praying every day for your continued good health and happiness,' she said, while giving him another long hug that he would never ever forget.

After supping lashings of tea from dainty china cups, together with an assortment of cakes and biscuits, the visitors were soon back in their chauffeur-driven car, frantically waving their last goodbyes. But this time there was no excitement on the road, no cattle, no nomadic tribe to colour the horizon. Nothing. Only dark clouds gathering as a strange silence filled the motor car, and a feeling of misconception and loneliness as John Paschal tried to comprehend the sudden appearance of a beautiful woman in his life – his mother.

Mother, he thought, why did you cry when I had to leave? And why does your face look so white? Why are you not like the rest of the people living out in the country? And why do you and all the other women in the Magdalene Home lead such strange lives?

Because of these and so many other unanswered questions, life for John Paschal would never be the same again.

CHAPTER FIFTEEN

As a result of Noreen Donnellan's successful escape bid, there was a serious rash of attempted breakouts from the home. All of them failed miserably because the nuns were ready for them and constantly on their guard.

It was a fierce blow to the Reverend Mother's pride that one of her most highly thought-of residents had managed to fool everyone – including herself – and got clean away. And unknown to Bridie Rodgers, her son's visit had almost come a cropper as a result of Noreen Donnellan's successful escape bid. And were it not for the fact that the Reverend Mother herself had given a personal commitment to her retired friend Sister Hortense in Tuam, allowing the visit of John Paschal to go ahead, then she would have cancelled the whole thing, fearing it to be just another ruse: an attempt by Bridie Rodgers to escape.

The Reverend Mother came to the conclusion that when an ungrateful penitent brat, such as Noreen Donnellan, was prepared to raise her right hand to God and swear that she wanted to become a consecrated penitent, then the rest of the inmates were fit for anything. They deserved no mercy. The cheek of that brat, she thought. Imagine! Imagine leaving a note like that! 'Gone to Winnamstown.' Winnamstown, my foot! Why leave such a silly note if she were going there? Clearly she never meant to go to Williamstown. Unfortunately it's too late now. I should have known she was up to no good: herself and her nineteen pounds, ten shillings and sixpence. God! What am I talking about? More like twenty-three or twenty-four pounds I expect by the time she left. It seems my Guardian Angel let me down after all. I knew I should have followed my own instincts and asked Sergeant Ruane to check the trains and buses that morning just in case she got on. Me waiting here like a fool for her to return. No. The mistake I made was handing her the savings book. God! When I think of the embarrassment of it all: having to report her to the Gardaí and the bishop as a missing person.

The Reverend Mother was still contemplating while she finished her cup of tea. I suppose I'm getting old, she thought, not able for this any more. A few short years ago I know what I'd have done: fleeced that lady good and proper and confiscated her little book. That would have taken the wind out of Miss Donnellan's sails, the ungrateful little brat. Oh, it makes my blood boil when I think of how good we were to that lady. And because of her, five more penitents thought they could make a run for it. But, thank goodness, I was ready and waiting. Imagine if they broke out, I'd probably be transferred to Dublin or Cork. Sure, where's the use in crying now? But the next one that tries to escape from the Magdalene is in for a rude awakening.

Peggy Neary came hurriedly out of the kitchen, carrying a small pot of Irish stew. She managed to slip quietly away from her real task of washing up, so she could be the first to relay the news. She knew that Sergeant Ruane was very highly regarded by most of the nuns, and in particular the Reverend Mother, whose close friendship with him she long suspected was one of an unhealthy nature. Nevertheless, Peggy was on the side of Church and State, and only too happy to align herself with the Reverend Mother in her admiration of the notable sergeant.

She also knew that many of the penitents, or what she herself called 'country bitches', hated Sergeant Ruane with a vengeance, just because he gave them a good lathering if they tried to escape from the Magdalene.

When Peggy reached the long tables in the centre of the dining hall she called out, 'Anyone for more stew?'

Immediately, there was a chorus of requests.

Bridie Rodgers called out, 'Have you any more bread? I'd love another cut, because there's nothing in this stew but peas.'

Peggy ignored the jibe and instead shouted back into the kitchen, 'Another slice of bread for Bridie Rodgers. No! Make that three. No! Four. Four more slices for tables seven and nine.'

Then, making her way over to Bridie, she lowered her head and whispered, 'Did you hear about Sergeant Ruane?'

For a brief moment Bridie was perplexed as she tried to recollect anyone having escaped or gone missing. Then the awful thought struck her.

'Oh God, don't say it's Noreen. She hasn't been caught, has she?'

'Arrah, what's wrong with you?' said Peggy, giving Bridie a playful dig of her elbow. 'Noreen's long gone, and well you know it. It's Sergeant Ruane. He's dead. He was killed yesterday. Run over by a bus. The poor man's as dead as a maggot.'

'What?' asked Bridie in total shock as the other penitents at the table began to crane their long necks to see if they were hearing things.

''Tis true. One of the drivers just told me. The Reverend Mother's beside herself. I couldn't make out what was wrong with her all morning. Promise me you'll not say a word, because some of them bitches over there,' she whispered, nodding her head to indicate the people at the back of the room, 'would dance on his grave and the poor man not buried yet.'

'But are you sure?' asked Bridie, still recovering from the shock, and half afraid it was just a wild rumour. To Bridie it seemed too good to be true. Though she never liked to hear a bad word about anyone, she had to admit to herself that Ruane was an evil thug and that perhaps this end was good enough for him.

'Here's your bread.'

'Thanks, Berni,' said Peggy, taking a slice of bread off the plate and handing it to Bridie. 'Amn't I after telling you he was knocked down. Killed stone dead,' said Peggy. 'Remember, blessed are those who have not seen but have believed. I have to go. I'll see you later. We'll go to chapel together and offer up a decade of the rosary.'

'If . . . if I have time,' answered Bridie hesitantly, as she didn't want to be seen associating with Peggy, who was widely regarded as a troublemaker and a gossip, though at the same time she didn't like to refuse. 'I'll ask Julie and Lilly – maybe they'd like to come too,' she added shrewdly, knowing Peggy didn't really care for her friends and wouldn't want to be seen dead in the same pew, never mind in their company.

Peggy half turned and gave Bridie a cutting glance as she dished out the last of the stew to a hungry penitent, saying, 'I don't mind your friend Julie, but that other toerag! Forget it.'

Then turning round, she headed straight for the kitchen, peeved that Bridie had rejected her reasonable request, and asking herself why she had even bothered to try to make friends with her. She's always the same: neither for you nor against you. Yet, she seems to have loads of friends. I just don't know how she does it.

Bridie sat finishing her dinner, mopping up the soggy stew with relish, while those around her asked if what they had heard was true. Bridie simply smiled and said, 'I don't know. If I was you, I'd take it like your dinner, with a good dose of salt.'

It was late that evening before Bridie, Julie and her friends had confirmation via one of the sisters that Sergeant Ruane had indeed been killed. At least Peggy was right in saying one thing, thought Bridie. Some of the penitents were indeed already dancing on his grave, and the poor man not yet buried.

For some weeks now, Josephine Finn had been sliding slowly but surely into the deep, dark throes of despair. This change in her personality went largely unnoticed by her friends and colleagues. They were always too preoccupied with thoughts and problems of their own to notice anyone else. Nobody knew that Josephine had been crying herself to sleep in the loneliness of the warm summer nights at the thought of a love lost. The shock of seeing Bridie's son coming into the home after twelve long years was almost too much to bear. It had awakened something deep inside of her. She felt as if someone had plunged a dagger through her heart because it brought home to her the awfulness of her own wasted years spent dreaming of a life outside the high stone walls of her imprisonment. Her life-long dream of going to London and Broadway, to meet her hero, Judy Garland, of seeing her name in big red lights, was seemingly so far away she thought, it was almost out of sight.

Unknown to herself, she had long ago eased the painful memories of her cruel parents and Cathal out of her head, concentrating all her energy instead on that foolish dream of becoming a major star, expecting all the time that the door to freedom would somehow magically open, or that a knight in shining armour, in the form of Mr Fincock from Dublin, would come to her rescue. Now she began to realise that it was all a pipe dream she had created to mask her own vanity, when all the time what she should really have been doing was plotting and planning her road to freedom, which in turn might have led to stardom.

Instead, she had resigned herself to her present fate for ever by giving up the fight. Look at Bridie, she thought. If I heard her say it once, I heard her say it a thousand times – how one day she'd be reunited with her son. And all I could think was, yeah, good for you, if you can settle for that, then so be it, but one day I'm going to be a star. Oh God! I've been such a fool, dreaming my life away. Even my own mother used to say, 'Josephine, you'll never come to anything, 'cause you're only a dreamer.'

Oh, why did John Paschal have to come to Bridie? He was just a baby the day the three of us came here, and he's thirteen or fourteen now. And Bridie is worried that in a year or two he'll leave home and she'll never see him again. But at least she had the pleasure of seeing him. To think, if only I'd run off with Cathal when we met in Tuam. We could have gone to England. We should have gone, I suppose; I *should* have run away from home. What's more, I should have made a run for it the day I was brought in here, because in the end nobody cares. Look at Julie Murray – at least she tried, twice. She'll surely get out yet. And look at Noreen – got away scot-free. Straight out the gate. I'll have to go too. I'll go straight out like that, because I can't stick this place another minute. Scrubbing floors and shirt collars, day in, day out, not to mention all the polishing and praying. And watching people fight over stupid things like rosary beads and food and money and clothes and cigarettes; even friends. But nobody fights over me, no one, because no one cares.

And as she lay awake in the early hours, thinking these horrible thoughts, she swung her bare white legs over the edge of the frail iron bed, and sighed wearily because she hadn't slept a wink all night. She knew dawn was already breaking and that soon they'd all be getting up and going down to the laundry to start another long day. Struck by the brightness of the early morning, she lifted her bedside chair, placed it quietly beside the tall window and climbed up on to the well-worn ledge so that she could peep out through the scratched spyholes of the painted glass. She could clearly see across the city rooftops the distant haze of an azure sky and hear the heart-warming chorus of songbirds nearby. For a long time she stood peering at the emerging blue sky of dawn and the drifting dark clouds rolling gently by. She began recalling the mythical words of her favourite song, which she had sung so many times for the penitents, especially at Christmas. Now she'd give almost anything, anything – even her own body – for some handsome fella to sing it to her. Then and only then could she ever believe in the lines of Judy Garland's song, that over the rainbow dreams really do come true.

She turned abruptly away from the vision and stepped down from the window-ledge. She'd had enough of dreams and rainbows, she told herself. She never ever wanted to hear that blasted song again. That's it, she decided, I'm leaving before this place kills me. Wouldn't it be a good one to climb over the wall and not say a word to anyone? No one knew Julie or Noreen were planning to escape, until they were gone. And now that Sergeant Ruane is dead, that's exactly what I'll do. I'll just vanish. Over the wall and I'm gone. It's as simple as that. I'll go to Dublin and find Mr Fincock and soon I'll be a star. I'm a good singer, I know, and in Dublin I'll be a real star. I'll ask Bridie and Julie for the loan of some money to buy perfume and cigarettes. They'll never deck it until it's too late, and by then I'll be gone. I'll be free.

Josephine sighed happily, as she climbed back into bed and dragged the ancient blankets up around her body. If only she could get some sleep now, she thought, before the excitement of this new day, then she'd really be elected.

'. . . Girls that reminds me, I was wondering if I could get the loan of a few bob off one of you. I want to get some nice perfume and make-up for the dance on Sunday. I've decided to treat myself to a good night out,' said Josephine to her friends, after she'd slipped away from the stifling heat and suds of the washroom. Julie and Bridie were only too glad to take a breather in the ironing room, the perspiration making the clothes stick to their bodies as they stood ironing garment after garment.

Julie and Bridie looked questioningly at Josephine. She never asked for money as a rule, and certainly never off Bridie because she knew all of her savings went on John Paschal.

'What dance? You mean . . . ?'

'Yeah! You know Sunday night! In the oul' hall, Lee O' . . . what's his name . . . Lee O'Byrne is playing. I heard it announced on the wireless.'

'Sure, I've only a shillin', if that's any good? You might get a man for that,' said Julie trying to inject a little humour into the conversation.

She didn't want to think about the money at all. She was fed up with people coming to her for the loan of fags, sweets, money, make-up and everything. You name it and they were after it, she thought. What harm, but half of them wastrels never gave it back.

'And I'm saving for Paschal's Christmas things. But I have two shillings. I'll lend that to you, if you promise me I can have it back soon.'

'Oh, I will! I will!' said Josephine eagerly.

'Besides, I think that perfume you're buying is awfully dear. Maybe the van drivers keep some of the money for themselves. Why don't you ask Sister Philomena to get it for you this time? You might get it cheaper?' said Bridie, reaching into the top of her blouse for the elusive purse, before handing Josephine the two shillings.

Josephine took the money and went back quickly to the washroom, ecstatic that everything was going according to plan. It was an ideal time to make a run for it, she thought, as she now had three shillings to her name.

As it was Tuesday, and last week's dirty washing was in full swing, young penitent girls were staggering to and fro up and down the long corridors under the weight of their trolleys, transporting the soggy masses of hotel linen to the big calenders in the drying room. Others were busy folding and stacking the freshly laundered curtains and drapes, ready to be sent over to dispatch for delivery. There, two of the nuns were overseeing the parcelling and speedy distribution of the city's laundry in time for the Galway races, where multitudes appeared overnight, eager to enjoy themselves and to seek accommodation in the city's hotels, guesthouses and private dwellings. The nuns knew they were being stretched to the pin of their collar to have everything washed and dried and delivered on schedule.

But that did not deter Josephine Finn. She slipped quietly away from her post by the sink, saying she was going to the lavatory, and disappeared instead out the rear exit and along by the side of the main building, towards Our Lady's Grotto. There she adopted a crouched position until she reached the nearest point to the high perimeter wall. Then she scurried across at an acute angle to the far corner of the floral garden, adjacent to the nuns' cemetery, where a large sycamore tree grew close to the wall.

She felt unbelievably calm as she stood for a moment to look around and see if anyone was watching. Perfect. It was just as she had planned. There wasn't a sinner to be seen anywhere as they were all too busy inside. The first city delivery having already gone out from dispatch, there was no prospect of any drivers or nuns approaching the main door, she thought.

All of a sudden she felt clumsy as she surveyed the most advantageous point from which to climb up on to the wall. She had anticipated that one good toehold in the ancient stonework and she'd reach the top of the wall. But as she gathered her long white gown and skirts around her, she wished she hadn't put on so many clothes.

Before going out to work that morning, Josephine had put

on an extra-large pair of knickers, an extra brassiere and two light jumpers, as well as her skirt and gown. She planned to remove the gown and cap the minute she was over the wall, and the extra clothing would come in handy when she was in Dublin.

Now she wasn't so sure if it was such a good idea. All morning she'd felt most uncomfortable working in all those extra clothes, but now she thought she'd suffocate and she hadn't even started to climb the wall yet. Placing one hand on the side of the tree and one hand high up on the wall, she levered herself upwards and spread her sore-infested legs to gain extra leverage. Then she wheeled her body round, and with a fierce struggle she managed to get a firm grip on the top of the wall and pulled herself up until her body lay resting across the top of it. She already knew the wall was very high from the outside, but when she looked down on to College Road and the sidewalk beneath her, she thought it was terrifying. The wall looked as if it was about to topple on to the sidewalk, as a result of being uprooted by the giant tree. She glanced instead across at the neat row of houses, which was called Mary Magdalene Terrace, and saw a little old lady, who was cleaning her window, stop and gawk at her. She just stood there staring as if frozen in time, holding up the lace curtain with her left hand, while her cleaning hand rested on the window. For a brief moment the two stared in bewilderment at each other, before Josephine realised she had to make up her mind quickly: turn round and go back or go ahead now and jump.

She looked to her left and saw that the wall appeared to take a slight turn left around a corner, not more than five yards away. If she jumped now, she thought, she'd better run off in that direction rather than go the other way, where she might run into one of the Sisters of Mercy collecting for charity.

She made up her mind. She'd have to jump now or face the prospect of a humiliating defeat, without having even tried to escape.

She manoeuvred her body sideways and adopted a sitting position ready to jump, aware that her every embarrassing move was being carefully watched by the old lady. She could already feel her cheeks flaming with embarrassment, especially with her having to swing her legs up and over the wall.

When she looked down she soon realised there was no way she could jump. It was too dangerous. She'd surely kill herself. But she was too far advanced now to turn back. Glancing quickly down, she couldn't even see the base of the wall, such was the angle. The only thing to do, she decided was to turn round and somehow lower her body gradually, seeking out a toehold before jumping the last few feet to freedom.

When at last she succeeded in turning herself round on the top of the wall, she got the land of her life. For in the twinkling of an eye she lost her grip and her body began to slither down the coarse stonework, which pushed her brassieres up off her breasts as she plummeted painfully to the ground. And because she landed so heavily on her feet, she fell backward, landing smack on her arse as her beautiful splayed legs flew into the air, exposing all her finery.

As if all that weren't bad enough, who should happen to be coming round the corner but two guards on their way to give evidence in the Galway Circuit Court. They immediately ran to her aid as a stunned Josephine moaned in agony. They lifted her up, helping her to her feet as she cried out, 'Oh, my feet! My feet!'

The guards, well aware of who she was and what her intentions were, carried her bodily to the main entrance of the Magdalene, despite her protests. They would have liked to help her escape, but they were duty-bound to do the right thing and return her to the Magdalene Home. The guards knew from experience that many of the inmates tried to escape by climbing over the wall. This was just another attempt.

The old lady continued to stare as if lost in something of a time warp as the heavy oak door opened in response to the doorbell and one of the reverend sisters invited Josephine and the guards to go right in.

The two guards escorted Josephine down to the infirmary ward where the nuns took care of her while the officers returned to their duty.

Soon Mother Superior appeared in the doorway and glowered for a moment at Josephine, lying on the bed.

'Well! Well! If it isn't Judy Garland herself! The latest escapee – or did you just pop out to the Galway races?' she said sarcastically, going to the foot of Josephine's bed. 'Aw, you poor thing. I suppose we'll have to get you a doctor.'

The Reverend Mother examined Josephine by grabbing hold of each leg and giving it a sharp twist to the left and right, much to Josephine's distress.

'If it's any consolation nothing appears to be broken, miss; more's the pity. It might have put manners on you, or better still, you might have landed on your head. That would surely have knocked a bit of sense into you and given you a bit of inspiration: something to think about 'cause, God knows, you're badly in need of it.'

Later the doctor was called. He confirmed that Josephine had no serious injuries. He said her hips and legs were severely bruised and they, together with her festering sores, would take a long time to heal.

The Reverend Mother's immediate response was to order the escapee's hair to be cut and her food rationed. Josephine remained in bed for several days, constantly moaning about her fate.

Julie and Bridie and a host of her friends came to visit her every day in an effort to cheer her up because they themselves were deeply affected by her sudden fall from grace, not to mention the loss of their regular songbird.

After a week she was back standing at her sink in the wash-room, but had little or no interest in scrubbing clothes. Instead she continued to moan about her misfortune and was then assigned by the Reverend Mother to carry out menial tasks. But Josephine point-blank refused to co-operate with anyone. After several rows with the sisters they decided she should see a doctor and he confirmed she was suffering from manic depression. He prescribed a course of medication and ordered her to take a complete rest.

Occasionally Sister Philomena would visit the infirmary ward to see how Josephine was, but each time Sister quickly turned away because of her own internal suffering. Not a day went by that she didn't recall the health inspector's visit and his desire to take Josephine to Dublin and to the theatre. But between listening to the Reverend Mother's lofty attitude and the priests' weekly sermon on man's wanton desire to consume the female flesh, she had done nothing for fear of doing the wrong thing. She knew now without a shadow of a doubt that she had done the wrong thing anyway, and it pained her even more.

Meanwhile, Bridie was desperate to have her two shillings back. She worried that she would never see it again. She did not want to ask Josephine to repay what she owed, but felt sure that she must still have the money, because she couldn't have spent it. She decided, she'd merely hint at it by saying she was looking forward to buying a few presents for John Paschal. If she got her money back it would make life so much easier, she thought. But the very minute she mentioned Paschal's name, Josephine flew into a rage.

'Ah, Bridie, will you shut up! I don't ever want to hear your boy's name again. Every time you open your mouth, it's John Paschal this, John Paschal that. You know you'd sicken anyone . . .'

'I'm sorry, love, I didn't mean to hurt your feelings—' began Bridie.

'Ah, you'd think no one in the world had a child but yourself. Cathal Swanick and I could have had half a dozen . . . and . . .'

'Ah, Josephine.'

'Ah, Josephine, me arse! 'Tis true. You'd think no one else in the wide earthly world had had a child but yourself. There are scores of women here who've had children and they never open their mouths about them.'

Bridie was disturbed and surprised at Josephine's onslaught. She was hurt by her suggestion that she spent too much time talking about her son, but she felt even more hurt by the realisation that her friend was still deeply disturbed in mind and spirit. Perhaps it was the medication, she thought. Nevertheless she would not let anyone talk to her like that.

'That may be so, but I'm different. I'll not—' she started to reply, but was again cut off in mid-sentence by Josephine, who looked as if she was going to have a fit as froth appeared at the corners of her mouth.

'How're you different? You think the sun shines out of your arse or something?'

'No, dear, I don't. And anyway, I'm not like that,' replied Bridie calmly, as she studied Josephine's contorted features. She knew her friend must be very down to talk like that to her. She'd have to try to help her; support her in her hour of need.

'Well then, shut up and leave me alone!' suggested Josephine.

But Bridie extended her hand and placed it tentatively on Josephine's, saying, 'I don't like to hear you talking like that. It's not like you at all to get upset. And, believe me, I know. You're feeling down, Josephine, after all you've been through. But we love you dearly. Many was the time when we were down, you cheered us up. If only you knew how much we've missed you at work. No other person in the laundry can cheer us up like you do: no one. I don't care what you say to me; you can call me all the names under the sun. You can tell me to buzz off because maybe I do go on a bit about John Paschal . . . too much for my own good.' Then giving her friend's hand a gentle squeeze she continued, 'But now it's you I'm thinking of. I want nothing more than to see you back on your feet and making us all happy again. Then we can plan for the future. I promised you once, if you remember, that I'd run away from here and that I'd bring two of my friends with me. And I intend to keep that promise,' she whispered.

'Oh, Bridie!' lamented Josephine, shaking her head. 'I . . . I have no future here. I fear God has deserted me in my hour of need and that I'll never know a day's freedom.' Taking a deep breath, she seized Bridie's hand in a vice-like grip, looking at her despairingly. 'Bridie, I don't want to die here. And if I do it will be because of a broken heart. Cathal Swanick and that other eejit from Dublin,' she started to babble, 'even my own mother . . . they all . . . deserted me.'

'Stop talking like that!' said Bridie, because this visit, this whole conversation, was too depressing. Soon she'd start to feel just as bad herself, she thought. And seeing Josephine's blotched, tear-stained face and red-rimmed eyes, she leaned over and kissed her lightly on the forehead, adding, 'Listen, love, you'll have to learn to pull yourself together and stop your raving. And the only one who can do it is you. I'll help you to start by going down to the kitchen and making you a nice cup of tea, with a thick cut of bread and lots of jam. Wouldn't you like that?'

The Reverend Mother came quickly into the ward, and saw Bridie huddled over Josephine's bed; the two of them in deep conversation.

'Bridie Rodgers, have you nothing better to do than going around disturbing my patients?'

'Sorry, Reverend Mother,' said Bridie as she bid Josephine

goodbye and the Reverend Mother continued on her rounds, visiting the sick and healing the afflicted. But Bridie had made up her mind: she'd be back with the tea and bread however she'd manage it. As far as she was concerned, friends came first and, apart from Julie, she had no better friend than Josephine.

CHAPTER SIXTEEN

J ULIE MURRAY WOKE from her slumber and slowly rummaged through her bedside locker for her toiletries. She could not find her towel. It wasn't there. She stood for a moment to try to think, as the rest of the inmates too eased their aching limbs from the creaking wire-sprung mattresses in response to the ward sister's call. Julie's memory appeared to have gone blank, and for a brief moment her heart gave a frightening lurch at the thought that she could be losing her mind. She knew for certain that she had a towel of her own. But where was it? It wasn't in her locker or hanging on the bed-rail where it should be. But what really began to bother her was the fact that she couldn't remember if she'd had a wash at all this past week.

Of late she'd begun to take liberties with her personal hygiene and refused to wash along with everyone else whenever the mood struck her. She didn't dare tell anyone that this rare act of defiance gave her a thrill. It's the stupidity of it all, she was fond of saying to Bridie.

'Sure, aren't we doin' the same thin' day in, day out? Washin' our faces and cleanin' our arses, and no one takes a blind bit-a-notice?'

But try as she might, she could not now recall whether or not she had had a wash at all yesterday. And as she began to dig deep into the dark recesses of her mind, she knew she was having some kind of a mental block; a block that disturbed her. Finally it came to her as a sort of hazy image. Was it something to do

261

with a stolen coat or broken window below in Kilmaine? No, she sighed, but it was something like that: something very close. She had had some sort of a dream, she thought; something to do with home. That was it, she'd dreamed about home; about her mother. Her mother! Then she began to remember how she'd woken up during the night and promised herself she'd recollect all the glorious details first thing in the morning. Only now she couldn't remember a thing. Pity. It seemed such a peaceful, tranquil kind of dream, where birds sang and horsemen rode leisurely by through winding country lanes festooned on all sides with wild flowers and acres and acres of green fields and golden corn. It seemed as if she had been to some sort of a party. But that was all.

The dream was like all the ones she'd ever had before, lost for ever in the mists of time. In desperation she turned to ask Lilly if she'd seen her towel or if she might have it. But Lilly was already gone to the washroom.

The oul' fecker, Julie thought. That lady hardly gives herself time to piss: runnin' an' racin', tryin' to keep in with the nuns. Nuns, me arse! Sure, she'll soon have that Bridie Rodgers as bad as herself. Turning round, she saw Bridie coming towards her.

'Bridie, did I have a wash at all yesterday? For the life of me I can't remember a thing and I can't find me towel any*f*where.'

'Here! Isn't this it?' said Bridie, reaching forward to pick up the crumpled towel mixed in with the bedclothes.

'Sure, I knew I left it some*f*where. Do you know *f*what it is, I must be losin' me memory,' she tittered before adding wryly, 'I can't understand *f*why them nuns don't give us an extra towel, bad cess to them, instead of goin' round the country collectin' money for the black babies. Sure *f*what good's a nice clean towel to that lot? Won't they still be as black as a pot?'

'You know 'tis true,' laughed Bridie, as they both went out the door. 'If the Reverend Mother hears you talking like that, you'll be the one as black as a pot.'

But the Reverend Mother, like everyone else, had a lot on her mind that morning. For some time she'd been suffering from aches and pains, which she'd put down to a form of creeping arthritis. But when she began to feel faint on more than one occasion she had to succumb and go to the doctor. The doctor gave her a stark warning.

'Sister, I don't wish to alarm you, but unless you step down from your position of authority, then I fear you'll fall down.'

Mother Superior didn't respond too well to that analysis as the reality that she was no longer able to cope with life's everyday woes had only slowly begun to dawn on her. But what bothered her most was who was going to replace her – if and when she retired. Who would she recommend or appoint as the new Mother Superior. Sister Stanislaus was the obvious choice. But there were times when she felt she was too lenient with some of the penitents. And besides, the new generation of nuns coming through the convent seemed inferior in religious matters and far too casual in their approach to their elders. She herself had already caught two of the young novices talking in the refectory; about crossroads dances, of all things, and God knew what else. And the way they go around the convent with their heads in the clouds, you'd swear they were going to a fancy-dress ball. Lord, between us and all harm, religion is not what it used to be, she sighed.

Today she faced a heavy work schedule, something she did not relish, but she had set aside today for tackling some of the thornier issues. Sitting in front of her were her two main advisors, Sister Stanislaus and Sister Philomena.

But first things first, she thought, I'll go through the mail. Who knows, there might be something to cheer me up while the sisters are sorting out their plan.

Sister Stanislaus and Sister Philomena had spent the best part of the week conducting a major survey into the running of the laundry as requested by the Reverend Mother. She informed them that His Grace, the bishop was looking for ways to help increase productivity in the laundry, in an effort to make it more profitable. He also wanted to raise money to help fund the proposed building of Galway's new cathedral and had turned to the Sisters of Mercy in the Magdalene Home Laundry, seeking their advice.

The Mother Superior held the sharply pointed letter opener in her right hand as she studied each envelope carefully, before deciding to slice it open. She was extremely proud of her ability to identify the source of each letter by its hand-written address and postmark. The letter she held at present seemed puzzling. The handwriting was indeed familiar, but for the life of her she could not put a name to the sender. And the postmark, New York, irritated her even more. Accepting defeat, she slit the envelope open with one clean thrust of her letter opener.

Dear Reverend Mother,

Thank you so much for your kind letter, which I received some time ago. If only you knew how relieved and happy I was to learn of my sister Julie's continued good health and recovery.

As you are well aware, for some time I've been deeply concerned for her welfare. Therefore, on receiving your written confirmation as to her overall good health I considered it an appropriate time to request her permanent removal from your care. In order to help speed up the process I further took it upon myself to telephone His Grace, the bishop, at his residence in Galway. He said he would be more than willing to accede to my request; on the understanding that I sign the necessary release documents when removing her from the Magdalene and that I, as her next of kin, take full responsibility as to her future wellbeing.

Furthermore, I would like to take this wonderful opportunity to thank you, Reverend Mother, most sincerely, together with all of your kind Sisters of Mercy staff in Galway for the care, dedication and devotion you have shown to Julie over a long number of years.

I've arranged to be in Galway city on Friday, 2 May, where I shall remove her from your care at midday. I shall, of course, speak to you by telephone prior to calling to see that everything is in order.

I do hope this will not inconvenience you in any way . . .

What in the name of God . . . ? thought the Reverend Mother, as she glanced up quickly at the religious calendar hanging on the back of her office door, as if she didn't already know the date. She felt her intestines heave, her stomach churn at the thought that the date was practically upon her, and that Sister Rosario had gone right over her head by corresponding directly with the bishop. Not just any bishop but her bishop!

Picking up the envelope again, she studied the postmark date in disbelief. She should have known. Three weeks in the post. 'Airmail, how are you?' she said beneath her breath; three lousy weeks.

Suddenly everything was up in a heap. She'd have to cancel this morning's meeting right away and talk instead to Julie Murray and have her fitted out with new clothes. More expense, she thought.

No! First she'd phone His Grace and demand to know why she wasn't informed about Sister Rosario's request to have her sister removed. Then she realised His Grace was probably out in Connemara somewhere, confirming school children, as his housekeeper had informed her earlier in the week that he had a very busy time ahead of him with confirmations and First Communions. She'd have to leave it and try later. Visibly shaken, the Reverend Mother buried her head in her large purple hands for a second in full view of Sister Stanislaus and Sister Philomena, who gave each other sideways glances before asking politely, 'Reverend Mother, is everything all right?'

The Mother Superior sprang to attention, before snapping, 'If you must know, it's not! Some people are so inconsiderate. I'm sorry, Sisters. Something very urgent has come about. I have no choice other than to leave this morning's business over for another day.'

As they began to leave the office, the Reverend Mother wished with all her heart they'd do so more quickly, as she did not want them to notice her state of anxiety.

When they had left, she again buried her head in her hands as she pleaded with God: Please, please don't let anybody disturb me for a few minutes.

Slowly gathering her thoughts, she sighed wearily. The doctor was right: I'm not able for this any more. Besides, I can't believe what's happening. Julie Murray about to walk free. That's surely the last straw. I never thought I'd see the day when my most able worker would be free to walk out on me; never thought I'd see the bishop accede to such an ill-considered request without first consulting with me. Undoubtedly Julie is the best worker I ever had and now she's being spirited away.

The Reverend Mother struggled to pull herself together. She leaned back in her favourite armchair because she knew it wouldn't be long before somebody disturbed her. They always did.

Picking up Sister Rosario's letter once more, she skipped through it. '. . . Friday, 2 May . . . from your care at midday'.

The cold-blooded cheek of that woman, she sighed. How could anybody be so inconsiderate as to go over my head like that? Flouting my authority. For all Sister Rosario knew, I could have been in South Africa. Then what would she do? Wait till I came back? Huh! Oh dear, oh dear. I don't know what the world is coming to. I must be getting old, I really must, when somebody can do that to me. What I need now is a strong cup of tea laced with a shot of whiskey. I'll ring down. I should have a drop left, she said to herself, as she pulled out the bottom drawer of her desk to reveal a small bottle of Powers whiskey hidden beneath the paperwork. For what seemed like the hundredth time in her life, she trotted out the same excuse to justify her actions: I know it's against my teaching, but if it was good enough for my father in times of stress, then it's certainly good enough for me.

Julie Murray dropped everything and went straight to the office at the Reverend Mother's request. She knocked on the glass-panelled door and went in, knowing full well that she was going to be asked to repair some gilt-edged garment belonging to some priest or bishop. 'Sure, I've performed more miracles than Our Lord,' she was fond of saying to Bridie after the completion of yet another delicate task for the Reverend Mother. 'You know I'd love to go and tell her, kiss me arse.' And Bridie would say, 'And why don't you, instead of you getting down on your knees every time and kissing hers?' And Peggy Neary, quietly listening nearby, would start preaching the same old mantra: 'Girls, please! Will ye stop using such foul language? Ye know well it's all for the good of the Catholic Church. Ye'll all go straight to hell if ye continue talking like that.' But Julie Murray loved to have the last word. 'Sure! An' if we do, can't we sit on the hob-a-hell warmin' our fannies while we're waiting for you?' Then everyone within earshot would break into peals of laughter as Peggy Neary fled the scene, hurriedly making the sign of the cross.

Now that Julie was sitting facing her boss she wasn't so sure that she'd been called in to do a special job after all. Her lady-ship has a sour look, she thought. God, have I been reported for usin' bad language again, or playin' tricks? That's the only other reason her ladyship sends for me.

But then Sister Antonia's sombre face broke into a faint smile. 'Well, Julie, how are you today?'

'I'm fine, Reverend Mother,' answered Julie nonchalantly, not knowing whether she was really good or bad.

'Well, well, my dear! You've been with us a long time!' said the Reverend Mother, lowering her eyes. 'How long has it been?'

Julie's first reaction was to wonder what all this fancy 'dear' business was about. Sure, that lady hardly ever said that. Then her mind moved swiftly to catch up with what the Reverend Mother was saying, but she could see that Sister Antonia looked wrecked.

Sure *f*what sort of a question is that? she asked herself. Gimme a minute until I think; how long has it been?

Julie, caught completely by surprise, hesitated for a long time. She knew every year, month, week and day of her imprisonment off by heart, but still she couldn't bring herself just to spit it out. It didn't seem right. She couldn't be there that long, she thought. It was as if she were afraid to tot up the total. But then she knew that she always added up her age and years in the Magdalene Home Laundry with important events that happened in her life. Things one could never forget. Mentally she began counting: I was fifteen years of age *f*when the priest put me here. I was eleven years here *f*when I escaped the first time. It was ten years after that *f*when I ran away again, that's twenty-one, and that was three years ago. Twenty-four, that's right.

'Twenty-four,' answered Julie, who was now coming to the conclusion, having deciphered the Reverend Mother's body language, that something good was about to happen. She was going to give her some money, or maybe make her a consecrated penitent. Only a handful of people were ever known to have received that honour. She began to push the latter from her head, deeming it too good to be true.

'Twenty-four years,' repeated Sister Antonia. 'Almost as long as myself. This is my thirtieth year here in Galway with the Sisters of Mercy,' she added proudly.

'Congratulations,' muttered Julie. She didn't know ƒwhat you were supposed to say to a nun who had spent that long on her knees, praying and shouting at them, and the devil knew ƒwhat.

'Well . . . needless to say, my dear, you've thought of freedom many, many times over the last twenty-four years,' said the Reverend Mother solemnly as she looked deeply into Julie's sea-green eyes, while thinking to herself what a loss she was going to be.

Julie sat staring at Sister Antonia. She was left speechless, wondering what she was supposed to say. If she agreed, she might be accused of trying to escape all the time, but on the other hand, ƒwhat sort of a statement was that?

Is she a biteen gone in the head, she wondered, or has she taken a supeen-a-the bottle. They say she does.

'Haven't you?' urged Sister Antonia.

'Yes,' croaked Julie in reply.

She was now positively afraid of what she might hear from the Reverend Mother. Maybe they were going to put her into a mental hospital. There was no knowing what this lady might do if she took it into her head. Then she saw the Reverend Mother's lips move again, as she said, 'Well, so have I! So have I!'

Christ, she must be leavin', thought Julie. Sure, as there's a grey rib on my head, she's leavin' and good riddance to her. And I beginnin' to think that maybe I'd get a few bob or somethin'.

Then Julie thought she detected a deepening sadness in the Reverend Mother's voice as her eyes began to drown slowly in tears. Don't say she's going to cry? She is. Glory bit-a-God Almighty, she's cryin'. Wait till the girls hear about this, thought Julie nervously as she watched the Reverend Mother's lower lip begin to quiver.

And as these mad thoughts went churning through Julie's head, the Reverend Mother reached out to her and said, 'Give me your hands, dear.'

Julie raised her hands tentatively, desperately afraid that something awful was about to happen. For a mere fraction of a second, she thought about getting up and running away, because whatever was wrong with the Reverend Mother, it wasn't good.

'You're leaving the Magdalene,' Sister Antonia whispered, as she took Julie's large white hands in her own great purple paws, holding them tightly as she struggled to control her emotions. But in spite of her best efforts a tiny tear cascaded down her cheek, washing away her shame; her years of guilt at having treated this penitent woman so appallingly. Continuing to look deep into Julie's eyes she realised for the very first time that this woman was made of iron. No other human being could have taken the punishment and work she had meted out to her. She shook Julie vigorously by the hands to jolt her back to a sense of reality.

'I said you're leaving us, dear. You've been granted your freedom. Your sister Kay – Sister Rosario – is taking you out of here tomorrow. Isn't that wonderful?' she whispered, trying to sound cheerful, though her soul was racked with pain and guilt.

During this time, Julie sat staring at the Reverend Mother in total shock and disbelief. She could not absorb or understand what the nun had just said. When first she heard the words 'You've been granted your freedom', a powerful surge of emotion rushed straight through her body. It started with her heart. It gave such a frightful lurch, it was almost like an electric shock: so powerful, it jumped violently in her chest, almost taking her breath away.

'You've been granted your freedom . . . You've been granted your freedom . . . Your sister Kay is taking you out . . . Your sister Kay is taking you out . . . Tomorrow . . . Tomorrow . . . Tomorrow.'

The words kept repeating themselves over and over again in her head. The mere thought that she was about to go free was both exhilarating and sickening all at the same time. Then Julie suddenly realised she had been in this situation so many times before. What if this was just another pipe dream? Her stomach heaved nauseously at that thought. She knew she had dreamed of a moment like this so many times, and had had so many false dawns, so many endless nightmares, she had given up all hope of ever being free.

It disturbed the Reverend Mother to see Julie's unchanging face, despite having given her such extraordinarily good news. Perhaps she was just overwhelmed, thought Sister Antonia. But what if Julie refused to leave? What if she was unable to accept that there was a *free* world out there, where people did as they pleased? The realisation struck her like an arrow that she herself was guilty of moulding this penitent woman into something resembling a zombie, a robotic figure now capable only of doing what she was programmed to do: scrub and wash; wash and scrub, and pray; pray and scrub and wash. She knew from her long years in the Magdalene Home Laundry and from her vast experience of human nature, that some penitent women, once regarded as the finest examples of womanhood, coming from the finest stock, were sooner or later reduced to pale shadows of their former selves. For the first time in her life, Sister Antonia clearly saw the enormity of her own sins. She now deeply regretted not having dealt with Julie in a more compassionate and humane way when she tried to run away. Perhaps it wasn't too late, she thought. She would try to make it up to her now, help to ease Julie's mind, before she left to go away for ever.

Standing up and coming out from behind her desk, she saw that Julie's bulging eyes followed her every move.

Extending her arms again she said in a faltering voice, 'Julie, you're free. From tomorrow morning, you'll be as free as the wind . . . as free as the birds in the air.'

The Reverend Mother stood facing Julie, an agonised look

upon her face, her arms still outstretched, waiting for Julie, who rose ever so slowly from her chair, never for one moment taking her eyes off the Reverend Mother until they were both firmly united in a warm, touching embrace. Sister Antonia patted Julie gently on the shoulder and said, 'I want you to know, Julie, that you've been a wonderful servant to God . . . and to me. I know that over the years I've been a hard taskmaster . . . at times. But you'll always be in my prayers.' Then, easing Julie away from her shoulder, she looked at her solemnly and pleaded, 'Julie, please forgive my faults and failings. I want you to pray for me. Pray to God for me to receive his forgiveness. Right now there's nothing more I want than God's forgiveness, because we're all sinners in the eyes of the Lord.'

After what seemed an eternity, Julie glanced briefly around the room, as if uncertain of her surroundings, before she turned once more to look at Sister's care-worn, pleading expression, and then in a barely audible whisper she said, 'I forgive.'

These two little words were more, much more than the Reverend Mother could ever have prayed for. She clasped Julie tightly to her bosom once more, and said, 'Thank you, dear! I hope and pray that God in his infinite wisdom will grant you a special place in heaven.'

Recovering her composure, she sat Julie Murray down and added joyously and with sincerity, 'Now that we have that little matter out of the way, we'll have ourselves a nice cup of tea. I've asked Sister Philomena to inform all of your friends in the laundry and tonight we'll have a little party in the recreational hall in your honour. Would you like that?'

Julie, still unsure whether or not it was all a dream, felt at that moment so utterly confused, she uttered, 'A party? Is it for me?'

'Yes, dear! Especially for you!'

The long years of confinement meant that Julie Murray could no longer accept anything said about freedom as fact. The only thing she could accept as reality was the here and now. If she was as free as Sister Antonia had just said, why couldn't she go now? What was she waiting for? Tomorrow?

Didn't me father once say 'tomorrow never comes'? If I go to bed tonight an' wake up in the mornin', sure, it'll all be forgotten. Fwhat will I do if all this oul' raimésh of birds and things turns out to be a cod; fwhat will I do then? As free as the birds . . . Your sister Kay . . . Sister Rosario is taking you out of here tomorrow. Sure, that sister-a-mine doesn't give two hoots. An' she in some oul' order hersel' over in America. Bridie, thought Julie excitedly, I'll go an' ask Bridie. Bridie an' Josephine will know *f*what to do. They'll know *f*whether 'tis true or not . . .

She rose from her chair and began to go towards the door.

'Where are you going?' asked the Reverend Mother, taken by surprise.

The words almost stopped Julie's heart. She froze in her tracks and placed her right hand on her chest as she turned to face Sister Antonia, terrified that she wasn't free after all.

'To see Bridie. I have to see Bridie,' she said, more out of fear than excitement. 'You said I could go home tomorrow.'

'Yes,' answered the Reverend Mother, seeing the disbelief still etched on Julie's face. 'It's true, you're going home tomorrow. But what about your tea, aren't you going to have a cup of tea? Sister Philomena's making it right now.'

Julie stood and stared. She didn't know what to do or say, and, seeing her dilemma, the Reverend Mother thought perhaps she'd be better off to let Julie go back down to Bridie and her friends, who by now would be well aware of Julie's imminent release.

Sister Antonia came from behind her desk to escort Julie back down to the laundry, but was met at the door by Sister Philomena bringing in the tea.

'Are you sure you won't have a cup?' asked the Reverend Mother, turning to Julie.

'I'd rather see Bridie.'

'Fine! Sister, would you ever be kind enough to stay here for a few minutes while I go down with Julie?'

When the Reverend Mother confirmed to Julie's disbelieving friends in the laundry what Sister Philomena had already told them – that Julie Murray was indeed leaving the laundry tomorrow – word spread rapidly through the entire institution.

In the wash house and the adjoining rooms, workers stood around in little groups whispering, while ageing penitents of nervous disposition stood peering questioningly from behind doors and curtains.

Only the brave and the bold came to congratulate Julie and enquire how such wonderful news had come to pass. But Julie, dazzled by all the attention, could hardly speak. She sat on a linen basket, while Bridie, Lilly, Josephine and Margaret Sherry tried to protect her by explaining to the others what was really happening.

Bridie herself hadn't yet had time to talk privately to Julie and was desperate for a word. Like most of the penitents, she couldn't come to terms with the fact that all of this had happened so quickly. If Julie was going to be gone by tomorrow, then she had better try to have a private conversation with her to arrange some secret code of correspondence. She had only ever had three letters from Noreen Donnellan, who was now over in England, and she felt somewhat cheated by this latest carry-on. She secretly thought that Noreen might have offered to help her escape by now. But now that Julie was about to leave she might have a better chance of escape through her, she thought. If Julie failed to support her, then she was really in trouble. Of all the girls in the laundry, Julie was her only true stalwart. They had been through so much together. That she was no longer going to be around the place didn't bear thinking about.

Bridie spotted Sister Stanislaus as she crossed the adjoining room. She ran out to her, calling, 'Sister! Sister! I was wondering if I could have the rest of the afternoon off, as it is Julie Murray's last day here?'

'Haven't you two got the evening long to be together? What about your work? Somebody has to do it and, from what I see, there's precious little of it being done at the moment.'

Bridie hesitated for a second. 'I know, but everyone will be around her this evening, blathering . . . and I thought if the two of us could be together . . . to go for a last walk . . .'

Sister Stanislaus's eyes widened even more at Bridie's gumption. She looked at her with renewed admiration. If there's one thing you have going for you, she thought to herself, it's fortitude.

'Whatever work you're supposed to be doing for Sister Philomena, will you please finish it, and then as far as I'm concerned you can have the rest of the afternoon off.'

'Oh, thank you, Sister. I'll pay you back later by helping out at the altar, or wherever you want,' said Bridie cheerfully.

Sister Stanislaus smiled sheepishly as she went about her business, while Bridie rushed back to finish her tasks and to tidy up, before escorting Julie away from the news mongers who were still turning up in droves to quiz her.

But Bridie did not have things her own way. Josephine and Lilly insisted on tagging along too. They felt as much a part of Julie's inner circle of friends as anybody else, despite Bridie's misgivings. They each wanted to know if she was going to America to live with her sister.

'Sure, I don't know anythin', except that she's comin' tomorrow. The devileen mightn't turn up at all,' she tittered nervously. 'America! I don't think I'd like America,' she added as her three friends fought like spoiled children for the right to link her arms while they walked around the back of Our Lady's Grotto, and round again to the front.

'I think we ought to kneel down and say a prayer to Our Lady for favours received,' said Julie.

'Don't forget, Julie, Our Lady is probably thanking you now for all the times you washed off the birds' you-know-what that landed on her head!' said Lilly, good-humouredly.

'Oh, yeah! There used to be loads of birdshite on her head and, Julie, you always got the job of washing it off,' said Josephine bluntly.

'But that was before they cut down that big tree,' said Bridie, trying not to deviate from the religious fervour she felt for Our Lady.

'And do you remember the time you had to kneel there half the night, saying fifteen decades of the rosary, because you asked the Reverend Mother was Our Lady the first unmarried mother?' said Lilly.

'Sure,' said Julie, remembering the brazenness of her youth. 'Wasn't I awful?'

'Why don't we make a wish now?' urged Bridie, trying to change the subject as they all knelt down giddily.

'What are we praying for so?' asked Lilly, 'That Julie will get herself a man with pucks of money?'

'And balls as big as a butcher's bag,' tittered Josephine, 'and . . . a fella that'll stay on top of her all night, and forget to get off.'

'Or better still, forget to take it out,' added Lilly, as they all started laughing uncontrollably, and Bridie glanced around nervously in case anyone saw them. She looked towards the convent and caught three elderly nuns looking out at them from the upstairs window.

The girls waved up at them and fell about the place with laughter. They hadn't had a giggle like this in ages and they were in no mood to end it now.

When they'd recovered their composure, having watched with glee the elderly nuns' continued observation of them, Julie said, 'Now, because this is my last day here, I think I'd like to put some flowers round Our Lady's statue. Blast you, will you give me a hand?' she urged as she began to pluck some flowers from the side of the garden, while the girls began to laugh once again at their own silliness.

Soon they had made a lovely heart-shaped arrangement of scented flowers at the base of the giant gilded statue, thereby adding colour and splendour to an already scenic shrine.

Later that evening, Julie and her friends gathered in the Great Hall, all mingling together and generally having a great time. They drank their tea from the finest bone-china cups as they and the Magdalene nuns chatted away blissfully while devouring an assortment of tinned biscuits and freshly baked scones. Then it was time for music. The ancient grand piano in the corner, though sadly out of tune and with one or two keys missing, was brought into use. Several people played tin whistles and accordions while others sang; but the best rendition of a song came from Josephine Finn. When asked to do something Josephine said that she never wanted to sing again now that her friend was leaving the Magdalene, but rather than be seen as a spoilsport, she'd sing one last song especially for Julie.

Coming towards the end of the night, Sister Stanislaus gave a few words on behalf of the Reverend Mother, who'd said good night and retired earlier. Then she asked Julie if she'd like to say a few words in return.

'No, I've nothin' . . . except to say thanks . . . to ever'one . . . for ever'thin',' she said before crumbling emotionally into the arms of her friends and turning her face away. But the round of applause she received from her fellow inmates said more about their love for her than a thousand words could have done.

When Julie and the rest of the penitents were locked in their dormitories for the night, Bridie, Josephine and Lilly stayed on talking and helping her to pack her personal possessions.

Earlier in the day Julie Murray had had very little to her name, but now she had loads of mementoes given to her by her many friends: a miniature silver-plated picture frame and photograph, several headscarves, earrings and bangles, pieces of crochet material such as place mats and tea cosies. And yet it all took no more than ten minutes to pack into the medium-sized, brand-new suitcase, together with some new clothes given to her by the Sisters of Mercy. Bridie gave Julie her one and only silk scarf that she actually wore to Mass every Sunday and which Julie had always admired. Bridie had bought it a long time ago while shopping in Tuam.

'What'll I do with all this stuff if that lady doesn't turn up?' asked Julie as she stood at the end of her bed, still trying to come to terms with the realism of it all.

'Have no fear, love,' said Bridie. 'If the Reverend Mother says she'll be here, then she'll be here. When John Paschal came to see me the nuns had it all arranged beforehand, so don't worry, it'll be the same with your sister.'

'Bridie, I hope you're right. Wouldn't I look a right *amadán* entirely, sittin', waitin', an' she not to turn up?' .

'She'll turn up,' Bridie reassured her again. 'Look! Are you going to write to us, or what? Or when can we expect to hear from you?'

'And in the honour of God, will you try to get us out?' urged Lilly.

'I'll do the best I can. But sure, I'm not out mesel' yet!' replied Julie.

'Well, when you do get out! Otherwise we might never see each other again,' said Josephine earnestly.

'And when will you write to me so?' asked Bridie, anxious to commit Julie to some sort of an arrangement.

'I'll write to Mr Hehir in a week or two. But sure, I don't know *f*where I'm going mesel'! It's hard to promise anything when I don't know *f*where I'll be,' answered Julie.

The four women went on talking in the semi-darkness of the dormitory late into the night. Some of the penitents complained about a lack of sleep due to all their talking, but they were more or less ignored.

Finally, the friends succumbed to what had been a long day, Bridie having arranged with one of her friends that they swap beds so that she could sleep near her Julie on this her last night in the home.

But Julie Murray did not sleep. She lay there thinking while trying to peer across the room at the steel-barred painted window, which was straight in front of her bed. She was far too excited and afraid to go to sleep in case she woke up in the morning and all this turned out to be a dream. Was all this really happening to her? She asked herself over and over; yes it was, she decided.

Tomorrow morning, I'll be as free as the birds, after twenty-four years. God! How many nights was that? Sure, it must be thousands. An' this is my last one. Then I'll be able to go *f*where I want. Buy *f*what I want. Imagine, I won't have to run away *f*when I see a guard or anythin'. I can even go home if I want. But sure, the neighbours will all be lookin' at me an' ever'thin', an' sayin', that's the one that stole the coat long ago, don't you remember? She stole a red coat from the shop. Oh God I'm not going back there ever, ever again. Arrah, hump the lot-a-them. They didn't worry about me . . . except me sister. At least she'd send an oul' card at Christmas. Isn't it wonderful, me own sister is takin' me out. I'll be like Bridie then, and John Paschal together again. An' janey mac, I'll be able to go dancin' an' ever'thin', an' get a man and sleep with him an' get married an' ever'thin'.

'Bridie, Bridie!' hissed Julie, in a low voice. 'Bridie, are you asleep?'

Bridie had nodded off, but she woke with a start and raised her head slightly to ask peevishly, 'What?'

'Bridie, it's me. Do you know *f*what?'

'What?'

'I'll be able to go and see Harry an' ever'thin'. An' I'm not runnin' away this time, if he comes after me,' she whispered aloud.

Bridie, half asleep, tried in vain to understand what Julie was on about.

'Harry . . . Harry who?'

'Harry! Sure, you don't be listenin'. Harry, the fella I was mad after when we used to meet at the bridgeen in Kilmaine ever'—'

'Oh, that Harry! I didn't know what you were on about. Listen, love, it's getting late and you have to be up early. So go to sleep. We'll talk about it in the morning. Good night.'

'Oh, good night! Might as well be talkin' to mesel'!' she sighed.

And as she slumped back on the pillow, and snuggled down once again, she began to dream of that glorious summer Sunday, long ago, when she'd have done just about anything for Harry's kiss. Just about anything. But didn't.

She stood at the door of St Teresa's dormitory and tried to interpret the momentary sounds of silence. She thought there was a strange atmosphere about the place. Everything seemed so quiet. She strained her ear and listened intently. She could just about make out the faint whirring sounds of the huge calender rollers and floor trolleys on the floor below.

She turned once more to pace up and down the dormitory, taking time to count all forty-nine beds, one of which had a sick penitent lying in it. All was quiet, except for the occasional moan out of Kitty Mulhare, the elderly woman who lay there. She'd been ill for days, but it was only in the vast stillness of the room that Julie saw her suffering for what it really was. She herself hadn't been alone like this in her own dormitory for a long time. With so many penitents lying on their beds resting of an evening, very little notice was taken of someone moaning or complaining, because someone was always moaning or complaining of a pain here or an ache there. But the sight of poor Kitty fading away there in bed frightened her like never before.

'Aaaaaah, aaaaaah! Water! Water!' moaned the sick penitent, raising a feeble hand.

Julie went to her aid, and held the old tarnished enamel mug to Kitty's parched lips as she struggled to swallow. The water dribbled down her sunken chin, and on to her frail chest. Julie tried to stem the flow with the soiled hand towel, and as she did so she felt the awful coldness of Kitty's seemingly lifeless hand, as she clutched hers in desperation.

'Sister! Sister!' she whispered in a barely audible voice, as her head sank back on the pillows and her eyes rolled up to heaven.

'This is Julie . . . Julie Murray. You remember me, don't you? Julie Murray.'

When she did not answer, Julie felt really frightened. She thought Kitty should be down in the infirmary, but she also knew that it was usually full and that sick penitents were being moved about all the time. Still, she thought, this was no place for her, and to try to hide her own guilt she decided she'd keep talking to her until Sister Stanislaus came up.

'I'm leavin' today! I'm goin' away, Kitty! I told you last night, I'm leavin'.'

'Sister, Sister,' moaned Kitty as she took hold of Julie's hand, mistaking her for one of the nuns.

When she relaxed her grip Julie turned quickly and went again to the door. In the name of God, will that one ever come and let me downstairs? she sighed. The hair stood on the back of her neck when she turned once more to look at Kitty. The dormitory had a weird feeling about it, she thought, and for the hundredth time in her life she was convinced she could get the stench of death about the place, which meant someone was going to die. She was sorry now that she hadn't agreed to work on this morning with her friends, until her sister Kay came to collect her. Instead she had been allowed to go back to her dormitory after Mass and breakfast to put on her new clothes and to be ready at eleven thirty. But when she looked at her new outfit now and felt the crisp twenty-pound note in her pocket, which had been handed to her by the Reverend Mother, she felt an awful lot better. Earlier Julie thought she'd like to walk the Magdalene grounds one last time before leaving. Now she thought she'd seen enough of it. She'd go straight to the chapel, and the penitents' graveyard instead, and say a prayer.

When at last Sister Stanislaus came upstairs, Julie asked if Bridie and Josephine could join her for a few minutes before she left the home so that they could pray together; her wish was granted.

Walking down the stairs for the last time she began to feel emotional as Sister Stanislaus carefully locked the intermediary doors behind them. So this was really it, she thought: after twenty-four years in the Magdalene Home she was being released.

The three women stood, arms linked together, on the edge of the penitents' graveyard. They stared at the small, black-painted metal crosses, which had the names of the deceased neatly painted in white. Some were of friends or elderly penitents they had known. For a brief moment they were afraid to speak, but unknown to each other they were thinking the same thought: there, but for the grace of God, go I; wondering in their own minds how they had survived at all. But Bridie and Josephine could not bear to dwell on the fleeting thought that flashed through their minds: they could end up being buried there themselves.

'You know, this place must be very old,' said Bridie, trying to lift the heavy gloom she was beginning to feel at her friend's eminent departure. She could see that the first person to be buried there died in 1887.

'I wonder how many people are buried here altogether,' said Josephine, wondering too if they were all Catholics, or if there were any Protestants amongst them. She wouldn't really mind being buried here, she thought, if only Cathal was buried beside her. At least they could be together in death.

'Sixty-five,' answered Bridie, the figure long-since engraved on her memory, after years and years of walking alone in the same grounds. 'I counted them one evening when I saw that lovely marble headstone there in the middle where it says, "6 November 1937, peacefully in her sleep, aged thirty-three." But I can't make out her name.'

'God! Sure the creature was only a young one,' said Julie.

Thirty-three, thought Josephine, almost the same age as me. I'm only a few years younger than Julie and look at her now. I never noticed it before but her hair is getting very grey, and she has bags under her eyes. It must be the sunlight, because I never saw her looking like that before. Soon I'll be as old and decrepit-looking as her. Jesus, am I ever going to get out of here?

'Come into the chapel, in the name of God, and we'll say a prayer. I don't care where I die, but the last thing I want is to be buried here,' said Bridie, suddenly feeling depressed and lonely.

As if reading Bridie's thoughts, Josephine tightened her grip on Julie's arm, rested her head against her ample shoulder and pleaded solemnly, 'Please, Julie, won't you try and get us out of here? Because if you don't we might all die here.'

The mere thought that herself and Bridie would no longer have Julie to console them in their hours of need was almost too much to bear. Julie had been such a tower of strength, such a shining example in her fight for freedom. And now after all these years her prayers were finally being answered.

Then a strange notion struck Josephine as the three of them entered the chapel: that what Bridie was always saying was probably true. Everything that happened in life came in threes. And if Bridie was right, then there was a very real chance that one of them could find herself walking out the door to freedom in the not too distant future. Noreen Donnellan had managed to escape; Julie Murray was as good as gone now; so that meant another of them was probably destined to go free. The thought alone began to warm the cockles of her heart.

The midday Angelus bell was ringing out loud and clear, and a small group of penitent women stood waving in the small corridor at the end of the main hall, as Julie, accompanied by Sister Philomena and two novice sisters, was escorted to the front parlour where her sister Kay was waiting to collect her.

'Goodbye! Goodbye, Julie! And don't forget to pray for us,' they shouted, as they watched her walk ever closer to freedom. Now the penitents poured out of their workrooms in earnest and stood huddled together, jamming the doorways as they waved their white handkerchiefs; frantically jumping up and down as Julie neared the corner. There, just before she disappeared from view, she turned one last time and waved to all her friends. But many of them found the moment too much to bear and turned their sad faces away.

Bridie, who had linked arms with Lilly, was totally lost for words. She had wanted so desperately to announce to everyone that if ever any penitent in the Magdalene Home deserved her freedom, it was Julie Murray. But somehow the words she had planned as a fond farewell lodged in her throat, and instead she ended up saying nothing.

Breaking from her friend, she too turned and sighed, 'Ah, well! That's the end of that! I only hope that if the man above had anything at all to do with Julie's good fortune, that we're next on his list.'

'Yeah, wouldn't it be great? I hope she doesn't forget to write. Where's Josephine?' asked Lilly, looking round.

She was nowhere to be seen. On entering the workroom they found her sitting dejectedly on one of the huge linen baskets. They said nothing because they knew, like themselves, Josephine had more than enough on her mind.

CHAPTER SEVENTEEN

I T WAS ALMOST three weeks since Julie Murray took those long steps to freedom, rescued by her sister Kay, the Very Reverend Sister Rosario. Would you ever believe it's that long? thought Bridie as she lay in bed resting after her hard day's work.

Ever since Julie went away she hadn't felt much like working, particularly at night or in the evening, when she was usually known to help her colleagues with the odd bit of dressmaking, knitting or sewing. Her friends still came, haunting her daily to lend a hand. Instead their half-finished dresses and cardigans lay wrapped in old newspaper and brown paper bags under her bed, because each day after work she told herself she'd do it later, tomorrow maybe. All she really wanted to do now was to be left alone with her thoughts.

One of these days, I'll have to get off me backside for good and try and do something about leaving here. No good depending on Julie. Not a word from her since she left. I can't believe it. Only God knows where she is now. She could be in Dublin, London or America. I'd say America, with her sister. I must be an awful eejit entirely myself that I didn't try and escape years ago. I can't spend the rest of me life in this place. Thirteen years I'm here, could you believe it? I'm nearly thirty-one years of age and as far away as ever from finding out who my mother and father were. As far away as ever from being reunited with my son, and as far away as ever from finding myself a husband. I'm useless, she sighed. Pure useless! I don't think I have the strength or desire to fight any more. Here I am, year in, year out, helping everyone else but doing nothing at all for myself. I'm pure stupid, I really am. If I don't leave here soon John Paschal will have left Williamstown and I won't see him any more. He'll surely stop writing to me, because he'll meet some nice girl and then that will be the end of me.

Ah, to hell with this, she thought, as she swung her legs to the floor and sat on the edge of the bed, thinking. It's time I started planning, because I'm going to run away from here one of these days: only I'm not going out on my own. I'll ask Josephine and Lilly to come with me. I always said I'd bring Josephine and Julie with me, but now that Julie has gone it will have to be Lilly. I'll do like Noreen Donnellan. I'll say nothing and keep quiet until the very last minute. Then the three of us will slip quietly away. I won't even tell the girls because they might tell someone.

Josephine Finn was returning from her trip downstairs. She'd been to see if the door in the corridor was unlocked so that she could sneak across to the pigswill barrel at the rear of the laundry to find something to eat. Unfortunately the door was locked. She was sorry now she hadn't put a bit extra in her pocket at tea time that evening.

As she entered Our Lady's dormitory she saw Bridie writing a letter. She was tempted to go to talk to her, but changed her mind. Bridie wasn't herself since Julie left: not near as friendly. I'm not good enough for her now, I suppose, Josephine thought. Besides, she won't let anyone else share her bed since Julie left; won't even let me cuddle up to her like she used to.

Josephine decided instead to go over and see what the rest of the girls were up to. The atmosphere all evening in Our Lady's dormitory was a bit like the weather: threatening, as if a storm was about to break. Little groups of penitent women hung around arguing endlessly while playing silly games on the floor. Others were trying to read snippets from old religious magazines. One penitent, however, had managed to get her hands on a Mills and Boon paperback. She had to read it quickly because if the sisters found it then it would get the fire; and everyone in the laundry would get a good grilling about how they came to acquire such filth.

Bridie had just about finished her letter to John Paschal – the second letter in a week – when one the inmates came and pleaded with her to join their group for a bit of a singsong and to bring over her mouth organ.

Bridie decided to pull herself together and join in as one of the young penitents in the corner squeaked, '"I'll Tell Me Ma",' and they all laughed, and the words were no sooner said than two young penitents grabbed each other and began to twirl wildly on the floor as they sang,

> 'I'll tell me ma when I go home
> The boys won't leave the girls alone.
> They pulled their hair,
> They stole their comb,
> But that's all right till I go home.
> She is handsome, she is pretty,
> She is the pride of Belfast City.
> She is courting one, two, three.
> Please will you tell me who is she?'

Soon the atmosphere was electric, which helped get Josephine into the mood and she made a suggestion.

'Why don't we have a dance and pretend we're at a real carnival? We'll pretend we're all having a big night out in the Seapoint out in Salthill.'

'Yeah! Yeah!' replied the girls enthusiastically. 'That's a great idea!'

'OK. Half of you go each side of the room,' said Josephine.

'Bridie, Mary Kelly and myself will be the band. And don't forget I want to see all of you out dancing on the floor.'

This proposal was overwhelmingly supported by the penitents because they knew from past experience that the best night's entertainment was usually of a spontaneous nature; people, it seemed, were less shy about expressing themselves when there wasn't too much expected of them.

'Bridie, you sit here on the left and, Mary, you sit on the right with the accordion,' said Josephine, eagerly arranging a chair for each of them. 'And I'll pull this bedside locker over to here so I can stand on it.'

Already the penitents were getting excited as Josephine made arrangements.

Turning to the band members, she whispered, 'I think we'll start with "Danny Boy". Give us the air to "Danny Boy" and we'll see. We'll pretend the place is packed with fellas and we're mad for it; and the music is blaring.'

Bridie and Mary began tuning up while keeping an eye on proceedings. Everyone was revelling in this impromptu form of entertainment.

Bridie was particularly pleased that Josephine seemed to have made a full recovery. Prior to her escape bid, Josephine was the life and soul of the place, but ever since then she wanted to portray herself as a tart, by dressing up gaudily in weird outfits that did not suit her at all. She would beg the nuns for fancy clothes, which of course they never had because they frowned on anything that vaguely resembled style. Despite that, Josephine always managed to get the loan of somebody's pleated skirt, silk blouse or horrid lipstick, so she could dress up and go to the recreational hall on Sunday night, and dance the night away listening to *Ceili House* on Radio Éireann, making believe she was in some famous dance hall. There was one big difference, however, which all of them hated, and that was the sight of three or four nuns sitting at the top end of the hall watching everything and showing them how to dance 'The Siege of Ennis'. And if it wasn't that, it was showing them how to behave in a ladylike fashion when invited to dance a jig or a reel by some imaginary man. It was bad manners to refuse, no matter how much you disliked the man, the nuns told them. And the nuns were always giving out to Josephine lately because of her gaudy make-up. She'd spend hours in front of the broken mirror below in the lavatory, preening herself. Bridie got a great kick out of these situations because Josephine was sometimes known to turn on the nuns like a viper, claiming, 'It's none of your business who I'm going out with tonight, or who I shagged last night.'

During these interludes, Bridie's deep concern for her friend's wellbeing would come creeping back. She'd ask herself why Josephine always had to put it on, or was her behaviour for real? Besides, Josephine often accused Bridie of being too plain and stupid, saying that she'd never be able to get a man anyhow because she was too dowdy, not like Josephine herself, who could have any man she wanted. Any man.

On the other hand, if Josephine was doing this to relieve the boredom and to have a little fun, then maybe Bridie herself should throw off the shackles and join in. Everyone knew Josephine Finn loved nothing more than to be the centre of attention be it acting the Mick, imitating Judy Garland or dressing up in some fine clothes. God! If only I had her confidence, I'd be elected, Bridie thought.

Josephine was now standing smiling on her makeshift stage, facing the audience. She was holding a small statue of the Blessed Virgin in her hand to use as her microphone.

'Good evening, ladies and gentlemen . . .' she began, but her introduction was interrupted from the floor by yahoos and wolf whistles. '. . . It gives me great pleasure here tonight, on this the last step of our Irish tour, to entertain you in one of Ireland's foremost venues: the Seapoint Ballroom, here in Salthill. As you're probably aware, this is my final appearance before starting a three-month tour of America. In a few days' time, together with my band, I hope to be walking down Broadway . . .' more clapping and cheering and shouting, '. . . so, for that reason I'd like to see you all out dancing, as we begin the night with that beautiful Irish melody, "Danny Boy".'

Almost immediately two girls start dancing as if they are in the great ballroom of romance, followed by several more couples, all of them dancing with the loves of their lives. And to add a bit of fun and excitement to the occasion, Breedge Courtney chooses a large pillow from one of the beds as her dancing partner.

As Josephine begins the second verse of her favourite love song, Bridie realises that any lingering doubts she had about Josephine's welfare were rooted in her own vivid imagination. After all, she thinks, when all is said and done, isn't it only a bit of fun? She can clearly see that, by getting up on stage the way she has just done, Josephine is living out her dreams, indulging in her own unique talents in a way she herself never could.

While out on the dance floor, Breedge Courtney is dancing away with her imaginary partner as if she were taking part in *Swan Lake*. But she soon gets carried away by the tempo of the music and begins to hold the pillow seductively to her bosom before lowering it and squeezing it lustfully between her thighs. And as herself and her imaginary partner begin to gyrate in a deeply sexual way, her friends start egging her on. 'More! More! More!' they scream in their desire for fun. As if to acknowledge their request, Lilly MacAlastair steps forward, snatches the pillow from Breedge, and throws it away before wrapping herself lovingly around Breedge, as a visible surge of excitement engulfs the crowd. Soon everyone is out dancing; and amid gasps of amazement, Lilly and Breedge start hugging and kissing each other in a passionate and deeply intimate way.

This real vision of people enjoying themselves sends the blood coursing through Josephine's veins. There's a rush to her head, and she starts to give the performance of her life, raising her voice several decibels.

'. . . And if you come when all the flowers are dying,
And I am dead, as dead I well may be,
You'll come and find the place where I am lying
And kneel and say an "Ave" there for me.
And I shall hear though soft you tread above me . . .'

Some of the penitents are so excited by the dancers' outlandish behaviour they start to cheer loudly, egging them on. But Peggy Neary can't take any more. She rushes headlong into the crowd, just as Lilly and Breedge are about to start exploring each other's bodies, and grabs Lilly viciously by the hair.

'You feckin' bitch! You leave my friend alone! You disgusting oul' whore!'

But despite being hauled backwards, Lilly manages to turn sideways, hanging on to her opponent for dear life.

'Who the hell are you calling a whore?' she screams, as she lunges back at Peggy, knocking her to the ground.

They both start flaying into each other while rolling around on the floor, before Lilly manages to get up on her feet. She starts to kick Peggy like a rag doll. *Kick!* 'You're nothing but a stupid nuns' pet.' *Kick!* 'A bloody weasel!'

Suddenly, Breedge Courtney decides to join in the fray and lands like a cat on Lilly's back. Meanwhile, the band has stopped playing. For a few moments they stand there, staring in total shock: Josephine having subconsciously dropped her Blessed Virgin microphone on the floor, where it explodes.

Breedge tries vainly to save her friend from Lilly's onslaught, but it's no use. In a matter of seconds Our Lady's dormitory has erupted into a full-scale riot.

Skin and hair go flying. Shoes, hairbrushes and pillows are used as missiles: anything that can knock the stuffing out of an opponent or put stars in her eyes is used.

Bridie is terrified she'll get hit by someone or be dragged into the mêlée, so she decides to escape by going around to the other side, while Josephine and Mary plunge straight into the row. Bridie jumps from one bed to the next in order to get away, stopping only briefly to pick up a pillow that has landed on the floor beside her. As Bridie is standing with her back to the wall, holding on to the pillow, the door suddenly bursts open and three nuns, led by Sister Stanislaus, enter the room.

For a fleeting moment Sister Stanislaus and Bridie's eyes meet before the nuns fully observe the wanton scene before them, as small groups of penitent women wrestle half-naked on the floor, some of them bare-breasted, their clothes hanging off their backs as they scream obscenities at each other, while at the same time desperately trying to remove the last vestige of decency covering their bodies.

Sister Stanislaus raises the bell high above her head and gives it such a vigorous, rhythmic jangle it would wake the dead. But only when the fighting has ceased and all eyes are on her does she lower the bronze bell and hand it to one of the novices, standing petrified beside her.

'What's . . . this?' exclaimed Sister Stanislaus in a loud voice, as she hurriedly made the sign of the cross with her large crucifix, before letting it jangle once more by her side. 'God Almighty protect us! And save us from the fires of hell . . . and the powers of Satan . . . Look at you! You're like a pack of wild animals! Have you all gone mad?'

There was complete silence as everyone diverted her gaze and tried discreetly to hide her shame. Everyone, that is, except Bridie and a few others, who had not been caught up in the rumpus.

Seeing Bridie holding the pillow, and assuming she was up to no good, Sister Stanislaus asked, 'Bridie Rodgers, what have you got to say for yourself?'

'Nothing . . . Sister.'

'Nothing! That's just what I'd expect to hear from the likes of you. Why are you holding that pillow? Ready to throw at somebody, I have no doubt.'

'No, Sister, 'twas on the floor—'

'On the floor! Whose idea was this? Whose? I'm not leaving here tonight until I get to the bottom of this. Now whose idea was it?' demanded Sister Stanislaus as she turned her attention to the unruly mob before her.

Bridie did not answer. Her blushes were saved however when one or two of the penitent women started tittering behind their hands at the mention of the word 'bottom'. In a way, they thought, that's what they were all trying to do: get to the bottom of someone's drawers.

Sister Stanislaus realised instantly that she had used the wrong word. She knew that if she pursued this line of questioning they would make a laughing stock of her in front of her novice sisters. She knew very well how it had all started. Jealousy. That was the venomous poison rampant among all of the penitents. If someone was over-friendly with the nuns, their friends were jealous. If some girl was very good at ironing church linen, her friends were jealous. If one was good at sewing or cooking, her friends were jealous. But most of all, if, like Josephine Finn, one was good at singing or switched her allegiance from one penitent to another, then everyone was jealous.

And that is why they must stamp out this terrible evil in their midst, she had told her novice sisters only earlier that day: and the only way to do that effectively was to get rid of the ringleaders. Ringleaders like Josephine Finn, Lilly MacAlastair and perhaps one or two others, who held sway and led by bad example.

'Some of them are certainly overdue a long holiday in

Ballinasloe Mental Hospital,' she told the novices, 'and now that I'm in charge I won't be half as slow in sending them there as Sister Antonia was.'

Sister Stanislaus ignored the tittering at the back of the crowd by pretending she hadn't heard. Instead she decided she would expose the chief suspect to show she knew who was behind the fracas. Then she'd leave well alone until she got each one of them on her own in the morning. She'd already made a mental note of the chief culprits from their demeanour when she came into the dormitory.

'Miss Finn, was this your idea?'

All eyes turned to Josephine, but she too pretended not to hear by remaining silent and instead began looking around. But when Sister raised her voice and repeated the question, she knew she could no longer ignore it.

'Miss Finn! Yes, you. Was this your idea of entertainment, or whose was it?'

'No, Sister.'

'No, it wasn't your idea, or no, you don't know who started it?'

'I don't know who started it.'

'Were you engaged in singing lewd songs earlier?'

'No,' answered Josephine hesitantly. 'I mean—'

'How dare you tell me such bare-faced lies? I distinctly heard you myself! As a matter of fact you could be heard abroad in Eyre Square.'

Then turning to her two novices, she said, 'I want you to lead these heathens into five decades of the rosary, and see that everyone of them retires for the night in a decent manner.'

To the penitents she declared, 'Tomorrow morning, I shall carry out a thorough investigation into tonight's unseemly behaviour. I'll take whatever steps I deem necessary, and I shall have no hesitation in calling the Gardaí tonight if I hear another sound. Have I made myself clear?'

The response was muted, but not for long, as the novice sisters led them into a night of fervent prayer because, for some, judgement day was but around the corner.

The early morning scream was terrifying. It was the most blood-curdling sound Bridie had ever heard. All at once it did three things to her: it woke her with a start; it made her heart beat viciously in her chest; and it transported her back to her childhood years in the orphanage out in Clifden, where often in the dead of night she'd been woken by screams of somebody having a nightmare or of a child being punished in a remote corner of the building.

Bridie looked to the far end of the dormitory and saw Lilly MacAlastair holding her chest. She seemed to recoil in horror at the sight of something and pointed to the bed.

'Where's Bridie? Where's Bridie? Bridieeee!' she screamed. 'Josephine won't move.'

'What's wrong?' Bridie heard the girls nearby say to Lilly, as heads sprang up all over the dormitory at the disturbance, terrified that something serious was amiss.

With a great deal of fear and trepidation, Bridie leaped out of bed and ran quickly towards Lilly, trying desperately to suppress the shocking thoughts in her head: that Lilly had suddenly gone mental or that, by the looks of it, Josephine was . . .

The women stood clutching each other beside Josephine's bed, unable to move as Bridie arrived. They were calling out to the crumpled heap, which lay motionless.

'Josephine! Josephine, wake up!' Lilly, barely able to speak now, whispered imploringly. 'Josephine! Ah, Josephine! Judy! Judy! Judy! Wake up.' Looking at Bridie with a terrified expression on her face, Lilly cried, 'She won't move! Bridie, she won't move!'

For a brief moment, Bridie herself thought she was going

to faint, but she willed herself to look down at Josephine. She saw immediately that she had a deathly pallor that seemed to indicate there was something seriously wrong with her. She reached out to touch her friend's haggard features, praying fervently that she could feel some warmth there. But she already knew in her heart what the result would be. Dead.

'Jesus, Mary and Holy St Joseph . . . she's dead! She's dead!' whispered Bridie.

Bridie's best friend was dead. The best singer in the whole world, Judy Garland herself, the one and only Judy, was lying there. Dead.

She reached down to clasp Josephine's cold hand, and as she did so she recalled her religious teaching, which specified that whoever finds the body of a departed soul should at once kneel down, and administer a good Act of Contrition into that person's ear, thereby absolving that person of all the sins of their past life.

Kneeling beside the bed she removed Josephine's decorative rosary beads from her bedpost and commenced her prayer.

'Oh my God, I am heartily sorry for having offended thee. I detest all my sins, because I dread the loss of heaven, and the pains of hell. But most of all because I have displeased thee, who art so good and kind and so deserving of all my love. I firmly resolve with the help of thy Holy Grace never more to offend thee and to amend my life. Amen.'

Slowly rising to her feet, she continued to look at the lifeless body of her friend, becoming more surprised each passing moment at how composed and calm she herself had become. Seeing her friend lying there like that, stone cold, made her realise how frail human life could be. She recalled something the two of them had discussed only three weeks ago, on the morning of Julie Murray's departure as they stood at the foot of the penitents' graveyard.

Their conversation springing to mind, she reflected all too clearly on the frightening significance of their spoken words. 'Come into the chapel, in the name of God, and we'll say a prayer. I don't care where I die, but the last thing I want is to be buried here,' she herself had said to Josephine.

And later that same morning they had discussed Julie's good fortune in being rescued from the home. And Bridie remembered confiding in Josephine that she firmly believed that everything that happened in life came in threes. Noreen Donnellan was free, Julie Murray was free, so that meant that another one of them was destined to go free.

Bridie tried to push the awful recollection from her head. She began to feel guilty as sin for having some strange power that enabled her to foresee or foretell certain things. She wished with all her heart that she hadn't convinced Josephine that one or other of them was soon destined to go free. She had probably caused Josephine to build up some false hope in her heart that she would be free to roam the world, free to meet her Cathal. Free, free, free. As Josephine herself used to say, free to walk the streets of Galway, or free to go and sing her heart out on Broadway.

Unable to speak to anyone, and with a heavy heart, Bridie turned away as a tidal wave of shock swept through the entire institution. Hardened penitents wept openly as concerned nuns suddenly appeared, flitting in and out of the room, whispering discreetly as they hurriedly arranged to escort Josephine's body down to the infirmary ward. And as they did so another recollection came into Bridie's head at something Julie Murray had once said. 'Sure, it makes no earthly difference, Bridie; once you're gone, you're gone.'

There's poor Josephine, only thirty-four years of age and now she's gone. I just can't believe it; lying there like that, stone dead, Bridie thought.

*   *   *

They were about to go haymaking when the telegram arrived. They didn't like telegrams because it usually only ever meant one thing: that someone was dead. Their minds raced, doing a quick count of ageing relatives, aunts and uncles. Come to think of it, they had very few left they thought, so who could it possibly be?

Josephine's mother tore open the telegram and flew through the contents.

'Mother of the Divine . . . it's Josephine, she's dead!' she said as she reached out to a chair for support.

'What?' exclaimed her husband in disbelief, as she handed him the telegram.

They'd not set eyes on their daughter since the day they'd put her away, and had long since resigned themselves to her loss; only ever briefly referring to her as 'that one'.

This was because *that one* had brought nothing but ruination on the good name of the Finns by aligning herself with them Protestant land-grabbers, the Swanicks. Now, after years of doubt, they felt justified in their actions, as Cathal Swanick had turned out to be nothing more than a drunkard. And, rumour had it, he frequently pledged his undying love for Josephine all over town, while wallowing in crates of Guinness and self-pity. It was also rumoured that he had fathered a child to some unfortunate girl in Tuam, and had point-blank refused to marry her.

Josephine's mother had at times felt a tinge of regret at not having made some attempt at a reconciliation with her daughter, but then the idea would balance itself out with the realisation that it could only ever lead to the reopening of old wounds. Josephine was sure to enquire about Cathal, and would make every effort to see him again.

The very notion of their reconciliation repelled her father even more. They were damned for ever if they let one of the Swanicks – Cathal, the womanising drunkard, and all that he

was – take their one and only daughter to breed a new generation of land-grabbing Swanicks. No. Never. This frightening
prospect had been trotted out time and again by John Finn to
his meek downtrodden wife, whenever she attempted to broach
the subject. Now it was all too late. Josephine was dead. The
only thing for them to consider was, would they go to *that
one's* funeral or not? And after a great deal of soul-searching
and debate, they finally decided that no useful purpose would
be served by attending. They'd had no contact with her since
they put her away, so where was the use in recognising her
now? Furthermore, they had a niggling suspicion that their
attendance at their daughter's funeral might mean they would
be expected to carry the costs of her burial. Then they thought,
what if the neighbours got wind of the news and decided to
go along to the funeral: that would show the Finns in a very
bad light – or would it? No, they decided, no one in the village
would know because telegram boys don't read telegrams; they
only deliver them. The only thing to do was sit tight and say
nothing; only make sure that it didn't appear in the death column
of the newspapers or local press. Instead, they'd send a Mass
card. No one in the locality would know anything until it was
all over and Josephine was safely underground. In a week or
two it wouldn't matter. They could simply claim it had been
a private funeral: family members only.

The procession was led by a large group of priests, dressed in
white, followed by the Sisters of Mercy dressed in black: their
long flowing habits swishing gently as they slowly swept down
the centre aisle of the Magdalene Home chapel.

The priests already occupied their positions round the main
altar as the nuns, their heads bowed, filed into the front pews
either side of Josephine's body, which had lain in state in front
of the altar overnight.

A strong smell of incense filled the air, as Mass candles danced and flickered on the tall, brass candelabra, which stood either side of the marble altar.

Soon the large congregation rose to its feet for the introductory hymn, led by one of the novices, Sister Concillio, which signalled the beginning of high Mass. Bridie and Lilly found it hard to control their emotion as they too sang the opening hymn from the same sheet.

Unknown to either of them, Cathal Swanick was standing just inside the heavy oak door; a lonely figure. He took in a deep breath as he surveyed the scene.

Women. God Almighty, I've never seen so many women together in all my life. Where have they all come from? So this is a refuge for women. Don't they have some quare places in Galway all the same, row after row after row of head-scarved women. You'd almost swear they were all nuns; except for the coloured scarves, and the fact that the real nuns are all in black, up at the head of the congregation.

Glancing nervously to his right, Cathal spotted two men kneeling by the tall church window. He wondered who they were. Did they live here with all these women? Were they married men, or what was their association with Josephine?

Unknown to him, they were two of the Magdalene's most loyal servants, Mr Hehir and Mr Tyrrell, both van drivers, who had each completed almost forty years' service with the Magdalene Home Laundry.

Mass was only beginning and already Cathal's throat felt dry, despite the fact that he'd had two quick ones at home in Lavally, whilst waiting for the taxi, as well as two more pints when he arrived in the city, just to give him courage to face the day. But it wasn't enough. He'd give anything right now to have another just to calm his fears.

He'd got such a shock yesterday when the postmistress waylaid him outside the post office to ask him if he'd heard the news. He'd told her he hadn't. She brought him into the office so

301

she could show him the rough copy of the telegram as written on her blotted note pad.

Regret to inform you Josephine Finn passed away last night. Peacefully in her sleep. Burial tomorrow after 11.30 a.m. Mass in the Magdalene Grounds unless otherwise requested. Signed Sister Stanislaus (acting Mother Superior).

'Unless otherwise requested.' Nervously, Cathal put his hand to his hip pocket to make sure the flask was still there, and to reassure himself that if the worst came to the worst he could always slip outside for a quick slug. But he knew it was a last resort. A pint, that was what he wanted. It was your only man for the thirst.

But where are the Finns? he asked himself, as he scanned the congregation again. They're not here. Hypocritical bastards. They thought that much of their daughter they wouldn't allow her to marry a Protestant, and yet they don't think enough of her to come to her funeral. You'd think they'd bring the poor girl home and give her a proper burial, and not have her buried here in a pauper's grave. I'm half-tempted to arrange it myself, but sure, there'd be ructions and blue murder if I said anything; I know there would. They'd gang up on me. It'd give them the perfect opportunity to slate me. Big oul' John with his viper's tongue would rant and rave: *Look here, Swanick, we don't need your Protestant charity around here. Is it what you want, to bury our only daughter? A decent grave, my arse: you buried poor Josephine thirteen years ago when you destroyed her life; as sure as they nailed Jesus to the Cross. So don't talk to me, Swanick, about charity, forgiveness or respect. You've no respect for yourself, so how could you have it for others?*

Cathal moved restlessly from one foot to the other. He was tempted to go outside so he could wet his lips. But one of the priests he felt was looking straight down at him. It made him feel uncomfortable.

Cathal meant only to hand in a Mass card to the convent but the nuns were so nice they persuaded him that he should attend Josephine's funeral service. He wished now that he'd stayed away altogether because all this singing and lamenting – keening, he thought they called it – was so mournful. And yet, in a weird sort of a way, he found it enchanting.

He continued to stand at the rear of the little chapel listening intently as the notes of the 'Kyrie' reverberated throughout the chapel as friends of the deceased dropped their heads to mourn softly into their tightly held handkerchiefs. He was even more mesmerised by all the religious fervour when, at that precise moment, a beautiful ray of sunlight filtered in through one of the tall church windows, casting a spotlight on the chief cele-brant and cantor as though he were the epicentre of some famous theatre production, to which his co-celebrants responded,

Chri-ste-e-e-e-e-e-e-e-e-e-e-e-e-lei-son.
Ky-ri-e-e-e-e-e-e-e-e-e-e-e-e-e-lei-son.
Chri-ste-e-e-e-e-e-e-e-e-e-e-e-e-lei-son.
Ky-ri-e-e-e-e-e-e-e-e-e-e-e-e-e-lei-son.

It was only when they had finished singing that the deep sense of shock and loss of his raving beauty assailed Cathal. He wished that he could just see her angelic face once more, dead and all, as she was lying there in a coffin.

The congregation began to file past her body on their way up to the altar to receive Holy Communion. He watched the long lines of penitent women return to their seats where they again knelt down before burying their faces in their pale white hands. He thought perhaps he too should try and make up for the sins of his past life. Yes, 'twas a good idea; only, not today. Some other time maybe. He started to feel restless and pleaded silently, in the honour of God, will the priest get on with it till I get outside for a breath of fresh air and, with any bit of luck, a pint of porter?

There was a brief lull, while everyone was seated after the Communion ceremony and Cathal realised to his horror that the chief celebrant was looking straight down at him, about to say something.

'My dear people, we are gathered here today to pray for the soul of Josephine Finn, who departed this life and who is now seated at the right hand of God. Today, I have chosen my words very carefully, because while most of us sinners can expect – at best – to spend a considerable amount of time in purgatory before being allowed into Heaven, Josephine Finn will have had no such burden placed on her shoulders. Josephine was by all accounts an exceptional human being. That we are all sinners in the eyes of God is without question. And yet, Josephine – from what I knew of her as a member of the Magdalene choir, and from accounts I have received only this morning from her friends and colleagues, and the Sisters of Mercy, whom she served so loyally and faithfully down the years – was a walking saint because of the great love and compassion she has always shown to her fellow human beings. She is at this very moment seated at the right hand of God, because he has ordained that Josephine should be one of his flock. In many ways it could be said that Josephine was one of his "Lost Sheep", who has now been found and returned to the fold.

'My dear people, in creating Josephine Finn, God bestowed on her one of his greatest gifts to mankind, that of a golden voice. She was and always will be remembered as a beautiful singer, who also had that rare ability to entertain. For as a great many of her friends and sisters in the choir said to me, "Truly, she had the voice of an angel." Alas, it's a voice we shall hear no more.

'But I did not have to hear those words today. Many, many

years ago I had the pleasure, or should I say the privilege, of hearing and seeing Josephine sing during a rare Christmas concert right here in the Magdalene Home. Wasn't it somehow appropriate that she should always sing the song that was first made famous by her heroine, Judy Garland, in *The Wizard of Oz*, a song all about wishing on a star? And wasn't it somehow appropriate too that in doing so she should connect us all to our secret dreams; to one day be free of all our cares, through her singing, her kindness and through her great love for us.

'Her visit on this earth was but a short one. Today, my dear people, may she rest in peace . . . Amen.'

Cathal could not hide the tears. His head sank onto his chest out of a deep sense of shame that anyone would see a grown man cry, but somehow the tears brought a strange sense of relief as they washed away the awful pain in his heart of the guilt of never having had the guts or the courage to come here to see her while she was still alive. He was amazed at how easy it had been to gain access to the convent this morning, and at the nuns' insistence that he have a nice cup of tea after his long journey. He had half expected to be turned away from the Magdalene as an unfit person to pay his last respects to a girl like Josephine.

But the priest's eulogy had flowed so eloquently that it had somehow exposed Cathal's own shortcomings like never before. He now saw at first-hand the errors of his ways, the futility of his life.

True, he had never heard his beautiful Josephine sing, but he knew the words of that famous song almost off by heart. It brought him back to their last meeting on that glorious summer's day long ago in the Mall, Tuam. He remembered her so clearly, standing there in the laneway, holding her bicycle, as her lovely floral dress swayed gently in the breeze. He remembered how their so-called love had been nothing more than a few brief encounters, smothered to death by their families' fierce hatred of each other. He remembered how he had allowed his love of her to grow, when what he should have done when he had first lost her was to let it go.

He knew he'd always been too weak; too lily-livered ever to stand up to the Finns. Even his own friends had said so. Afraid too to stand up to his own parents, who, while they never actually stood in his way, always frowned on him whenever he cast his eye on anyone other than a girl of his own religious denomination.

At long last, the Mass was over. Cathal turned quickly, slipped outside the door of the little chapel and stood for a moment, surveying the scene. Everything was so quiet and peaceful, he thought, as a little group of men stood waiting beside an open grave a short distance away. So, his great love affair with Josephine was finally over. Maybe it was time to make a new beginning. After what he'd just witnessed, he decided he'd change his life. He'd go back to Tuam this very day and offer to make a decent woman of Mary Burke, who had borne his child. He'd already destroyed one life; he couldn't bear to ruin another. Reaching into his pocket, he took out the flask, unscrewed the cap, went across to the grass verge and watched the bane of his life drain away. He shook out the last drop of poisonous liquid with a vengeance. Time for a new beginning, he sighed as the congregation emerged from the church.

Bridie stood at the graveside without showing a single trace of emotion, while all around her young and old wept openly. Lilly and Margaret clung either side of her, as the priest said the final prayers. But something made Bridie turn away from the mourners. She had had enough and could take no more. She began to walk back towards the laundry. She felt like she was past caring any more, because there was nothing to live for.

Making her way back, Bridie mumbled aloud to herself in her heartfelt grief, 'Look at me now! I've no one! No Paschal. No Noreen. No Julie. No Josephine. No nothing. But I swear to you, Almighty God, I'm leaving this place before the year is out. I swear on the Holy Bible, because if I don't, I know that I'd be better off dead.'

CHAPTER EIGHTEEN

I T WAS WHILE helping Sister Perpetuo – one of the new nuns – to sort out the County Clare parcels for distribution that Bridie was slipped an envelope by Mr Hehir, the van driver. Bridie in turn slipped the folded white envelope into her pocket, much to the relief of Mr Hehir, who'd kept the letter in his pocket for almost a week, awaiting his chance to see Bridie.

When Mr Hehir and his lorry had pulled out into the yard, Bridie asked permission to be excused, saying she wanted to go to the lavatory. When she reached the cubicle she tore open the letter.

Nurses' Home
Merlin Park

Dear Bridie,

I'm after hearing about Josephine's death, and I'm not worth tuppence. The girls here in Merlin said that a girl had died in the Magdalene. They said she was supposed to be a great singer. When I heard that, Bridie, I nearly died. I walked all the way to Mr Tyrrell's house to ask him if it was her. I brought one of the girls here with me because I was afraid the nuns might see me. When he told me it was Josephine, I cried and cried. She was such a good friend, and so good to me, even though we often had our rows. I only hope that God will forgive me for all the horrid things I used to say to her. Sure 'tis hard to be good all the time. I fell out with me sister Kay because I wouldn't do what she wanted and go to America. I said hump America, I want to stay near Bridie. She got me into the Merlin Park Hospital in the end. A girl who ran away from the Magdalene worked here for a while years ago, but left when she heard the nuns were looking for her. I live in the nurses' home because one of the doctors said I should stay here. I cry ever night, Bridie, when I think of our dear friend Josephine, and you still in there. Maybe you should write to that nice man you used to work for. Sure where's the harm? He might come and take you out. I asked the van driver if I wrote a letter would he give it to you. He promised he would. I've stuck in five pounds in case you get out. I hope you don't lose it. Write a letter quick, and give it to Mr Tyrrell and tell me what's happening or how Josephine died.

Goodbye for now, from Julie.

PS. I pray ever day that you'll soon get out and we'll go to the Seapoint. I've been to a nurses' dance and met a fella. But he kept dancing, I mean standing on me feet and everthing. The nurses call him Johnny Two Shoes.

After receiving the five pounds, Bridie's faith in human nature was greatly restored.

She thought long and hard about what Julie had said, about writing to Mr O'Malley at Conly House in Tuam. She'd already thought about it herself, but had ruled it out. She thought she could never see him getting in touch with the Magdalene Home Laundry to take her out, especially after all these years. He probably had enough problems of his own. And anyway, if she did write and he came to take her out, he'd probably want her to live and work in Conly House for ever, looking after the farm hands, and she didn't want that. Besides, the O'Malley children would be grown up and gone, so they wouldn't want her. From now on she'd make her own way in the world, she decided.

First she'd write to Julie and thank her for the money.

Dear Julie,

Thank you very much for the gift. It was so thoughtful of you. I was killed wondering where you were and if you knew about Josephine. I think she died of a broken heart. Wasn't it awful? I don't think I'll ever be the same again. It was bad enough when you went away but Josephine's death really put the tin hat on it. Everything's the same since you left. Work! Work! Work! I don't know in the name of God how we stick it. Half the girls got the flu and I had a touch of it myself for a few days. I pray every day for a miracle like yours. If anything happens I'll let you know straight away.

Goodbye for now, and thanks again for your gift. I'm sure I'll make good use of it.

Love, Bridie

After weeks of careful consideration, Bridie decided she should commence her own plan of action. Now was as good a time as any she thought, particularly as several new inmates and nuns had arrived. One of the new nuns, Sister Kieran, was appointed ward sister in place of Sister Philomena. Sister Philomena was supposed to have gone to Dublin, although she disappeared without warning and no one knew for sure what had happened to her. Some inmates claimed she had left the order altogether. Bridie had great respect for Sister Philomena because she'd gone out of her way to help her keep in touch with John Paschal when no one else cared.

Bridie's only close allies now were Lilly MacAlastair and Margaret Sherry. She decided she'd try to make a pact with them, to swear them to secrecy about her plans for the three of them to escape. If ever there was a time it was surely now, she thought, before things get any worse.

Having heard nothing from Noreen Donnellan for a long time, Bridie was delighted to receive a secret letter from her via Mr Hehir. To Bridie's astonishment, Noreen encouraged her to run out the gate and enclosed five pounds to help her on her way. Bridie immediately tore off the address in England and hid it with John Paschal's lock of hair before flushing the rest of the letter down the lavatory. But of one thing she was sure: if she escaped she would not go to England. She'd stay in Ireland so she could be near John Paschal. But she'd keep hold of Noreen's address just in case she changed her mind.

The three penitents were sitting on the grass as the sun slowly slid down the broad evening sky, supposedly planning their escape. But Lilly and Margaret were very sceptical. True, they claimed they wanted their freedom more than anything else, but Bridie sensed that, like the majority of the women in the laundry, they were being slowly conditioned into accepting their lot and becoming institutionalised. She could almost empathise with their fear of the unknown and their reluctance to come on board. She knew if she failed to convince them she'd end up questioning her own ability to launch such a daring plan.

'But what if the O'Briens won't let us stay? They might call the Guards,' suggested Margaret.

'They won't! I know they won't. I can tell by the letters,' replied Bridie as she nervously plucked a few sun-drenched blades of grass and tossed them over her right shoulder. 'They're nice people. I know I can trust them. Besides, they've looked after John Paschal for years, so why wouldn't they let us stay with them?'

'I don't care what you say, Bridie, I think we'd be a lot safer – that's if we ever get out – to go straight to Julie Murray in Merlin Park. I know where it is; it's not far at all from here.

Sure, Williamstown is miles and miles, according to Noreen Donnellan,' countered Lilly.

'No! NO! You're not listening to me!' said Bridie, raising her voice in her annoyance. 'I've already told you it's not safe. That's the last place we should go. I know 'twould be lovely to be with Julie and everything, but the nuns and the guards would go straight there, because they know we're good friends. And even if we managed to hide there for a day or two, and then they saw us, they could have us brought back anytime because we escaped. Julie told me in one of her letters that a girl who had escaped from here and was working in the hospital, left there because the nuns were trying to bring her back. You see, it's different for Julie. Her sister signed her papers and took her out. Only a relative can get you out.'

They continued to argue, going over and over the same old ground for almost a week. Bridie was adamant that together they could make a run for it, while Lilly and Margaret were of the opinion that the whole thing was too risky. Three of them together! Whoever heard of it? One, maybe two, but three? No.

'Besides, we're not ready,' objected Margaret.

'Look!' said Bridie, desperately pleading with them to see a bit of sense. 'If we stick together we have a great chance. But if I have to go out on my own then I will. I'll not say anything to anybody and then the two of you will be sorry. I won't even bother me backside writing to you or anything,' she added as a levering ploy.

'But if we do get out, how will we get to Williamstown?' asked Margaret.

'I don't know! And I don't care! The thing is to concentrate on getting out of here. If we can do that the rest will follow. I don't want to spend the rest of my life in here. I've sacrificed everything for the last thirteen years for the sake of John Paschal. And I've only ever seen him once. He'll be going to work somewhere soon – maybe Galway or Dublin or England. And if he goes while I'm still in here, I might never see him again. Please! Do it for me!'

'Maybe you're right. What have we to lose? There was a time when I wouldn't think twice about it,' said Lilly as she began to extract a cigarette butt from her secret hiding place in the hem of her dress. 'Arrah, to hell with it! We'll take a chance! We could talk about it till the cows come home and not do anything about it.'

'I don't care. It's up to ye,' said Margaret with a shrug of resignation.

'It's not up to us. Why is it up to us? We can't go and leave you on your own,' retorted Lilly. 'You might tell on us – where would we be then?'

'Will you stop talking stupid! Why would I tell anyone? I'll go too if it makes ye happy. I don't want to be left on my own. Only thing is, if we get caught, we'll get a fierce hiding from the guards, and the nuns will leather us and cut our hair. That Sister Stanislaus can be right vicious, you know. She'd give us a good hammering because she loves showing her authority, and then the whole place would be laughing at us.'

'No! No! The first thing to do is stop thinking like that. We're going out of here the first chance we get. Are we agreed on that?' asked Bridie quickly, in case they changed their minds.

'Yes.'

'OK. Whatever you say.'

'And if I hear one word about it from anyone I'll say nothing but go out on my own. So, don't breathe a word to anyone,' whispered Bridie. 'I'll pick the time and the place, and because it was my idea, I'll go out first.'

Bridie concluded that it was better to move quickly. The longer they waited, the greater the risk that one of the girls might open her mouth. She could already see how excited they were getting, as they would sometimes jokingly ask, 'Anything happenin'?' whenever they met in the corridors.

As there was no obviously suitable time in which to strike for freedom, Bridie had to figure it all out and make a decision soon. Saturday seemed to her to be the best day, particularly as the Galway races were over and the laundry was returning to normal after the busy summer season. Saturday afternoon, when all the scrubbing and choir practice had taken place was an ideal time to escape.

It was Friday evening when Bridie took out the goatskin purse from her blouse. It contained the lock of her son's hair she'd kept for all of thirteen years. She sat on the edge of her bed for a moment. She wanted to feel its soft texture and to study the tiny photograph, whispering to herself, 'Son, some day soon this will be yours. I have sacrificed so much for you, Paschal. You are the nearest thing to my heart.' She kissed the delicate strands of hair, which still retained a glint of gold, despite the passing years.

She checked to make sure she still had Noreen Donnellan's address and the five-pound note, together with Julie's fiver, and put them all back together again. Looking round, she saw some of the elderly penitents polishing the brass door knobs that had never once grown cold from the dint of polishing over the years. She knew these silent robotic creatures spent hours every day wiping away imaginary dust and dirt from their doors and bedside lockers, and rummaging under their beds for old clothes, knitting needles or misplaced balls of wool.

Bridie slipped discreetly out of the room and went down the stairs and across the grounds to say a quiet prayer at the penitents' graveyard. She wanted to say a special one for Josephine, asking for her support in her hour of need and thanking her for making her life in the laundry more bearable with her humorous songs and ditties.

Bridie circled the Magdalene grounds to admire everything

for the last time: her favourite tree – the huge cherry that flower-ed so beautifully in the spring and that always attracted the birds and the bees. She had a fierce passion for nature and couldn't wait to see what life was like in the outside world. Then she climbed the stone steps to Our Lady's Grotto to ask for her guidance and forgiveness. She reached up to touch Our Lady's strong yet delicate hand before leaning forward to kiss her well-worn feet. Accepting that she'd done all she could, she returned to her dormitory in silence.

Tomorrow was Saturday, the day she planned to climb over the wall and away to freedom.

She had one eye on the wall clock and was nervously counting down the hours and minutes. Then something unforseen and unnerving happened. The new Reverend Mother, Sister Stanislaus, whom none of the penitents had seen all morning, suddenly appeared out of nowhere accompanied by a young penitent half-wit, known as 'Hang on Mary', who usually went round with one of the nuns ringing a small bronze bell to announce their presence. 'Hang on Mary' was like a child with a new toy. She loved showing off and flaunting her role as assis-tant to the Reverend Mother.

When the bell ceased ringing the Reverend Mother came forward, her firmly starched white coif and veil looking as if it might strangle the very life-blood from her face. All eyes in the ironing room were on her as her long black habit made a slight rustling noise and her heavy crystal rosary beads clinked as she slid her hands tightly into the deep dark folds of her sleeves and spoke with an authoritarian air. 'Girls, what day, is it tomorrow?'

Bridie felt her heart palpitating and wondered if the Reverend Mother knew something. Was the Reverend Mother going to put a spanner in the works? Please, not now, when we have everything planned, she thought. Some of the penitents glanced nervously from one to the other and raised their eyes to Heaven as if to say, 'Here we go again.' Most of the girls in the ironing room were caught unawares and were unsure what the Reverend Mother meant.

'Sunday,' squawked one of the penitents in a birdlike voice. It did not go down too well with Sister Stanislaus.

'I know it's Sunday, dear. I know that well, but it's also a very important Sunday. Now, what date is it, and whose birthday is it the day after that?' asked the Reverend Mother as 'Hang on Mary' stood behind her, gesturing wildly to Bridie.

A chorus of voices rang out, 'It's Our Lady's birthday!'

'How right you are. It's the Sunday before the eighth of September, which is Our Lady's birthday.'

Alarm bells rang in Bridie's head and her heart began to thump. She lowered her eyes so the Reverend Mother wouldn't meet her gaze because she knew what was about to happen.

She glanced sideways at her two friends as the Reverend Mother continued, 'At least you've learned something and managed to retain it in your heads. Which is why I'm looking for volunteers for this afternoon to help erect a special altar to Our Lady for tomorrow morning's Mass. I would like you to put some nice flowers on the altar, and lots more around the statue, as we have a lot of Sisters of Mercy nuns from the schools coming in to visit us in the afternoon.'

Several penitents put up their hands straight away, crying out, 'Me! Me! Me!'

'And Bridie,' suggested 'Hang on Mary' brazenly, while still gesturing with her hand that she wanted Bridie to assist her in her task.

Normally this was a job Bridie did without fail. She loved Our Lady with a passion and was devoted to her; but not today of all days. Yet how could she refuse? There seemed no way out. She'd be expected to be the main devotee among the penitents tomorrow.

Before Bridie had time to realise what course of action to take, she could hear herself talking, and began to turn crimson at the sound of her own voice.

'Reverend Mother, maybe I could be excused today . . . I'm not feeling that well . . . Besides, I think it's only fair that others get a chance with the altar, as I'm always doing it.'

The Reverend Mother's eyebrows shot up in surprise as she turned swiftly to look at Bridie.

'Certainly there's nothing wrong with your tongue,' retorted the Reverend Mother, and the penitents all laughed. 'What way are you not feeling well?'

'I . . . I feel kind of sick . . . a bit dizzy at times,' lied Bridie.

'Dizzy! When did you first notice it?'

'Yesterday, Reverend Mother.'

'And pray tell me, why didn't you inform one of the other sisters or myself?'

'I didn't want to trouble you . . . I thought it might go away.'

'Would you like to go to bed for a few hours?'

'I think I would,' replied Bridie, not knowing what she was going to do, as her plans for today's attempted escape were blown to smithereens.

She could have kicked herself. Why couldn't she have kept her mouth shut, carried out her task, and then tried running away as she'd planned? How could she possibly escape now? And what about Lilly and Margaret?

As Bridie was immersed in these thoughts, the Reverend Mother turned to Lilly MacAlastair and said, 'Lilly, would you like to take Bridie's place?'

'Yes, Reverend Mother,' replied Lilly enthusiastically, not knowing that Bridie had other plans for that afternoon.

'So would I,' said Margaret Sherry quickly, not wanting to be seen to be the odd one out.

'Very well! So, we have Mary, Christine, Josephine Rabbitte, Bernadette Comer, Lilly MacAlastair and Margaret Sherry. You're to meet with Sister Aloysius and Sister Consillio over in the chapel right after you've had your dinner. The rest of you can carry on scrubbing the floors. Bridie, will you come with me and I'll walk you to your dormitory?'

While Bridie was being led back to her dormitory she could not believe how stupid she'd been to refuse to erect an altar to Our Lady. She felt a deep sense of guilt as she watched the Reverend Mother unlock the intermediary doors before leading her upstairs to her dormitory

'I'll get you an aspirin and a hot drink,' the Reverend Mother was saying, as she prepared to lock the door behind her. 'One of the Sisters will bring it over to you, and if the dizziness gets any worse be sure and let me know right away.'

'Thanks, Reverend Mother,' said Bridie trying desperately not to look the sister in the eye in case she detected her deceit.

There's nothing for it but to go to bed and sit it out until Lilly and Margaret have finished work, thought Bridie. Nothing much has changed. My big mouth still gets me into trouble every time.

After Sister Aloysius brought Bridie the glass of warm water and an aspirin, she lay in bed thinking long and hard about what she had done, and she came to the firm conclusion she didn't even know her own mind. She was teetering on the edge of darkness because for weeks the voices in her head had been telling her to go, go, go, but she was terrified of the consequences. What if she failed and let down her two friends? After all, it was her idea. What if she ran away and was captured? What if she fell off the wall – like poor Josephine – and landed on her arse? Would she too go mad and, like her friend, end up being buried in the black-clad graveyard of the Magdalene grounds? The thought sickened her beyond belief. If she was going at all, she'd have to go now, she told herself.

She jumped out of bed because she could no longer control the thoughts going through her mind. She felt such pressure within her chest she thought she'd pass out at any moment. Yet another day, another opportunity had presented itself and she hadn't the courage to take it. Today's chance was gone – or was it? She'd have to wait and try again next Saturday, she thought.

After pacing the dormitory for a long time, Bridie was relieved to hear Lilly and Margaret returning with the other inmates. They couldn't understand why Bridie claimed to be unwell when clearly she hadn't said anything to them. They were ready to demand an explanation on entering the room, half afraid that Bridie might not even be in the dormitory; that she had pulled some stunt, in order to get away herself. And they were mighty relieved to see her sitting waiting for them.

'No! No! I had nothing planned. But I was fed up with being taken for granted,' she replied to their many questions. 'Listen, it's a lovely day outside, why don't we go for a walk?'

'A walk! Are you mad! It's too warm, and besides, I'm too tired. Later on, maybe.'

But Bridie insisted. She almost had to drag them with her, such was her overwhelming desire to flee the Magdalene Home once and for all. The awful stress and pressure she was feeling was like that which had engulfed her body years earlier when the nuns were about to remove John Paschal from her. The time had come for her to make a stand and scale the Magdalene wall to freedom. She'd waited far too long, wasted almost a lifetime, living every single day of her life in fear: fear of failure, fear of the unknown, fear of the nuns and fear of being betrayed by one of her fellow inmates. Yet some overpowering force was urging her to go: to go now.

The three women went out the rear door of the building and stood for a second in the wavering heat. The sunlight seemed to dazzle Bridie for an instant. When she looked up she thought she saw the sun as a clear figure of a child looking down on her, its warm rays spreading out across the broad expanse of infinity. She could feel its glorious energy entering her body.

She turned to her friends and almost half-heartedly said, 'I think we'll go now.'

'Go where?' asked Lilly and Margaret as Bridie turned to walk in the opposite direction to the one they normally took when going for a stroll. Suddenly the realisation struck them that perhaps Bridie was about to make a run for it, that this was the moment they were all waiting for. But it couldn't possibly be happening now, with no warning.

'Where do you think?' answered Bridie nervously. 'Come on, quick!'

'But we can't, Bridie, we can't. Look, they're watching us.'

'And look at all the people!' added Margaret, who thought Bridie must be mad even to suggest such a thing.

'I don't care so long as there are no nuns about. I can't stick this place another minute. I'm going whether you like it or not.'

'Bridie, do you realise what you're saying? We're bound to get caught! We've no clothes or anything. You couldn't have picked a worse time, as far as I'm concerned. Why don't we wait till the morning? It'll be grand and quiet then,' suggested Lilly.

'I thought we agreed we'd go together. If you don't come now, I'll go on my own,' insisted Bridie. 'We've wasted enough time. I'm here thirteen years, and every time I walk down by Josephine's grave I get sick. I know if I don't get away from here this minute, then I'm going to die.'

The words 'Josephine's grave' were too much for Bridie's friends. They began to walk hesitantly behind her as if strolling about, towards the furthest corner of the enclosed grounds.

'Listen!' said Bridie. 'You two lift me up on the wall and then I'll try and pull you up. If we can manage that, then you can hold on to me while I try to slide down the other side. Once I get over I'll help you.'

320

Acting as a human chain, they pushed and pulled and dragged each other until they were halfway over the wall. Looking back, they noticed two or three penitents standing watching them from the far side of Our Lady's Grotto. They just stood there staring in bewilderment, wondering what they were trying to do. Minutes later all three of them had disappeared completely from view.

The first thing to hit the three escapees when they were safely over the wall was elation, followed quickly by panic. They could not believe that they were actually free. They wanted to shout for joy as they fled, breathless as thieves in the night, along College Road. They wondered if they were going the right way as they quickly removed their white caps and gowns and stuffed them under a hedge. When they caught up with an elderly lady returning home with her shopping bags, Bridie asked her if this was the way to Tuam. It was. Then they decided it was better not to be seen to be in too much of a hurry, and to act as normal as possible in case they were reported.

To them the outside world was a frighteningly new place full of strange sights and sounds. And were it not for the fact that they'd seen lorries and buses at close quarters from the Magdalene Home Laundry they would have been terrified for their lives. Even the sudden sound of a motorbike and sidecar tearing along behind them, left them terrified.

'What was that?' gasped Margaret as she stood looking.

'A motorbike, I think!' answered Lilly 'But that noise! I used to think it was the buses.'

'Buses, me arse! Come on! We'll have to move faster and see if we can get a lift or something. Me shoes are killing me,' said Bridie.

Hitching a lift was something they'd never done before and the last thing any of them wanted to do now, but somehow they had to.

321

When they saw a car coming down the hill behind them, they decided to jump out in front of it and wave the driver down.

'Are you going to Williamstown? We missed the bus,' said Bridie brazenly.

'Williamstown? Where's that?' enquired the young driver.

'I don't know,' said Bridie. 'I think it's near Tuam.'

'Tuam! I know where Tuam is, but you're on the wrong road. What bus were you supposed to catch?'

The women looked at each other in a confused state before Bridie blurted out the first thing that came into her head.

'It was a green one.'

'Sorry, I can't help you and, like I said, you're on the wrong road. Just take the next left and then turn right and you're on the Tuam road,' said the driver, pulling away hurriedly as he was holding up traffic behind him.

After a heated debate about which was left and which was right, the escapees made further enquiries regarding Williamstown and Tuam. Soon they found themselves getting a lift in a huge lorry, the driver thinking all his birthdays had come at once when he saw three damsels in distress. Giving them a lift was no problem, he said. But despite that, they were packed in like sardines in the front of the lorry.

'Where do ye work?'

'We work in a factory,' answered Lilly in response to the driver's query.

'It's our first day,' added Bridie, conjuring up enough lies and stories to see them safely all the way to Williamstown.

The driver had informed them that he was going via Tuam and Castlerea all the way to Donegal and that if they wanted a lift with him then they were more than welcome.

It wasn't until they had jumped down from the lorry in the small village square of Williamstown that they began to realise it had probably been the most audacious escape attempt ever made from the Magdalene Home. Making their way on foot up the winding byroad to the O'Briens' house, they soon realised, was one thing: keeping ahead of the law was quite another.

When John Paschal came home in the evening, having spent a long hard day in the bog, he got one hell of a surprise. Instead of seeing his place set at the table, he found three strange visitors, stuffing themselves with lovely home-cooked ham and tomatoes. He wondered if there would be anything at all left for him. And when he saw his mammy offer the visitors yet more ham, saying, 'Eat up now, let ye, 'cause there's no knowing when ye'll get the next bite,' he was rightly disgusted.

He was halfway across the floor when Bridie said, 'Glory be to God Almighty, is this him? Paschal, love! How are you?' She stood up and gave him a fierce hug. 'God, but I wouldn't know you! You've got so tall!' And seeing the shock on John Paschal's face, she asked, 'Do you not know me? I'm your mother!'

Paschal made a show of acknowledgement before she again hugged and kissed him.

After Lilly and Margaret shook his hand, he stood there embarrassed, not knowing what to do, while his mammy pampered them with yet more tea and sweet cake and biscuits.

'We'll have ours later,' she announced, seeing John Paschal's questioning gaze, as Edward O'Brien leaned forward every so often with a little piece of paper towards the fire in an effort to keep his pipe lit.

But I want it now! Paschal's stomach screamed. He'd made short work of the tea and sandwiches in the bog and deeply regretted having scoffed half of them before he had even got there that morning. The trouble was he loved the blackcurrant jam sandwiches and would eat them until they came out his ears.

God knows when I'll get a bite now, or how long they're

staying, he thought. How come they've no car? I wonder how they got here.

'I believe you're a great worker altogether. Why don't you come and sit down here beside me?' said Bridie, making room for John Paschal.

Instead, he looked at his mother and father for guidance and to see if they had any objections, but they just smiled at him.

When he made no move to sit down, Mrs O'Brien said, 'Why don't you sit down and join them? You must be near kilt working, 'cause you're as black as a pot. On second thoughts, why don't you go out and wash the muck off your face so Bridie and her friends can see what you look like?'

The visitors laughed and John Paschal's ears turned a bright red as he made his way into the back kitchen. He listened to their every word as Edward, in between blasts of smoke, spat into the open fire and said, 'I think the best thing ye can do now is get the train and go to Dublin. Ye can get the boat from there to Holyhead. Ye'll have no trouble at all gettin' work over there.'

Edward had a particular reason for suggesting this course of action. Ever since John Paschal and his real mother began to communicate with each other, Kate O'Brien had lived in dread that one day Bridie would turn up on her doorstep and claim him as her own; and she after rearing him since he was knee-high to a grasshopper. 'It would be a devil entirely,' she had said to him, 'if Bridie were ever let out of the Magdalene Home, and she were to come down here and try to claim him, after all I've done for him.'

I know Kate is cranky an' everything, and a devil an' hell to live with, but she's clever enough, Edward thought. She could see this happening and I couldn't. So I best use me influence and persuasive powers to divert Bridie as far away as possible from here, otherwise there'll be hell to pay.

'Oh God! I don't think I'd like to go to England. Maybe we

could get jobs here in Williamstown. But I'd be afraid we'd get caught and sent back to the Magdalene again,' said Bridie.

'I don't think I'd like to go to England either. Maybe if we went back, we might get a job in Galway,' said Lilly anxiously.

'Can't we stay here a while and maybe get some kind of a job in Williamstown?' suggested Margaret, trying to come up with a solution that would suit everyone.

'Is it what ye want, to be arrested and sent back to Galway? If ye are reported to the Gardaí in Galway, this is the first place they'll come looking for ye. So if I was ye, I'd hop it fairly lively, because the people round here seem to know everything,' said Edward, deep concern in his voice.

'And believe me they already know who ye are, and where ye came from,' intervened Kate, appalled at the prospect that John's mother would have access to him now, and that herself and Edward would become the laughing stock of the whole parish if that scenario ever came to pass.

'I'll tell ye what we'll do,' suggested Edward, assuming full authority on the issue once more. 'I'll give ye a few pounds and arrange a lift to the station in Castlerea later on this evening. The train will bring ye as far as the boat in Dubland, where ye can catch the night sailing. That will bring ye to Holyhead and ye can get whatever train ye want, and go to London, Liverpool, Birmingham or Coventry. Ye know ye'll always be welcome to come here anytime ye want, and we'll not say a word to anyone. No one will know where ye are. And besides, when John's a biteen older, he'll be going to England because there's nothing for him around here. What do ye say to that?'

The three escapees looked at each other, the same thoughts going through their heads: Jesus, they're going to give us money and a boat to England. We'll be miles and miles away from the Magdalene and no one will ever find us. Besides, Noreen Donnellan is in Northampton and we can go straight to her.

'You know, I think it's a great idea. I think we should go,' said Bridie to her friends, before turning to Edward.

'That's very good of you, Mr O'Brien. And we promise to pay you back when we get work, and thanks very much to the two of you for looking after John Paschal so well.'

'Ah, thanks yourself,' said Mrs O'Brien.

John Paschal took his time washing his face in the back kitchen because he didn't want to go back into where the women were eating, and where he'd be expected to sit beside his mother like a sissy. Instead he stood quietly, listening attentively to every single word.

'The Gardaí . . . is it what ye want, to be arrested . . . if ye're reported to the Gardaí . . .'

What the hell is going on? he wondered. They must be criminals. And Mammy wants me to wash myself and sit beside three criminals. And if the guards happen to come looking here, I'll be caught as well. What the hell is going on? I don't understand it at all. They must have escaped and run away. They've no car or anything. I wonder how they managed to get here because the Galway bus doesn't come until seven o'clock. It's only half-past five yet. And they've no money for a bus or train. God! I've heard of many a thing, but this is a mystery. And to make matters worse, they're eating my dinner.

His mammy called aloud, 'John, what in the name of God are you doing out there? If it took me that long to wash me face, you know I'd think I'd drowned mesel'.'

John Paschal reappeared, sheepish and red-faced, and stood in the middle of the room watching them all tittering and laughing at him. It was the most mortifying moment of his entire life. He'd have to sit with these people now, who were obviously some sort of convicts, who'd escaped and were wanted by the Gardaí and were about to flee to England. And to complicate things further, the nicest one of them was supposed to be his mother. His mother! That couldn't be right.

Why are people saying that Bridie is my mother? he thought. Oh, I wish to God I'd stayed in the bog another hour or two. I could have come home then this evening and with any bit of luck they'd have all gone to England and I could have had a right good feed. If I have to sit down beside Bridie now, I'll be squashed. And if any of my friends happens to call for me to go playing football they'll see me sitting beside her and tell everyone in school how I was sitting on some woman's lap. And I'll say, that was my mother who lives in Galway. She was down to see me. No, no, I can't say that. Nobody has two mothers. Mammy is my mother, or is she? How come I've no brothers or sisters? If only I could ask someone, but who could I possibly ask? I can't pretend to my friends that I'm that dumb that I don't even know me own mother. It sounds ridiculous.

He went and sat down beside Bridie, but only because he had to. Immediately she put her arms around him and gave him a gentle squeeze.

Edward rose from his chair, spat into the fire, and said, 'I'll go as far as the town and see if I can get Michael Kirrane's hackney car to run ye to the station in an hour or so. Ye could go in the morning, of course, but I think it's better for ye to go this evening. You never know, the Gardaí might come looking for ye, and 'twould be a devil entirely if ye got caught and ye after travelling all the way from Galway.'

With that, Edward jumped on his bicycle and headed straight into town to make the necessary arrangements, so that little more than an hour later, Kirrane's hackney stood ticking over in the street, waiting to take the three women to the boat train.

'Paschal, love,' said Bridie, clasping her son tightly, 'I'm sorry I have to go. Won't you promise me faithfully that you'll write to me and that when you're old enough to go to England, that you'll come and see me?'

'I will.'

Gently holding him at arm's length and caressing his sunburned cheek, she pleaded, 'That's all I'll ever ask — that you write to me,' as a deepening sadness crept into her eyes. 'You're all I have in this world. You know I could never live without you,' she whispered before quietly slipping a half-crown into his hand, together with a small harmonica.

Then Bridie and her friends got into the hackney, and waved goodbye as John Paschal watched the gleaming black car disappear down the narrow laneway that wound out by the lake.

In little more than half an hour, the three escapees would be seated on a boat train bound for England and a strange new world.

CHAPTER NINETEEN

I T WAS EARLY in the morning when the slowing rumbling locomotive ground to a halt. A fierce cloud of vapour sizzled beneath the train's grimy chassis as carriage doors sprang open and weary passengers spilled out on to the platform. This was Northampton, their final destination.

It was here, amid a welter of excitement, that youthful passengers met their mums and dads, brothers and sisters, before helping each other to carry their luggage to waiting taxis. When all these arrivals had nearly disappeared, three lonely-looking women stood in bewilderment on the platform.

'What will we do now?' asked Lilly. 'Where will we go?'

'I don't know. We'll have to get a bus, I suppose.'

'A bus! A bus! Don't say we have to catch a bus or I'll die. Can we not get a hackney?' asked Margaret sheepishly.

'This is Northampton?' asked Lilly in obvious distress, as a small dapper-looking man came sidling up to them.

'Excuse me,' said Bridie, 'do you know how we can get to Barrack Road?'

'Yes, my love, it's just round the corner; five minutes and you're there. You want a taxi?'

'Oh, yes please!' replied the girls eagerly, as Lilly picked up the small brown suitcase that Mrs O'Brien had given them and which contained all their worldly possessions.

'OK! Let's be having you. Follow me,' ordered the taxi driver, as he escorted them out of the station.

When they reached Barrack Road, they knocked at number forty-nine but there was no reply. After several more tentative knocks the taxi driver urged them to knock louder and when that didn't seem to work he stepped forward and gave the door knocker an almighty clatter, which brought immediate results. The three escapees could scarcely believe their luck when their lifelong friend Noreen Donnellan opened the heavy hall door, wearing her dressing gown and hair curlers. In a fit of unbridled joy they hugged and kissed before paying the taxi driver. And as they sat in the cold of a downstairs living room they told Noreen of their daring flight to freedom and how they hoped to start a new life for themselves in England.

Bridie and her friends soon found themselves jobs. They were taken on as packers in a large shoe factory, but they were not happy. One by one they managed to find alternative employment, working alongside Noreen in the kitchen of St Andrew's Hospital, and for a while it was almost like old times.

Life, they thought, was really wonderful, except for the one thing: the superior attitude of the English, who seemed to detest the Irish – describing them as thick and ignorant, and a pure nuisance for coming over to England in the first place to steal their jobs.

Regrettably the allegations, as far as Bridie and her friends were concerned, were not without foundation. They knew they were downright stupid with regard to everyday affairs in Ireland – never mind England – because of their long years in the Magdalene Home. They didn't know the value of money, or how to count it. They were unable to use a telephone, and had never even seen a television set, let alone a television programme. They didn't know what a pressure cooker was, and when asked to cook something special in one of these new-fangled cooking pots it usually turned out to be a disaster. And although they could bake the finest bread and make a decent pot of Irish stew, they were looked down upon because they were unable to make

Cornish pasties, shepherd's pie, Yorkshire pudding, hot pot or spotted dick. The management sometimes showed a degree of latitude to a young girl coming into the job for the first time, but they couldn't accept such stupidity and ignorance in grown-up Irish women such as Bridie and her friends. Their co-workers expected them to already have large families of their own, and when the local girls found out that the Irish girls hadn't a husband or a single boyfriend between them, they looked on them with a jaundiced eye. And as time went on this attitude forced Bridie and her friends to retreat more and more into themselves.

Even in the house, which they shared with several English girls, they kept very much to themselves, because a discussion on an Irish political figure or a famous theatre figure left them completely tongue-tied. They didn't know who John F. Kennedy was, they didn't know who Mary Quant was, and they didn't know what it was to vote.

Even after a couple of years in Northampton, Bridie and her friends had to admit to themselves they didn't know anything. But as Noreen Donnellan said to them 'Ye'll soon learn, yet, so ye will.' So, they stuck together as a family unit, prepared to hide behind their past and to dream about the future: a future that would include men; hopefully lots of men.

Only finding the right one was one hell of a problem, thought Noreen.

'I keep telling you, Bridie, them fellas you're after in the Irish Centre are no good, yet. They're only interested in porter, gallons of it. They only smile when they're looking at you over a big pint, don't you know?'

Bridie did not answer, because she was too ashamed and embarrassed by the fact that again she had been conned by an Irish charmer whose spiel flowed as smoothly out of his mouth as the creamy pints of Guinness flowed into it. Before that she had fallen head over heels for another Irish man, only to discover that he was already married. And she had lent money to a man whose mother was supposed to be dying in Ireland.

'I'm telling ye, girls,' continued Noreen in her motherly fashion, 'we'd be better off in Ireland, somewhere: maybe in Dublin or Galway or Limerick. All a man over here wants is for someone to wash his shirt, don't you know, the lazy oul' feckers.'

Bridie was on her knees in front of the fire because she was perished with the cold, despite her mug of hot tea and a packet of fags. She continued to stare into the fire, taking Noreen's criticism with a pinch of salt. Although she knew that Noreen was speaking the truth, she wondered what would happen if she herself turned the tables on Noreen. Bridie knew that Noreen had stayed out several nights with some fella, but she decided to say nothing.

She was a lot happier when the girls changed the subject slightly and started talking about going back to live in Ireland.

'You know, I think we really would be better off at home. God, just think of it! Wouldn't it be lovely to be dancing away in the Seapoint, or Hangar, and not have to be listening to some old crooner below in St Brendan's, crying like a Banshee, '"If We Only Had Old Ireland Over Here",' sang Lilly with enthusiasm.

'Oh, I hate that song!' said Margaret. 'Over here, me arse!'

'So do I,' added Bridie quickly. 'Every time I hear it I get so lonesome I want to go back home to Ireland. But sure, we can't. You'd think they'd play something decent. And if it's not that it's "I'll Take You Home Again, Kathleen" or "The Siege of Ennis".'

'Oh, I like "The Siege of Ennis", yet,' said Noreen cheerfully.

'Did you tell Noreen about your new man and the drink you got the other night?' asked Lilly, out of the blue.

'No,' answered Bridie, slightly embarrassed.

'Tell Noreen. Noreen, are you listening?' insisted Lilly.

'I am, yet. Go on.'

'Lilly, I'll kill you,' said Bridie. 'Why did you have to open your big mouth?'

'Ah, go on! Isn't it only a bit of fun, a bit of oul' codology; it could happen to any of us.'

'Let me think, yes, 'twas last Saturday night, I had a date with Tomás. We were in the Irish Club and he was after buying me two Babychams; and as he had brought me home the night before, I thought I'd like to treat him. He was drinking pints of beer but I wasn't too sure what they were, so I said to him, "What'll you have? I'll treat you to this one." And he looked at me, a bit surprised, like, that I was treating him at all. Then he said, "I'll have a Bush." Of course, I thought I was hearing things, or that he was pulling my leg, because I didn't know you could get such a drink. I said, "A *Bush*?" And he said, "Yeah, a Black Bush," and I thought, that must be what he was drinking. Anyway, when I went up to the bar I asked the barman for a Babycham, first – to give me a bit of courage – even though I didn't want another drink myself. Then I asked for a pint of Black Bush. Well, I nearly died,' said Bridie, laughing. 'You should have seen his two eyes. He said, "A pint of Black Bush? We don't sell pints of Black Bush. You can have a small one or a bottle; which is it?" Lucky enough, I said a small one. But if you saw the little drop he put in the glass: it would hardly wet your finger. And I was thinking about changing it for a bottle when the barman asked if I wanted to add some water to it. So I told him to fill it up, because I didn't want to go back down to the table with the little drop that was in the glass or Tomás would think I was mean. I never knew that Black Bush was a whiskey until Tomás told me . . .'

'And what did Tomás say to you? "I'll have another, yet,"' suggested Noreen, trying to egg Bridie on.

'Oh, he wasn't a bit pleased,' laughed Bridie, lighting another

Park Drive cigarette. 'He told me that I had killed a good whiskey and that it tasted like mare's piss; and that I was stupid to have put any water at all in it. He said he liked his whiskey the same way as he liked his women, nice, neat, and naked.'

'Now there's gratitude for you,' laughed Noreen, heartily. 'What did I tell ye, yet? We'd be better off in Ireland, so we would.'

'Well, then, why don't we go, and stop talking about it?' suggested Lilly.

''Tis true,' agreed Margaret Sherry. 'We'd be able to meet Julie Murray in Merlin Park. She might get us fixed up with jobs. Who knows, we might end up having to dress some good-looking doctor.'

'You mean undressing him! Sure, you're not able to dress yourself,' suggested Lilly mischievously.

'Oh, shut up, you. You've men on the brain,' retorted Margaret.

'But what about me? I can't go,' said Bridie in a distressed tone. The very mention of Julie's name sent a wave of emotion searing through her. Julie was great company and Bridie feared that her friends might desert her.

'Why not?' asked the girls in unison.

'Because of John Paschal. He's in Manchester now. Remember I told ye I had a letter from him last week and he said he might be coming down to see me?'

'Oh, that's right. You did, you did, yet.'

The three girls looked at each other in silence before Margaret plucked up the courage to say, 'But can't you come home with us for now, and maybe come back here again for a holiday?'

'No!' replied Bridie, disappointed that Margaret could come out with such a mouthful. 'I'll stay here because I want to be near Paschal. I promised myself in the Magdalene, a long time ago, that I'd follow him to the ends of the earth if I ever got out of there. I only agreed to leave Ireland and come to England because the O'Briens said he'd surely come here when he was old enough. Besides, I've never seen him properly, even though he's near seventeen now.'

Again there was a strained silence, as each of the girls considered her lot. Deep down, none of them liked the idea of leaving Bridie alone. They had been together so long and been through so much, it was almost unthinkable. But the reality of the situation was that they couldn't wait to get away; away from Northampton's smog and the constant smell of shoe leather, for which the city was noted. As the months and years went by, they realised that they needed to carve out lives of their own; that they were no longer bound together, being dictated to by a group of nuns, and that they were all bound together now only by their shared finances. Bridie was determined to stay in England, despite the prospect of not being able to meet Julie Murray, who had continued to write regularly, asking her to come and live in Galway. Even the comings and goings of romantic life in the Seapoint Ballroom, as conveyed by Julie's letters, wasn't enough to persuade Bridie to pack her bags.

'I'll tell you what. You go home and I'll stay here. I'll wait until I can meet John Paschal. Then, when I have a few pounds saved up, I can go home for a holiday and meet you all. You never know, John Paschal and myself might end up going back to live in Ireland.'

'Right!' said Lilly. 'Whatever you think yourself.'

Noreen and Margaret agreed.

The three girls set sail in the spring. Their parting was a tearful one, but they hoped they'd all meet again in the not too distant future. Bridie told them she looked forward to meeting her son John Paschal. And if things went well, she might even find the time to go to Dublin and look for her mother and father.

All she had ever wanted in her entire life, she said, was to be part of a nice family.

John Paschal had been in Manchester but a few short months, and was fast learning that life for a sixteen-year-old in a strange English city was not an easy one. Up at six a.m. of a cold frosty winter's morning, ready to leave the company depot at seven a.m., he'd sit for an hour in the freezing canopy, on the back of an open lorry with some of the toughest men he was ever to meet. They would be driven to various building sites within a forty-mile radius of Manchester – Buxton, Liverpool, Leeds, Ellesmere Port or Chester. Forty miles in traffic jams and freezing fog, while Keane, the lorry driver, laughed contentedly, listening to his cronies in the comfort of the warm cab.

When they arrived on site, the heavy wooden toolbox would be opened to reveal a mangled heap of forks and shovels that were all welded together with frozen muck. And there was usually a mad scramble to get hold of the best and cleanest-looking implement as they were considered less painful to begin digging with.

John Paschal invariably ended up with the meanest-looking implement of all. He barely had the strength to lift a dirty shovel out of the box, such was the severity of the cold, while cold hard chaws stood swaggering in their opened-necked shirts, awaiting instruction on where to begin. The majority of these men, John Paschal soon found out, were habitual dossers who only ever worked enough days each week to pay for booze and rent.

Their breakfast consisted of steak and onions, consumed while standing around a big open fire, which always brought some respite. There were times when the workmen fought over their food like prairie dogs over a fatted carcass.

One morning John Paschal saw an ageing beer merchant knocked to the ground by a young fella who was holding a knife to the man's throat. Having forcibly removed the juicy steak dangling from the man's mouth, he began ranting, 'You thieving poxy bastard! You're the cunt that's been taking my steak every fuckin' morning.'

'No! No! It wasn't me!'

'Own up to it, you miserable poxy bastard! Own up!'

'No! 'Twasn't me, I swear!'

The young fella straddling the suspected thief held him by the hair of the head with his left hand, while his other held aloft the sharply pointed steak knife. He began hopping the man's head off the ground.

'Own up, you whore's melt, or . . . or I swear I'll slit your throat from ear to ear, you dirty dog's knot. You're too mean to shite. Own up!' he roared, banging the man's head off the ground again.

'Maybe 'twas a mish-take,' the man pleaded, his eyes two holes of terror.

'Aha! I knew it was you, me bucko. Mistake, my arse! Let this be the last time you do that to me . . . because the next time . . . I swear on my mother's grave, I'll gut you . . . so I will.'

With that the young fella, or Connemara, as he was more commonly called, picked up the piece of steak that was lying on the ground and fired it in the general direction of the sea-gulls. At that moment a huge cheer went up from the rest of the gang, due to the entertainment they had derived from the incident.

'I declare to Jesus, some people would take the bit out of your mouth,' quipped a gleeful Keane, before one of his cronies, added for good measure, 'Musha, 'tis true for you, Martin! 'Tis true for you! 'Tis hard times when a dacent man can't get time to feckin' chew, and the landlady cocking her snoot when a man goes home after a hard day's work and maybe fourteen pints-a-stout. Huh?'

After the excitement of a good early morning row, dinner

on site was usually a hurried sandwich, quickly followed by four or five pints of Guinness in the nearest pub. Then it was back to digging, or pulling heavy cables for the rest of the day. All of which meant it was often a tired and broken John Paschal who returned to his digs late into the evening.

During these hard times he wrote long rambling letters to the O'Briens in Williamstown, slipping in the odd few pounds whenever he could manage it. Correspondence with Bridie, however, practically ceased, even though she continued to bombard him with letters, begging him to stay long enough at the same address so that she could come up to visit him. But of course he never did. He didn't like the idea and wrote back saying he was very busy, what with work and attending night classes and the devil knew what.

But in truth, such was his hatred of digging the roads and the gang he worked with, he set about looking for something more meaningful, and in early spring he found himself a new job, working on the buses.

On more than one occasion, he was taken to task by the depot inspector and threatened with dismissal unless he made a marked improvement in his accounting practices.

What upset John Paschal most of all was that things seemed to be getting worse in his mathematical returns, not better. It didn't make sense to him. He thought he was clever and good at figures but these reports were proving him wrong. Yet when he applied for the job as a bus conductor, he was told he had done exceptionally well in his aptitude test, and after his six weeks in school and a further six out on the road with a qualified instructor, they said he had the potential to work his way right to the top. But at the rate things were going, John Paschal knew he'd soon be working his way to the bottom.

Obviously, he was doing something wrong. He wasn't counting his money properly. There were occasions when he would count his takings up to three times at the end of a shift, and make mental notes to keep the dates in mind. But then when he'd check the shorts list again the following week he'd discover he was down half a crown on that particular day.

His morale was taking a fierce hammering. He felt like walking away shame-faced, but he couldn't, because all his friends, particularly the girls, knew how much he loved the job. They would definitely think he'd been sacked. But if he stayed much longer without improvement, he surely would be shown the road.

In desperation he had a quiet word with the cashier and informed him that it was the ticket machine that must be at fault. It was the ticket machine that had stated he was one and sixpence or one and ninepence or half a crown short. The cashier disputed this. Ticket machines don't lie. If the machine stated that he was short, then he was short and that was that.

'John, stop worrying! Every bus conductor is short in his takings at some time or other!'

'But I'm not every bus conductor. I want to be able to do the job properly.'

'Ye bleedin' Oirish, ye're always fighting or arguing,' said the cashier in jest. 'John! You know that lovely pair of leather gloves that you handed into lost property, and the camera, and that umbrella? They've not been claimed, and they've been here three months. So you can have them. Here! Take them away with you!' he added, reaching under the hatch and pushing the items towards John Paschal.

'No, I don't want them.'

'Here, John, don't be stupid! They'll only go to auction!'

'No, I can't take them. It doesn't seem right, and anyway, I don't want them.'

John Paschal wouldn't take them. Not because he didn't want them, but because it didn't seem right to be taking something that didn't belong to him. If he wanted a thing that badly, he knew he could always go to the auction room where he'd probably pick them up for a song.

For a short while his accounting miraculously improved. He was in heaven. Then he looked at the shorts list again after some wisecrack whispered in his ear, only to discover that he was short nineteen shillings and sixpence. The figures, in bold red lettering for all to see, made him sicker than he ever could have imagined. The depot inspector hauled him into his office, where the friendly cashier witnessed John Paschal getting a right royal telling-off.

Later that night, John Paschal engaged his friend Nobby Clarke, bus driver and ex-conductor, to crosscheck his takings. They were, as expected, spot on.

The following afternoon, when he went to start his late shift, he again went to the cashier and asked how things had gone the night before.

'Paddy! What are you playin' at? You were down another shillin' last night. You really should be getting the hang of it by now.'

Paddy didn't say anything because he had that awful, sinking feeling that he was being done and there wasn't a whole lot he could do about it. Someone was diddling him. In that case, he thought, there was only one thing to do and that was to walk away.

Despite changing his home and his job frequently, John Paschal still managed to find himself new girlfriends. Life couldn't be better, he thought, if only they'd stop asking such awkward questions; about his mother, about his father, about his whole family. He knew he had no real mother or father but he didn't care. He knew he had no brothers or sisters, aunts or uncles, nieces or nephews, or another living relative in the whole wide world, but still he didn't care.

Not so his latest girlfriend. She seemed to care about everything.

They are standing in the doorway of the nurses' home at Withington Hospital, where she works, with their arms lovingly entwined around each other, when she asks how many brothers and sisters he has.

Paschal says the first thing that comes into his head: twelve – because it sounds so virile, and because there were twelve apostles, and besides, most of the married men he knows have twelve children. She wants to know the names of John Paschal's brothers and sisters, their ages and if he's the youngest. He tells her, as far as he can remember, he's somewhere in between, right slap-bang in the middle of the lot.

A week later she catches him out telling lies. An argument ensues and that's the end of a beautiful relationship

Next time he meets a girl, he thinks, he won't be so smart. That's until he meets the beautiful red-haired Sally. She too wants to know the names of his brothers and sisters, their ages, and surely they're not all girls. Well, no, not all. How many brothers are in England; and America? John! I don't believe you! Surely they're not all living in Ireland. They can't be. Everyone has at least one brother or sister in America.

So he decides to spread his relations all around; until, weeks later, he's caught out again.

And it's with a heavy heart he decides it's time to change tack, completely. He meets Teresa Brady and decides it's time to tell the truth. He tells her how he's an only child. But she's not impressed. Not impressed at all.

'You must have brothers and sisters!'

'No. I haven't.'

'But you must have! You must! Everyone has at least three or four brothers or sisters.'

'No. Honest, I'm the only one.'

'And are your mother and father still alive?'

'Yeah.'

'They must be real big shots then, if they wanted only a son.'

'Well, they're sort of separated. Anyway, I don't like talking about them.'

'Oh! And how come you never told me before?'

'Because you never asked.'

'John! I shouldn't have to ask, if you were honest with me. But you're hiding things. You're always hiding things.'

'I'm not!'

'You are!'

'I'm not!'

'OK. So where are they now?'

'Teresa, would you ever stop asking questions?'

'No I won't! Where are they now?'

'If you must know, my father lives in Galway, and my mother's in Northampton, OK?'

'Why are you getting so upset? Are you ashamed of them, or what?'

'No, I'm not! Why would I be ashamed of them?'

'I don't know! They're your parents! Did they get separated in Ireland?'

'Yeah.'

'Well, that's a lie for a start. You can't get divorced or separated in Ireland; so there! I knew you were telling lies!'

Every day John Paschal feels as though his past life is coming back to haunt him. He's so ashamed of his family background he wants to run away for ever. Each person he meets is a potential friend until it comes down to the awkward questions. And sooner or later they have got to be answered. But how can he answer them when he doesn't know how to answer them? Especially when his new-found friends insist on introducing him to their brothers or sisters. They even invite him to their homes for the weekend. All of a sudden life's wonderful again: great altogether, until they in turn ask if they can come and stay at his place in Galway. They believe Galway's a magical place. Are you sure, John, your old pair won't mind? No! No! Not at all!

But how does he explain that he's not like them? That he never really had an old pair. Instead, he tells them that his 'Mother' is not that well; that she has taken a turn for the worse; that perhaps it would upset her to have two or three visitors coming into the house on top of her.

But Teresa Brady does not give up that easily. She wants to know why she can't come and visit each of his divorced parents; so one day he decides to come clean, and he tells her every-thing.

They're hiding beneath the stairs in Teresa's house, because her landlady is very strict, and says there are no visitors allowed, particularly men. Teresa has her arms around his shoulders and whispers caringly that it doesn't really matter about him not having any brothers or sisters, aunts or uncles. That it's not really his fault. She says she understands everything because she herself doesn't know who her own mother and father are; where they live or where they came from or anything. Teresa says she was reared with her two older sisters in County Mayo and now the three of them are over here in England.

Her two sisters are married, one to a Spaniard. They have a lovely son who's a year old now so that makes Teresa an aunt, which in turn makes her a normal human being like everyone else; whereas John Paschal is still a lost soul, but she forgives him anyway. Her other sister's husband, she says, is from Cork and he comes home every single night drunk as a skunk and belts the shite out of her, while at the same time she has to cope with their four screaming kids. Despite that, Teresa herself thinks that she'd love to get married and have lots and lots of children.

It's early spring and the birds are singing sweetly; daffodils are in bloom and romance is in the air as John Paschal and Teresa go strolling hand in hand around Manchester's beautiful Piccadilly Gardens. And because it's Saturday the streets are thronged, and shades of Carnaby Street, Mary Quant and Beatlemania waft from every store and window. And like everybody else, Teresa and John Paschal go window shopping, admiring the clothes, the shoes, the fancy hats and the jewellery; particularly the jewellery. Outside the jeweller's Teresa turns to John Paschal and says she'd love to get engaged.

'Engaged! Why would we get engaged?'

'Because, John, it's time! We're going out six months, we should be engaged.'

'But, Teresa, people only get engaged if they're going to get married and we're . . .'

'You mean . . . you don't want to get married?'

'I do! I do! Sometime . . . but not . . .'

'Then what are we waiting for? I get the feeling, John, if I waited for you to ask, I'd be waiting for the rest of me life. Oh, look! look! Isn't it beautiful? Look at that ring there! Oh, I'd love to get that one! Why don't we go in and buy it . . . and get engaged?' she asked, looking at him longingly. 'Please, John! Please!'

'But, Jesus, Teresa! Will you look at the price of it! And besides I've no . . . Let's wait till I save up a few pounds.'

'Ah, for God's sake, I'll buy it myself! You know, John, you're pure useless. You've no proper job, no money, no nothing. Well, I'm buying the ring whether you like it or not.'

So in they went. Out they came. Half married; because now they were officially engaged. They celebrated by dining on burgers in Wimpy's famous burger bar across the street.

The following week they drove down to Northampton to see John Paschal's mother and to convey the good news – Teresa wearing her sparkling diamond, and John Paschal wearing his new pin-stripe suit, which he could ill afford, but which he bought anyway, to keep the *quare one* happy. In Northampton, they both smiled and Bridie's camera rolled. They were treated like the royal family.

And, in a private moment, Bridie whispered that she'd love

to visit him in Manchester; and that whatever he did, he shouldn't get married too soon. 'You're still young, love, and have plenty of time.'

Bridie said she might go up and live in Manchester, where she could wash his socks and iron his shirts and cook his meals – because, Paschal, I love you and nothing in this world matters more. I want to do everything I can to help you. I've waited all these years to be with you; I prayed every single day that sooner or later, you'd come back to me and now my prayers have been answered.'

Yes.

John Paschal drove back to Manchester late that Sunday evening in his big Consul motor car, feeling anything but contented. He was deeply disturbed in both mind and spirit and couldn't figure out what possessed him to go all the way to Northampton to see someone he neither knew nor loved. He was deeply concerned about the hatred he felt for everyone; especially his mother. He thought he was developing some form of mental illness. What was wrong with him? Every fella he knew simply adored his mother. Their mothers were like gods to them. But he didn't want to see his mother ever again. Never ever, he thought.

He glanced furtively at Teresa as she lay sleeping content-edly on his shoulder. The powerful Ford Consul cruised majes-tically on the motorway as they overtook car after car after lorry. He tried to tell himself he was now a man of the world and, at eighteen years of age, officially engaged. But he didn't feel engaged. And he most certainly didn't want to get married. Maybe he should see a doctor. Could a doctor tell him why he never wanted to see his own mother again? Could a doctor tell him whether or not he was ready to get married? And, for God's sake, could a good doctor tell him what being in love was because trying to find the answer himself was killing him.

For weeks, John Paschal lived in constant fear that his mother would turn up at his flat in Manchester and ruin his life. He moved out at the earliest opportunity and wrote home urgently, instructing the O'Briens to inform Bridie that he had moved without leaving any forwarding address.

He started to drift aimlessly from one building site to another all over the city in search of suitable employment, only suddenly to walk away again because he hated the bullying foreman, he hated the job or he hated them both. But most of all he hated 'the gimp'.

'The gimp' was an image he was meant to portray when looking for a job in the building industry. Prospective workers would congregate on the corner of a noted street in the city slums at 6.30 a.m. surrounded by a vast array of buses and lorries. Dressed in their heavy hobnailed boots and mucky trousers, they'd hang around and wait for the boss to arrive. Then one by one they'd boldly step forward; their two thumbs hooked into the bottom corner of their trouser pockets. But that wasn't enough. If they wanted to get a job they had to display a sort of a workman's swagger, with their shoulders slightly stooped. They traditionally wore a white, dirt-stained shirt – from previous exploits – which should be opened all the way down to the waist to denote a touch of class; and if it happened to be six degrees below freezing, so much the better.

There were usually scores of men looking for work. And as soon as you spotted your prey you were expected to go forward and say in a broad West of Ireland accent, 'Any-chance-a-the-start' in the hope that you might find a kindred spirit.

Needless to say, John Paschal was very backward at going forward and when he did, it was minus 'the gimp'. In a soft gentle tone of voice he would mumble something like, 'Have you got any jobs?'

The West of Ireland gaffer would stop and blink, look and stare, as if he were an alien. And if he was really desperate for men and he thought you had any bit of a shoulder at all on you, he'd rant, 'You! Take the third wagon on the right. You're going to Ellesmere Port. Come on! Come on, men! I haven't all day! What the fuck are ye waiting for?'

On one occasion when John Paschal asked – after being told that he was being hired for the day – how much he was being paid, the gaffer lost the rag entirely. He began ranting and raving, as if dancing an Irish jig in the middle of the road, which John Paschal enjoyed better than any stage presentation.

'Jesus Christ Almighty! Amn't I givin' you a cuntin' start! Jump on that wagon *there*, before any more of them poxy bastards jump off. Ye're like a fuckin' shower-a-cripples, the lot-a-ye! Ye're not fit enough to send to Lourdes, never mind to an oil refinery. Hup! There, lads. Hup! Come on, boys, hup!'

But John Paschal would think long and hard before jumping on any particular wagon, given what kind of a day's slavery it might bring. The general going rate was reckoned to be a fiver a shift, but when he heard some of the men grumbling about having been paid only four pounds and some of them only three ten, then he'd lose all heart and go straight home. Other days he'd stand around in the freezing cold and wait until almost every man was hired, and pray silently that when he'd ask for a job he'd be refused: only then to go home to his flat, fully convinced that he had done his level best to find a job.

A lot of these men, John Paschal soon noticed, had the appearance of being half human and half ape, from years of hard work and heavy drinking. Instead of a nice T-bone steak for dinner they'd consume six, eight or ten pints of Guinness at an alarming rate, followed by an afternoon of ranting and raving, and those who worked with them took their lives into their own hands. These mad men were usually rewarded for their hard work and heavy drinking exploits by being made a foreman or ganger, which meant they drank even more and worked less. And it seemed to John Paschal that from London to Glasgow, Manchester to Hull there were mad Micks everywhere. He wondered how he could ever describe them individually. To him no poem could ever do them justice; and in his idle hours, at home he'd happily scribble on the wall.

THE IRISH IN BRITAIN
Cold hard chaws
What romanticism in a name
Instead I found big brutish monsters
Who'd work you like a slave – some dame
Who'd skin you alive for the price of two pints of porter.

THE BEAR
Big bad Jimmy, his legs askew
He'd shout at you,
'Take that fucking dumper off that poxy bastard.'
Standing, his arms agape
I'd ask myself, is he really a monster, a shite, or a hape.

Then John Pascal would stand back to admire his handiwork and, if the mood was on him, he'd scribble another line or two, making the print smaller and smaller in the hope that the owner of the house wouldn't see it, and he'd dream that perhaps one day he'd become a poet or a writer, because deep down he felt that was all he ever wanted to do. To write, write, write.

But then, turning to go out the door and down the road again, he realised it was only a foolish dream; that it wouldn't help to put bread and butter on the table. No, sir, it would not. Only a decent job could do that. But where would he find one of them?

CHAPTER TWENTY

A ROUND ABOUT THE same time as John Paschal was
contemplating looking for a new job in Manchester, a
group of women sat spellbound in the sitting room of their
home in number 49 Barrack Road, Northampton. Arms neatly
folded they were too deeply engrossed in the unfolding saga
of *Coronation Street* to notice who it was that had entered the
front door.

Coronation Street, however, was the last thing on Bridie's mind
as she carefully checked the mountain of out-dated bills strewn
on the hall table; still, no letter from John Paschal. Glancing
into the room she couldn't make up her mind whether to join
the girls, or go upstairs to be alone with her thoughts. But then
the thought of sitting alone in her room repelled her. Instead,
she'd stay downstairs and try and think things through.

It was weeks and weeks since John Paschal and Teresa had
come to see her. She remembered being so overcome, so over-
joyed at having seen him again. It was as if all her birthdays
had come at once. Although she had some misgivings about
his intention to get married, she thought it better not to intervene. She would have liked him to wait a while longer, at least
until he got to know his real mother again. Eighteen years apart
was such a long time. Yet, she had only ever seen him three
times in all those years. And even then, for only a few hours.

But since that memorable weekend visit, she'd heard nothing.
Not a word. Was he ill? Had he been involved in an accident

at work? Had Teresa whipped him off to Ireland to get married? No, she thought. John Paschal would never do that without letting her know. But then why hadn't he written? He always wrote.

Sitting in the corner, she began to regret not having gone up to Manchester, as she'd planned. It was her intention to surprise John Paschal. But then her boyfriend, Tomás, would not hear of it. She had to cancel the idea at the very last minute because of him. She couldn't dare tell Tomás that she had a nineteen-year-old son, born out of wedlock. To do so would be akin to going around with a sign round her neck that read, 'I am a tart.' Even when John Paschal and Teresa came to see her, she had to postpone her date with Tomás and claim she had cousins staying with her. And when she hinted she was going up to Manchester on a return visit he accused her of seeing another man. In the heat of the moment she cancelled the whole idea, feeling it was better to stay with Tomás.

Deep down, she knew she needed Tomás as much as he needed her. On the surface he appeared to be the life and soul of every party, yet he suffered fierce bouts of depression and alcoholism. She found it hard to make up her mind whether she liked him enough to stay around. There were times when she convinced herself that she loved him, and others when she knew she could never share the same house with him.

'Bridie? Did you have your tea or would you like a cup? I'm putting the kettle on,' said Beryl Foster, as the TV commercials came on.

'Oh, I'd love a cup, dear, if you're making one.'

Going out into the kitchen, Beryl shouted, 'Bridie! There's a letter here for you. I picked it up off the floor when I came in.'

'Oh, thanks be to God!' answered Bridie excitedly, going to claim it.

Climbing the stairs with her fresh cup of tea she was a bit

disappointed to see that the writing was not John Paschal's. But then again a letter from her friend Julie Murray was almost as good any day, she thought.

Dear Bridie,

You're great for writing. I don't know how you do it. Sure, I'm pure useless, but I know you don't mind. Anyhow, I had to write quickly and tell you the awful news. Lilly was attacked and raped the other night She was nearly strangled. The guards were here in the hospital and everything. She's in an awful state, black eyes, and cuts, and lumps, everywhere, and she won't talk to anyone.

I was so upset when I went to see her in the hospital. I'm not the same since. You might write as soon as you can and cheer her up. Sure, she's such a wonderful person, I don't know how any man in his right mind could do such a thing.

I go to the Seapoint, every weekend. Men! Sure you never saw the likes. Packed with them, but awful hard to meet anyone right. They haven't a spark of sense between them. Drink, and a hand up the skirt is all they want. Sure, I had to give one of them a clatter last weekend, but I was sorry after, because he was gorgeous. Is that spelled right, Bridie? Sure, I'm hopeless at spelling.

Why don't you come back to Galway? I'd love if you were here with me. I get lonesome when I think of the times we had in the Magdalene, and them oul raps of nuns. Sure I can't stand the sight of them nuns here in the hospital: they always seem to be whispering and praying and everything.

But the doctors and nurses are wonderful. They're always treating me and everything. I have no more news. Besides, I have to go to confession now, or I'll be late. Won't you say a prayer for me that we'll all be safe from that mad yoke that attacked poor Lilly? And think about what I said about coming back to Galway, or are you still going out with that drunkard? I don't mean that, Bridie. Honest, I mean the same fella. Sure you know what I mean. I had to laugh when you said he was gorgeous, but a biteen of a drunkard, and that you hated drunkards. Sure, Bridie, they're all the same, except there are a lot of pioneers here in Galway. But they're nearly all snapped up.

It's too late for confessions now I think, so I can't go. But with any bit of luck, I'll have something besides impure thoughts to tell the priest the next time. Bridie, I often wonder, do they, you know, like other men? There's one of them here in Galway and he's supposed to be at it all the time. I wouldn't like that, would you?

I'm going now. Goodbye. Write to Lilly. Don't forget, because she's always talking about you. Try and come to Galway; you keep promising. Goodbye and God Bless,

From your best friend, Julie xxx

PS. How is Paschal? Tell him I was asking for him.

Bridie gasped when she read about Lilly. She read that part of the letter again so she could get a clearer picture, devastated that such ill luck could befall her friend. The mere thought that anyone could do such a thing upset her.

The thought of being attacked by some madman terrified her. She knew she herself harboured a deep-seated fear that it could happen to her. She knew only too well what the result of something like that might be. As it was, Tomás was forever trying to get her to go to bed, and she was forever making excuses. She'd say that she didn't really know him well enough yet; and then he'd get into a bad mood and she'd be sorry afterwards.

She'd heard all about contraception and 'Frenchies', but Tomás would never mention them. She often thought that if only he'd offer to use one of them things, then she might take a chance, because God knows, she often felt like doing it again. But the fear of getting pregnant and being put into a home and being made to work for the nuns was always uppermost in her mind. Then again, she thought, if she could meet someone nice, who was interested enough to marry her, things would be different. Maybe she should go back to Galway, to her friend Julie. The lines from her friend's letter jumped into her mind. '. . . I can't stand the sight of them nuns, here in the hospital . . .'

The words echoed her very own thoughts. Nuns and homes, and priests and babies, and laundries and Galway were all too close to the bone for her to ever think seriously about going back to Ireland. Especially Galway. Who knew, they might even lift her off the street and put her in there again, just because she ran away?

Anyway, she could never leave John Paschal here and go home. And when she thought of her son again, her heart began to ache. She had that uneasy feeling that something was seriously wrong. Why hadn't he written to her? It had been eight weeks, eight long weeks and not a single word.

In an effort to improve his station and because he hated working nights in Kellogg's Corn Flakes factory, John Paschal took a job as a machinist in Dunlop's rubber factory. And at the end of his twelve-hour shift he would flee out the door, thankful to be away from all the racial aggro that seemed to go with the job. Back to the lodging house, where he and his friends would listen to the Beatles, and Gerry and the Pacemakers. On Saturdays he'd go shopping; buying mod clothes and the latest LPs.

But then on Monday morning it was back to the rubber curing department of Dunlop's factory where two Northern Ireland workers passing through his department would have a go at him again.

'What's a Fenian bastard like yous doing over here? Och aye, you'll take the Queen's shilling all right.'

Every day the same insults kept piling up: 'Yous still here! You papish prick. Why don't yous go back home, back where yous belong, back to the Republic?'

There were other times when he just happened to be alone in the toilet and the two Protestant workers would come along, and try to push him around, saying, 'Is it true yous Fenian bastards wash your mouths out with soap? Have yous heard of Harland & Wolff? No Fenian bastards need apply. Och aye! Good sound Protestant State: part of the British Empire, ya know. Why don't you fuck off outa here, you scumbag?' they'd scream, trying to draw a kick on him as he went out the door.

On and on it went, day in, day out, week after week, month after month.

One day a loyal Protestant Orangeman declared, 'Hey! You papish scum! Don't you ever set foot in Belfast, or we'll cut your Fenian throat. Och aye! There's only one place for yous papish prigs. That's at the bottom of the River Lagan.'

Paschal could see the venom in their eyes, but he never once responded to their goading. He just stood there and looked them straight in the eye, or if he happened to be working, carried on as if they never existed. Whenever he saw them coming through his department, he would hide discreetly behind the huge rollers of his machine. But each time they spoke, his pride was deeply wounded. Yet he felt he could hold his head up high and thank God that, if nothing else, he'd had a decent upbringing in the South of Ireland; free from all forms of rancour and hatred.

Day after day they still strode arrogantly by, dressed in their pinstripe suits, hair neatly oiled, which only seemed to highlight their sickly-looking, down-turned mouths. Instead of him washing his mouth out with soap – as they claimed all papists did – he thought he'd love to ram a few bars of the horrid carbolic stuff down their own throats.

No such luck, he thought. After working there for almost a year he was offered promotion, only to turn it down flat because he knew he could no longer work alongside such despicable people. Instead he gave in his notice and walked out the gate. And in a matter of weeks he suddenly found himself without a job, without a penny, without a room, without a bed to lie on.

And it was during these semi-turbulent times that Teresa would castigate him for being such a useless oaf. They seemed to have rows about everything. But then they'd make it up again quickly, only to start all over again the next day. He hardly ever drank except on social occasions. He just loved dancing and music and going to the pictures.

He would arrive at the nurses' home adjacent to the hospital to take Teresa out and everything would be grand. He'd arrive back again in a day or two to be attacked for his appearance. If it wasn't his hair, it was his shirt. If it wasn't his shirt, there was something wrong with his trousers.

'John! It looks awful! I'm not going out with you dressed like that. If you had any respect at all for me you wouldn't come dressed like that. Whoever saw a fella wearing a shirt with a belt on it? Is it that you think you're a bit of a pop star or something?'

'If I was a pop star, I suppose that would be all right?'

'Yes, it would, because then you'd be something. As it is you're nothing,' she replied.

'That makes two of us.'

'Oh, shut up!'

Occasionally the ornaments went flying as he stormed out of the room and went home. But then they'd make it up again the next day.

He's twenty years old and they're strolling through the park of a summer's evening, where they end up rolling around on the grass with not a care in the world, when straight out of the blue, Teresa asks, 'When are we going to get married?'

Paschal, somewhat taken aback, sits up and looks at her.

'I'm not sure.'

'But for God's sake, isn't it time we talked about it? You never even mention it. Not a word. You carry on as if it didn't matter.'

'But it doesn't matter! Sure you can get married any time. Today. Tomorrow. There's no law saying we have to do it now! We can do it next year,' he adds with a shrug of his shoulders.

'John! Be serious. I'm talking about us! When are we going to get married?'

'Teresa! I don't know! I have no desire whatsoever to get married . . . yet, and that's that! OK!'

'But you're twenty years old, for God's sake! I'm nineteen! Do you want me to wait until I'm an old woman or what? You're living here this last three or four years with nothing to show for it . . .'

When she gets like this, his blood rises. He wants to run away. Instead he sits there, trying hard not to listen to her tirade, or see the picture she's trying to paint. It pains him so much because everything she says seems to have a marked grain of truth about it.

' . . . You've no proper job! No money! No house . . . and no notion of getting one. You had a good job on the buses and you left! You had a good job in Dunlop's and left! All you do now is go from Billy to Jack. You just don't seem to care about anything. John! Are you listening to me?'

He says nothing because he is incapable of thinking. His mind and body are in turmoil. He doesn't know what he wants. The one thing he doesn't want is commitment. He wants to be free. Yet he wants more than anything else to love and be loved. Deep down he knows he is very unhappy because he had such high hopes of success when he first came to Manchester.

'I said, are you listening to me?'

'Yeah! Yeah! Yeah! You're like a flipping gramophone!'

'And what are you going to do about it?'

'Teresa, would you ever leave me alone, for the love of God?'

'No, I won't. What are you going to do about it?'

At that precise moment, he wants to grab her by the throat just to shut her up. He doesn't know in God's earth how such a small, beautiful-looking creature can inflict so much pain. He's terrified he'll reach breaking point, and maybe end up killing her. He doesn't ever want to hit a woman, any woman. It isn't right. He knows in his heart of hearts that it isn't right. He thinks that maybe there is something wrong with him. Why does he feel so terribly lonely at times like this? Scores of fellows would give anything, *anything*, to be like him: young and free, with a beautiful girl hanging on their arm. Yet, he's not happy. Maybe he should consider getting married. But how can he get married when he doesn't know anything about the world? He doesn't know if he loves Teresa. He thinks he loves her, but he could never say it to her the way they do in the films at the Apollo cinema. He wants so desperately to be able to say those words to a beautiful girl, but he knows he can't. Not even to Teresa Brady. He craves a million and one things in life but he can't put them in any order. He starts to think how he loved working on the buses. He'd love to work in a shop, or a department store. Sometimes he thinks he'd like to be a musician, or a pop star, like the Beatles.

He takes a sneaking look at Teresa lying there on the grass, hands under her chin, eyeing him up, probingly, as if reading his mind.

'Look at you! You don't know whether you're coming or going. You know I never met the likes of you, John. Never! What's wrong with you? Is it that you're afraid to commit yourself or what? I know . . . you're afraid of responsibility, and you want me to do everything. I even had to tell you when it was time to get engaged! And you're waiting for me to arrange the wedding now, I suppose. Well, I'm not feckin' doin' it. You can arrange your own wedding.'

He looks at her longingly, and pleads, 'Teresa! Why are you so hard on me? So hard on yourself? Aren't we all right the way we are? Haven't we a whole lifetime ahead of us? Can't we wait a while and see what happens, see how we get on? I'll get a proper job as soon as I can. Something good will turn up, you wait and see.'

'No we won't! I'm fed up with the way you carry on! And I'm sick of listening to you saying how you'd love to do this and love to do that. But you've never once said you loved me.'

Paschal thinks it sounds horrid when she puts it like that. All he can do is shrug and say, 'Well . . . you know.'

'Well, what?'

'You know.'

'Know what?'

'I like you.'

'But do you love me?' she asked.

'Yeah . . .' He knows it has a very hollow ring to it.

'Well, say it then.'

Choosing his words with care, he finally says, 'I like you.'

'Say you love me.'

'I won't.'

'Please, John, just once. Say you love me.'

'I won't!'

'John, I'll throw this ring back at you if you don't say it.'

'Teresa! Would you ever shut up and leave me alone?' he shouts. 'You're turning out just like your feckin' sisters.'

She rises quickly to her feet in obvious shock, flicking her beautiful mane of raven-black hair over her shoulder.

'My sisters!' she exclaims. 'What have my sisters got to do with it?'

John Paschal hasn't meant to say anything about her sisters.

It just slipped out, and now that he has said it and can see the effect it is having on her, he can't resist turning the screw.

'Well, one of them married a Spaniard, had a child, then he left her. Your other sister got married, had four children and he has left her. And I'm damned, Teresa, if I'm going to be a third. No feckin' way.'

'John!' she squeals. 'That's an awful thing to say. How could you say such a thing?'

Bursting into tears she takes off the engagement ring and throws it in his face, saying, 'You can keep your lousy ring. I never want to see you again as long as I live,' and she storms off across the park.

John Paschal sighs deeply, rises to his feet and starts walking dejectedly towards the exit gates, leaving the diamond ring lying on the grass. He has no desire to pick it up or to say sorry. Yet he can't resist turning round to deliver one parting salvo.

'Teresa! When I buy a ring it's because I really am getting married, and not thinking about it.'

Embarrassingly, he hears the echo of his voice reverberating across the park. Walking towards the exit he sees the park keeper waiting patiently by the grass-green gates, ever ready to bind the chains around another trying day.

Arriving back in his lodging house John Paschal is surprised to see a telegram waiting for him on the table. With a trembling heart he tears it open to learn that Edward O'Brien, the only father he has ever known, has quietly passed away.

Bridie's theory that all things come in threes was again verified after she received yet another rotten letter. First, the news about Lilly MacAlastair, then a telegram about Edward O'Brien, and now *this*. She felt she couldn't go on and decided to take a few days off work at St Andrew's Hospital. The work was energy-sapping and demoralising; scrubbing the same old pots and pans seven days a week, for breakfast, dinner and tea. Things were bad enough before all this, she thought, what with breaking up with Tomás, but this letter was something else.

Sitting alone in the front parlour of number 49 Barrack Road, she tries to make sense of it all. She has each disturbing word and syllable of the letter firmly engraved on her mind. Yet she takes it out of her pocket one more time, in the hope that its contents will somehow dissolve the awful pain she feels in her heart.

Dear Bridie,

Just a few lines to inform you John Paschal has left Manchester and is now living in Australia. He came home from England for my husband's funeral a few weeks ago. He asked if I'd write and tell you how sorry he was that he hadn't been in touch with you lately. He thought it best to go away and say nothing. He left no forwarding address, so God knows if I'll ever hear from him again. He says he intends to settle there for good.

Bridie, I know it won't be easy but you'd really be better off to forget all about him. I don't think he really knows what he wants. He was very close to Edward and we thought he'd settle on the land, but no. John didn't want to work it, so there was no reason for him to stay. I don't expect I'll ever see him again. Australia is such a terribly long way to go. Perhaps it's for the best. He'll probably meet a nice girl over there and settle down.

I don't particularly like being the one to bring you this news. But he asked if I'd let you know, so I suppose that's that.

I wish both yourself and John Paschal all the best in the future.

Yours sincerely,
Catherine O'Brien

★   ★   ★

It's still the same rotten letter, thought Bridie. Still as bad as ever; no matter how many times I read it. My only son has rejected me.

She had never felt so low in her entire life. How could John Paschal do that to his own mother, his own flesh and blood: cut her out of his life entirely; at twenty years of age; and all she did for him? Where had she gone wrong? '. . . *You'd really be better off to forget all about him . . .*' How! How in God's holy name could anyone say such a thing?

She went to the sideboard and opened her jewellery box, took out the goatskin purse that contained her son's lock of golden hair and held it lovingly between her fingers; feeling the soft silken strands as she recalled that fateful morning long ago when she cut it off, prior to their separation.

It would soon be twenty years, she thought as a single tear ran down her cheek. And all for nothing. Will I ever know a single day's happiness? Will I? She wondered if she should just throw the hair into the fire and start anew. No, she sighed. I can't do that. If nothing else I'll keep it in memory. He was a good son; my only son. Gone now for ever, she sobbed, as she broke down and wept openly on the rug in front of the fire.

She took out her handkerchief to wipe away the tears. How could any son do that to his own mother? she cried. It must be the influence of that Teresa, or someone. John Paschal would never do that to me; after all I have done for him. All the letters and parcels I sent from the Magdalene. Oh God! How I suffered in that place, because I had you, my love; locked away for thirteen long years. Oh, how I begged and borrowed off poor Julie, and now this. There must be a reason, there has to be a reason. Why didn't he just write himself from Manchester? Why?

She slammed the door behind her and went for a walk in the park. She felt so utterly dejected that she didn't really care if she walked out in front of a bus, because at the end of the day no one cared; not even her own son.

She sat there alone in the park, staring into the wide-open

expanse of oblivion. There was really nothing to live for any more. Life would have been so much easier if she'd just given him up completely, instead of getting to know him, only to lose him in the end.

She thought briefly of Tomás. He was gone. She thought of her dear, dear friend Josephine Finn; dead and buried. And now her son, John Paschal, was lost for ever. Even her friend Lilly MacAlastair had been raped. Dear Lord, was there no end to it?

She'd have to pull herself together somehow, she thought, otherwise she'd lose her job. The very thought of having to catch the early morning bus appalled her. What if she didn't go back to work? What if she went back to Ireland instead, to Galway maybe? It seemed there was nothing here for her any more.

Slowly making her way out of the park she tried to control the mounting desolation; tried desperately to make sense of it all. There must be something I can do, she thought, because I swear I will not give in; not now, never. I'll do whatever it takes. But what can I do?

Suddenly she stopped in her tracks to extract the letter and to read it one more time.

'. . . I don't think he really knows what he wants . . .'

As sure as night follows day, thought Bridie, in sudden heart-felt relief, he's confused.

'. . . He was very close to Edward . . .'

That's what's happened, Bridie decided. The poor lad is totally confused. And as for that bitch Teresa Brady, unless I'm greatly mistaken, she was no help to him at all. Confused, that's it. He's confused. I'll go to Ireland for a few days and see poor Lilly. Maybe I'll stay a while longer and see all my friends. If I know Paschal at all, despite what anybody else says, he'll write. The only question is, when?

CHAPTER TWENTY-ONE

BRIDIE SAT UP and breathed a deep sigh of relief. She was feeling so much better now after her week in hospital. The doctors had told her she was severely rundown and suffering from physical and mental exhaustion. They had also advised her to change her job, otherwise it would kill her. Twelve hours a day was too much, they said. And while she was considering their advice, she collapsed at work in St Andrew's Hospital shortly after her return from Ireland.

Deep down she knew it wasn't the work that was killing her, but the stress and strain of the past few months, waiting every day for a letter. She recalled there were days when she was overwhelmed by the sheer hopelessness of it all. She felt she had lost everything. All she ever wanted in life was to *know* what it was really like to love someone. To *know* if she had a real mother or father; to *know* if she had a brother or sister; to *know* if her own son, her own flesh and blood, ever really loved her.

But now suddenly everything seemed so bright and beautiful. Beryl, her lovely English friend from work, had visited her every single day in her hospital bed, promising each time to introduce her to her brother, Gordon, who'd recently divorced.

At last she brought him.

'Bridie, this is Gordon. You know, when I first told him about this beautiful Irish friend of mine, he simply insisted on coming along because he said he'd like to meet you,' smiled Beryl proudly, tipping a wink at Bridie.

'Wha' you been doin' then, heh?' said Gordon cheerfully, his broad smile already putting a glow on Bridie's pale complexion as he extended his hand in greeting.

'Hello, Gordon. It's lovely to see you,' she replied, taking his warm hand in hers. 'Gosh, Beryl, he's just like you – the same features and everything.'

'I know. He hardly ever drinks, he's just mad about cars and loves to go for long drives in the country.'

'How abou' it then? You and I go for a drive when you get better, heh?' suggested Gordon.

'Oh, Gordon,' enthused Bridie, 'that would be lovely, 'cause I hardly ever go anywhere. And I love the countryside and I love looking at the animals and everything.'

'Right then, that's settled,' said Gordon, rubbing his hands together in anticipation.

And on their first outing, they went for a long drive in the country, where Bridie gave Gordon the gift of a lovely little toy dog that he placed in the back window of his car. She was so pleased when she saw him smile at the sight of the little dog's head bobbing.

The following Sunday they went for another long drive, followed by another the week after, until one day they both agreed they were deeply in love. Bridie, in particular, was so happy to have met someone who loved her for what she was. And so, so happy when Beryl helped her to set up in a nice flat, and gave her bits and pieces of furniture.

After two years touring the countryside, and whispering sweet nothings over wild flowers and picnic baskets, Gordon asked Bridie if she'd like to become Mrs Foster. Without hesitation she said yes, because Gordon was the kindest, most caring man she had ever met, who didn't drink the way the mad Irish did. Then the two of them drove in Gordon's Morris Minor to the register office where they were married with two friends as witnesses: Beryl as bridesmaid and Gordon and Beryl's brother Raymond as best man.

Gordon was Church of England, but Bridie didn't care, though she did care that she hadn't had a church wedding. Even after they were married, she never gave up hope that one day they could marry all over again in a Catholic church, she dressed all in white. It was one of two things she prayed for last thing at night before going to sleep: that, and to be reunited with her son for ever.

'Byedee! It doesn't matter! All weddings are the same! They're just a money racket,' said Gordon in response to her continuous goading, as he slapped another length of wallpaper on the living-room wall.

'I know, love, and I'm pleased we got married, but a register office isn't the same. I'd still like to have a proper church wedding.'

'Byedee,' replied Gordon, raising his voice in anger, 'I've told you a dozen times! We can't get married in a Cat'lic church! I'm not Cat'lic, Byedee!'

'But we could if you weren't so stubborn. You could easily become a convert.'

'Aw, Byedee, give over. Pass me that cloth a minute.'

Instead she went into the back kitchen and pretended she hadn't heard him.

When he saw the disappointment etched on her face, he tamely added, 'Gimme time to think abou' it; you know it'll cost a packet; an' we barely got enough to get by as it is; wha' with the mortgage and everythin'.'

After months and months of cajoling, Bridie got her wish. Marching down the aisle in her beautiful white wedding gown, she felt more radiant than at any time in her entire life. She was very happy to have Julie, Noreen and Beryl as her bridesmaids this time; while Gordon's friend John was best man.

Putting together her wedding album, Bridie feigned contentment, because she couldn't bear to tell Gordon that her heart
still ached in the absence of her son. She knew that no album
would ever be complete without a recent photograph of him.
She would have given the whole world just to have him walk
her down the aisle. She didn't care that it would have been
strange to have her twenty-odd-year-old son giving her away
or that people might whisper behind her back. He was her son
and she was proud of him. But sure, where was the use in
thinking that now when she didn't even know where he was –
and he didn't seem to care either? It had been years since she
had last seen or heard from him. But who knows, perhaps he'll
turn up one of these days, she thought.

After they were married Gordon insisted that Bridie give up
her job at St Andrew's. There was the offer of an easier job
working for the City Council, looking after the elderly in their
own homes. The hours were much shorter and she would be
more or less her own boss.

Bridie took the job. She almost cried with relief at the
thought she would have no more early mornings, and if she was
lucky Gordon might just be in the door before her in the
evenings and have a nice fire on. Being a one-time chef in
the defence forces, Gordon could rustle up a tasty morsel in
no time at all; particularly his favourite recipe of pork pie and
mash with loads of gravy and Yorkshire pudding.

And while Gordon did all the cooking Bridie wrote to her
friends Noreen and Julie. Still lamenting the loss of her John
Paschal, she would ask them to be on the lookout in case he
ever returned to Ireland.

On her last working day at St Andrew's Hospital, Bridie had
gone up to the main office in the administration department
to collect her wages.

'Mrs Foster, you know you're entitled to a bonus of one
pound for every year of service?'

'That's right,' said Bridie, thinking a pound seemed such a miserly sum when she considered the long hours and years of loyal service she had put in.

'And as you've been here ten years that means—'

'Eleven,' corrected Bridie firmly, before the wages clerk looked questioningly at her. 'I'm here eleven years!' she re-iterated.

The wages clerk went to the filing cabinet to study her employment record. He consulted his colleague in whispered tones, and returned with a triumphant look on his face.

'Actually, Mrs Foster, you've only been with us ten years.'

'Eleven! As true as God is my judge, I'm here eleven years, and I think I should know.'

'I'm afraid that's not quite so. You're actually one week short of eleven years. Therefore that constitutes ten years' bonus.'

'Well,' replied Bridie, feeling very embarrassed at not having got her facts right in the first place, 'I hope none of you ever die with the hunger. To think of all I did for you! I washed and scrubbed from morning till night seven days a week. And no patient of mine ever went hungry and no doctor ever went to work of a morning without being offered a nice cup of tea . . . and that's the thanks I get. You know, when I think about it, my husband was right. He said killing people, you are, with work, not kindness.'

'Now, now, Mrs Foster! That's not a nice thing to say,' replied the wages clerk, feeling somewhat peeved as he handed two pay packets to Bridie. 'I'm sorry, Mrs Foster, but these things are completely outside my control. You see, it's not up to us. It's Department of Health regulations and we must apply the rules.'

But Bridie was still angry.

'How much is in that?' she asked, indicating the small brown envelope marked 'Bonus'.

'Ten pounds! It's your bonus for length of service and this

here is your two weeks' wages, together with your holiday pay and superannuation.'

Pushing back the envelope marked 'Bonus' Bridie said, 'Here, you can keep it! It looks like the Department of Health needs it a lot more than I do.' Then, turning on her heel, she stormed out the door.

A week later she received a cheque in the post from St Andrew's Hospital. It was made out for the sum of ten pounds sixteen shillings and sevenpence.

After the breakup of John Paschal's romance with Teresa Brady, he moved around so fast he never knew himself where he was going, and never stayed anywhere long enough to call it home. He never wrote to Bridie or had any desire to contact her again. Instead he drifted aimlessly from one part of the country to another before emigrating to Australia.

In Australia he was as fleet-footed as ever. Working first in the sprawling gold mining fields of Kalgoorlie in Western Australia, he then went south to Albany; then to Melbourne, where he worked as a conductor and tram driver for a year or more before packing his bags yet again. This time he lived and worked in places as diverse as Sydney, Brisbane, Townsville, Ayr and Cairns. And it was during one of these flights of fancy that he decided he was going nowhere. He had become disillusioned with life in Australia.

He made up his mind to return to England, where he soon got himself a good job working on an oil rig in the far north of Scotland. He managed to survive the arctic winter conditions long enough to save up a few pounds to buy himself a lorry and start a haulage business.

But before making any major decision he decided to take a short holiday in Ireland – only to learn on his arrival that his beloved adoptive mother, Catherine O'Brien, had passed away a few days earlier.

A year later, after he got over the shock of Mrs O'Brien's demise, John Paschal decided to spend a few days with his long-time friend Joe Hennessy down in Kilkenny, where he thought the craíc was always good. And it was there that Joe introduced John Paschal to some of the best watering holes in Urlingford, frequented by many of Joe's cronies. But one evening John Paschal was more interested in a young lady he spotted walking down the other side of the street.

'Jesus, lads! Look at that! Who is she?'

'Oh! That's Julie,' laughed Richie Brennan, perched on his high stool. 'Keep your shagging eyes off that lady. I'm bringing her to the dance tonight . . . so you've no chance, JP.'

'OK, OK. I'll tell you what we'll do, just to make the thing fair. We'll go fifty, fifty. One of you chaps can take Julie to the dance, but I'm taking her home. Isn't that fair enough?' laughed John, to which a loud alcoholic cheer went up in the bar.

'Fair play to you, JP. You never lost it. You know it's her eighteenth birthday today, so you'll have to buy her a big box of chocolates,' added Richie.

'Yeah, and a massive bunch of flowers, I suppose. Do ye know something, lads, you're the greatest shower of hoors I ever met. I wouldn't like to believe one solitary word that comes out of yeer filthy mouths,' replied John Paschal.

This line was followed by yet more jibes and laughter, until Joe said. 'Come on, lads! Drink up! Time for the road.'

John Paschal and his friends drove straight into Thurles and went to the Anner Hotel, where John Paschal looked eagerly around to see if he could see Julie anywhere. No such luck. Then, half an hour later he spotted her being escorted into the hotel by a male friend, but she was soon lost in the midst of the huge crowd, whose laughter grew louder as the beer flowed free. And as the band continued to pound out rock-and-roll music, John Paschal slipped quietly away from the bar to have a few dances and maybe, with a bit of luck, meet somebody nice. But most of all he wanted to meet Julie, to find out if she was committed to anyone or not, as he couldn't accept the word of his friends. She was the finest-looking girl he'd seen in a long time. But what was she like to talk to?

He spotted her not more than a few feet away as he ordered himself a drink at the small cocktail bar. She had her back turned to him and was leaning across a table talking to her female friends. There they were, blathering on and on; he thought they'd never stop. He was really desperate to talk to her, and knew that if he didn't act quickly the opportunity would be lost.

But he couldn't just tap her on the shoulder and ask her to dance. To do that would be to give all her friends the chance to laugh and snigger when she refused, which she might well do. Jesus, he thought, will she ever stop talking? He knew what he was going to do. It was something he'd never done before and could result in him getting a slap across the face. But, on the other hand, he'd be guaranteed a quick response.

Seeing the exposed flesh of her lower back, where her white top had ridden up, he reached forward and poured a small drop of his bottled Guinness on to her bare flesh. She sprang to attention immediately, turned and looked him in the eye, while all her friends sat with their vodkas, laughing their heads off.

'Hi, Julie! Sorry about that. but desperate times call for desperate measures. I had to talk to you.'

'Well, Jesus! You'd better start talking fast. You realise you have me drowned. What made you do that?' she smiled, as she tried drying the small of her back.

'Desire! An overwhelming desire to . . . talk to you . . .'

'And who are you? Do I know you?'

'You do now. My name is John. I'm a good friend of Joe Hennessy, whom I believe is a neighbour of yours. I saw you walking down the street earlier today, and I thought I'd like to get to know you.'

'Well, did you now?' she smiled broadly. 'Isn't that strange? And I saw you walking down the street yesterday and I thought I'd like to get to know you too.'

Placing his drink on the bar counter he turned round and said, 'Good! That's what I like to hear. Let's go and have a dance.'

They had several dances before returning to the bar. There he treated her to a cocktail, as it was indeed her eighteenth birthday. Then they danced the rest of the evening away before he waltzed her out the door and gave her a lift home in his white vintage motor car, with its chrome wire wheels, which he'd brought over from Manchester.

A week later John Paschal decided that, having met the woman of his dreams, he had no desire to return to England: preferring instead to set up his haulage business in Dublin from where he commuted up and down to Kilkenny to see Julie.

Then one sunny afternoon, almost two years later, in the grounds of the Dublin Annual Spring Show, in Ballsbridge, he asked her to marry him.

She said yes.

Her mother didn't approve, though. 'Who is he, Julie?' she said. 'You're going with that fella two years or more now, and you don't even know the first thing about him. And him not having two pennies to rub together and nobody belonging to him. And now you're telling me he has no mother or father; that he was reared God knows where . . . above in county Galway. Faith, if I was you, Julie, I'd think long and hard before I'd have anything at all to do with a fellow like that. Long and hard, so I would.'

'Mother! I'm marrying him! I don't care whether you like it or not!'

Despite that major hiccup, they got married in Rome and later decided to buy a house in Williamstown. It was on a

Friday, the thirteenth day of April, that they moved into their
new home

Time to start a brand new life, thought John Paschal.

The scene was as old as the universe itself. A very old woman,
frail and decrepit-looking almost beyond belief, was going
through every dustbin in the bowels of the city, trying desperately to uncover something that would reveal the whereabouts
of John Paschal. As he stood there watching her, she continued
her painstaking search, going from one rat-infested alley to
another, checking every crumpled letter and piece of paper for
news of his whereabouts . . .

John Paschal sat bolt upright in bed as a cold sweat ran down
his forehead. What was really terrifying about the whole thing
was that he was seeing the face of his own mother, Bridie. Not
only that, but it was the image of a woman steeped in poverty,
and it was poverty of the mind that was destroying her, not
hunger. She was slowly starving to death for news of her son.

In an effort to banish the hideous scene from his memory
he got out of bed, dressed quickly and went down stairs to
prepare breakfast for his three young children.

Julie knew instinctively that something was amiss. After much
coaxing John Paschal disclosed to her his terrible dream and they
both put it down as just a nightmare; something over which he
had absolutely no control. But, although he never admitted it,
John felt that it was indeed a message from the other side.

Fortunately, when he first met Julie he had told her everything about his mother, and how he had walked away from
her: disowned her entirely. He felt telling Julie was the right
thing to do. He knew he couldn't live a lie. Julie understood
this and the subject was never mentioned again.

But when, three weeks after the nightmare, the self-same
dream occurred again, it threatened his state of mind. No one
could fail to be affected by such a dream. He lay there in bed,

his body swathed in sweat. He knew it could mean one of two things: he was slowly entering the realms of madness; or else it was a clear sign that his mother was looking for him. He chose to believe the latter. Something, somewhere was clearly amiss. As he played the image over and over again in his mind, and saw her rummaging through the litterbins, he equated that with the numerous parcels she had sent to him over the years and the countless letters she had written. Thinking about it made him feel ill with guilt. He felt unworthy of her name. Nobody in their right mind could have been so selfish, so rotten as to ignore their own mother. Yet that was what he had done. He had disowned his own mother, and all she had done for him.

'How long since you've seen her?' asked Julie.

'Oh, too long I fear!' replied John as he paced up and down the kitchen. 'I have to try and think. This has to be a clear sign that she's dead or something.'

'Oh God! Don't say that!'

'It is! It is! I know it is! It's a clear sign. But what it is I don't know. And, if she *is* dead, how am I going to find out? I have to go and find her. The problem is it's been such a long time. It's twenty years since I last saw her in Northampton, and I've had no contact with her since.'

'What about her address? Maybe you should write, if it'll make you feel any better.'

'No, no! I've got to go to England. Besides, I don't know where she lives; all I have is a vague memory of where it was, but that was such a long time ago. And, believe me, this is urgent. To dream about her once is just chance; to have the same dream a second time is telepathy. I know it is. She is calling out to me. Perhaps she's in a home somewhere, with no one to look after her. She may even be homeless or on the streets, or seriously ill in hospital or worse still, maybe dead.'

'So what are you going to do?' asked Julie, struggling to feed Síle, the youngest of their three children.

'I'll go straight down to the bank, draw out a few pounds and go over to England on tonight's sailing, and while I'm over there I'll pop down to London and buy a few canvas paintings for framing. That way the trip won't be a total loss.'

'Well, I don't care what you do, so long as you're happy about it. But I think maybe you should wait a while, think it over and not rush into anything. You must have had some reason for not keeping in touch with her in the first place. And what if you find her and she wants to come here and live with us, how will we manage?'

'No, no! It was my fault. I was in the wrong. I was a bit too young and I couldn't cope with it all,' admitted John as he prepared to put a rasher in the pan and to make breakfast.

'As regards her wanting to come and live with us,' he added, 'we'll cross that bridge when we come to it. Besides, twenty years is a hell of a long time. It might not be that easy to find her. But whatever it takes I know I've got to track her down and that's that.'

Julie, having finished feeding Síle, said, 'Well, darling, she's your mother; and whatever you decide to do, I wish you the best of luck.'

A few hours later he was on his way to England.

CHAPTER TWENTY-TWO

T HEY WERE SNUGGLED up on their brand-new couch at number 34 Cloutsham Street, Northampton, having a nice cup of tea while half watching television and discussing their respective family ties. Bridie had decided it might be a good time to disclose to Gordon a little bit more of her past life, a little more of her secret dreams and desires.

'Did I ever tell you how I cut off a lock of my son's hair the day I had to leave him?'

'Your son's 'air!' exclaimed Gordon. 'Wha' you on abou', Byedee?'

'I cut off a lock of my son's hair the morning I had to leave him. I keep it in my jewellery box upstairs. You see, I had a dream the night before he was taken away that if I kept something belonging to him he'd come back to me and that's why I've kept it all these years. I thought I told you about it before?'

'Aw, Byedee, everybody's got dreams! They're just a waste o' time, as far as I'm concerned.'

'I know you don't believe in them, Gordon. But I'm different. I'll never ever give up on him. Even when I go to bed at night, it's the last thing I think about. I pray every night, Gordon, that he'll return or write to me – only I wouldn't like to be an old woman when it happens. I wouldn't like to have to wait that long.' Slipping her arm lovingly around Gordon's shoulder, she continued, 'I know, love, it's hard for you to understand, what with your own family, and your ex-wife and everything, but sometimes that's all I ever think of. And it upsets me when I hear you giving out to your grandchildren. They're only young, Gordon; at least you can talk to them every day. If only I could talk to John Paschal, I'd be the happiest woman in Ireland . . .'

'Island, Island! Wha' you on abou'?' chuckled Gordon, unable to pronounce his Rs.

'Sorry, love, I meant England. You know well what I mean. But, isn't it funny, I keep trying to figure out where in the world he might be. Sometimes I think it's like standing on top of a tall pillar and looking down on to the streets of London, watching the millions of people go by, trying desperately to pick out the one you're looking for. And it's far worse when you don't even know which country they're in. It makes it so much harder to reach out to them in your prayers.'

'Why not go to Island then? Someone must know if he's been abou'.'

'Oh, Gordon, that would be lovely. Maybe next year we could go on holiday to Galway and I could make enquiries. But I wouldn't like to meet up with him without first letting him know. It's up to him to find me, if he wants. You know, he could be in Ireland, England or Australia at this very moment. The last I heard of him, he was supposed to be in Australia. But somehow I feel he'd never stay there. He might be back living in Ireland now or maybe Manchester.'

Bridie leaned over the side of the couch to pick her cigarettes off the floor. And as she lit up another Park Drive for herself, and one for Gordon, she continued, 'All I know is, Gordon, I shall never stop praying. I know that my prayers will be answered, but that the time has to be right for the two of us. The last time we met I think I may have frightened him away because he was young and didn't know me. Did I ever tell you I was psychic and had the power to know certain things at certain times?'

'Wha'? You a medium?' laughed Gordon. 'Cor blimey! That's

a good 'un. I'll have to take you to the market on Saturday; we'd make a packet!'

''Tis true, Gordon. Did I ever tell you – and please don't laugh – that I met a man when I was, what . . . about sixteen or seventeen, who was very good to me? I remember his words to this very day. He said, "I can tell you, Bridie, that you'll never be rich, but then again you'll never be poor. But someday, perhaps years from now, when you'll least expect it and need it most you are going to win." And isn't it a funny thing, I don't think he meant money – although I keep doing the pools and every free competition, just in case. I think he was talking about Paschal even though he wasn't even born then. But it was the way he looked at me; I know he meant every word of it.'

'Was he a gypsy or something?'

'He was a gentleman farmer I used to work for. He had a wife and three lovely children. I'll never ever forget how kind he was to me. Somehow I always feel that his words will come true and that John Paschal will come back to me. I'm sorry, Gordon, to keep going on about it, but I just know that if I could reach out to him, he'd come running.'

'I doubt it,' sighed Gordon wearily. 'But you never know, do ya?'

He was tired of listening to Bridie. He had enough problems of his own, he thought, without dwelling on hers any longer. 'That's it! Move your backside, Byedee, I got to be in Abington Street in the morning at eight o'clock. You go on up; I'll put things away.'

But Bridie stayed there, lying on the couch. She was in no mood to get up as she savoured one last puff of her cigarette, while trying to imagine what it would be like if her son were ever to walk in the door of her living room. It would be absolute heaven, she thought. Absolute heaven.

★   ★   ★

The Holyhead boat train swooshed its way past unsuspecting hamlets, as it sped across the English countryside, bound for London. Its dimly lit carriages were packed to capacity, mounds of luggage strewn here there and everywhere. Trying to make sense of it all while studying the toothless gaping features of his fellow passengers was John Paschal. He wished at that moment he were an artist, for truly the late night scene was a cartoonist's dream. Yet, despite the enormous pleasure he derived from looking at the human form, he could not rid his head of that awful dream. The very thought that he had deserted his own mother and was now going to England to try to right the wrong made him feel ill again. He had an uneasy feeling that his past might be coming back to haunt him. No, no, that wasn't a fair assumption, he thought. His mother would never haunt him like that; and it all happened such a long time ago. But what was it that made him feel so bad? It was as if he had committed some heinous crime. A crime he couldn't explain. And the very thought that he wanted to be reunited with his mother brought back memories of a word he hated more than any other in the English language. *Illegitimate.* He'd heard so many crude inter-pretations of the word as a youngster. It was the legal term for a bastard; a child born out of wedlock. And here he was himself, a bastard, going to England aboard the night train to look for his mother. He wondered if there were any more bastards on the train. Sure, the world is full of bastards, and mother-fuckers, and sons-of-bitches who wouldn't even write to their own mothers never mind their grannies. So in both senses he was a bastard.

Would he be proud of his mother when he saw her? If she was going to be anything like the image portrayed in his dream he wasn't so sure. He prayed with all his heart that the dream was no more than a secret sign; a sign that he must save her. But save her from what? From sickness, from death or the twilight zone? The twilight zone, like death, was one of those subjects people were loath to talk about. But that horrid dream he'd had made him recollect a frightening memory from years ago, when he lived in Manchester.

He remembered how he was returning home from work one evening when he saw a bowed elderly figure pushing a rickety old pram laden with rags down the cobble-stoned alley at the back of the house where he lived.

The old man was calling out in a clear voice, 'Rag-bone . . . rag-bone . . . rag-bone . . . !' The very sight of that man, whom he had never seen before, frightened the life out of him. For some strange reason, he thought the piercing tone of that man's voice was synonymous with death. Later that same night, on his return home from an enjoyable night out, he suddenly developed an uneasy feeling as he neared his house. There was something eerie about the deserted, dimly lit street that made him break into a run, as the hair stood on the back of his neck. Something or someone was following him, of that he was sure: not a human form but a form none the less. He reached the house safely and was never so glad to go to bed.

He'd only been in bed a short time when he heard the most awful cry of lamentation coming from the front of the house. He thought it was the most terrifying wail he had ever heard. It made both himself and the man he was sharing a room with rear up in their beds with sheer fright. He could clearly see the silhouette of his roommate in the bed beside the window, as he exclaimed, 'Jesus Christ, John! What was that?'

'I don't know, it sounds horrid,' replied John Paschal, in fearful dread. 'It must be some old drunkard.'

'But I can't hear or see any fucker. There's no one around,' said his roommate, looking out the window. For a few moments they both sat there, terror-stricken, as the neon city lights cast hypnotic shadows across the room. Then they quickly buried their heads beneath the blankets to hide the ghostly shadows dancing on the walls of their abode. But when John woke in the morning, his roommate was lying there dead.

And that dream he had had of his own mother was the nearest he had ever come to reliving that horrible moment. He didn't want to relive that dream ever, ever again, and he prayed that it wasn't a premonition of his mother's death.

If so, he didn't know how he would ever cope with the knowledge that he had denied his own mother. And the reason he now felt so bad, he knew, was because of this stain on his character, this sin on his soul. There was only one way he could redeem himself, and that was by finding her. He would have to find her at any cost, before it was too late. Maybe it wasn't too late, and she was still alive and living in Barrack Road. But what did he know about her, he asked himself. Damn all. And apart from a few old photographs, he had nothing to show that his mother ever existed. No letters, rhymes or poems, and certainly no mouth organ. Absolutely nothing. And all the letters she had written – there must be hundreds, no, thousands of letters. She was forever writing. And after all that, it was sad to think he didn't have one solitary letter of hers to his name.

But I'll find her, he promised himself as the train slowly ground to a halt, and a pleasant voice came over the public address system, announcing, 'All passengers bound for Northampton change at Rugby. All passengers bound for Northampton change at Rugby; Rugby next stop.'

It was around seven thirty a.m. when he arrived in Northampton. He decided that first and foremost he'd try to find some suitable accommodation in a cheap hotel or guest-house. Regardless of how things were going to go for him during the day, he'd be stopping in Northampton for the night, so he could leave his luggage there now. Then he'd hire a taxi and go straight over to Barrack Road and see what sort of a response he'd get. Knowing his luck, he thought, the place would probably be demolished.

Oh God, he pleaded, don't do that to me. I don't think my ailing heart could take it. At least if the street still exists, somebody somewhere might know of her whereabouts.

He knew that solving this great problem was destined to be the most critical moment in his entire life. Not only was he endeavouring to find a blood relative, he was also trying to turn the clock back, and to make amends for lost time.

Three hours later, John Paschal turned a key in his hotel bedroom door, happy to have got rid of his luggage. Then he ran downstairs again and jumped into a waiting taxi. 'Barrack Road, please.'

'Very well, sir. Which end of Barrack Road would you like sir?'

'I'm not sure. Number 49, wherever that is.'

Number 49 was a neat, red-brick house situated about halfway down the road. It was part of a continuous block that stretched to one hundred houses, with another block on the other side of the road. The houses were fronted by rows of cars and vans.

The newly painted green door of number 49 had a ship's anchor door knocker as well as a bell. John Paschal weighed the ship's anchor for the pleasure that was in it and let it fall heavily on the door. He did it again and again and when no one answered he rang the doorbell.

From somewhere a voice said, 'They're at work, mate. They'll not be home till late.'

When John Paschal turned he saw a small elderly man standing outside the house directly across the way.

'Oh! I take it you live around here. I'm trying to find a family relative, who used to live in number 49. Bridie Rodgers. Do you know if she still lives here?'

'Bridie Rodgers?' The man shook his head. 'Never heard of her. Alec and Winifred live there now ... a long while ... elderly Jamaican couple. Ain't no Bridie ... what's it ... ?'

'Rodgers.'

'Rodgers? Ain't no lady by that name, not that I know of, anyroad, an' I've been here ten year or more.'

'Ten years!' exclaimed John Paschal. 'How long have this couple been here then?' he asked, realising too late that it was a stupid question.

'About six . . . maybe seven year. They won't know aught. Nah, mate. No woman by that name lived about here, anyroad,' said the little man. 'You could ask Jack; lives in number 59,' he said, pointing to a house a few doors down the street. 'He's lived here all his life, he might know summat.'

'OK, mate, thanks.'

John Paschal went straight to Jack's house and cursed his luck because there was no one there either. Nothing for it now, he thought, but to knock on every door. He tried the doors either side of number 49 and those directly across from it. But he got nowhere, because hardly anybody was at home. He took note of those that weren't; he'd have to call back later. Somebody was bound to remember her.

It was fast approaching dusk and he had tried every house in the street, including the paper shop on the corner. He felt exhausted, having knocked on so many doors, and having asked so many questions, while at the same time giving away as little information about himself as possible. In desperation he went back to Jack's house for the third or fourth time. Jack appeared to be the key to everything. Finally, he collared him on his way home from work.

'Bridie Rodgers?' queried Jack thoughtfully, while John Paschal tried to figure out what class of a tradesman Jack was. A coal man, he decided, as unmistakable rings of dust shrouded the man's bright blue eyes.

'I never knowed what lady's second name were,' he said, shaking his head thoughtfully, 'but I remember a lady what used to live at number 49. A lovely lady she were and all: Irish lass, black 'air. She were a Bridie, I think, wha' used to work in St Andrew's.'

'That's her! That's her! Where did she go, or how long is she gone?'

'Aw, mate, haven't seen her in years. All moved out of area, see, wha', ten years or more ago. Been lots o' changes since then, lots o' changes.'

'Well, thanks for your help, anyway. I'll probably try St Andrew's first thing in the morning. They'll surely have some idea.'

'Sorry, mate.'

'No problem. Thanks.'

The next day, John Paschal made his way to St Andrew's Hospital, and hung around the reception area for a long, long time. Nobody seemed interested in his query, and the lady he first spoke with never came back to him.

After repeated enquiries to various members of staff as to the likely whereabouts of Bridie Rodgers, he was at last approached by a dour-looking matron who told him, 'Bridie Rodgers left here years ago. She used to work as a domestic. That the lady?'

'Yes, yes! That's her! Do you know where she went?'

'Sorry. I've no idea, and even if I did, I'm not at liberty to give out that sort of information.'

'I know, I know. And I appreciate that. But I'm her son, and I'm trying to find out where she has gone. Have you any idea where she might have lived?' pleaded John.

On hearing this, the matron's eyebrows drew down and her thin lips curled in distaste as she raised her ample chin and replied, 'I'm sorry, sir, you must be in the wrong place, or else it's somebody else you're after. The Bridie Rodgers what worked here had no family so how could you be her son? The lady wasn't even married.'

'I know that, but I *am* her son! And all I'm trying to do is find my mother. It's very urgent.'

'Well, you've come to the wrong place,' retorted the matron, before adding, 'Now, if you don't mind, I have to get on with my work.'

'OK, I understand. But maybe I could speak with someone else . . . one of her friends. They might be able to help me,' suggested John hopefully, lowering the tone of his voice.

For a moment the matron's eyes blazed as she studied him. Then she replied, 'Sir, I've already told you. We do not give out information on any of our staff. Now, if you don't go away I'll call the security men and have you removed from the premises.'

John Paschal turned away, devastated. His face, he surmised, like many before him, didn't fit. Now where do I go? he asked himself, as he sat atop a red bus all the way back to town. He went to a café and sat thinking over a refreshing cup of coffee. After some serious deliberation he appointed himself commander-in-chief of this investigation. He began work immediately by drawing up a long list of possible sources of information, beginning with the deaths register because there wasn't much point in searching for someone if they were already dead. After that he would proceed to check the marriage register. With a bit of luck she might have got married, he thought.

Paschal spent the rest of the day going from one records office to another, and in the heavy downpour it wasn't easy. His feet ached like never before. He felt as if he'd walked miles and miles, and yet he had nothing to show for it. What if she was still living and married? What if she had married, but had since passed away? She'd then be listed in the deaths under her married name. It would take days to check all the registers. There were so many permutations to deal with it was almost beyond comprehension.

That night he went through his list again: death registers, marriage registers, social welfare and taxation records and any number of hospitals where she might be working.

Then over a beer it occurred to him that she might not be

in Northampton at all. What if she had moved and was now living in London, Leeds, Birmingham or Manchester? If that was the case then there was no hope at all, particularly if she was married and using her married name. Then he had a brain wave; the voting register. They usually have records of every family name and every street. He would begin with the list of residents for Barrack Road. That would surely shed some light on the matter.

It didn't, though he checked all the names going back light years. Then he checked the tax offices, haphazard and all as they were; and again, nothing. And again the problem arose: what if she had married and had given the marriage register a false name? Then he might never find her. Someone suggested the Salvation Army as a great source of help. He merely cringed at the idea. He had started this investigation and he would finish it. Again he went back to the deaths and marriage records: a futile exercise.

He had now spent three whole days on the beat, and was absolutely exhausted, both mentally and physically. His body ached as he lay flat out on his hotel bed. He was hungry, but the prospect of dining out, knowing he did not deserve it because he hadn't earned it, killed his desire to eat anything. How could one possibly eat anything nice when one had worked hard for three whole days and had made no progress whatsoever? To do that would be to accept defeat. He decided instead to go out and buy himself a newspaper. He'd read it first to take his mind off things and hopefully starve himself into submission. There was no other way.

Returning to his hotel room with the *Evening Echo* tucked under his arm, he again lay down on the bed to ease his aching limbs. He read the *Echo* from cover to cover and was about to cast it across the room out of sheer boredom and frustration when something caught his eye. It was the Personal Column in the small ads section. He sprang from the bed in sheer excitement. Why hadn't he thought of this before? He would run an advertisement in the *Evening Echo*. That was surely the key. But how would he phrase it? If nobody on Barrack Road could remember Bridie Rodgers or knew of her whereabouts, then who else would bother to answer it? Would she herself be likely to see it? No, but perhaps some of her friends or work colleagues would. But the chances of that happening were negligible. Pacing up and down the room, he knew that this could be the defining moment. Placing an advertisement in a newspaper was an extremely long shot, and he would have to sweeten it because people were always open to persuasion if they were to gain something from it. What address would he use for a reply? He didn't like box numbers because he felt there was something secretive about them, and there was little point in using the hotel as an address as he'd have to hang around Northampton for days, waiting for a reply and he couldn't afford it anyway. Nothing for it but the old reliable, he thought.

Next morning John Paschal delayed his trip to London – to buy some canvas paintings – long enough to submit his advertisement.

REWARD OFFERED to anyone knowing the where-abouts of Ms Bridie Rodgers, last known address No. 49 Barrack Road, Northampton about 1966. Please contact John Rodgers, Main Street, Williamstown, Co. Galway, Éire.

He paid for the insertion and requested that the newspaper run it for two days. From now on, he told himself, the matter was in the lap of the gods.

Beryl Foster was relaxing at home with her evening newspaper. It was a pleasure she enjoyed more than any other: to be able to read in the quiet of her own home when the evening chores were done. She always read the daily news, followed by the gossip columns, before considering the merits of a nice cup of tea and tasty biscuit. She was about to put away the newspaper when something caught her eye. It was the two words in capital letters 'REWARD OFFERED' in the Personal Column.

As Beryl began to read she did a double take. My God, 'Ms Bridie Rodgers . . . 1966 . . .' – that's Bridie, that's my sister-in-law. She reread the article again and again.

It has to be our Bridie. She has a son, John, John Paschal. That must be him, John Paschal Rodgers. God! I wonder if Bridie knows. A reward offered. Gosh, I wonder how much it is. I know Bridie would give anything to see him. I don't think she has heard from him in years. I wonder if that's really him. Bridie and I used to live on Barrack Road. That's where she was living when we first met, herself and a few of her friends. Gosh, I can't believe this, in the *Evening Echo*.

She checked the date at the top of the page in case she was making some horrid mistake, but there was no doubting her eyes. It was there in black and white.

She must ring Bridie right away. But then she thought, no, she would drive around to Gordon and Bridie's instead, so Bridie would be able to see the advertisement for herself.

She put on her shoes. Then she decided to ring first just in case they had visitors, or had gone out visiting.

'Hello, Hello, Bridie! I was just checking to see if you were at home.'

'Hello, Beryl. How are you, dear?'

'Everything's fine, Bridie! Do you mind if I pop round to see you? I've something to show you. I'm not a hundred per cent sure but I think it may be good news.'

'Oh! Is everything all right?'

'Yes, dear. There's nothing wrong: nothing that a nice cup

of tea won't put right. I'm on my way over then . . . See you in ten minutes.'

When Beryl arrived, she couldn't wait to see Bridie's face. She didn't know which of them would be the more excited – Bridie on reading the good news, or herself as the bearer of warm tidings

'I think, Bridie, you'd better sit down,' she said breathlessly, 'and get your glasses on. Read this.' She thrust the newspaper in front of Bridie.

'What's up then?' enquired Gordon, seeing the excitement mounting on his sister's face, as he stood in front of the fireplace. 'Won a free holiday or wha'?'

'Gordon! Listen, please.'

'Jesus, Mary and Holy St Joseph! It's John!' exclaimed Bridie, looking up from the newspaper. 'That's my John.'

'John?' asked Gordon in bewilderment, as the two women looked at each other starry-eyed for a few moments.

'It's my son! John Paschal! Gordon, I've found him. Oh, Beryl, it's him! It's him! Oh, thanks be to God Almighty. How can I ever thank you?' Bridie clasped her hands together and raised her eyes to Heaven. ''Twas God sent you, the first time we ever met.' She stood up and the two of them fell into each other's arms in unbridled joy.

'Gosh, Beryl . . . what will . . . what will I do now?' she gasped, wiping away the tears of joy that were cascading down her pale cheeks.

'Reply, of course! Reply straight away, dear! This is your golden moment. This is what you've been waiting for.'

John Paschal phoned Julie at a neighbour's house from London and told her of his disappointment at failing to locate his mother. But he was adamant that he could still find her, with more time and resources. Somebody somewhere was bound to know her, he said. It was more a question of time and patience.

'When are you coming home, that's what I want to know? The children miss you terrible. They keep asking, where's Daddy and when is he coming home?'

'The day after tomorrow, all going well.'

'Oh, I'll look forward to seeing you then. So make the most of it while you're over there, 'cause I don't want you running off on me again. You might get fond of it over there. And don't forget to bring me something nice.'

'What! Bring you something nice! You know I can't do that. There's nothing in the whole of London good enough for a lady like you,' he laughed.

'Well, you could always try! Surprise me. Make believe you're buying something for yourself.'

'What! A pair of frilly knickers! I don't think they'd look good on me.'

'Well, seeing that you've mentioned knickers, it's not such a bad idea.'

'Listen. I have to go now. My money's running out. I'll see you on Monday morning, before midday, please God.'

'OK, give me a quick call, so I'll know what time to expect you.'

'All right! Bye.'

John Paschal was almost there. Another three miles and he'd be home. He wondered if there would be any response to his advertisement. Perhaps it was too soon to expect anything. Maybe a letter might come over the next few days. That's the problem with not having a phone, he thought, as he rounded the last bend before home. He was so glad to be getting off the road. He was sick of travelling. He'd been travelling all his life, and where had it got him, he wondered, as he pulled up on the footpath in front of the house. He was early. He inserted the key into the front door and opened it in silence. Almost immediately the children came running. Within seconds all three of them were around him. Their eager eyes said it all.

Roisín, the eldest at five years of age, turned and ran back into the kitchen, calling out excitedly, 'Mammy, Mammy! Daddy is home!'

And not to be outdone, the others said, 'Daddy! Mammy said you might bring us presents from London if we did the dishes. Were you really in London?'

He made them wait a second. He had to find out if they'd been really, really good: did they deserve presents?

'And where's my kiss? Have you forgotten all about me?' teased Julie, coming forward to give him a big hug. 'Welcome home. It's great to see you again.'

'How could I forget you, bossy-boots? Sure, I'd never hear the end of it. How are you, anyway? Did you miss me at all?'

'Well, I'm delighted now that you're here. I've cooked a lovely breakfast, or have you eaten? I thought you might phone to let me know what time you'd be here.'

'No, I had nothing to eat. Where would you get a breakfast this hour of the morning coming down from Dublin? And anyway, I figured you'd probably have something ready, so where was the point?'

Before eating, he dished out the presents to his children and then gave Julie hers.

'Oh, at long last! Chanel No. 5! I never thought you'd get it for me. Well, fair play to you. You know I've always wanted a bottle of the real stuff. But it must have cost you a fortune. Thanks very much.' She beamed, as she planted another kiss on his cheek.

'What do you mean, you never thought I'd get it?' he joked.

What John Paschal didn't say was that he'd got it in Bond Street, off some wheeler-dealer con artist who'd disappeared at the first sight of a policeman and with John Paschal's money safely in his pocket. For all John knew, he might well have purchased a bottle of Lourdes water. Still, there seemed to be a decent enough pong off it: not bad for a tenner and if it kept the *quare one* happy, then who cared?

'And now I've a little surprise for you,' she said, handing him an envelope. 'Danny delivered it yesterday evening. It's addressed to you, so I couldn't open it.'

'A telegram!' he exclaimed in glorious surprise, examining the envelope carefully before attempting to open it. But there were no clues because it had come via the local post office.

His hands trembled slightly as he tore the envelope open. He prayed that it wouldn't convey bad news. Could it possibly be connected to his mother, so soon? He read it silently. 'Please phone 0604 24772 immediately. Signed Bridie Rodgers.'

His raised his eyes to Heaven in thanksgiving, as overwhelming emotion gripped his entire being. It was as if a tidal wave was washing over him, removing him from all the debris of his past life. He was powerless to control the unbelievable sense of joy flowing into his heart, rising higher and higher until it over-flowed and ran down his sallow cheeks. He felt almost whole again; a normal human being with a real mother.

'Congratulations, dear,' whispered Julie, taking the telegram from him and wrapping her arms around him. 'You did it! You did it! And that's all that matters!' They held each other as they both wept openly for a long time.

'How does it feel?' whispered Julie, handing him a white handkerchief as the children sat around quietly, concern clearly etched on their tiny angelic features.

'I think this has to be the greatest single moment of my life,' he joyously replied. 'It's not every day that you find your long-lost mother.'

'Well, it's certainly one for the family records,' said Julie as she reached for the chart hanging on the back of the press door, which contained all the family's notable records such as birthdays; the date they had moved into the house; when they had had the mumps, the measles, the chicken pox and every other disease under the sun. But this particular bit of good news would go under the heading. 'Memorable Events'. It would take pride of place all on its own.

Julie wrote, 'Monday 13 June 1983. John found his mother. Amen.'

'The next entry now will be when ye finally meet,' she added as she finished, admiring her handiwork.

John Paschal sat at the breakfast table and cuddled his three children.

Roisín, worried, asked, 'What's wrong, Daddy?'

'Nothing, love; nothing in the wide earthly world.'

'Then why were you and Mammy crying?'

'Well,' he replied slowly, 'it is because we got some really good news, and now I'm going to share it with you.'

'I know, you've brought us another present,' ventured Óisin.

'No! No! It's better than that, Óisin. You know how ye have a lovely granny down in Kilkenny?'

'You mean Nan Nan?'

'Yes. Well, I've just discovered ye have a brand-new granny over in England. What do ye think of that?'

'And what's her name?'

'Can we still keep Nan Nan down in . . . down in . . .'

'An' will we be able to see our new granny?'

'As sure as night follows day! We'll all be able to see her . . . and when we do we'll all have one big party.'

'When?' they cried. 'Can we have it now?'

'No! We'll have to wait a while yet. But soon! Real soon!'

The three children stood looking questioningly at their father, before their small features broke into beaming smiles.

CHAPTER TWENTY-THREE

B RIDIE WAS KNEELING on the hearthrug in the small down-stairs sitting room, entering yet another free competition. She was happier now than at any time in her entire life, and knew that she was having the best of all worlds. She'd already received letters and photographs from John Paschal, his wife Julie, and their three children, on an almost weekly basis. And for the past two weeks her old friends Julie Murray and Noreen Donnellan had been staying with her.

On Gordon's days off they'd go for long drives in the country, while at weekends they'd go shopping in Abington Street or to the open-air markets on Kettering Road, the visitors buying toys for their relatives and friends back home. This gave Bridie an opportunity to rummage through piles of bric-a-brac, looking out for miniature bronze dogs, cats and birds, and fancy pieces of jewellery. And if she saw an old brass picture frame or a picture postcard of a dog or cat, then she had to have that too – so that every inch of space on the sideboard, the mantelpiece and windowsills was chock-a-block.

Julie and Noreen were upstairs, studying the latest photographs of Bridie's extended family, having finished packing because they were going home tomorrow.

'She was very lucky, yet,' said Noreen. 'And Gordon's such a fine man. Look at the way he has the house beautifully painted and everything. And will you look at the ceiling; isn't it beautiful? Like I said, you can't bate a man about the house, so you can't.'

'Sure, 'tis wonderful entirely. An' Gordon can turn his hand to an'thin'. Fwhere did *we* go wrong, I wonder,' tittered Julie light-heartedly. 'We were too choosy, that's fwhat was wrong.'

'But where would you find another man like Gordon, yet? They don't make them like they used to,' said Noreen.

'Are you comin' downstairs? You know I'd love a cup a tea. I wonder, has she the kettle on?'

Bridie was still kneeling, filling in the relevant details in the free competition when Julie and Noreen came into the sitting room. She told them what she was doing.

'It's a free competition, I just love doing them. Besides, it passes the time for me, and it doesn't cost me anything.'

'God, but you're great.' said Julie. 'I'm no good at that sort a thing. I've no patience or an'thin'. Sure, I can hardly write me own name.'

'Did you ever win anything, yet?' asked Noreen, as she and Julie threw themselves down on the settee.

'No, not really,' replied Bridie. 'But I know that someday I'll win something big . . . maybe the pools or something.'

'Wha' you on about, Byedee? Wha' about the nags? Tell 'em abou' the nags,' suggested Gordon.

'Oh, that's right. I won a few pounds on the horses. Gordon, you tell them,' she laughed.

'Julie, you should've seen our Byedee a few months back,' said Gordon enthusiastically, turning to the visitors. 'There I were one Sat'day, tryin' to paper the kitchen an' Bridie's curled up by the fire, like she does, sticking a pin in an 'orse here, an 'orse there, weren't we, Byedee?'

'That's right. I remember I was frozen with the cold and all I wanted to do was kneel in front of the fire to try and warm meself, while I picked out a few horses.'

'And there's me up on ladder, covered in bleedin' wallpaper an' paste, wan' I, Byedee?' laughed Gordon, turning to Bridie for confirmation. 'I said, "For God's sake Byedee, give us a hand." But she wouldn't. Ain't that right?' he laughed. 'Instead she goes off to the bookies . . .'

'That's right' confirmed Bridie, laughing heartily at the good of it all. 'Honest to God, you won't believe it, but I won two hundred and ten pounds on a Yankee—'

'My, you should have seen 'er,' interrupted Gordon. 'She goes into bookies with thirty pence, an' comes out with this great big bundle a dosh. I thought, my God, wha' she done? She's gone and robbed the joint! I were expectin' cops to come knockin' on the door any minute, weren't I, Byedee?'

'Honest to God, 'tis true. Gordon wouldn't believe me when I came back with the money. You know I love to have a bet, especially of a Saturday: usually ten or twenty pence. But I always think you're better off putting it on a Yankee; you've a far better chance.'

'God! Aren't you great? I must think a' that now fwhen I get home. A Yankee,' said Julie thoughtfully. 'Is that horse from America, or fwhat?'

'What's wrong with you? You oul' *amadán*! You can't be that stupid, yet,' intervened Noreen, giving her friend a good dig in the ribs to shut her up. 'A Yankee's a bet, not a horse.'

'An' how's it you didn't put a bet on it yoursel', if you're so smart?' retorted Julie, annoyed that she'd been up-staged once again by Noreen, whom she thought was a right show-off whenever they were in company.

When they had ceased laughing at her gaffe, Julie quickly turned the subject to something which she knew would please Bridie greatly.

'There's a new thin' at home now, fwhere you can buy a ticket for a pound, and win a mill'on pounds,' said Julie, anxious to prove that she wasn't as stupid as some people thought. 'An' you can buy a scratch card in any shop or post office an' win an'thin', from two pound to ten thousand.'

'That's right,' endorsed Noreen, sorry that she herself hadn't thought of telling the story in the first place. 'A friend of mine, Mrs O'Keeffe won one hundred pounds, don't you know, and she only bought the one ticket, yet. Straight out-a-the shop, so she did.'

'God, it sounds great, and I never even heard tell of it. I must get you to send me two tickets when you get home.'

'Byedee! Byedee! It's no good! You can't use 'em here! Be a waste of money, because Island's a foreign country,' said Gordon angrily, annoyed that Bridie should waste money on tickets.

'Well, I don't care, Gordon. I'd just like to get one or two . . . out of curiosity.'

'You never know, Gordon,' countered Noreen. 'It's the winning that counts, don't you know? Maybe in God ye'd be lucky, yet. I'm sure I heard Mrs O'Keeffe say you can send them all over the world, so you can.'

'Sure, there's no harm in havin' a go an'way? If you don't chance your arm, you can't break a leg,' tittered Julie.

'And if we didn't win itself, 'twouldn't be the end of the world,' added Bridie, which reminded her she'd better finish the competition she was at, before she started making the tea.

'Bridie, before I forget, do you think you could parcel up me oul' coat and send it home to me? Sure, I'll be kilt, murthered entirely if I have to wear it goin' home, an' the weather so warm. I didn't realise I'd so many things for the little ones. Sure, I could hardly close me suitcase!'

'Of course I will, love. I'd be only happy to do it. When do you want it?'

'Arrah! So long as you post it before the frost sets in, that's all I care,' laughed Julie. 'An' I'll give you the money now.'

'An' why don't you bring it yourself, yet? What'll you do if it rains?' asked Noreen, who couldn't understand Julie at all. That lady's always doing things arse-ways, she thought.

'Sure, I've no room. Me suitcase is bursting and I've a load of bags besides. An' how can I go home without little gifts for the nephews?' said Julie, annoyed that Noreen couldn't understand her predicament.

Bridie stood up to get the tea ready, and left the two women at it. It was the visitors' last evening, so she wanted to be sure to give them a good send-off.

It's not every day that I have my life-long friends visit me, she thought. And no two people deserve it more. Besides, won't Gordon and myself be going home to Ireland shortly to meet John Paschal, and with any bit of luck we'll stay a night or two in Galway with Noreen and Julie. Oh God, I look forward to that day so much I don't know how I can stick it, she sighed to herself: to see my own flesh and blood again, after all these years.

She had risen at the crack of dawn and the thoughts going through her head were ones of contentment. Bridie loved looking after the elderly on behalf of the City Council. She worked on her own, and could come and go as she pleased with no one to say a cross word as long as she carried out her duties. As well as that, the early morning shift always gave her a chance to do a little bit of shopping on the way home, with time to marvel at the way her life had evolved over the last few months. Now she'd done her morning's work, she could enjoy the rest of the day off, she thought to herself as she made her way home, taking a short cut down a narrow side street.

She had enjoyed her Irish visitors' company so much, but what she was really looking forward to now was a reunion with her son, and meeting his his wife and, in particular, her three grandchildren. She was expecting another letter from John this morning. Letters, she thought, made the world go round. She adored letters, both writing and receiving them. Perhaps if things had been different when she was young, she could have made something of herself, instead of being a slave all her life, because she loved books and art and reading and puzzles.

Stopping to draw her breath for a moment, she stood at the glass-panelled front door of her house and inserted the key. She gently pushed open the door and closed it behind her. Home at last. Just time to rest and have a nice cup of tea before starting to get the dinner ready. I think I'd like a piece of fish today, she thought – and then she saw the letters: two of them, strewn at the back of the front door. Wonderful. She recognised the writing immediately, one from John, and one from Julie Murray. Four more weeks now and she'd be going home to Ireland, to see her son for the first time in more than twenty years. *Was* it really twenty years?

Funny how time plays tricks on one. I always thought I could remember everything; especially the years I was separated from John Paschal.

She made herself a mug of tea, and knelt on the hearth rug. She opened Julie's letter first and read the contents carefully before admiring the enclosed scratch cards. She had requested them from Julie when she posted home the coat, making sure to enclose the two pounds for them. She was forever scratching cards, unknown to Gordon, usually for the blind, the handi-capped or some social club, like the British Legion. How could she refuse them, for twenty or thirty pence, when they were for such a good cause? But these new ones cost a pound a piece. She wondered which she should scratch first. They looked the same. So, like a child, she reverted to an old rhyme to help solve her dilemma. Separating the two cards on the floor, she began: '"Eenie, meanie, minie, mo. Jump, on, a, buggie, and, away, we, go." That's Gordon's, this is mine,' she said as she picked up her ticket and scratched it with a silver coin. 'Match any three figures or symbols,' it said, to win that amount. She had two fifties, two fives, a thousand and a hundred. Nothing! Ah well, better luck next time. She looked at Gordon's ticket, and thought she'd love to scratch it too. Would he mind? Sure, where's the harm? If there's nothing in it, it doesn't matter, and if he wins anything it's his and I'll tell him. So she scratched and scratched.

God! Was she seeing things? She reached for her glasses, but she couldn't be sure. She got the little magnifying glass out of the drawer. She went over and stood by the window and read the rules again. God! It seemed unthinkable to her. She'd have to wait until Gordon came home, to see what he thought of it.

And when Gordon did come home, worn out and breathless after his busy morning on the beat as a traffic warden, he was none too ready for Bridie's extraordinary remark.

'Gordon, love, I know you won't believe this, but I think you've just won ten thousand pounds on a scratch card.'

Gordon took a sidelong glance at Bridie as he hung up his warden's hat, before replying, 'For God's sake, Byedee, wha' you on abou'?'

''Tis true, Gordon! Look at this! I've been sick waiting for you to come home. It was your card and I scratched it because I thought there'd be nothing in it.'

'Wha's for dinner then? Byedee! Wha'? Wha'?' asked Gordon aloud, as he recoiled in irritation at some item Bridie was thrusting in front of his nose.

'Just look at it.'

'Wha'? Wha' you playin' at, Byedee? I hardly have time for me dinner.'

Gordon took the ticket reluctantly, then examined it very carefully before turning it over to read the rules, as Bridie stood nervously by.

Then he turned to her and said. 'Cor blimey! Byedee! Looks like we've just won ten grand! But where'd you get the ticket?'

'Julie Murray. You know how I posted home the coat she left after her? Well, I slipped in two pounds and asked her to get me two tickets because she was on about them when she was here.'

'Cor!' said Gordon, still studying the ticket. 'I can't believe it! Ten thousand quid; just like tha'!'

'But, Gordon, do you remember – I'm sure I told you before – I met a man once who told me that I'd win. He said that when I'd least expect it and need it most, I'd win. And I never gave up hope. I have never stopped praying, and now my prayers have been answered.'

'But how do we get the money?' asked Gordon, as he sat down in a daze, still holding the ticket and staring at it in disbelief.

'I think I've it all worked out, if you'll agree to it,' she said, as she went quickly into the kitchen to fetch two glasses.

'I'll tell you what I think later. Here! Take this,' she said handing him a glass of Bailey's Irish Cream. 'Cheers!'

'Cheers!' he smiled. 'I knew first time I saw you in hospital, you were a good 'un. I knew you'd bring me luck. That's why I married you. I could see ten grand etched across your forehead,' he laughed heartily.

'I know, love! I know. But I could see the money long before you; only I never told anyone.' She laughed too, as she sat down beside him. And as she kissed him on the cheek she added, 'I think the dinner might be a bit late, but I'm sure you won't mind, now that we're ten thousand richer.'

Gordon's smile said it all as he slipped his arm around her shoulders and pulled her that bit closer to him.

Bridie was packing her bags in the small upstairs bedroom, getting ready for her trip to Ireland the following day. She stopped momentarily to admire the large framed photograph of her son, his wife and their three children, which took pride of place on her bedside locker. She was trying to decide what she'd say to them when they'd meet to make it a memorable occasion. But whatever she was going to say to her new family could not be said the first day, because it just wouldn't be right. Later on, if everything went well, she'd choose her moment. She could not believe that at last a day was dawning when all of her dreams were about to come true. Seeing her daughter-in-law's kindly image in the photograph and having read her soothing words in many of her letters she felt sure they would understand each other. She put down the photograph and began checking her luggage once more, double-checking to see that all her clothes and gifts were carefully packed. This time tomorrow, she sighed, I'll be in Ireland.

John Paschal sat at the breakfast table reading the daily newspaper. He was trying to catch the very latest on the sporting scene, particularly the state of play in Galway football. After only a few minutes he folded the newspaper and threw it aside because his heart wasn't really in it this morning. He was feeling nervous and trying hard not to show it, but Julie could sense the uneasiness in his every move.

In a little over an hour, Bridie and Gordon would arrive on their doorstep to spend two whole weeks with them. He'd never met Gordon before. And as for Bridie, he figured he hardly knew her at all, having met her only two or three times in his entire life. He couldn't help but wonder how they'd get on. What if he didn't like her? What if the children were nasty to her? John Paschal could never imagine them doing that, but children were children and might show their displeasure by ignoring her. It was one hell of an 'if' he thought. And what about Gordon? Julie in particular had found it hard to understand a single word he'd said to her on their new house phone.

Time and again John Paschal tried to reassure himself that things would work out all right. For God's sake, stop worrying, man, and grow up, he told himself. Haven't you met all kinds of people before on your travels, and didn't you get on with them? Yes, yes, but this is different. These people are staying with us – for two whole weeks. We've never had that before, and besides, Julie might not like them. They're my people, my family. And sure, I mightn't like them myself. Gordon, too, might feel awkward being here. How much of my mother's past does he really know? How much do I know? Nothing. Somehow I could never imagine her telling Gordon how she had been institutionalised for years and had only escaped to England by climbing over the wall with Margaret Sherry and Lilly MacAlastair.

John Paschal thought he heard the screech of brakes outside the house and when he looked out the window he saw a red Morris Minor Traveller parked outside; the driver waving in at him, smiling. They'd arrived.

'Jesus! They're here!' he exclaimed. 'I thought they weren't supposed to be here for another hour.'

'Well, open the door before they start knocking,' suggested Julie, as she hurriedly tried to clear away the last residue of dirty dishes from the draining board.

John opened the front door and saw a small, dapper man get out of the car, and begin to stretch his aching limbs, before turning to meet John.

'Morning,' he said, beaming from ear to ear as he extended a limp hand, forgetting that he'd left Bridie sitting in the car. 'You must be John, then? Wha' a bloomin' drive. You should've seen the roads, great big potholes, and the traffic in Dub Linn . . . cor blimey!'

'Yes. Gordon, it's wonderful to meet you, you're very welcome. Bridie, is she able to get out of the car?'

Gordon turned quickly and went to the offside door. 'Byedee! Byedee! Wha' you playin' at?' he said, opening the door reluctantly for her.

'I'm sorry, Gordon, but I can't get used to that door handle. I much preferred our old car.'

'Aw, Byedee, Byedee! Our old car were clapped out, wern' it? Hardly bring us to bottom of the street. I changed it so you could come on holiday, an' still you're moanin'!'

'I'm not moaning, Gordon, far from it,' retorted Bridie, stepping gingerly from the tiny estate car. 'But you shouldn't leave your wife locked in the car and she supposed to be on holidays,' she laughed. But he ignored her by turning to John.

'Nice little motor then? Wha' you think?' But before John had time to reply Gordon added 'Two and a half hours from Dub Linn; forty-eight miles to the gallon. Not bad goin' then, if it wasn't for those bloomin' potholes. I'm not kiddin' you, it were hardly safe to drive down here in a bleedin' tank never mind a bloomin' car,' he beamed.

'Forty-eight miles to the gallon . . . not bad at all. Bridie, how are you, dear?' said John, going forward to welcome his mother. For a split second they both stood looking at each other, before giving each other a great hug.

'Oh, Paschal! It's been such a long time! It's wonderful to see you again, and thank you so much for getting in touch. You'll never know what it means to me.'

John could not speak when he heard her say that. Instead he hugged his mother again and kissed her on the cheek. When he heard her say those magic words, 'You'll never know what it means to me,' his first thoughts were, and you'll never know what that telegram meant to me.

'I thought I'd lost you,' he whispered. Recovering his composure, he turned and said, 'This is Julie.'

Julie was already welcoming Gordon and talking to him about the children.

'Bridie, how are you? You look great, all out in your lovely suit, your fancy brooch and everything,' said Julie, giving her a hearty hug and handshake. 'And this is Roisín,' nodding towards the little girl who was edging closer to meet her new granny, and beaming like the morning sun.

'Oh, how are you, love?' asked Bridie clasping Roisín's hands and raising her eyes to heaven. 'You look gorgeous. Just like a little princess. And you must be Óisin, my little grandson. Come here till I give you all a hug.' She kissed each of them on the cheek. 'And this must be Síle – how are you, dear?'

And Síle, for what seemed like the first time ever, smiled ever so shyly, as she took Bridie's hand.

'Julie, I can't get over the likeness. Roisín is the spitting image of you. And Óisin is so like John Paschal when *he* was small. And as for Síle; I don't know who she reminds me of: probably takes after both of ye.'

The children got uncontrollable fits of laughter when Bridie called their father Paschal. What a silly name, they whispered to each other. Wait until their granny in Kilkenny heard that their Daddy had a new name, they giggled as they raced excitedly through the house.

'Julie and John, they're a credit to you. They're so neat and tidy, and mannerly,' said Bridie.

Eventually they all traipsed into the house, depositing the luggage in the hallway, and on into the kitchen where the kettle was soon put on and fresh tea made. They weren't really hungry, they said, because they had eaten an early breakfast on the boat and had stopped briefly for another bite on their way down from Dublin. Soon their heavy luggage was undone, and gifts for John, Julie and the children were distributed, while Gordon spoke of the high cost of petrol in the Republic, compared to England. It was the EEC, he said. Ireland should never have joined.

Later in the day, Julie confided in John how she thought his mother looked lovely and cheerful – for her age. John Paschal, on the other hand, thought Bridie looked very pale and worn-looking. But, of course, he never said, deciding that perhaps his wife's judgement carried more weight. Anyway, it made no difference. All that mattered now was that he gave the two of them a right good time while they were there.

They began with a sumptuous meal that evening, followed by another on Sunday. On Monday the whole family escorted them to Galway city, while on Tuesday they brought them to Salthill and Connemara, because the weather was promised warmer still.

Inside a few days, John Paschal instinctively knew that, next to his wife and children, Bridie was going to be the single most important person in his life. He'd already accepted her as his real mother. He adored her smile and her easy manner. In a word, he thought she was wonderful.

The weather in Salthill was glorious, as they all played about on the beach and Julie took Gordon for a walk along the promenade to get some ice cream for themselves and the children; which gave John the perfect opportunity to talk to his mother and to apologise for having ignored her for all those years. He placed his arm around her and told her he'd never ever desert her again, and that if herself and Gordon ever chose to come and live in Ireland, then they'd be more than welcome.

For a long time, they sat confiding in each other, while keeping an eye on the children playing in the sand. It was during these precious moments that John sensed his mother had a special gift: that of perception. She could suss out a situation or character she'd never previously met very, very quickly.

And when Bridie and Gordon told John and Julie of their great win on the Irish Lottery, John could see why Bridie did the most audacious thing ever in claiming their prize. Their first inclination, they said, had been to fly into Dublin with the ticket. But Bridie thought that as her good friend Julie Murray had purchased the tickets for them in the first place, it would be unlucky to leave her out of the equation. So, she wrote to Julie, enclosing the signed scratch card. She then promised Julie £1000 if she went to the post office and claimed the winnings on Bridie and Gordon's behalf, with strict instructions to lodge the winnings in both their names. Consequently, they now had

£9000 sitting in the Post Office, thanks in no small measure to the two ladies' life-long loyalty to each other. Any woman who could do that successfully, thought John Paschal, could do anything.

Later on in the week, Bridie arranged for Gordon to collect Julie Murray and Noreen Donnellan in Galway city and to take them out to Williamstown to meet John Paschal and the family. But then Gordon's 'nice little motor' began to play up and he had to take it to Brennan's garage instead, which gave Bridie the perfect opportunity to do something she had always wanted to do. When Gordon asked her if she wanted to go with him to the garage she declined, saying she wanted to play with her grandchildren.

Gordon had no sooner gone out the door than Julie put the kettle on and Bridie ran upstairs on the pretext that she had forgotten something. She was particularly pleased that John Paschal was at home pottering about the place, and in and out to his workshop at the back of the house. And as he prepared to deliver some framed pictures and mirrors to a nearby hotel he heard Julie ask his mother if she'd like a cup of tea.

'Oh, I'd love a cup, if you don't mind,' answered Bridie. 'But I'll make it for you, if you like, while you hang out the washing.'

'Don't be silly,' suggested Julie. 'Jesus, Mary and Holy St Joseph, if we can't find time to sit down and talk to our visitors, sure there's no hope at all for us. Maybe, John, you'll have a cup before you go on the road?'

'Ah, sure, I might as well while the going is good,' said John as he sat down for a minute to join in the conversation.

'Oh, that would be lovely, because I want to do something now that the two of you are here,' said Bridie. 'I don't know if I ever told you this or not, John, but when you were just a baby, I cut off a lock of your hair and kept it as a memento all these years. I guarded it with my life wherever I went. You know I never once gave up hope. I prayed night, noon and morning that one day we'd be together again. This is it . . . I have it right here' she added, opening her jewellery box to take out the small goatskin-type purse, which had a clear, plastic front on it, so that you could see the contents without taking it out. 'This is it, I made this purse, especially for it . . . years ago,' she said proudly, as she held up the lock of golden hair.

'You mean to say that's John's, from when he was a baby? I don't believe it!' said Julie, taking the purse in her hands. 'Imagine that! Do you mind, Bridie, if I take it out?'

'No! Not at all! I'd love it if you did.'

Julie took out the half-moon-shaped lock of John Paschal's hair from its purse and felt the delicate strands between her fingers. She could not believe how it had retained its full colour and texture all these years. All the while, John Paschal sat in the smoker's chair, gob-smacked. He vaguely remembered his mother saying something about it, years ago. He wondered, would he ever really know his mother or what drove her or gave her the power to surmount the terrible hurdles life had placed before her?

'Oh, Julie, if you only knew how hard it was. He was only thirteen months old at the time, and it nearly broke my heart to have to part with him; which is why that morning I grabbed a pair of scissors and cut off his beautiful bob, so that he'd always be with me, in spirit at least. Even in my darkest hour I could never ever part with it, because somehow I always knew that one day he'd come back to me.'

Then, turning round, Bridie went to John Paschal and gave him a hug, before handing him her most treasured possession. He thought it felt weird and strange, almost surreal, to be holding a part of his own being from, what . . . thirty-eight years ago now. He knew that the gods were looking down on him. He felt deeply grateful that he'd had the courage of his convictions to go to England in response to her spiritual calling and to make her happy.

Yet the feeling was nothing compared to what he felt when his mother turned to his wife and said, 'Julie, love, I want you to take this,' squeezing the lock of hair into her fist, 'as my special gift to you. I prayed all my life that God would grant me the pleasure to have a proper family of my own, because I had no one belonging to me. You see, as long as I held this treasure, John Paschal was always mine. I'm so sorry, dear, I wasn't there for your wedding. So I'm giving you this now, as a symbol that he's no longer mine but yours, and I hope that you'll both be very happy.'

'Bridie, dear,' said Julie in an emotional voice, 'I'm very happy to accept it. It's something I shall treasure all the days of my life. Talk about baby-snatching!' she laughed tearfully, trying hard to suppress her feelings. 'I can always say I knew my husband since he was in the cradle.'

Witnessing this scene of love and devotion between the two most important women in his life was almost too much for John Paschal to bear. He had to struggle violently within himself to control his outpouring of joy. To have got up and left the room he felt would have been the easy option, but it would also have been an act of cowardice. Yet a grown man doesn't cry because of what his mother is saying. He takes it on the chin. But Christ, he thought, who could take this? You'd want to be made of iron or have a heart of stone because he knew within his heart that what he had just seen was his mother exorcising the ghost of her past life. It was the culmination of a lifetime's pain and suffering: an embalming of old wounds, a washing away of years of pain, of torture, of loneliness, of begging and praying on bended knee, of crying oneself to sleep, in the hope that a great day like this would somehow come to pass, and now it had, at last.

John Paschal left the kitchen, knowing that no pictures would be delivered now. Instead he went quietly into his workshop and took down from the shelf a small personal diary he'd kept hidden away. He immediately penned his own thoughts and desires. Flicking back through the pages, he thought briefly about the few songs, poems, the odd short story, the feature articles he'd had published in the press. For a while he'd even run with a play. But what he'd wanted above all else was to write a book, a good book, on his mother's life. This diary contained many passages and notes that he wished to use. Though he never quite knew how his book would end he always knew it would be called *For the Love of My Mother*, as a tribute to the three bravest women he'd ever known, and in particular to his mother, who'd sacrificed so much to ensure that as a child he wouldn't be sold into slavery – for a mere £100 – or sent to America to pacify some well-meaning, childless couple. He knew that perhaps his book might take years to write.

It did.

And now at last, I'm happy to say, I did it. And I'm glad.

Now you can buy any of these other bestselling non-fiction titles
from your bookshop or *direct from the publisher*

FREE P&P AND UK DELIVERY
(Overseas and Ireland £3.50 per book)

Don't Wake Me at Doyles   *Maura Murphy*   £7.99
The remarkable memoir of an ordinary Irish woman and her extraordinary
life. From her early days running wild in the countryside, to her destruc-
tive marriage to a hard-working, hard-drinking womaniser, the birth of her
nine children, and a life-or-death choice that would change her forever.

The Boy with No Shoes   *William Horwood*   £6.99
This heartbreaking story of a boy's struggle with early trauma is based on
William Horwood's own remarkable childhood in an English coastal town
after the Second World War. Using all the skills evident in his modern
classics, he has written an inspiring tale of a journey from a past too painful
to imagine to the future every child deserves.

Life, Interrupted   *James McConnel*   £6.99
A memoir of obsession, compulsion, loneliness, alcoholism, music, the quest
for identity, the search for love, some very fine jokes and late-diagnosed
Tourette's.

Pete Doherty: My Prodigal Son   *Jacqueline Doherty*   £6.99
Nothing can break a mother's love for her only son. The mother of Britain's
most notorious drug addict talks for the first time about what she calls
'the Peter problem' in a deeply moving account of his very public self-
destruction, and her endless love and hope for him.

To order, simply call 01235 400 414
visit our website: www.madaboutbooks.com
or email orders@bookpoint.co.uk

Prices and availability are subject to change without notice.